W9-DDH-790
DISCARDED

FOURTEENTH CENTURY STUDIES

Maude Violet Clarke

Aet. 42

Emery Walker Ltd. ph. sc.

FOURTEENTH CENTURY STUDIES

BY

MAUDE VIOLET CLARKE

EDITED BY

L. S. SUTHERLAND
FELLOW AND TUTOR OF
SOMERVILLE COLLEGE

AND

M. McKISACK
FELLOW AND TUTOR OF
SOMERVILLE COLLEGE

Essay Index Reprint Series

Originally published by:

OXFORD
AT THE CLARENDON PRESS

BOOKS FOR LIBRARIES PRESS, INC.
FREEPORT, NEW YORK

First published 1937
Reprinted 1967

Reprinted from a copy in the collections of
The New York Public Library
Astor, Lenox and Tilden Foundations

LIBRARY OF CONGRESS CATALOG CARD NUMBER:
67-30181

PRINTED IN THE UNITED STATES OF AMERICA

PREFACE

THE Principal and Council of Somerville College, in publishing the collected essays of Maude Violet Clarke, have two ends in view. They wish in the first place to commemorate a distinguished Oxford scholar and member of the College, whose characteristic intellectual approach and deep knowledge of the fourteenth century gave unity to all her writings. Some of these essays are now recognized to be unusually important discussions of difficult and crucial themes. All are valuable contributions to our knowledge of the period. Secondly, by bringing together articles unpublished or scattered in learned periodicals, it is hoped to make the fruits of her learning easily accessible to scholars. Mr. Woodward's biographical study not only enhances the value of the book to Miss Clarke's many friends and pupils, but remains a memorial to a fine scholar and a rare personality.

Our task as Editors has been light, thanks to the able assistance of Miss M. D. Legge, Mr. V. H. Galbraith, and Miss E. Evans, who has compiled the index.

L. S. S.
M. McK.

SOMERVILLE COLLEGE
May 1937

CONTENTS

LIST OF PLATES

M. V. CLARKE

LONG ago, the wisest of the Greeks defined contemplation as a form of action, the action of the directing mind. Yet the contemplative life, of which the scholar's life is an example, cannot signify much to those who measure action by standards of external displacement. A scholar's life is set in quiet surroundings, with little outward stir. It resembles in many ways the life of the professed religious. It is not a life of day-dreams, but its richness and consolation, its excitement and accidie are removed from the stresses and vanities of the practical world, and may be understood only by those who know, directly or by analogy, the discipline which it exacts. This form of knowledge at least is remembrance. If you try to describe the contemplative life to any one unfamiliar with such a discipline, you might be describing to an audience unfamiliar with the theatre the voice and gestures of some player long dead.

The analogy of a stage, an actor or actress whose power, once absolute, over their hearers can never be recovered directly (as one may recover something of the power of a sculptor by looking at his work), applies particularly to those forms of the contemplative life lived by women. Whether by historical accident or necessity, the modes of social life or deep physical causes, it has happened that an artistic interpretation of experience is more common among men than among women. There are notable exceptions; they remain exceptions. It is still true that, for the most part, women are silent about themselves.

On the other hand, at a time when women have had more opportunities than at any other period in history to pursue, on equal terms, the life of contemplation outside the sphere of professed religion, it is fitting that some record should be kept of those who made good use of their opportunities. If one generation is to leave to its successors an image of the world of its time, the world of imagination as well as the world of politics, corn exchanges, and hospitals, there should be many personal records of these lives withdrawn from what are commonly called public affairs. Otherwise history is little more than an account of the struggle to live, or of the corruption of power peculiar to a given age; an account which at least one of the greatest English historians has called a narration of 'the crimes, the vices, and the follies of mankind'.

Maude Violet Clarke, the writer of the essays and studies collected in this book, and one of the women of her time most eminent in historical scholarship, was born at Belfast on 7 May 1892. In this year her father was Rector of Trinity Church, Belfast. His family came from County Cavan; their name was, originally, O'Clery; the O'Clerys were hereditary historians of the O'Donnells, and wrote the *Annals of the Four Masters*. Maude Clarke's mother was the daughter of J. T. Jessop, J.P., of Mount Jessop, County Longford. The Jessops were a Yorkshire family which had settled in Ireland in the reign of Charles II. Canon Clarke accepted the living of Carnmoney, on the outskirts of Belfast, in 1903; his three sons and Maude, his only daughter and second child, grew up at Coole Glebe, the rectory house. From Coole Glebe Maude once walked, hand in hand with her youngest brother, to a neighbouring gipsy encampment, hoping for adventure, and greatly disappointed when the gipsies made no attempt to hold them up for ransom. She was taught Greek, and helped in Latin at home by her father. She went to school in Belfast, and, in 1905, to Alexandra School, Dublin. In 1910 she matriculated at Queen's University, Belfast, where she took first-class Honours in History. At Belfast she had the good fortune to work under Professor F. M. Powicke, who advised her to go to Oxford. She won the first scholarship in the

Lady Margaret Hall examination of 1912, and came into residence in the autumn of 1913. She read the Modern History School at Oxford in two years. In 1916, when Professor Powicke was called to London for war work, Maude Clarke took his place as deputy-professor. She held this post until 1919. In this year she was appointed History Tutor at Somerville College. She became Vice-Principal of Somerville in 1933. It is probable that, if she had lived, she would have been elected in due course Principal of the College. She held a University Lecturership in medieval history from 1930. She was elected a Fellow of the Society of Antiquaries in 1934.

Her main interests were in English medieval history, though from her childhood she had read very widely in all periods from the end of the Roman Empire to the present day. Her first published work was a paper on *Irish Parliaments in the reign of Edward II*, read in December 1925 to the Royal Historical Society. Her first book, *The Medieval City State*, was published in 1926. She had already begun to write a life of Richard II; one may notice that many of her studies in the art and institutions of the Middle Ages were suggested by the unsolved problems of Richard's reign and age. In these years she was doing a great deal of teaching, and her time for research and writing was limited by the task of keeping up with the great mass of literature in the fields in which her pupils were working. The appointment of one of these pupils, Miss Lucy Sutherland, as a second tutor at Somerville in 1927 lightened this burden of work. Miss Sutherland was able to share the history teaching and to take over those undergraduates who were reading for the Modern Greats School. This appointment gave Maude Clarke a close personal friend, as well as a colleague with whom she could work in complete harmony. The return of Mr. V. H. Galbraith to Oxford in 1927 also meant a great deal to her. Mr. Galbraith knew the subjects upon which she was working; he could discuss technical questions with her, and suggest new material.

In 1928 Maude Clarke read a paper to the International Historical Congress at Oslo on *The Lancastrian Faction and the Wonderful Parliament.* This paper was a by-product of the book on Richard II, but for the time other interests put Richard into the background. A short note written for the *English Historical Review* (January 1930) on *Henry Knighton and the Library Catalogue of Leicester Abbey* led to further work on monastic libraries, and the plan of a catalogue of the contents of these libraries. Mr. R. B. Mynors, of Balliol College, collaborated with her in this study of manuscript material; the catalogue was not finished, but Mr. Mynors has put the notes into shape, and has left a copy of them in the Bodleian Library for the use of students.

In 1930 her main work was an edition of the *Dieulacres Chronicle*, which she edited with Mr. Galbraith. In an introductory essay the editors made out a conclusive case for abandoning the traditional Lancastrian account of the deposition of Richard II. This argument, which was the subject of a leading article in *The Times*, attracted considerable notice. About this time, when she was at the height of her power and work, Maude Clarke began to take a special interest in iconography, and gave a good deal of attention to the problem of dating ancient Irish crosses. A few years later, it happened that she was asked by the Board of Faculty of Modern History at Oxford to report on a thesis dealing with the figure sculpture of these crosses. She took immense trouble over the report. She read for herself most of the authorities used in the thesis, and spent some time in Ireland, visiting and examining the most important crosses. Before this study was made she had turned with equal interest to a branch of the history of art directly related to the age of Richard II, and had written an article on the Wilton diptych (*Burlington Magazine*, June 1931).

In 1930 Maude Clarke wrote the historical part of an

introduction to the edition of the *Kirkstall Chronicle* which she published in collaboration with Mr. N. Denholm-Young, of Magdalen College. She also did a good deal of work for a paper on *Forfeitures and Treason in 1388*, read to the Royal Historical Society in 1931. This study of forfeitures led to some interesting excursions into the inventories of confiscated goods, and resulted in a number of transcriptions of these inventories. The transcriptions are now in the library of Somerville College.

During 1930 Maude Clarke decided to write on the document known to scholars as the *Modus tenendi parliamentum*. At first she did not plan a large book, but she had already come to the conclusion that the Irish version of the *Modus* deserved closer study. She began by making an intensive examination of the Irish background. She wrote, after leaving Oxford for Ireland in the Long Vacation, that she had 'stuck firmly in the bog of Irish taxation'. In this letter she enclosed a scheme of her proposed book. The book was growing under her hand and she was able to publish some preliminary work on these Irish problems in a paper to the Royal Irish Academy in April 1932.

At the beginning of 1933, after another six months' work at her book, she fell ill. The illness was diagnosed as cancer, and she went to London for an operation in the early spring. She recovered very slowly, and could do little work during the summer, though she managed to correct the proofs of two important articles; a paper on *The Origin of Impeachment* for the volume of essays presented to the Rev. H. E. Salter, of Magdalen College, and another paper on *Committees of Estates and the Deposition of Edward II*, for a similar volume presented to Professor Tait, of Manchester University. During the Michaelmas term Maude Clarke was unable to go back to full work, but she began to revise the *Tristernagh Chartulary* which she had promised to edit for the Irish Manuscripts Commission. About this time she also undertook, at the request of friends, to edit for publication, with

Miss Sutherland's help, some work on St. Albans left unfinished by the late Professor Elizabeth Levett.

Throughout the winter of 1933–4 she was far from well, but after Easter she seemed to have regained her strength. She began work again on the *Modus*, which she had been compelled to leave untouched for many months. She went to Ireland in July hoping to give the greater part of the Long Vacation to the book. This respite did not last long. Before the year was out the malignant symptoms reappeared. A course of treatment in London tried her severely, but gave at least some hope of a permanent cure. She missed most of the Hilary term, though she was at Somerville to take part in the scholarship examination in the early part of the Hilary vacation. After the examination, which tired her a good deal, she crossed to Ireland. She had been asked in 1933 to write the volume dealing with the fourteenth century in the new *Oxford History of England*. She was looking forward to this work, as a survey on a larger scale than anything she had undertaken hitherto, and as an opportunity to use her general, as well as her specialized, knowledge, of a fairly wide period of English history. She had further plans in her mind and wanted to get the book on the *Modus* cleared away. On Easter Day, 1935, she wrote from Greencastle, where she was staying with friends: 'I have read nothing except Chaucer, who has made me very keen to get on with the fourteenth-century volume.'

A short while afterwards her doctors found that the treatment had not stamped out the disease, and that she could hardly hope to live more than a year. She came back to Oxford in the summer term, and kept her intention of telling only the Principal of Somerville the verdict from which there was now no chance of escape. She was not doing full work, but was able to finish the remaining chapters of her book on the *Modus*. She saw as much as possible of her friends, though towards the end of term she was very ill.

She left Oxford for the last time in July, and went to her father's house at Carnmoney. The disease made rapid progress, and in July she was just able to dictate to Miss Sutherland her final collation of manuscripts for the book. She was distressed by the inevitable pain of her friends, and by the thought of her father with whom she had been always on terms of the closest affection. She had twice known pain as heavy to bear; once in her twenty-first year, and again, in 1924, at the death of her brother. She spoke of her own death calmly, without fear, and without resentment. She died on 17 November 1935.

Les plus belles choses ont le pire destin. Those who see a life of much achievement, and still greater promise brought to an end in this way, find it hard not to think in such terms. There was a time when Maude Clarke would have passed a similar judgement. In the year before her illness, when she was in the full vigour of thought and energy, and after a period of indifference, she had returned to the religion in which she had been nurtured. The comforts of this religion fortified her in her last months. There had been nothing feverish or spectacular about this change of view. It was the result of intellectual conviction, of the winnowing of experience. My wife and I, who knew her well and saw her often, did not know for a long time that her opinions had changed. Yet this change can be described only in terms of illumination. A very close friend, who had known her for more than twenty years, used most aptly the words: *sero te amavi, pulchritudo tam antiqua et tam nova, . . . fugasti caecitatem meam, tetigisti me, et exarsi in pacem tuam.*

The greater part of Maude Clarke's scholarship belongs to a field which for some time to come must be remote from the ordinary reader of history and histories. It is inevitable that, at the present time, medieval studies should appear to the layman fragmentary and almost esoteric. There is a rhythm in the progress of every science which is not always understood by those who are impatient for large syntheses. These syntheses are necessary in their place; they are indeed the end and purpose of history. Historians want a building and not a quarry-heap of roughly worked stones; but progress in history, which is both a science and an art, matter for research and matter for divination, must follow a certain order. Every attempt at synthesis must be followed by a more critical examination of known material and the exploration of new evidence. In some fields of historical work even the first wide surveys have not yet been written. For the history of the institutions of medieval England this preliminary work has been done. Scholars as masterly as Stubbs and Maitland have provided a halting-place, and left their successors for some time to come with innumerable problems of detail. These problems cannot be solved easily. Until they are solved, the historian of the English constitution, the study in which Maude Clarke did her most complete work, must deal with minutiae. An attempt to write on any other scale would bring indeed, if not mere repetition, a series of unanswered questions. These limits, set by the condition of the subject, explain why Maude Clarke gave, as other medievalists of our day are giving, their best work to the composition of monographs or of learned books for the use of the learned. The time will come when the fruits of this work will be harvested, and the scattered learning will again be shaped into complete artistic form for the pleasure and the general good of the many. A jewel must be cut and polished before it is set. Moreover, the qualities necessary for the work of examining detail are more rare and diverse than mere patience and application. The detail has little significance unless you see it not merely in dissection, but in its general relationships. These tasks of observing, collating, guessing, verifying need delicate and quick imagination. They involve drudgery, but such drudgery is the background of all scientific and artistic work, and, in the case of the historian, has rich enough reward in the discovery of meaning and order where at first sight there is only confusion, the dust-heap and debris of the past.

This philosophic outlook, strengthened by a remarkable memory and very wide reading, could be seen in Maude Clarke's work with her pupils as well as in her research and writing. The Oxford tutorial system, though it taxed her time and slowed down the pace of her research, exactly suited her gifts, and gave her a chance of using her skill in discerning the meaning and interconnexion of a thousand different facts. She set her pupils a high standard; like most good teachers she never minded slowness, as long as the pupil was doing her best and working in the right way. She was easily tolerant of the pleasant self-confidence and *panache* of youth, but she could be sharp enough when any one tried to disguise idleness under a flashy show. All her pupils were 'persons' to her, not candidates reading for an examination. I worked with her for a good many years in choosing history scholars for her College. I used to think sometimes that she had almost too high a standard; but she knew what she wanted, and she convinced me well enough that in the interest of the education of women these standards must be exacted. Moreover, her standards were never mechanical, and never required too much in the way of positive knowledge of fact. She wanted her scholars to show something of her own powers of relating various fields of study and of keeping their knowledge always in play. She would make every allowance for differences of environment and opportunity; but upon qualities of imagination she insisted with a rigour which I never wanted to break down. She took care to explain her aims to the schools from which the scholarship candidates were drawn, and to give a reasoned defence of her standards and methods of choice.

Research, writing, and teaching are not the only work of an Oxford tutor. At any time, and particularly in these days when it is not easy for those under twenty to settle for themselves their attitude towards received opinion in every subject open to clever, honest, and inquiring minds, the relationship between a tutor and his or her pupils must have a general importance, and extend beyond the reading and criticism of essays. Each generation goes its own way, and the last thing an Oxford or Cambridge undergraduate would think of doing would be to accept *en bloc* his or her tutor's views on questions of conduct or judgements upon public affairs. Yet undergraduates are influenced more than they know, or more than they will admit, by the method of approach and temper of mind as well as by the technical attainments of their tutors and professors. From the elder man or woman's point of view, the difficulty is often to keep alive the pupil's independence. It is not easy to teach a man to think and at the same time to avoid suggesting to him a set of opinions. It was common knowledge among Maude Clarke's friends that her pupils, and not only her pupils but her colleagues, put much store upon her judgement and her advice. This advice was wisely given; it was given after a lavish use of time and thought. There was no attempt at domination. There was nothing of the 'I told you so' attitude, if the advice were not taken; no unhealthy desire to form a coterie of admiring disciples. If one were to single out any special aspect of her relations with the College of which she was a member, one would say that she applied to the corporate life of a woman's society of the present day the lessons she had learned from the study of institutions in past history. She was concerned with the form, and not merely the spirit, of an institution. She insisted always upon the dignity, the permanent value of external observances and conventions as safe-guards against sentimentality or drift. During Maude Clarke's time at Oxford the women's societies increased suddenly in numbers, status, and importance. It is difficult to exaggerate the value to a college, during this period of expansion, of one whose mind was steeped in the history of community life, and knew its problems and its special needs and dangers.

To her friends Maude Clarke was not only an historian of established reputation, with a record of published work already remarkable in quality, a good tutor, whose influence was felt outside her own College and University, and a wise counsellor in matters personal or general: Maude Clarke was a woman of charm and distinction. You would not forget the impression she made on you; the life and colour of her eyes, the poise of her head. She had a quiet voice, a quiet and noble style; there was every subtlety, but nothing of cheapness or malice or arrogance about her.

The first twenty years of her life had been spent in Ireland, and she reflected in countless little ways the great beauty with which she had been surrounded. Coole Glebe, until very recent times, was wholly outside Belfast; the house belonged to the Antrim hills, the country of the Cuchulain stories, and not to the city near at hand. Maude Clarke knew this country from childhood. She knew the people of the country and of the town. From her father, a clergyman who would have delighted Joseph Addison or Oliver Goldsmith, she had learned a quick, easy sympathy with the quick, vivacious Ulstermen; there was no self-consciousness or class consciousness on either side. A close contact with the many-coloured life of an Irish parish, where every other beggar talks better English than most English graduates, put her at her ease in every kind of society. She took all her father's interest in rather mischievous but harmless sinners. She had indeed a very strong sense of mischief, though she could not be tiresome, and an Irish power of sharp, rapid description. She was on excellent terms with children, her own nephews and nieces, and the children of her friends. If she had learned charity from her upbringing, she had also learned kindness, a shining, delightful kindness which had its related quality in her anger at insincerity, or callousness, or bullying.

Coole Glebe was not a rich house in Maude Clarke's girlhood. Miss Helen Waddell has described these days to me: 'It was an old house as bare as Argo, full of echoing, uncarpeted passages, and great low-ceiled rooms. All its richness was in its multitude of books, and in the walled garden on the southern slope, looking across the Lough to the delicate sea-coast of the Ards. Here Maude and her three brothers grew up, and her friends and theirs who were continually about that hospitable house still remember the clatter of feet down the long corridors, the talk that whirled round the table, the sudden exotic head of Shah the peacock at the dining-room window, and the Canon's spare figure darting to give him his expected crust of bread.'

Maude Clarke was not less happy in England than in Ireland. It chanced that few of her nearest friends were wholly English, but she made her friends without distinction of nationality or politics. She thought the English the most complicated, and perhaps the most interesting people in the world; like Burke, she had read about these people before she knew their country for herself, but she never thought of any one or any place, Irish or English, in merely abstract terms. After coming to Somerville, she had more money to travel, and she enjoyed travel on land and at sea. At first these holidays were taken with her youngest brother; a man of very great gifts, and her inseparable companion. Her brother's death happened just after one of these expeditions, a walking tour across Albania to Greece. Maude came home with a broken leg, badly set by a Greek doctor. She had left her brother in Greece, and was told the news when she reached England. None of her friends could take this brother's place; their interests and associations, their likes and dislikes were so close. Each had the same powers of withdrawal and contemplation.

These powers of withdrawal and contemplation were to me Maude Clarke's most remarkable qualities. They led her on a long journey to an end which, in the high days twenty years ago, she would have thought beyond her acceptance. Her scholarship seemed to me something more than an intellectual interest in the past. I can describe this scholarship only as possessing the nature of moonlight; a reflected and exquisite light, but the real source remains hidden. Maude Clarke might have chosen other modes of expression. Two very acute friends said, at different times, that she was a born diplomatist. She might have excelled in the pointed, Italian diplomacy of the renaissance; she would have looked the part she was playing. Yet the shifts and shams of this diplomacy, the half-measures and false smoothness were far below her, and would soon have wearied her. I think that by temperament and by natural gifts she belonged much more to the type of woman who ruled a medieval abbey. She was indeed as modern, as directly a child of her own time, as these medieval women were children of their age; but, with all the difference in circumstance, she had this medieval sense of a rule and a law, the belief that one's inner freedom is not diminished but enhanced by submission to the life and service of a community.

During her last illness I thought not only of those women who combined a contemplation of the divine order of things with the fulfilment of duty in this world, and did not exclude laughter either from heaven or from earth: I thought also of certain anchoresses who lived in deliberate inner seclusion, though, again, not refusing to teach their wisdom to others. Particularly, for these last months, I thought of the Lady Julian of Norwich, and her confidence that 'all shall be well'.

I

IRISH PARLIAMENTS IN THE REIGN OF EDWARD II[1]

AT the death of Edward I Ireland was, in theory, equipped with institutions on the English model. The various parts of the machinery of Irish government had been assembled and put together in the century following the Conquest. Imitation of English institutions was necessarily close, as the Anglo-Norman colonists were not content with anything less than their full share in the constitutional rights enjoyed by themselves or their kinsmen in England. From the first, the head of the English government in Ireland was the Justiciar; his duties were vice-regal and he obviously borrowed his title from the Anglo-Norman officer who acted as royal deputy in England. He was *ex officio* president of the King's Council in Ireland, a body which normally consisted of the chief officers of the Crown, but which was sometimes afforced by the attendance of the magnates and free tenants of the colony.[2] The *curia regis* in Ireland was represented by the Court of the Justiciar; pleas which in England would have been called *coram rege* were heard by him and entered on the Justiciary Rolls.[3] The oldest of the committees of the *curia regis* in Ireland was the Exchequer, which was probably constituted very soon after the Conquest.[4] There was apparently one Itinerant

[1] Read before the Royal Historical Society on 10 December 1925, and reprinted from the *Proceedings* of that Society by kind permission of the President and Council.

[2] In 1228 the Justiciar was commanded to summon the magnates, knights, free tenants, and bailiffs of the several counties of Ireland to hear the reading of Magna Carta (Close Roll Eng. 12, Hen. III).

[3] The first recorded Justiciar was Hugh de Lacy in 1172 (Hoveden, ii. 34), but the earliest plea-roll extant was for 23 Ed. I. A calendar of the rolls for 23–35 Ed. I was published by the Stationery Office.

[4] The first reference to the Exchequer in Ireland is dated 1200 (*Calendar*

Justice in the reign of John and with him two others were associated in 1221.[1] Justices De Banco are not mentioned by name before 1251; they were perhaps set apart for the first time in the previous year when a special escheator was appointed for Ireland.[2] Before 1232 there was no separate Chancery for Ireland and, perhaps, no Irish Chancellor. In that year the Chancery of Ireland was granted to the English Chancellor, who was to execute the Irish office by a deputy. In 1245 the appointment of an Irish Chancellor was made by the king himself.[3] The law of these courts and of the local courts established in counties, towns, and liberties was the same as the law of England.[4] The appearance of the Parliaments of 1297 and 1300 was the logical conclusion of a century of constitutional development.

The Irish Parliament developed out of the Magnum Concilium, under royal direction and in imitation of the English representative system. Its organization followed the Model Parliaments of Edward I so rapidly that there can be no doubt that the king regarded it as a necessary aid to government. The first Parliament for which there is record was held, probably at Dublin, in 1297.[5] Writs of summons were sent out not only to the prelates, earls, barons, and other chief persons of Ireland, but also to the sheriffs of ten counties and the seneschals of five liberties,

State Papers, Ireland, vol. i, no. 118). The earliest Pipe Roll, extant in 1922, belonged to 13 Hen. III.

[1] *Pat. Roll* 9 John. Rolls of the Itinerant Justices were extant for the years 36 Hen. III to 5 Ric. II and for 13 Hen. IV.

[2] *Cal. Doc. Ireland*, vol. i, nos. 985, 3209, 3077. De Banco rolls were extant from 6 Ed. I.

[3] Ibid., no. 2796. The earliest Chancery roll extant was that of 31 Ed. I.

[4] See Maitland's *Collected Papers*, ii. 81–3, 130–4. A register of between 50 and 60 writs current in the English Chancery was sent to Ireland in 1227. It was accompanied by a royal ordinance declaring that all seeking legal redress in Ireland should have justice according to the custom of the realm of England, cf. *Early Statutes of Ireland*, pp. 3, 4, 20–1.

[5] *Early Statutes*, pp. 194 seqq. Credit for the work of organizing the Irish Parliament ought, probably, to be given to John Wogan, who was Justiciar from 1295 to 1307 and again from 1309 to 1312.

commanding them to cause to be elected in the full court of the county or liberty two of the most honest and discreet knights of the several counties or liberties to come to the assembly with full power from their communities to do and receive (*ad faciendum et recipiendum*). The sheriffs and seneschals were also commanded to be present in person. No representatives were summoned from the cities and boroughs. This Parliament enacted twelve statutes, most of which dealt with the maintenance of order and frontier defence. Three years later (Easter, 1300) the financial demands of the king led to a further development in parliamentary representation. Edward I caused writs to be issued to the prelates, magnates, cities, and boroughs of Ireland, demanding a subsidy for the Scottish war.[1] The Justiciar issued writs for a general Parliament at Dublin summoning prelates and magnates to come in person. The communities of the counties were commanded to send two, three, or four representatives, and the communities of the cities and boroughs two or three. Before Parliament met the Justiciar visited in person the cities and boroughs and extracted from them promises to contribute a fixed sum towards the subsidy. Twenty-three towns in Leinster and Munster were thus visited and made promise of contributions varying in size from 260 marks promised by Drogheda and one mark promised by Modreeny (Co. Tipperary). When Parliament met it excused itself from granting the subsidy and requested the Justiciar to make a second tour to raise the rest of the money demanded by the king.[2] This was accordingly done, and pledges of payment were extracted from the lords of liberties, the religious houses, and cross-lands (ecclesiastical estates) throughout Leinster and Munster. This curious procedure suggests that the power of representatives to bind the communities they represented was not yet established in Ireland. The Justiciar certainly found it easier to overawe the local groups one by one

[1] *Early Statutes*, pp. 228 seqq. [2] Pipe Roll of 31 Ed. I accounts for this subsidy.

than to coerce a general assembly. A similar plan was adopted by Philippe le Bel when raising subsidies for the Flemish war in 1303 and 1304;[1] though the States General was twice summoned for the purpose, the townspeople were consulted locally.

At the accession of Edward II the Irish Parliament resembled that of England very closely, yet political conditions in the colony made it improbable that it would develop on precisely similar lines. It was still little more than a council of magnates and had no tradition of responsibility behind it. It did not actually take shape as a constitutional body until after 1307, and for this reason its history during the twenty years of Edward II's reign is worth some attention. There is record of eleven *Parliamenta* in Ireland between 1307 and 1327, but of these only four are known to have been full Parliaments for which legislation is extant.[2] The material for their history is scanty and dispersed. No statute roll exists before the fifth year of Henry VI's reign. Earlier statutes have been collected from a variety of sources, but their preservation has been accidental and unsystematic. All those hitherto discovered have been edited by Dr. Berry for the official publication known as *Early Statutes of Ireland*. Some supplementary evidence can be gathered from official records, ecclesiastical registers, and the meagre comments of Anglo-Irish chroniclers. Enough has been preserved to enable some general conclusions to be formed about the composition, procedure, and business of Edward II's Parliaments and to trace their relations with the government of England.

From the first the Irish Parliament was exclusively colonial in its composition; throughout the Middle Ages no Irish names occur in the lists of magnates summoned. Bishops or clerical proctors of Irish birth may sometimes have been present, though the jealousy with which the

[1] P. Viollet, *Institutions Politiques et Administratives de la France*, iii. 183.
[2] See Appendix I for list of Irish *Parliamenta* in Edward II's reign.

native and Anglo-Irish clergy regarded each other makes their presence improbable.[1] In a letter from Edward II to the Pope, written in August 1316, it is stated that if an Irishman became archbishop of Cashel English authority would be seriously endangered. As in the same letter the native Irish (*puri Hibernici*) are described as *bestiales et indocti*, it seems unlikely that writs of summons were often issued to Irish prelates. The Irish had no share in the election of members of Parliament, as they were excluded from county courts and governing bodies of cities and boroughs. The conclusion reached by Sir John Davies in 1613 seems to be correct.

'Before the thirty-third year of Henry VIII', he wrote, 'we do not find any to have had place in Parliament but the English of blood or English of birth only. For the mere Irish of those days were never admitted . . . because their countries, lying out of the limits of counties, could send no knights, and having neither cities nor boroughs in them, could send no burgesses to Parliament. Besides, the State did not hold them fit to be trusted with the counsel of the realm.'[2]

The Irish Annals do not contain a single reference to Parliament in the reign of Edward II, but we know that its existence and purpose were understood by the native princes. In the complaint addressed by Donald O'Neil, King of Ulster, and the princes and people of Ireland to John XXII, reference is made to 'the common council of the King of England . . . in the city of Kilkenny',[3] and the statute excluding Irish from monasteries among the colonists is accurately quoted, though its revocation by the Justiciar in the same year is ignored.[4] The words

[1] Rymer, *Fœdera* (Rec. Ed.), ii. 294. This jealousy is illustrated by constant complaints that Irish were excluded from Anglo-Irish religious houses, and vice versa. An Act of Exclusion was passed by the Kilkenny Parliament in 1310 (3 Ed. II, cap. 10); it was mentioned in the complaint of the Irish princes to John XXII in 1317 (Fordun, *Scotichronicon*, Lib. XII, cap. 26). [2] Sir John Davies, *The Irish Parliament*, p. 401 (Morley's edition).

[3] *Scotichronicon*, Lib. XII, cap. 26.

[4] 3 Ed. II, cap. 10. The real object of the petition was to induce the Pope

inter Anglicos are added to the phrase *per consilium totius terrae Hiberniae* which concludes the statute, an addition suggesting consciousness of exclusion. The only occasion in the reign when the Crown attempted to conciliate and make use of the Irish chiefs was during the invasion of Edward Bruce. In 1315 Letters Close were issued to Nial O'Hanlon *dux* or prince of Orion (Armagh) and twenty-one other Irish *duces* requesting them to give credence to the Justiciar, Chancellor, and Treasurer of Ireland, who will explain to them by word of mouth certain of the king's affairs, which they will carry out and expedite.[1] Similar letters were sent at the same time to sixteen prelates, thirty-six Anglo-Irish magnates, and the governing bodies of seven boroughs.[2] As it was obviously difficult to communicate locally with these eighty-five persons by word of mouth while war was raging in every province of Ireland, it may have been the intention of the Government to summon an assembly of notables to organize general resistance to the Scots. One of the letters is printed by Rymer as a parliamentary writ. There is no evidence that such an assembly was convened, but the documents suggest that the possibility of summoning Irish princes to discuss the affairs of the realm in a central assembly was considered by the executive.

Although the Irish chiefs and their subjects were excluded, the Parliaments of Edward II were not oligarchic, or even feudal, in composition. Though detailed evidence is lacking for every Parliament except that of 1310, enough has survived to show that the colonial population was fully represented. No doubt political conditions made it important for the Justiciar to win the support of

to withdraw the excommunication launched against adherents of Robert and Edward Bruce.

[1] Lascelles, *Liber Munerum*, vol. i, pt. iv, p. 7. The summary in *Cal. Cl. Rolls, 1313–18*, p. 218, is curtailed and mangled. Nial O'Hanlon is called Duke of Erche.

[2] The boroughs were Dublin, Waterford, Cork, Ross, Drogheda, Kilkenny, and Trim.

the whole free community for the legislative measures brought before Parliament. As a result the Anglo-Irish seem to have been more fully represented in Parliament than the English even at a much later date. An unusually large number of persons, lay and ecclesiastical, were summoned by special writ. The counties were represented by two members and possibly their sheriffs;[1] the liberties returned two members and possibly their seneschals;[1] the boroughs in both counties and liberties sent two members; and the cathedral chapters and diocesan clergy probably sent proctors to Parliament from an early date.

The Irish Patent Roll of the third year of Edward II's reign contains a list of eighty-eight secular[2] persons summoned to the Kilkenny Parliament of 1310 by special writ, thus making it possible to discover who were entitled to be summoned by such writs. When the majority of these persons are identified and their conditions of tenure ascertained it becomes clear that writs of summons were issued arbitrarily and not in accordance with feudal or legal rules. All who held *per baroniam* were not summoned. Neither Edmund Butler, who held his estates in Tipperary by twenty-two services, nor Theobald de Verdun II, who held the western half of the liberty of Meath, was summoned.[3] Both were of full age and acted as Justiciars in 1314 and 1315 respectively. Roger Mortimer of Wigmore also received no writ, though he held the liberty of Trim[4] and the honour of Dunamase in Offaly. No one of the three great absentee noblemen,[5]

[1] The sheriffs and seneschals were certainly instructed to be present with the elected members of 1297 (*Early Statutes*, p. 196), but it is doubtful if this practice was continued.

[2] *Early Statutes*, p. 258. Henry, bishop of Clogher, is included in the list, but this is certainly a mistake as there was no such bishop of Clogher in 1310.

[3] 'Irish Exchequer Memoranda', *E.H.R.* xviii. 505.

[4] Meath (West Meath and the liberty of Trim) was held by fifty services (*E.H.R.* xviii. 505).

[5] In 1310 most of the liberty of Carlow was held by Thomas of Lancaster, the liberty of Wexford by Aylmer de Valence, earl of Pembroke, and the

who held portions of the Marshal inheritance in Leinster, was summoned nor was Richard de Clare, who was then fighting a losing battle against the O'Brians to retain the land of Thomond.[1] There can be no doubt that in Ireland as in England the possession of a barony did not confer the right to be summoned to Parliament.[2]

As in England the summons was not limited to those who held *per baroniam*.[3] Irish Exchequer Memoranda of the reign of Edward I contain a list of persons owing knight services to the King of England. Certain of the names occur also in the list of those summoned to the Parliament of 1310, and in nearly every instance the tenant owed far less than the thirteen and a half services which constituted a barony. For example, Walter le Bret was summoned to Parliament in 1310, though according to the *Memoranda* he held his lands of Rathfarnham in the Vale of Dublin by only one service and seven-tenths. The writ of summons was not even limited to those who held their lands directly from the Crown. Of the eighty-eight persons summoned not more than eleven can with any certainty be described as tenants-in-chief, while by far the greater number of them were the vassals of the nine or ten great feudatories who held honours, liberties, and provinces in Ireland. Almost a third (twenty-five out of eighty-eight) can be proved to be vassals of Anglo-Irish tenants-in-chief, chiefly of the earl of Ulster and Roger Mortimer of Wigmore.[4] The proportion of sub-tenants would probably be still greater if all the tenements held by those summoned could be identified.

liberty of Kilkenny by Gilbert de Clare, earl of Gloucester and Hereford (Orpen, vol. iii, chap. 26).

[1] Thomond is the modern County Clare. It was held of the king by ten services, and therefore may not have been reckoned a barony.

[2] *Report on the Dignity of a Peer*, i. 241.

[3] *E.H.R.* xviii. 497 seqq. The case of Thomas Furnivall (1326) is cited by Anson to prove that in England the king's right of summons was not limited to persons holding *per baroniam* (*Law and Custom of the Constitution*, vol. i, p. 204, 1922 edition).

[4] For a list of sub-tenants see Appendix II.

Thus a rough analysis of the list of persons summoned to the Parliament of 1310 shows that tenure imposed no limitation on the royal right of summons. This conclusion seems to run counter to the feudal theory that only the tenants-in-chief of a lord were members of his court and council. The Report on the Dignity of a Peer suggests that in England tenure was not a condition precedent to summons, but the only example cited in proof is that of Warin de Lisle, who held the manor of Kingston Lisle as a mesne tenant.[1] The Irish Parliament furnishes a number of examples showing that the Crown was able to call upon all classes of tenants for advice and counsel. No doubt the great number of sub-tenants summoned was due partly to the small number of tenants-in-chief, certain of whom were permanent absentees.

As there were then very few counties and boroughs in Ireland, the number of members returned by election was bound to be small. It seems probable that the Executive hoped to use the commoners to counterbalance the magnates, who dominated the country by their great territorial influence. Judged by its legislation, the main object of Edward II's Irish Parliaments was to restore public order by compelling the magnates to protect the marches, control their retainers, and abandon private war. The country gentry or sub-tenants formed the largest class among the colonists.[2] During the thirteenth century they had shown themselves to be loyal to the Crown and prepared to obey the orders of royal officials. As those who had most to lose by rebellion and war, they were ready to support any measures likely to bring about peace and security.

It is impossible to determine whether the same plan was followed for the other Irish Parliaments of Edward II, as no writs of summons have been preserved. From what

[1] Pike, *House of Lords*, p. 116 seq.

[2] Geoffrey de Geneville was able to lead 2,000 vassals from Meath in 1276 (*Cal. Doc. Ireland*, ii. 257).

we know of Edward III's reign, the number summoned seems to have decreased steadily. Only forty-two special writs were issued to secular persons in 1374, thirty in 1377, and twenty-four in 1382.[1] By the end of Edward III's reign the Crown seems to have abandoned its claim to call the lesser gentry to Parliament. In 1377 Walter Lenfaunt was fined for failure to attend Parliament when summoned by special writ. He petitioned against the fine and pleaded in the Justiciar's Court that he was not a tenant *per baroniam* and therefore ought not to have been fined for non-attendance. The Court decided that it was not the custom in Ireland that those who did not hold *per baroniam* should be summoned to Ireland or fined for non-attendance.[2] The legal doctrine of barony by writ was apparently not adopted in Ireland.[3]

It is difficult to ascertain the names and number of prelates and other clergy who were present at Edward II's Irish Parliaments, as no writs of summons are extant. Five are mentioned by name as present at the Parliament of 1310, but there must have been many others present and still more summoned.[4] There were four archbishops and twenty-nine bishops in Ireland at the beginning of the fourteenth century. The standing feud between the native clergy and Anglo-Irish ecclesiastics excluded the bishops and clergy of dioceses in Irish hands from any

[1] *v.* Betham, *History of the Constitution of England and Ireland*, pp. 316, 323, 328. It is possible that the transmission of the *Modus Tenendi Parliamentum* may have led to the adoption of a uniform system of summoning only tenants *per baroniam.* Unfortunately the history of the Irish version of the *Modus* cannot be traced back beyond the sixth year of Henry IV's reign (*v.* O. Armstrong, *Proceedings of the Royal Irish Academy*, 1923). [Miss Clarke discusses the Irish *Modus* more fully in *Medieval Representation and Consent*, 1936, chapters v and vi.]

[2] Cl. Roll, Chancery, Dublin, 51 Ed. III, cited by Lynch, *Feudal Dignities*, pp. 123 seqq. 'Non est juris seu consuetudinis in dicta terra nostra hactenus usitatae, quod aliqui, qui per baroniam non tenūnt (*sic*) ad parliamenta nostra summoneri seu occasione absenciae suae ab eisdem amerciari deberent.'

[3] Lynch, *Feudal Dignities*, pp. 126 seqq. No instance of a claim to a barony by writ is known in Ireland.

[4] *E.H.R.* xviii, loc. cit.

contact with the colonial Church.[1] Yet it would not be safe to infer that bishops whose dioceses were among the Irish never came to Parliament as sometimes Englishmen were appointed or provided by the king or the Pope. Fortunately the Irish Pipe Rolls for the reign furnish a clue, as they record the names of all sees of which the temporalities were in the king's hand at the time of a vacancy. The sees where the custody of temporalities was in the hands of the metropolitan certainly sent no prelates to Parliament and were known as dioceses *inter Hibernicos*. Thus by compiling a list of dioceses *inter Anglicos* and testing it from a list of episcopal vacancies in the reign, the names and number of prelates summoned to Parliament can be reasonably conjectured.[2] According to this calculation all four archbishops and nineteen bishops were *inter Anglicos* and probably received writs of summons. Of the nineteen bishops two belonged to sees which are described on the Pipe Rolls as 'situate among the Irish where no Englishman dared to distrain or act for the king's advantage'.[3] The bishops of seven other sees during the reign did not receive Letters Patent informing them of changes in the Executive, and as their dioceses were remote and poor it is improbable that they came to Parliament.[4] This deduction leaves a total of sixteen prelates, which perhaps represents the average number summoned. Ten were summoned in 1359 and eighteen in 1374.[5] The Cathedral Chapters and diocesan clergy *inter Anglicos* probably returned proctors to Parliament in Edward II's reign. The

[1] In the complaint to John XXII (1317) it is stated that Anglo-Irish ecclesiastics, especially the archbishop of Armagh and the abbots of Inch and Granard, were in the habit of preaching 'that it was no more sin to kill an Irishman than to kill a dog'.

[2] See list of dioceses *inter Anglicos* and *inter Hibernicos* in Appendix III.

[3] The dioceses of Killaloe and Ardagh. Report 42, Deputy Keeper, pp. 45 and 58.

[4] The bishops of Clonfert, Emly, Ross, Annadown, Achonry, Connor, and Clonmacnoise.

[5] Lynch, *Feudal Dignities*, pp. 315, 323. Copies of writs of summons.

earliest record of their summons comes from the register of the archbishop of Armagh in the year 1375, though the practice may date from the origin of Parliament.[1] They continued to sit in Parliament until the Reformation. It is impossible to ascertain the names and number of religious houses represented in Edward II's Parliament. The Priory of the Hospital of St. John of Jerusalem (Kilmainham) alone is mentioned by name.[2] The number probably varied very greatly as only two were summoned in 1359 and fourteen were summoned in 1374.[3]

The system of summoning elected representatives was apparently standardized in 1310. In 1300 the communities of the counties were commanded to send two, three, or four representatives, and the communities of cities and boroughs two or three.[4] In 1310 the number of selected representatives was fixed at two from every community summoned through the sheriffs. The liberties, which returned members in 1297,[5] are not mentioned by name in 1310, but it is hardly possible that they were not covered by the term *comitatus*. They returned members regularly to the Parliaments of Edward III and Richard II.[6] In 1310 there were five[7] great liberties or counties palatine in Ireland, comprising the most prosperous part of Leinster and the whole of the colonized portion of Ulster. After Bruce's invasion Kildare, Desmond (Kerry), and Louth were made liberties, and Tipperary was given as a liberty to James Butler at the end of the reign. These nine liberties may not all have returned members to Parliament; in the reigns of Edward III and Richard II writs

[1] *Calendar of Sweteman's Register*, p. 285.

[2] *Early Statutes*, p. 264.

[3] Lynch, *Feudal Dignities*, pp. 315, 323.

[4] *Early Statutes*, p. 230.

[5] Ibid., p. 194.

[6] See Writs printed in Lynch's *Feudal Dignities*, chap. xi.

[7] Wexford, Carlow, Kilkenny, Meath (divided into West Meath and Trim), and Ulster (modern counties of Antrim and Down). Kildare had been a liberty until 1297, when it was made a county by Act of Parliament (*Early Statutes*, p. 199, 25 Ed. I, cap. 1). These five liberties returned members to the Parliament of 1297 (ibid., p. 194).

do not seem to have been issued to more than six. The sheriffs of the cross-lands within the liberties were frequently instructed to return members,[1] but there is no evidence to show that this practice was followed in Edward II's reign. There can be no doubt that the number of liberties as large as counties in Ireland made it necessary for the Crown to check the growth of the palatine rights which were enjoyed by Chester and Durham.[2] In England the lord palatine held his own courts for his subjects and did not permit them to attend Parliaments either as peers or as commoners. In Ireland the Crown retained much more legal control, though in practice nearly all the great liberties were completely independent of the Crown by the end of the Middle Ages.[3]

In addition to the nine liberties there were five counties in Ireland in the reign of Edward II—Dublin, Waterford, Cork, Limerick, and Roscommon. Connaught was reckoned a county in 1297,[4] but as its sheriff did not render any accounts during the reign of Edward II, and as it does not appear to have had any writs of summons in the reign of Edward III and Richard II,[5] it is improbable that it returned any members in the fourteenth century. Like Thomond, Wicklow, Leix, Offally, and the whole of Ulster west of the Bann, Connaught was not made shire ground during the Middle Ages. Fourteen counties and counties palatine may have returned members to Parliament between 1307 and 1327, but it is more than possible that members from distant counties ignored the writs of summons.

[1] Lynch, *Feudal Dignities*, writs in chap. xi. The liberties returning members were Meath, Ulster, Kilkenny, Kerry, Wexford, and Tipperary; Carlow and Kildare seem to have relapsed into counties.

[2] The whole subject of Irish Liberties has not yet been investigated. Considerable material exists for a study of the liberty of Meath.

[3] For example, the earl of Desmond was virtually sovereign in West Munster by the end of the fifteenth century, and claimed the significant privilege of 'never attending Parliaments nor entering any walled city'.

[4] *Early Statutes*, p. 194; *Cal. Justiciary Rolls, Ireland, 1295*, i. 73.

[5] See Lynch, *Feudal Dignities*, chap. xi.

No names or numbers of Irish cities and boroughs returning members in Edward II's reign have been preserved, though a record of their summons through the sheriff or seneschal has survived for the Parliament in 1310. At that period the cities of the colony were prosperous, loyal to the Crown, and very hostile to the magnates. The presence of burgesses in Parliament was no doubt intended to assist the Executive in passing legislation to reduce the power of the magnates. In the reigns of Edward III and Richard II, the number of cities returning members increased from nine to twelve between 1359 and 1392.[1] Accounts from only seven[2] cities appear on the Pipe Rolls of Edward II, and probably not more than that number returned members to Parliament. According to these calculations, between forty and fifty commoners should have been returned to Parliament, though no doubt the number of those who actually attended was considerably less.

The Irish Parliament ultimately took over from the Council a great mass of judicial business. The details of this transference cannot at present be traced as the evidence is not available. The Justiciary Rolls for the last twelve years of Edward I's reign contain four sets of entries,[3] entitled *Pleas of Parliament.* These pleas were heard before the Justiciar and council and represented a variety of subjects brought forward in the form of petitions. Most of them are appeals against actions of Crown officials, especially the Escheator of Ireland. It is still impossible to trace the development of this jurisdiction, as the Justiciary Rolls were not published or calendared after 1307 and have now been destroyed. The only Roll of the Irish Council, earlier than the reign of Elizabeth,

[1] See Lynch, *Ancient Cities and Towns of Ireland*, p. 31.

[2] These were Dublin, Drogheda in Louth, Drogheda in Meath, Waterford, Youghal, Cork, and Limerick. Reports of Deputy Keeper, numbers 39 and 42. Accounts were not rendered from any boroughs in Connaught or Ulster.

[3] *Cal. Justiciary Rolls, Ireland*, vol. i, pp. 303 seqq., 382 seqq., 450 seqq.; vol. ii, pp. 350 seqq.

that has been preserved, belongs to the year 1392–3[1]. It consists of petitions and, sometimes, endorsements for the redress of grievances of particular persons. There is no reference to Parliament throughout the Roll, and it seems probable that judicial business was still monopolized by the Council. Only two private petitions to Parliament, dated 1375 and 1380, have been discovered for the fourteenth century;[2] another belongs to 1421 and is recorded with a number of general provisions.[3] In Henry VI's reign private petitions occur very frequently and continue to increase in number to the end of the century. Probably the decay or disappearance of other courts of justice[4] accounts for this increase. The facts suggest that in Edward II's reign judicial business did not come before full Parliament, but was dealt with by the Justiciar and Council. The failure of Parliament to acquire the prestige of a high court of law probably retarded its general development, though it does not seem to have interfered with its legislative activity or to have prevented the demand for frequent sessions.[5]

In Edward II's reign Irish Parliaments were not summoned to grant taxes. The only piece of evidence suggesting that financial business ever came before them deals with a purely local levy. In 1326 a Parliament at Kilkenny granted for the county of Tipperary an aid to repress rebels and felons within its borders.[6] The statutes of the reign and the financial records do not contain a single reference to parliamentary grants of money. The entries on the Pipe Rolls show that the Crown derived its revenue from a variety of other sources[7] and was com-

[1] Edited for the Rolls series by James Graves, 1877.

[2] *Early Statutes*, pp. 588–9.

[3] Ibid., p. 582.

[4] No rolls of Itinerant Justices or Judges of Assize have been found for the period 1412 to 1509.

[5] *Early Statutes*, p. 288, 1320. Cf. Pollard, *Evolution of Parliament*, pp. 42–3, 118–20.

[6] *Early Statutes*, p. 588 (Pat. Roll, 20 Ed. II, § 22).

[7] See Appendix IV for the sources of Irish revenue in the reign of Edward II.

pletely independent of parliamentary subsidies. The practice of asking Irish Parliaments for money grants does not seem to have begun before the second half of Edward III's reign. The elaborate negotiations which were necessary to secure a subsidy in 1300[1] seem to have caused the Irish Executive to disregard for a time the financial possibilities of Parliament.

Recent historians regard early Parliaments primarily as courts of law; an older school represented them as mainly tax-granting assemblies. The Irish Parliaments of Edward II's reign will not fit into either of these categories, as their main purpose was always legislative and political. The Irish Executive seems to have determined that Parliament was the only means of solving the problems of chronic disorder amounting to civil war. Mr. Goddard Orpen, the historian of Anglo-Norman rule in Ireland, concludes his four learned volumes with a eulogy of the *Pax Normannica*, which he claims was established in the country by the beginning of the fourteenth century.[2] A study of Irish statutes of the period does not support this conclusion. Almost every enactment has the same burden; the Irish magnates are oppressing peaceful persons, they are protecting and abetting felons, they are constantly waging war with each other, and leaving the marches undefended. Statutes dealing with these evils were first passed in 1297, and they were re-enacted persistently throughout the fourteenth century with only slight verbal alterations.[3] It is usual to explain the collapse of Anglo-Norman rule in Ireland by reference to the demoralization following the Scottish wars of 1315 to 1318, the murder of the last De Burgh earl of Ulster, in 1333, and the preoccupation of England with the Hundred Years War. The early appearance of legislation against civil war and colonial degeneracy shows that

[1] *Early Statutes*, pp. 228 seqq.

[2] G. H. Orpen, *Ireland under the Normans* (Clarendon Press, 1920), vol. iv, chap. 39, pp. 262 seqq.

[2] *Early Statutes*, pp. 194 seqq.

the true causes of disintegration were in existence at the end of the thirteenth century. An increasing number of magnates were absentees and the Executive was too weak to curb the lawlessness and greed of those who remained. The native population had recovered from the shock of invasion; they had adopted a system of military organization and were prepared to take every advantage of the geographical weakness of the colony, with its long, ill-defined frontiers and *enclaves* of unconquered Irish in every county.[1]

The Irish Parliaments attempted to arrest the process of disintegration by passing again and again statutes against 'English rebels' and 'Irish enemies'. The following may be quoted as typical:

1310. 'And whereas merchants and the common part of the people of this land are [much] impoverished and oppressed by the prises of great lords of the land, who take what they will through the country, as it pleases them without making reasonable payment or satisfaction with those from whom the things are taken; and also whereas they will sojourn at their pleasure, and lodge with the good people of the country against their will, to destroy and impoverish them, It is agreed and assented that no such prises be henceforth made. . . .'[2]

'It is also agreed and assented that if any men enfeoff another of his land, with the intent of going to war or committing any other felony, and after the commission of the felony, to have again his aforesaid land, that such manner of feoffments be held for nought. . . .'[3]

[1] The beginning of the Irish rally must be dated before 1262, when the Celtic princes invited King Hakon of Norway 'to free them from the thraldom of the English' (Sturla). Cf. the invitation to Robert Bruce in 1314. The chief causes of the Irish success in winning back land from the colonists were: (1) A return to a system of military organization. Foreign mercenaries called *gallowglasses* were brought from Argyll and the Isles and Irish troops called *bonnaughts* were employed on permanent service. (2) The domestic policy of the chiefs was strengthened by the adoption of the custom of tanistry. (3) Irish military leaders began to realize that feudal armies were unsuccessful in broken country or in winter. See E. MacNeil, *Phases of Irish History*, chap. xii.

[2] *Early Statutes*, p. 267, 3 Ed. II, cap. 1.

[3] Ibid., p. 271, cap. vi.

'It is also agreed and assented that those who have lands in the march, cause their marches to be guarded, and if any, by their negligence and their open default, and so as to destroy their neighbours and their neighbour's lands, wilfully and of malice, suffer their said marches to be destroyed and taken by Irish felons or others, whereas they might have defended them, and they do it not nor are willing to do it; but by their open default, the passes and the roads used by merchants and others who are in the King's peace, are stopped. And thereupon entrance is given to Irish felons into lands at peace, who thus shall take and destroy the neighbouring lands; in such case, it shall be lawful for the King or the chief lord, of whom the said marches shall be held, if they conquer the said marches, to hold them in their hands until the charges be paid them, which they shall have expended as well in conquering the land as in securing and guarding it.'[1]

1320. 'And whereas the common people are much troubled by idle men[2] and others who bear rents of divers people of the land, for being of their avowry and protection by their letters patent, and who thereby are emboldened in evil doing and burdening their neighbours and the people, on account of which none can enjoy their goods, prosecute or defend their rights for fear of such kind of patronage; it is agreed that none henceforth grant protection, except the King and the lord of the liberty.'[3]

No doubt one reason why Irish legislation was almost exclusively concerned with problems of defence and penal measures against the magnates was that a considerable amount of legislation was still imported ready-made from England, sometimes in the form of statutes and sometimes as ordinances of the king in virtue of his preroga-

[1] *Early Statutes*, p. 273, 3 Ed. II, cap. ix.

[2] *Udynes gens*, called elsewhere *homines ociosi*, 25 Ed. I, cap. 6. They were the retainers of magnates who were billeted on their tenants in time of peace. The custom was known in Ireland as *coigne and livery*. By this means the armies used against the Scots were maintained in 1314 to 1318. See Sir John Davies, *Ireland before 1603*, pp. 228–36 (Morley's edition). Cf. the phrase *archers et autres gentz udifs* used in an ordinance against extravagant housekeeping issued by Edward II on 6 Aug. 1316 (*Annales Londonienses*, p. 239).

[3] *Early Statutes*, p. 285, 13 Ed. II, cap. iv.

tive. In Edward II's reign various statutes, some of them dating from previous reigns, were transmitted to Ireland.[1] Certain of them were confirmed by the Irish Parliament, but others were published by the authority of the king and Council. The Ordinances of the Staple (1326) applied to Ireland as well as England and Wales. Ordinances dealing specially with Ireland were issued in 1308, 1321, and 1323; they were concerned with administration and the interpretation of the law.[2] It is stated that the assent of the Council in Ireland had been given to the Ordinance of 1323; that of 1321 was in response to a petition to the English Parliament. Many petitions from Ireland are recorded on the Parliament Rolls, and others occur among the records of the king's Council.[3] Nearly all are from private persons, asking for favours or seeking redress of personal grievances. A few general petitions from the king's lieges in Ireland are enrolled.[4] These petitions to the English Parliament and the transmission of statutes and ordinances show that the Justiciar and Parliament of Ireland were in no sense a sovereign body. It is still doubtful at what period the king's ordinances completely yielded to the more constitutional authority of parliamentary statutes: probably not before the reign of Henry V. The first formal declara-

[1] The Statutes of Winchester (1307), York, and Lincoln (1324). The Statutes of Westminster I and II, Merton, Marlborough, Gloucester, and 'other statutes made in England by the king and Council', were confirmed by the Dublin Parliament of 1320, 'saving always the good customs and usages of the land' (*Early Statutes*, p. 283).

[2] *Early Statutes*, pp. 244 seqq. and 292 seqq.; *Rot. Parl.* i. 458–9.

[3] Baldwin prints certain examples in the Appendix to *The King's Council.*

[4] For example, *Rot. Parl.* i. 386, 1320, and iii. 85–6, 1379–80. The petition of 1320 prays that the king and Council will ordain: (1) No pardons shall be issued for the death of Englishmen except by the king's special grace. (2) The Irish (Irreis) who wish may enjoy English law concerning life and limbs. (3) Men learned in law (*sachauntz de la Ley*) may sit on the Common Bench. Though favourable answers were given to these petitions, the Irish, excepting particular individuals, were denied English Law until the reign of James I. See Sir John Davies, *Ireland before 1603* (Morley's edition, pp. 268–75). He contrasts Edward I's Welsh policy.

tion that Ireland was not bound by English Acts of Parliament, unless they had been accepted by the Irish Magnum Concilium or Parliament, was made in 1460. Poyning's Law, passed over thirty years later, destroyed all claim of the Irish Parliament to be an independent legislature. Its period of freedom from English control does not seem to have been much longer in the Middle Ages than it was in the eighteenth century.

The place of meeting of the Irish Parliament was determined by the Justiciar and Council. This practice was confirmed by Act of Parliament in 1320,[1] and at a later time was sometimes abused in order to secure a docile assembly by summoning it in an inconvenient place. In Edward II's reign one Parliament met at Kildare (1309), three in Dublin, and seven at Kilkenny. The time of meeting and the frequency of Parliament seem to have been determined by the Executive. During the first part of Edward II's reign Parliaments were summoned only for some special purpose; for example, four were summoned during the years 1315 to 1317 to organize defence against Edward Bruce's invasion. In 1320 it was enacted 'that there be a parliament each year . . .[2] times at least'. This enactment was perhaps in imitation of one of the articles of the English ordinances.[3] Sometime before August 1316 the people of Ireland had petitioned the king and Council that a Parliament should be held in that land annually. The law of 1320 was probably not enforced. There is record of only four Parliaments between 1320 and 1327, and legislation is extant for only four Parliaments during the thirty-eight years of Edward III's reign. The dissolution, prorogation, and duration of Parliament were not subjects of any special legislation and were probably entirely under the control of the Executive. The duration of a parliamentary session in Edward

[1] *Early Statutes*, p. 288, 13 Ed. II, cap. 7.

[2] MS. torn. Probably the words *two or three*, as in the Ordinances of 1311, should be understood.

[3] *Cal. Cl. Rolls, 1313–18*, p. 358.

II's reign appears to have varied from four days to a month.[1]

As information about early Irish Parliaments is drawn mainly from isolated statutes it is difficult to form conclusions about their procedure. The Justiciar probably acted as President and explained to Parliament the wishes of the king and the purpose for which it had been summoned. He acted in close co-operation with the Council, and on at least one occasion in Edward II's reign withdrew to confer in secret with Councillors while Parliament was in session. It seems unlikely that there was any division into houses, as there is nothing in the evidence to suggest it. Evidence from later reigns goes to show that the estates continued to sit together at least until the reign of Henry VI. For example, in the following complaint made against the Lord-Lieutenant of Ireland in 1373 it is mentioned incidentally that Parliament met in a single chamber:

> 'At the Parliament at Ballydoyle held [in 1371] . . . there was not in the place any building, but a small chapel, wherein the parliament was held, with the intention that, as the Commons of Ireland, who ought to be called to the said parliament, could not find lodging or other necessary accommodation there during their stay, they might the more quickly grant the subsidy required of the prelates, magnates and commons . . . and, although the said commons excused themselves for two or three days from granting a subsidy, yet, being worn out by the tedious stay in that inconvenient place [at length] they granted to the King £2,000.'[2]

In the same document complaint is made that the knights elected by the county of Meath had at the Parliament of the previous year been forced by threat of imprisonment to agree to grant a subsidy. No mention of privilege is made in the statement of grievances. It seems probable

[1] The Kilkenny Parliament of 1310 sat from 8 Feb. to 12 Feb.; the Dublin Parliament of 1320 sat from 30 Mar. to 30 Apr.

[2] Public Record Office. Parliamentary and Council Proceedings, Chancery 47/50 Ed. III, Roll 3, nos. 20–5, summarized *infra*, p. 222.

that the privileges of the House of Commons, the Speaker, and the division of the estates appeared together for the first time in 1449, when they were formally demanded by the Commons in a Protestation recorded on the Statute Roll.[1] Irish privilege was put on a statutory basis in 1463.[2] Degrees of precedence among those summoned by special writ seem to have been determined in the fourteenth century, perhaps as early as the reign of Edward II.

The Kilkenny Parliament of 1310 was distinguished by an important deviation from normal procedure. When Parliament had assembled the Justiciar and Council presented on behalf of the king a request (*petitio*) which ran as follows:

'Whereas all things saleable are become so excessively increased in price . . . our said lord the King, by his Justiciar and his Council here present, prays the prelates, earls and barons, and other good men of the community who are come by summons, that . . . they will . . . see into the defaults, and on this and on other things . . . afford such counsel, remedy and aid as may be for the honour of God and of Holy Church, and to the common profit of the King and of the people of his land of Ireland aforesaid. And forasmuch as it seems a cumbrous proceeding (*acombrose chose*) that all those who have come by summons should be ordainers of these things, our lord, by his Justiciar and Council . . . prays that all the assembly choose two prelates with two other men of note, and that these four choose of themselves and others the wisest that are here, sixteen who best know how, are willing and able, by the assent of the community aforesaid, to afford counsel, aid and remedy [in conjunction] with the King's Council.'[3]

In accordance with the royal request Parliament elected (*eligerunt*) five persons, three prelates and two laymen, who chose eleven others to make up their number to sixteen.[4] This Council, 'being specially sworn for

[1] *Statute Roll, Hen. VI*, pp. 110 seqq.

[2] Ibid., *Ed. IV*, pp. 142 seqq., 3 Ed. IV, cap. 47.

[3] *Early Statutes*, pp. 263 seqq., 3 Ed. II.

[4] No less than six members of the Committee were commoners, not summoned by special writ.

this purpose, treated together with deliberation, and ... with the assent and consent of the Justiciar and Council ... and of the community ... ordained and ... enacted certain ordinances. ...' The delegation of authority to an inner council of representatives suggests a parallel to Scottish practice. From the habit begun in 1367, of appointing commissions composed of persons 'elected by the Estates to hold the Parliament', the institution known as the Lords of the Articles developed.[1] In Ireland the use of a committee of Parliament was apparently an experiment which was not tried again. Its adoption would, as in Scotland, have given too much power to the magnates and thus defeated the main purpose of Irish Parliaments.

A more characteristic irregularity of procedure occurred at the Dublin Parliament of 1324.[2] The Parliament had been summoned primarily to reconcile contending factions, and its legislation took the form of an indenture or agreement between the king and certain lords of Parliament. It is clearly stated that the enactment has the assent of 'the prelates, earls, and barons and all the common people in full parliament', but the whole responsibility of its execution is undertaken by seventeen 'earls, barons, and other magnates of lineage' (*grauntz de Lynnage*). They pledge themselves that until the next Parliament they will take and cause to be taken the felons, robbers, and thieves of their own family and surname (*de lour braunche e sournoun*) and all other felons and notorious evil-doers who shall be found and received in their lordships. The royal seal was affixed to the part of the indenture remaining with the magnates and their seventeen seals were affixed to the part remaining with the king.

To the same Parliament of 1324 belongs the only surviving account of an Irish parliamentary debate in

[1] V. R. S. Rait, *The Parliaments of Scotland*, chap. iv.

[2] *Early Statutes*, pp. 306 seqq.

the reign of Edward II. It occurs in a contemporary narrative of proceedings against Dame Alice Kyteler, prosecuted for sorcery by Richard Ledrede, bishop of Ossory.[1] Internal evidence makes it almost certain that the narrative was written by the bishop himself. The Kyteler case was the *cause célèbre* of fourteenth-century Ireland and involved many of the most important personages in Leinster and Munster. In 1324 the bishop of Ossory, an English friar, brought accusations of witchcraft and sorcery against Dame Alice Kyteler of Kilkenny, the cathedral city of his diocese. The lady had then been four times married, had outlived three of her husbands, and was known by her maiden name of Kyteler.[2] Her last two husbands, Richard de Valle and John le Power, were both important enough to be summoned by special writ to the Parliament of 1310, and were members of great families in Tipperary and Waterford. It was alleged that, with the help of a certain demon called Robin Fitz Art, she had caused the death of the first three husbands, after inducing them to bequeath all their goods to her and her first-born son, William Outlaw,[3] and that the fourth husband was already wasting to death when the sorcery of his wife was discovered. William Outlaw, the son, was also accused of aiding and favouring his mother and her accomplices, but he was able to call upon powerful persons to protect him. Roger Outlaw, Prior of the Hospitallers' house at Kilmainham and Chancellor of Ireland, was a near relative, and Arnold le Poer, Seneschal of the liberty of Kilkenny, was a close ally. Arnold le Poer was a leader of the Despenser

[1] Edited by Thomas Wright and published by the Camden Society in 1843 under the title of *Proceedings against Dame Alice Kyteler for Sorcery*.

[2] Kyteler was a Flemish name. A William le Kyteler of Ypres was trading in Ireland in 1277 (*Cal. Pat. Roll*, 5 Ed. I, p. 223). There was a *villa Flamingorum* at this time in Kilkenny. *V.* Orpen, *Ireland under the Normans*, vol. iv, p. 218, n. 2.

[3] Her first two husbands were Will. Outlaw, a wealthy banker and money-lender in Kilkenny, and Adam le Blund, who probably held estates in Offaly, now King's County.

faction in Ireland;[1] he was supported by the De Burghs of Ulster and Connaught and opposed by the Butlers, the Geraldines, and the Berminghams. In this way the Kyteler case became part of the general quarrel between the Despenser party and that of Roger Mortimer.[2] The seneschal of Kilkenny refused to lend the bishop the support of the secular arm to punish the heretics, and even went so far as to cause the bishop to be imprisoned. In the spring of 1324 the bishop was cited to appear before the court at Dublin (probably the court of his metropolitan), to answer the appeal of Dame Alice against the charges of heresy and sorcery brought against her. While the case was pending the bishop was also cited to appear before Parliament: he seems to have disregarded the formal summons to attend with the prelates from fear of being ambushed by his enemies on the way. In order to reach Dublin he was forced to travel by night and hide by day in woods and marshy places. When he arrived he found that the whole Curia Regis and even the archbishop's court were hostile to him. Arnold le Poer was cleverly justifying his incarceration of the bishop by disputing his authority to demand the support of the secular arm. The claim was based on the decretal of Boniface VIII, *Ut inquisitionis negotium*, the decretal by means of which William Sautre was burnt in 1401.[3] Le Poer hoped to convict his adversary of working on the anti-clerical and nationalist prejudices of Parliament. What followed is best described in the bishop's own

[1] At this time the castle and liberty of Kilkenny were held by Hugh Despenser the younger, in the right of his wife, Eleanor, eldest daughter and one of the coheirs of the late earl of Gloucester (Orpen, iv. 223).

[2] Roger Mortimer of Wigmore had been Justiciar of Ireland from 1316 to 1318 and from 1319 to 1321. Through his great-grandmother, one of the Marshal heiresses, he inherited the honour of Dunamase (modern Queen's County), and by marriage with Joan de Geneville he was lord of the liberty of Trim (Meath) (Orpen, iii. 103–4).

[3] C. 18 in Sexto, 5.2. *V.* Pollock and Maitland, ii. 550, and Maitland, *Canon Law*, pp. 176–7.

words, though, no doubt, he has pruned down the speeches of his opponents and made the best of his own eloquence.

'. . . While the Justiciar and King's Council held private session apart (*privato separatim existentibus*) the prelates, earls, barons and other magnates of Ireland were in the hall.[1] To them came Lord Arnold [Le Poer], bringing in his train . . . William Outlaw and carrying in his hand a written statement (*cedula*) as if on behalf of the King's Council. He brought forward three propositions relative to the case to be discussed in Parliament; the first of them being that it was the will of the King that the Church should enjoy her liberties as set down in Magna Carta. Whereupon Lord Arnold at once added a statement on his own account. "Observe," he said, "the King says not any liberties whatsoever, but such as are comprehended in Magna Carta; for if any vagabond (*trutannus*) from England or elsewhere procures a bull or privilege from the papal curia, we are not bound to obey it unless it be issued to us under the royal seal. I say this because you well know that in the land of Ireland no heretics were ever found, but it was wont to be called the island of saints. Now, forsooth, comes some foreigner from England and says we are all heretics and excommunicate, and brings up to prove it some papal constitutions that none of us have ever heard of before now; and because the disgrace of this country touches every one of us it is the duty of all of you to take part against him." Thereupon the other bishops began to urge the bishop of Ossory to answer somewhat to his opponent and not suffer him to flaunt his victory over the cause of faith before such a multitude. Then spoke the bishop of Ossory in the presence of them all. "Reverend fathers and lords," he said, "though many arguments have been put before you by this noble and powerful lord, all are not borne out by the facts; for the privileges of the Church are indeed many and are not readily to be comprehended once for all in one little charter (*parva cartula*). It is beyond all question that even as the kings

[1] This hall was probably the Great Hall of Dublin Castle, which had been roofed and had its gutters repaired sometime between 1299 and 1302 (*Pipe Roll, Ireland*, 1 Ed. II. Report 39 of the Deputy Keeper, p. 25). The Council may have been sitting in the 'chamber of the justiciar' referred to in the same account.

and princes of this world dispose as they will of things temporal (*de suis temporalibus*) and establish laws and statutes, so our Lord the Pope, who is the Vicar of Christ, has it in his power to dispose and decree in things spiritual, and above all in the matter of faith. . . . And his third point, that we declare you all heretics and excommunicate to the disgrace of your country and yourselves, is not, with all reverence to so great a man and so mighty a power, true; for that ill men should be found among the good bringeth no disgrace upon the good, unless the good foster and protect them in their malice. . . . And we in our own diocese, amidst many good and upright men, have found a nest of the devil, fouler than hath ever been in the kingdom and dominion of the King of England; which when we set ourselves to purge . . . it fell to our lot to suffer calamities unheard of in modern times. For when, having in mind the power and wealth of our opponents, we came in full pontificals, bearing in our hands the body of Christ and with a great following of priests and religious, to that place where you sat, my Lord Arnold, to implore your help against the aforenamed heretics . . . you not only omitted all reverence to your creator but with insult and clamour drove out from your judgment hall[1] (*aula judicialis*) the Lord and Master of us all, and even your father the bishop. . . . For which cause know that you have brought on your head the sentence of Canon Law; and do not think that the bishop sent you by our Lord the most holy Vicar of Christ and nurtured under the wings of the Holy Roman Church, is such a one as to fear in the cause of faith your power, your threats, your terrors, but rather, if need be, is prepared to suffer, by the help of God, not only prison but death itself. We leave it to your judgement, my lords and prelates, whether these be the deeds and tokens of the faithful or of others."

'This spoken, Lord Arnold rose in fierce anger and made answer to the bishop. "Full, full will be the reckoning that is coming to you wherever you go." The bishop replied: "Come against me with your hirelings when you will, you shall find one ready to counter you with quiet and joyful mind on behalf of the faith of Christ." After which Lord Arnold with his following

[1] The Court of the seneschal of the liberty of Kilkenny. Cf. *Proceedings*, p. 13: '. . . senescallus . . . in civitate Kilkenniae in aula ejusdem judiciali sua teneret placita.'

and the aforesaid William, withdrew from the hall, the rest of the Parliament remaining in session.

'Now though many, indeed one might say all, encouraged the bishop to stand fast in the cause of faith, yet there was not one among them with courage to say so openly. . . . The bishop of Ossory approached the bishops and other prelates in Parliament . . . asking their counsel and help. . . . The Vicar General [of the Church of Dublin] advised that, as Lord Arnold . . . was a man of great power in Ireland, it would be wise first to make peace between him and the bishop, and then it would be possible to deal more freely with the ecclesiastical question. . . .'[1]

This advice was accepted and a committee of five persons, all ecclesiastics, was appointed to arbitrate between the bishop and Lord Arnold.[2] As a result of their negotiations Lord Arnold asked the bishop's pardon for all injuries done to him. 'Peace was made between them and they embraced each other in the presence of the prelates and all the members of the King's Council.'[3]

It seems probable that the bishop's account of the debate can be relied on as evidence for political and parliamentary conditions in the reign of Edward II. He describes the Justiciar and Council consulting apart while Parliament was sitting and intervening only to preside over the formal reconciliation of the chief opponents. He makes no special mention of the commons, though they were certainly present;[4] he obviously considers his grievance as an affair for the prelates and the magnates. He also describes a separate consultation of the clergy in order to formulate a policy for the defence of the liberties of the Church. His description of the committee of arbitration and the formal reconciliation that followed throws light on the way in which the indenture to maintain the peace was arrived at by the same Parliament.

The most important function of the Irish Parliament

[1] *Proceedings*, pp. 17 seqq.

[2] The committee consisted of the dean of St. Patrick's Cathedral, Dublin, and the bishops of Ferns, Kildare, Emly, and Lismore.

[3] *Proceedings*, p. 20.

[4] *Early Statutes*, p. 306.

seems to have consisted of arbitration of this kind. The Parliament of Kildare (1309) made peace between Arnold le Poer and the relatives of John de Boneville, whom he had slain.[1] The Parliament of Kilkenny (1316) is described by one chronicler as 'allaying great strife that had arisen among certain magnates of Ireland'.[2] The Kilmainham Parliament of 1317 released the earl of Ulster and negotiated peace between him and his chief enemies.[3] In 1324 there was an attempt to reconcile the contending factions of Despenser and Mortimer. The attempt failed as the Despenser faction became more and more confident of their superior strength. In 1325 writs were issued to Maurice Fitz Thomas and Arnold le Poer commanding them to desist from gathering together men-at-arms and foot-soldiers to attack each other.[4] A year later writs were issued to four sheriffs and five magnates forbidding rebellious conventions and conspiracies.[5] In 1327 the two factions were engaged in open war. The chroniclers give as a cause that Arnold le Poer used 'monstrous language' (*enormia verba*) about Maurice Fitz Thomas,[6] calling him a *Rymour* or mischief-making poet. The real cause was the general struggle between the Mortimer and Despenser factions. The Kilkenny Parliament of 1327 made another attempt to end the war, but it continued until the death of Mortimer in 1330.[7]

The reign of Edward II was remarkable for a persistent effort to solve the problems of Irish disorder by means of Parliament. The failure of the experiment was due much less to Parliament itself than to external causes.

[1] *Annals of St. Mary's, Dublin*, p. 339. [2] Ibid., p. 294.

[3] Ibid., pp. 302, 354–5.

[4] *Cal. Pat. and Cl. Rolls, Ireland*, 18 Ed. II, Cl. Rolls 99 and 100.

[5] Ibid., 20 Ed. II, Pat. Rolls 20–2. The four sheriffs were those of Cork, Limerick, Tipperary, and Waterford.

[6] *Annals of St. Mary's, Dublin*, p. 364. Maurice Fitz Thomas was the head of the Geraldines.

[7] Ibid., Baldwin (King's Council, p. 473) prints an order in Council to suppress the feud between the Geraldines and the Poers, 24 June 1328. Cf. *Rot. Parl.* ii. 53, 1330.

The geographical peculiarities of the colony, the weakness of the Executive in both England and Ireland, the Scottish wars and the Irish rally against the colonists, combined to render Parliament impotent and to destroy confidence in all political institutions. The effort was continued half-heartedly during the reigns of Edward III and Richard II, but Parliament steadily declined in size and importance. In the fifteenth century it became little more than a law court for a steadily shrinking number of colonists. Reconquest by the Tudors was necessary before any effective central government could be established.

APPENDIX I

LIST OF IRISH PARLIAMENTA IN EDWARD II's REIGN

Regnal Year	*Date*	*Place*	*Authorities*
1. 2 Ed. II	1309	Kildare	*Ann. Dowling*, sub anno 1310. *Ann. St. Mary's, Dublin*, pp. 291, 339.
2. 3 Ed. II	1310, from Feb. 9	Kilkenny	*Early Statutes*, pp. 258 seqq. *Ann. Dowling*, s.a. 1311. *Ann. St. Mary's*, p. 294.
3. 9 Ed. II	July, 1315	Kilkenny	*Ann. Clynn*, s.a. 1315. *Ann. St. Mary's*, p. 349.
4. 11 Ed. II	August, 1316	Kilkenny	*Ann. St. Mary's*, p. 300. *Cal. Cl. Rolls, Eng.*, 1313–18, pp. 358–9.
5. 11 Ed. II	1317	Kilkenny	*Ann. St. Mary's*, p. 301.
6. 11 Ed. II	June, 1317	Dublin (Kilmainham)	*Ann. St. Mary's*, pp. 302, 354–5. *Cal. Cl. Rolls, Eng.*, 1313–18, p. 476.
7. 13 Ed. II	Mar. 30–April 30, 1320	Dublin	*Early Statutes*, pp. 28 seqq., 588. *Cal. Pat. and Cl. Rolls, Ireland*, 13 Ed. II, Pat. Roll No. 46.
8. 17 Ed. II	April 15–May 15, 1324	Dublin	*Early Statutes*, pp. 306 seqq. *Proceedings against Alice Kyteler*, pp. 13–22.
9. 18–19 Ed. II	June 24–July 11, 1325	Kilkenny	*Early Statutes*, pp. 311 seqq.

10.	19 Ed. II	June, 1326	Kilkenny	*Early Statutes*, p. 588. *Ann. St. Mary's*, p. 364.
11.	20 Ed. II	April, 1327	Kilkenny	*Ann. St. Mary's*, p. 365.

APPENDIX II

SUB-TENANTS SUMMONED TO THE PARLIAMENT OF KILKENNY IN 1310

Walter de Valle. Held Moneday of Jas. Butler, Earl of Ormond, in 1339. Inq. Post Mortem, 1339.

*Richard de Valle. Sheriff of Tipperary, was perhaps a Butler tenant. *Pipe Roll, 16 Edward II*, R. 42, Deputy Keeper, p. 42.

Jordan de Exeter II (Senior). Held lands in Connaught from Richard de Burgh, Earl of Ulster. *V.* Orpen, iii. 197, 211.

Jordan de Exeter III (Junior). Son of Jordan II.

Matthew de Caunteton. Held Lythlainee in Wexford from Roger le Bigod. Inq. Post Mortem, 1306.

Simon de Geneville. Held lands in Meath from Roger Mortimer of Wigmore. *Gormanstown Register*, pp. 171–4.

Walter de Lacy. Held manors in Meath from Roger Mortimer. Orpen, iii. 174; *Gormanstown Register*, p. 11.

Hugh de Lacy. Held manors in Meath from Roger Mortimer. *Gormanstown Register*, pp. 53 seqq.

Richard de Tuit. Held Killallon, Meath, from Robert Mortimer. *Gormanstown Register*, p. 11.

Walter de Cusack. Held lands in Meath from Roger Mortimer. *Gormanstown Register*, p. 28.

John de Boneville. Held Typercathan in Oboy (Leix) from Roger le Bigod. Inq. Post Mortem, 1306.

Richard Tuit. Held Sunnagh, West Meath, from Roger Mortimer. *Gormanstown Register*, p. 11.

Baldwin le Flemyng. Held Slane, Meath, from Roger Mortimer. *Stat. Roll*, p. 37; 2 Ed. IV, cap. 15.

Richard Taaf. Did suit of court at Trim in 1306. Tenant of Roger Mortimer. *Gormanstown Register*, p. 169.

* Marks doubtful examples, of which there are nine. Counting these nine, thirty-four persons summoned to the Parliament of 1310 can be proved to be vassals of Anglo-Irish tenants-in-chief. Probably if all the tenements of those cited could be identified the proportion of sub-tenants to tenants-in-chief would be still larger.

Thomas de Mandeville. Ulster tenant of Richard de Burgh. Orpen, iv. 178.

Hugh Byset. Ulster tenant of Richard de Burgh. Orpen, iv. 151–2.

John Byset. Ulster tenant of Richard de Burgh. Orpen, iv. 163.

Alan Fitz Warin. Ulster tenant of Richard de Burgh. Orpen, iv. 209.

*Philip de Mandeville. Ulster tenant of Richard de Burgh.

William le Fitz Warin. Ulster tenant of Richard de Burgh. Seneschal of Ulster, 1272. Orpen, iv. 9.

*Walter de Sey. Probably held land in the Nynch, Meath, and tenant of Roger de Mortimer. *Gormanstown Register*, p. 31.

Nicholas le Blund. Held Rathregan, Meath, from Roger Mortimer. *Gormanstown Register*, p. 139; Lynch, *Feudal Dignities*, p. 268.

John de Mandeville. Ulster tenant of Richard de Burgh. *Cal. Pat. and Cl. Rolls* (Ireland), 1326, p. 7.

*Adam de Logan. Probably Ulster tenant of Richard de Burgh as the family held lands in Antrim.

Thomas le Tailleur. Held lands in Meath from Roger Mortimer. *Gormanstown Register*, pp. 96–7.

*Hugh Byset. Ulster tenant of Richard de Burgh.[1]

*Peter de Mandeville. Ulster tenant of Richard de Burgh.

Roger de Holywood. Ulster tenant of Richard de Burgh. Holywood is in County Down. Roger was killed in 1315. *Annals of St. Mary, Dublin*, p. 346.

Michael de Kylkenan. Ulster tenant of Richard de Burgh. Kylkenan is in Island Magee (Antrim).

Hugh of Ballydonel. Ulster tenant of Richard de Burgh. Ballydonel is in Down.

John, son of Alan de Logan. Ulster tenant of Richard de Burgh. Orpen, iv. 184, 245.

*Richard le Savage. Probably an Ulster tenant, as the family held lands in Antrim.

*William Byset. Ulster tenant.

*Hubert Byset. Ulster tenant.

[1] The Bysets held lands in the Glens of Antrim.

APPENDIX III

BISHOPRICS *INTER ANGLICOS* FROM 1303 TO 1388

The temporalities of the following archbishoprics and bishoprics were seized into the king's hand during vacancy:

Deputy Keeper's Report	*Page*	*Diocese*	*Pipe Roll*	*Date*	
39	23	Armagh	1 Ed. II	1306–8	Archbishoprics
39	62	Dublin	12 Ed. II	1314	
42	14	Cashel	12 Ed. II	1314	
39	42	Tuam	6 Ed. II	1311	
39	29	Leighlin	3 Ed. II	1307–9	
39	43	Ferns	6 Ed. II	1311–13	
42	19	Ossory	12 Ed. II	1317	
44	54	Kildare	8 Ed. III	1334	
42	57	Clonfert	18 Ed. II	1323–6	
39	29	Emly	3 Ed. II	1307–9	
45	48	Waterford	11 Ed. III	1338	
39	29	Lismore	3 Ed. II	1307–9	
35	45	Cloyne	16 Ed. II	1323	
35	35	Cork	15 Ed. II	1321–3	
44	57	Ross	7 Ed. III	1337	
39	43	Achonry	6 Ed. II	1311–13	
39	43	Limerick	6 Ed. II	1311–13	
42	17	Killaloe	12 Ed. II	1317–20	
42	58	Armagh	18 Ed. II	1323–6	
35	32–3	Meath	15 Ed. II	1322	

Connor. Restored to temporalities in 1324. Ware and Harris.

Down. Restored to temporalities in 1305 and 1329. *Lib. Mun.* ii. 16.

Clonmacnoise. Restored to temporalities in 1303. *Lib. Mun.* ii. 13.

BISHOPRICS *INTER HIBERNICOS* FROM 1309 TO 1327

The temporalities of the following bishoprics were not seized into the king's hand during vacancy:

Connaught:
- Killala. Vacant, 1309. *Cal. Pap. Reg.*, p. 59.
- Killmacduagh. Vacant, *c.* 1323. *Cal. Pap. Reg.*, p. 228.
- Elphin. Vacant, 1310 and 1313. *Cal. Pap. Reg.*, pp. 70, 108.

Munster	Ardfert. Vacant, 1331. *Cal. Pap. Reg.*, p. 356. Killfenora. Vacant, 1323. *Lib. Mun.* ii, pt. v, p. 79.
Ulster	Dromore. Vacant, 1309. *Lib. Mun.* ii. 25. Derry. Vacant, 1316 and 1319. *Lib. Mun.* ii. 29. Raphoe. Vacant, 1319. *Lib. Mun.* ii. 26. Kilmore. Vacant, 1307 and 1314. *Lib. Mun.* ii. 20. Clogher. Vacant, *c.* 1322. *Cal. Pap. Reg.*, p. 219.

APPENDIX IV

SOURCES OF IRISH REVENUE UNDER EDWARD II

THE Summary is based mainly on the calendars of Pipe Rolls published in Reports 39 and 42 of the Deputy Keeper of Irish Records. A few additions from other authorities are added.

1. Escheats, wardships, and temporalities of vacant sees and religious houses.
2. Accounts rendered by sheriffs from thirteen counties. The number varies from six to two per annum.
3. Accounts rendered by seneschals from six liberties. The number varies from none to two per annum.
4. Accounts rendered by officers of seven cities and boroughs. The number varies from one to four per annum.
5. Revenue drawn from thirteen royal manors. The number varies from one to eight per annum.
6. Great New Custom, called in England *Antiqua Custuma.* It was granted to Edward I by Parliament at Westminster in 1275. Its collection in Ireland was a considerable addition to the revenue. Accounts were rendered of it four times in Edward II's reign. In 1325–6, £695 2*s.* 4½*d.* was paid in from Dublin, Drogheda, Ross, Youghal, Wexford, and Cork (R. 42, p. 78).
7. Little New Custom, called in England *Parva* or *Nova Custuma*, a tax on foreign merchants first levied in 1303. Accounts for it were rendered once in Edward II's reign (1325–6) from Dublin, Youghal, and Drogheda. The total amounted to £21 12*s.* 2¾*d.* (R. 42, p. 78).
8. Twentieth levied on the clergy by permission of the Pope. Accounts rendered from the dioceses of Ferns,

Ossory, and Cloyne, and the prebends of St. Patrick's, Dublin, in the year 1325–6 (R. 42, p. 76). The total was £141 4*s*. 8¼*d*.

9. A forced loan was demanded from certain prelates and commoners in 1322. *Cal. Cl. Rolls*, 1318–23, 3 April, 1322, p. 530.

II

THE LANCASTRIAN FACTION AND THE WONDERFUL PARLIAMENT[1]

UP to the last quarter of the fourteenth century the importance of the English Parliament was primarily functional; it gave judgements, granted taxes, and made laws, but its traditions were still unformed and it had little inherent or corporate life of its own.[2] It did not become a living and independent force in constitutional development until it was transformed into a political assembly, and it is characteristic of the whole trend of English parliamentary evolution that the change should have come about through the friction and stress of party conflict. The main interest of Richard II's minority lies in this beginning of English party politics, a beginning that may be seen most clearly through a study of the Lancastrian faction.

Lancaster's organization of a political party dates back to the Good Parliament. He was then the only member of the royal house fit to come forward as the champion of the monarchy, and he had been goaded into action by gross personal slanders and by the impeachment of his friends. Through his vigorous policy of reprisal the reign of Edward III had ended, not in the anarchy of parliamentary control, but in the restoration of royal dignity. In Parliament and at Richard's coronation, theories of the Prerogative and of Divine Right were skilfully set forth, but these would have carried little weight if they had not been supported by a strong Lancastrian party in the country. The nucleus of the party was Gaunt's own household and retinue. Round it he drew together a

[1] This paper was read before the International Historical Congress at Oslo in July 1928.

[2] [It is probable that Miss Clarke would later have modified this statement. Cf. her *Medieval Representation and Consent*. Longmans, 1936.]

group of able and influential men whose lands lay about the honour of Richmond and who were connected by ties of marriage and common interest. John Neville, lord of Raby, was Gaunt's retainer; his brother, Alexander, was archbishop of York; Richard Le Scrope of Bolton married his son to Neville's daughter and his own wife was a sister of Michael de la Pole. Wycliffe, already famous as a teacher and as a reformer, came from a parish in Teesdale half-way between Raby and Richmond. The Percy family, then almost paramount on the Border, had intermarried several times with the houses of Neville and Lancaster. Other powerful members of Gaunt's retinue were Dacre of Greystoke, Latimer of Cleveland, Roos of Hamelak, and Welles of Lindsey. The whole group constituted a body of northern lords far more formidable than the western Marchers whom Mortimer had led in the Good Parliament. Outside the northern alliance, Gaunt had support from certain magnates of the south, notably his brothers of Cambridge and Buckingham, Stafford, Mowbray, and the bishops of Chichester and Exeter. Through Wycliffe he was in touch with Oxford anti-clericalism and in London he was the patron of the faction led by John of Northampton.

It is easy to see that the party was far from homogeneous. Prelates, officials, professional soldiers, and courtiers were forced into partnership with Border raiders, Oxford heretics, and London drapers. The Percies were the weakest link in the northern alliance, as they were frankly indifferent to the public interest and careless of the trust granted to them perforce. The head of the family had supported Mortimer in the Good Parliament and had been bought over only by the office of Marshal and the title of Earl of Northumberland. He was never a loyal subordinate, and jealousy of Gaunt's position as King's Lieutenant in the Marches[1] led to his desertion during the Peasants' revolt. A bitter quarrel

[1] *Rot. Scot.* ii. 27.

was patched up by Percy's public apology, but it is doubtful if he was ever again a trusted member of the party.[1] His neutrality, if not his friendship, was bought by a long series of favours. In 1383 he was made one of a syndicate of four who had the custody of the Mortimer lands;[2] in 1384 Gaunt signed an indenture which gave him temporary control over all the Marches;[3] in 1385 he was granted a full pardon for twice losing Berwick to the Scots;[4] finally, in 1390, he and his son Hotspur were appointed Wardens of the East, Middle, and West Marches.[5]

In the south, Gaunt's allies in Oxford and in London were a source of danger rather than strength, as it was the weaker factions that he had taken under his protection. Northampton's party in the City was almost bound to give way before the attacks of the wealthy monopolists whose financial aid was necessary to the Government. Through Brembre, the king's 'grocer friend', the victuallers had an increasing share of royal favour and were thus drawn into the larger intrigues of Court and baronage.

Wycliffe was at once the most energetic and the most damaging member of the party. His sermons and polemical tracts show that he gave Lancaster vehement and continuous support, though by training and by temperament he was utterly unfit to handle concrete political problems. When asked to lop off a branch he invariably set himself to cut down the whole tree. His arguments against the Norwich Crusade held good equally against Gaunt's Spanish voyage;[6] his peace propaganda turned into a denunciation of all war;[7] in defending the imperial alliance, he raised the Emperor above the Papacy;[8] hor-

[1] Armitage Smith, *John of Gaunt*, pp. 244–59.

[2] 16 Dec. 1383. *Cal. Cl. Rolls 1381–5*, p. 533.

[3] Rymer, *Fœdera*, vii. 425. 23 Apr. 1384.

[4] Ibid., p. 463.

[5] *Rot. Scot.* ii. 105, 110; R. R. Reid, 'Office of Warden of the Marches', *E.H.R.* xxxii. 479–96.

[6] *Pol. Works*, *passim*.

[7] *Sermones*, iv. 34 seqq., 209 seqq.

[8] Ibid. i. 132.

ror at the Schism made him see both Urban and Clement as Anti-Christ.[1] Again and again he gave to Lancastrian policy an heretical twist which exposed its weakness to the opposition.

A party made up of such diverse elements was bound to be 'unsafe to touch and unsure to stand on', and it is not surprising that Lancaster's policy was often hesitating, tortuous, and incomplete. Though in foreign and commercial matters positive lines of action can be discerned, it is difficult to generalize about the attitude of the party to domestic issues. Professor Tout has shown that while de la Pole was Chancellor the *expensa hospicii* were lower than at any other period of the reign.[2] On the other hand, the tables recently published by Mr. Steel suggest that nothing was being done to check the 'pernicious process' of assignment; in fact between Michaelmas 1382–3 and Michaelmas 1384–5 cash payments fell to a point considerably lower than had been touched since the sixties.[3] Probably both economy and assignment represent a policy, not of choice, but of obligation. For quite different reasons the way was barred to any settlement of ecclesiastical disputes. Gaunt and de la Pole were in close alliance with Wycliffe, yet they themselves did not believe that drastic changes in the organization or doctrine of the Church were either possible or desirable. Their policy was, therefore, half-hearted and insincere. They were strong enough to punish Norwich and to protect Wycliffe as long as he lived, but they failed to drive the prelates out of politics and could not escape the disgrace of fellowship with idealists and heretics.

[1] *Sermones*, iv. 173; *Op. Evang.* i. 383.

[2] Tout, *Chapters in Administrative History*, iv. 207.

[3] *E.H.R.* xliii. 179–80. A decrease in assignments began after Michaelmas 1385, possibly due to the Scottish expedition. The special receivers appointed by Parliament in 1385 made nearly all their payments in cash. It is perhaps significant that the two keepers were grocers and therefore probably anti-Lancastrian.

The commercial policy of the Lancastrians was at least more definite in intention. De la Pole's hostility to the Middelburgh Staple is perhaps our best angle of approach. The Middelburgh Staple was the outcome of the revolt in Flanders and the Norwich Crusade. When the men of Ghent proposed an Anglo-Flemish alliance in the autumn of 1382 they made it a condition that the Staple should be permanently in Flanders, and for the first three years at Bruges.[1] Parliament at once ordered it to be moved from Calais,[2] but the disaster at Roosebeke made location at Bruges impossible and it was natural that Middelburgh in Zeeland should be chosen as the 'convenient town and place' in the Netherlands. After the Norwich Crusade the Commons were promised that if peace were made the Staple would be fixed at Calais, if otherwise, it should be in England,[3] and two years later de la Pole spoke openly in Parliament against the Staple at Middelburgh.[4] Though it was agreed that it should be in England when and where the Council should think fit,[5] it remained in Zeeland until 1389. There is no direct evidence to explain why de la Pole was opposed to the Middelburgh Staple nor why he was unable to get rid of it, though he probably disliked it from the first as a consequence of the Flemish alliance which he consistently opposed. In Parliament he argued that an overseas Staple meant a loss of 1,000 marks a year in custom and a pauperizing export of specie.[6] Perhaps convinced by Wycliffe's tracts, he was a strict bullionist and saw danger in the fact that English money was worth less at home than abroad. But these reasons do not really explain his opposition, as the export of bullion was already prohibited[7] and the enforcement of the law and efficient collection of customs were purely

[1] Froissart, *Œuvres*, ed. Kervyn de Lettenhove, x. 464.
[2] *Rot. Parl.* iii. 136 *b*.
[3] Ibid., p. 159 *a*.
[4] Ibid., p. 203 *a*.
[5] Ibid., p. 204 *b*.
[6] Ibid., p. 203 *a*.
[7] *Statutes*, 5 Ric. II, § 2.

administrative problems. It is more likely that his underlying motive was political and that he wished to thwart the group of merchants chiefly responsible for the organization of the Staple at Middelburgh.

Evidence drawn from a variety of sources suggests that many of these merchants belonged to the party opposed to John of Northampton in London. The two London envoys sent to Albert of Zeeland in 1382 to negotiate about Middelburgh were a fishmonger and a pepperer.[1] The fishmonger, William Brampton, became governor of the Merchants of the Wool Staple at Middelburgh in April 1384[2] and he retained office until the Staple was moved in 1389. Figures recently published by Mr. Miller show that in the year 1382–3 only 191 sacks were exported[3] to Middelburgh, but in the following year the number rose to 16,000 odd. The change synchronized with a change in City politics: in October, 1383, John of Northampton was driven from office and the grocer, Brembre, was elected Mayor of London.[4] It is even possible that Northampton's followers were actually expelled from Middelburgh, as his turncoat secretary, Usk, refers in the *Testament of Love* to former friends whose expenses he had paid 'til they were tourned out of Selande'.[5] The little we know of the organization of the Staple points in the same direction. The first recorded convoy of ships to Middelburgh was entrusted to six London citizens—three grocers and three mercers—who were to organize it at the expense of merchants.[6] After Northampton's fall the convoy was paid for by the government and was commanded by two grocers and a mercer.[7] The governor was a London fishmonger, and seven out of nine London merchants trading with

[1] Rymer, *Fœdera*, vii. 374.
[2] *Cal. Pat. Rolls, 1381–5*, p. 397.
[3] *Cambridge Historical Journal*, ii. 65 (1926). The destination of 9,000 other sacks is unknown.
[4] *Cal. Letter Book H*, p. 219.
[5] *Chaucerian and Other Pieces*, ed. W. W. Skeat, p. 34.
[6] *Cal. Pat. Rolls, 1381–5*, p. 302 (6 July 1383).
[7] *Cal. Cl. Rolls, 1381–5*, p. 364 (24 Jan. 1384).

Middelburgh between 1383 and 1388 were either grocers or vintners.[1] At least there can be no doubt that the London victuallers were deeply interested in the wool trade, a fact that helps to explain their wealth and political importance.

If it be admitted that the Middelburgh Staple was organized and supported mainly by London victuallers, de la Pole's opposition to it falls into line with what we know of the rest of his commercial policy. The victuallers were striving to enforce a monopolist system of trade: their opposition to home staples was probably due to fear that the wool market would be more difficult to control if the growers could escape the capitalist middleman. De la Pole seems to have believed in open trading and in the encouragement of foreign traders. The chroniclers heap abuse on him for the treacherous favour he showed to certain Genoese ships, though entries of the Patent and Close Rolls show that he merely intervened to protect friendly foreign traders from being plundered.[2] It is also probable that he was responsible for cancelling the charter which gave Yarmouth the monopoly of Kirkeley Road fishing dues. He had been a member of the commission which advised the revocation of the charter in 1382; he almost certainly advised the Parliament of 1385 not to renew privileges granted temporarily at the beginning of the year; significantly, soon after his fall, Yarmouth recovered her monopoly by the charter of December 1386.[3] When de la Pole was accused in the Salisbury Parliament of taking bribes from a fishmonger, the victuallers were trying to ruin him, perhaps as a by-plot to the unravelled mystery of the Carmelite friar.[4]

[1] John Philipot, Richard Odiham, John Chynford, John Sutton, Thomas Heyward, Nicholas Brembre, William Ancroft. *Cal. Cl. Rolls, 1381–5*, pp. 270, 542, 614; *Cal. Cl. Rolls, 1385–9*, p. 400; *Cal. Pat. Rolls, 1385–9*, p. 434.

[2] Walsingham, *Hist. Ang.* ii. 146; Knighton, *Chron.* ii. 211; *Cal. Pat. Rolls, 1385–9*, p. 255; 10 July 1386; *Cal. Cl. Rolls, 1385–89*, p. 339; 29 July 1387.

[3] *Select Cases before King's Council*, ed. Leadam and Baldwin, p. xciii.

[4] *Rot. Parl.* iii. 168.

In opposing the victuallers de la Pole was closely following Lancaster's lead. The frequent appeals of Northampton and his followers to Gaunt show plainly that they looked on him as their champion. Though he was unable to annul Brembre's election (as he was asked to do) or to prevent the arrest and trial of the party leaders, he was strong enough to save them from the death penalty.[1] After they had been condemned as traitors in the Tower it was de la Pole himself who came to the Council to announce a reprieve.[2] Up to the eve of sailing for Spain, Gaunt was trying to win for them full pardon and restoration of civic rights, and as late as September 1387 the Mayor and citizens found it necessary to try to extract a promise from the king not to pardon Northampton or any of his followers.[3]

In contrast to his domestic policy, Lancaster's handling of foreign and military affairs was relatively far-sighted and constructive. His first and bolder diplomatic combination had come to nothing before de la Pole was Chancellor. He had tried to use the Great Schism to organize a Grand League of Urbanists against France. Treaties were signed with the Emperor, the Rhine princes, Charles of Naples, and Fernando of Portugal and, with de la Pole's help, Richard's marriage to Anne of Bohemia was arranged.[4] The scheme looked well on paper but was never practicable. Wenzel's indolent and eccentric character and the internal and frontier wars of the Emperor made active German intervention impossible.[5] In England the idea of an Urbanist League was probably not understood. The chroniclers write about the marriage with hostility or veiled contempt, an attitude due partly to the cost of the match and partly to Wycliffite propaganda.[6] Wycliffe seems to have hoped

[1] *Cal. Letter Book H*, p. 307.

[2] Higden, *Polychronicon*, ix. 48.

[3] *Cal. Letter Book H*, p. 313.

[4] Rymer, *Fœdera*, vii. 262, 280–1, 283, 304, 354.

[5] Lindner, *Deutsche Geschichte unter den Habsburgern und Luxemburgern*, ii. 108–12.

[6] e.g. Walsingham, *Hist. Ang.* ii. 46.

that the Anglo-imperial alliance would be followed by a confiscation of Church property in both countries,[1] and in a Lollard tract, *De Schismate Extinguendo*, it was maintained that the Emperor, as the Pope's superior, had the right either to decide between Urban and Clement or to call a General Council.[2] This revival and extension of claims made for Lewis of Bavaria must have spread distrust of Gaunt's foreign policy among the clergy and roused them to organize public opinion on behalf of the Flemish Crusade.

When the disasters in Flanders enabled Gaunt to recover control of foreign affairs the military and diplomatic situation looked blacker than at any time since the outbreak of war. The Scots had just signed a new treaty with France by which they were promised an expeditionary force and a subsidy of 40,000 gold florins.[3] De la Pole reminded Parliament that, not only Scotland, but 'three of the greatest kingdoms and countries of Christendom, France, Spain, and lately Flanders, with all their adherents and allies which are innumerable, [are] mortal enemies of this little realm of England'. Deliberately stressing the English claim to suzerainty, he outlined a plan of campaign with the subjugation of Scotland as its main objective.[4] Gaunt understood that, though his first policy of encirclement had failed, an honourable peace might be secured if France were weakened by the defeat or desertion of her allies. He set to work to strengthen the will to peace on both sides of the Channel and to keep France out of the war by a series of truces, while England's forces were concentrated first against Scotland and then against Castille.

It was this policy that the Lancastrian party forced through in the teeth of growing, though divided, opposi-

[1] *Sermones*, i. 132. Had Wycliffe heard of Wenzel's proposal to assume the administration of vacant sees?

[2] [The editors have been unable to trace this reference.]

[3] 20 Aug. 1383. Rymer, *Fœdera*, vii. 406–7.

[4] *Rot. Parl.* iii. 149–50.

tion. By skilful diplomacy, Gaunt included Flanders and excluded Scotland from the Truce of Lelinghen.[1] The two expeditions against the Scots, though without spectacular victories, reduced the country between the Forth and the Border to a desert, taught the Scots that the French would not face the English in the field, and brought them round to the idea of a permanent peace.[2] At the same time a great effort was made to break up the formidable combination of French allies. In November 1384, John Boucher was sent to Ghent as Warden of Flanders in the hope of encouraging resistance to Burgundy.[3] In January 1385 an attempt was made to frighten the Duke of Brittany back to the English side by opening negotiations for the release of his rival, John of Blois.[4] In February a mission was sent across the Alps to beg for the active support of the Pope, Charles of Naples, and the cities of central Italy.[5] Charles of Navarre was evidently coming round to the English alliance, as in the same spring he sent two minstrels to Paris to poison the great French admiral and leader of the war party, Jean de Vienne.[6] Still more promising were Portuguese appeals for help against the succession claim of Juan of Castille. Envoys from Portugal were allowed to raise troops in England and transports were supplied for the little band of English archers which destroyed the Castillian army at Aljubarrota.[7] News of this victory reached England just after the second Scottish expedition and Gaunt at once began to prepare for a Spanish campaign. It was generally believed that he was bent on making himself king of Castille, and the real purpose of the Spanish voyage was probably known only to a few. His real purpose is clear enough in the treaties

[1] 26 Jan. 1384. Rymer, *Fœdera*, vii. 421.

[2] In June 1386 the Scots signed a truce to last until March 1387 (Rymer, *Fœdera*, vii. 526–7).

[3] Rymer, *Fœdera*, vii. 448–50.

[4] Ibid., pp. 454–5.

[5] Ibid., pp. 455–6.

[6] Terrier de Loray, *Jean de Vienne*, pp. 183–4.

[7] Rymer, *Fœdera*, vii. 450, 453; Walsingham, *Hist. Ang.* ii. 134–5.

he signed with the king of Portugal and with Richard in the spring of 1386. Portugal bound herself to perpetual friendship with England, promising aid and comfort against all enemies except Pope Urban, the Emperor, and Gaunt himself.[1] To Richard, Gaunt pledged himself never to recognize Juan as king of Castille unless the Castillians agreed to pay a heavy indemnity for damage done to English shipping during the war and to enter into perpetual alliance with England.[2] By this means the southern frontier of Gascony would be secured, and the danger to English commerce from the Franco-Castillian navy would be brought to an end. Gaunt set sail from Plymouth with an army of 10,000 men, but the fact that two unmarried Lancastrian princesses accompanied the expedition shows that he was putting his faith as much in the bait of matrimonial alliances as in force of arms. His purpose was fulfilled and Iberian friendship won when he married one daughter to the king of Portugal and the other to Henry, son and heir of Juan of Castille.[3]

The diplomatic triumphs of the Lancastrian policy were bought at a heavy cost, for in the struggle to force the consent of Court and of Parliament the smouldering jealousies of faction were fanned into flame. As the implications of the peace policy became clear, the bishops were able to draw into their ranks men like Arundel and Warwick who had grown rich on the profits of war. Their chivalry was neither an 'unbought grace' nor a 'cheap defence' and they had been kept in good humour since 1376 only by a lavish distribution of Crown perquisites and war salaries. The truce of Lelinghen already began to have a half-permanent look; it originally covered the period from January to October 1384, but it was extended first to May and then to 1 July 1385.[4]

[1] 9 May 1386. Rymer, *Fœdera*, vii. 515–23.

[2] 7 Feb. 1386. Ibid., p. 495.

[3] Knighton, *Chronicon*, ii. 208.

[4] Rymer, *Fœdera*, vii. 418–21, 438, 466.

Barons who were professional soldiers began to murmur about the national disgrace of any surrender of towns or territory to France and to suspect the Council of treacherous negotiations for a dishonourable peace. On the other hand, the young king was already organizing a Court party, made up chiefly of personal favourites like de Vere and the clerical members of his household. The Carmelite plot of 1384 and the conspiracy to arrest Gaunt on a charge of treason in 1385 show that this group had become madly jealous of Lancastrian influence. Though the peace policy was welcomed by the courtiers, they were anxious to hurry it through without the preliminary campaigns against French allies which Gaunt thought essential. They were also in touch with the victualler party in the City, who were probably attracted by the commercial advantages of peace. For a time Richard was inclined to throw in his lot with the prelates as not even Wycliffe's exalted ideas of royal power could reconcile him to any taint of Lollardy. He supported the Flemish Crusade and, in spite of de la Pole, restored the temporalities of Norwich to the bishop.[1] But the combination of clergy and secular magnates prevented any permanent alliance and made him increasingly eager to take power into his own hands. At this stage his motives were probably still personal, though he had already mastered the Lancastrian conception of the Prerogative and was prepared to use it against those who thwarted him.

Opposition to the Lancastrian party was thus steadily growing in the Court, in Parliament, and in London, though the prestige and overwhelming territorial influence of Gaunt kept much of it underground. The Scottish campaign of 1385 had served as a demonstration of Lancastrian military power as over a third of the whole army had been Gaunt's retainers.[2] Neither the Court

[1] Walsingham, *Hist. Ang.* ii. 141.

[2] Armitage Smith, *John of Gaunt*, pp. 437–46.

nor the magnates dared to risk a conflict without the help, or at least the neutrality, of this great retinue, and no doubt recognition of this helps to explain the general consent to the Castillian expedition. When Gaunt sailed for Spain in July 1386 with an army of about 10,000 men he left the remnant of his party without material support. He was either indifferent to its fate or else confident that its ascendancy was due to the ability and experience of its leaders rather than to latent force. When the Wonderful Parliament met in October it was at once clear that without Lancaster and his retainers the middle party could no longer exist.

As soon as de la Pole had asked for supply the Lords and Commons made a concerted attack on the Lancastrian ministers and the Court. In the prolonged and obscure parliamentary crisis that followed Richard fought hard for his prerogative rights of choice of ministers and of dissolution, but finally agreed to dismiss the Chancellor, de la Pole, and the Treasurer, Fordham, bishop of Durham, probably in return for a guarantee of immunity for his personal friends.[1] De la Pole's impeachment was certainly intended to be an exposure of the whole policy of his party, but the articles were drafted with careless haste and it was found that the general charges could not be pressed.[2] The three articles dealing with the conduct of war and expenditure of supply were dropped, as it was admitted that responsibility lay not with the Chancellor alone, but with all the Council. Mr. Lewis has recently explained the glaring injustice of the charge of failure to send help to Ghent,[3] and it is perhaps significant that de la Pole's reply to this article was not entered on the Parliament Roll. By dropping the general charges, Parliament gave up the attempt to censure Lancastrian policy as a whole and in this way probably won over recruits from the wreck of the middle party.

[1] Walsingham, *Hist. Ang.* ii. 152.

[2] *Rot. Parl.* iii. 216–20.

[3] *E.H.R.* xlii. 402–7.

The trial degenerated into a personal attack on de la Pole's use of his power as Chancellor. Three specific charges were brought against him, behind each of which private interest seems to have been at work. He was accused of sealing a charter for Dover Castle which contained franchises prejudicial to the Crown and to the Common Law. An entry on the Patent Rolls shows that on 14 October 1386, the Constable of Dover had been granted the liberty that all pleas of trespass and real and personal actions in the King's Court there might be terminated before him or his deputies; the profits of justice were to be used to pay for the repair of the Castle.[1] This allocation to the Constable of cases that should go before the Judges of Assize was certainly an abuse, though it is not very different from the fairly common practice of assigning fines and amercements to royal creditors. De la Pole's share in the transaction was purely formal and Parliament accepted his plea that the patent of a Chancellor or the decision of a judge might be cancelled without punishment of the officer who gave it. The fact that the king's favourite, Simon Burley, was then Constable of Dover probably supplies the true reason for the charge; his enemies were satisfied by the withdrawal of the grant.

A more complicated accusation related to the transfer of an annual charge of £50 on the Hull customs transferred from Tydman de Limburg, a German merchant, to de la Pole, and to the further exchange of this annuity for the manor of Faxfleet, alleged to be worth £200 a year. Tydman had been involved in intricate financial dealings with Edward III and William de la Pole. In 1344 he had been granted the charge on the Hull customs and sometime before 1377 he had alienated it to Michael de la Pole to meet a debt of 1,000 marks. The

[1] *Cal. Pat. Rolls, 1385–9*, p. 225. The Constable was also authorized to use the writ of attaint and the franchise was issued by signet letter (14 Oct. 1386).

transfer had been made without a licence to alienate, but it was ratified by letters patent in May 1385.[1] Three months later de la Pole had exchanged it for two-thirds of the manor of Faxfleet and ten marks of a rent, then valued jointly at £50 a year.[2] The propriety of the whole transaction was challenged on five counts, of which the most serious was that de la Pole had gained £150 a year by exchanging the Hull annuity for the manor of Faxfleet; but the king's ratification of the transfer from Tydman legalized all the earlier stages of the business, the alleged valuation of Faxfleet was dubious and it seems that de la Pole's principal offence was that he had used his influence with Richard to recover a bad debt of long standing.

The third accusation concerned the allocation to de la Pole of the alien preceptory of St. Anthony, London; it has a special interest as illustrating how little his family affairs were influenced by Wycliffe's teaching. Before he became Chancellor the king had granted the Hospital of St. Anthony, at a farm of 20 marks a year, to de la Pole for his youngest son, John. In 1385 John, who was then in his twelfth year, was provided to a prebend at Beverley and it was at first intended that he should also become preceptor of St. Anthony.[3] While negotiations with the Pope were pending, de la Pole agreed to waive his son's right to the collation in favour of a certain Richard Brighouse. In return Brighouse bound himself to pay 1,000 marks and an annuity of £100 to Michael and John for the term of their lives.[4] The charges based on the whole transaction were extraordinarily confused and suggest that Parliament did not know whether or not the king ought to enjoy all the profits from alien houses, though the practice of letting them out to farm

[1] *Cal. Pat. Rolls, 1381–5*, p. 570.
[2] *Cal. Pat. Rolls, 1385–9*, p. 32 (20 Aug. 1385).
[3] *Cal. Pap. Letters, 1362–1404*, pp. 409–10.
[4] *Cal. Cl. Rolls, 1381–5*, p. 593.

was firmly established.[1] An attempt was made to prove that the agreement between de la Pole and Brighouse was illegal and it was compared to the case of Chief Justice Thorp who in 1350 had been sentenced to death and forfeiture because he had taken bribes from litigants in his court. But on this point Parliament was compelled to accept de la Pole's defence that the case had come before him, not as Chancellor, but as 'father and friend' of his son. The real ground of complaint was that de la Pole had admittedly held the preceptory of St. Anthony at a rent far below its value and that he had driven a hard bargain with Brighouse before giving it up. Such charges could not justly be magnified into crimes, and the fact that the profits of the bargain were transferred to the king was a tacit admission of its validity. It is not easy to see why the whole affair was worth an inquiry. The explanation may be connected with the fact that two clerks of the Privy Seal had been drawing an annuity of £10 from the farm of the house since 1385.[2] One of them, John Macclesfeld, was a Cheshire man who soon afterwards became king's secretary and then succeeded Brighouse as preceptor of St. Anthony. He was a shameless pluralist and it is at least possible that he saw a chance of forwarding his greedy intrigue for promotion by offering information against de la Pole.[3]

Thus the impeachment, which dragged on for at least a month, degenerated into three badly sustained and trivial charges, behind each of which motives of malice or private interest may be suspected. Neither de la Pole's able defence nor the strong speech of Scrope reminding his judges of thirty years of hard and honourable service as soldier, diplomat, and statesman could save him from the heaviest sentence of imprisonment and forfeiture which Parliament dared to inflict. His

[1] For example, Wycliffe's reference to it (*Sermones*, iii. 391) and Patent Rolls, *passim*.

[2] *Cal. Pat. Rolls, 1381–5*, p. 553.

[3] Tout, *Chapters in Administrative History*, iv. 386, n. 1.

condemnation completed the ruin of the Lancastrian party, driving its members into one or other of the surviving factions. York, Gloucester, and Scrope were made members of the Commission Council and they carried with them younger men like Derby and Nottingham.[1] De la Pole and Archbishop Neville were forced to join with the king's friends and, in self-defence, to give their help to plots for revenge. It is possible that de la Pole was the brain behind the attempted *coup d'état* of 1387, as the questions put to the judges at Nottingham merely carried one stage further the conception of the Prerogative outlined by Gaunt in 1377.

[1] *Rot. Parl.* iii. 221 *a.*

III

THE DEPOSITION OF RICHARD II[1]

(IN COLLABORATION WITH V. H. GALBRAITH)

I

AN interest far in excess of its historical value, or so it seemed, has always attached to an anonymous chronicle published more than eighty years ago by Benjamin Williams as an appendix to the *Chronique de la Traison et Mort de Richard Deux*.[2] It was only a fragment, without beginning or end, drawn from a corrupt seventeenth-century transcript, and it contains little more of value than a description of the revolution of 1399. But the writer, if hardly an eyewitness of these events, was at least a contemporary, and historians have valued it above all as the unique statement, the French chronicles apart, of the point of view of Richard's supporters.

It is the original text of this chronicle which is here[1] printed from a fifteenth-century MS. (No. 9) in the Library of Gray's Inn; and the discovery of the original, it will be seen, has both rescued much of the chronicle, before and after 1399, that was unprinted by Williams, and has made it possible to fix definitely its date, provenance, and value. These points are dealt with below in the first part of the paper, and are of some complexity since the chronicle turns out to be the composite product of two writers of strongly opposed views. Indeed, it almost seems as though a rare chance has revealed to us within a Cistercian Abbey the clash of opinion during a

[1] This essay was written as an introduction to the edition of the *Dieulacres Chronicle* (Gray's Inn MS. No. 9) published in the *Bulletin of the John Rylands Library*, vol. xiv, no. 1, January 1930. We have to thank the Editor for permission to reprint it.

[2] *Chronique de la Traison et Mort de Richard Deux* (Eng. Hist. Soc., 1846), pp. 280–5.

revolution and the partisanship which it is natural to suppose were reflected in monastic life, but which can so rarely be proved. But the chronicle is something more than a literary curiosity. In the work of editing, we were persuaded that it supplies weighty evidence for a restatement of the facts regarding Richard II's deposition. Other neglected or unknown material which came to light showed a similar inconsistency with the accepted story, and the convergence of such various and independent evidence suggested the reconsideration of the fall of Richard which is the second portion of this paper.

The small but precious collection of Gray's Inn MSS. was catalogued by A. J. Horwood in 1869. It was this little-known catalogue which called our attention to the chronicle. In a full description of MS. No. 9 it is mentioned as follows:

'From 142 *b* (accession of Richard II) the MS. proceeds very much in the style of the "Brute" chronicles. Down to the death of Rich. II it is by a partisan of that King; then, 145 *b*, col. 1, is an interpolation by the copyist or the composer of the following portion, stating that he finds much in his copy that is untrue, "et hoc scio pro certo, quia in multis locis interfui et vidi." The chronicle ends on 146 *a*,[1] after describing the battle of Shrewsbury and the execution of some of the rebels. . . . There is nothing to show the ancient owner of this volume.'

It is remarkable that Horwood, his interest once aroused, did not track down his text to the extracts which had been published some twenty years earlier. It is even more remarkable that he failed to discover its provenance, which appears from an analysis of the relevant section of the MS. It falls roughly into two parts, of which the first (ff. 1–86) is a well-known Latin poem, the *Speculum Humane Salvacionis*,[2] and the second is of a miscellaneous historical character.[3] The second section

[1] *Recte* 147 *a*.

[2] Ed. J. Lutz and P. Perdrizet (1907), 2 parts. The Gray's Inn MS. was not known to the editors.

[3] The *Speculum* may not originally have been bound up with the rest of

can in turn be divided into two parts. Of these the first (ff. 88–128) consists chiefly of large extracts from Henry of Huntingdon's chronicle, and the second (ff. 129–46), with which we are alone concerned, is a tripartite chronicle divided as follows:

Part I: ff. 129–36 is headed *Excerpciones de diversis auctoribus de monarchia anglie de orbe terrarum et de ejus demensione et divisione*. It is a general description of England, its laws, customs, geography taken from Bede, Higden, and Geraldus. It ends on f. 136: *Explicit prima pars*.

Part II: ff. 136–41 is (chiefly) a history of the earls of Chester and of Dieulacres Abbey, written in the thirteenth century by a monk of that house.[1] Therein is a list of the kings of England with the lengths of their reigns, which gives the year of Henry IV's accession but not that of his death. It ends on f. 141: *Explicit secunda pars*.

Part III: ff. 141–7 is a history of England from 1337 to 1403, headed *Incipiunt guerre inter Angliam et Franciam*.

After several blank leaves the volume ends with a short theological tract describing a 'Tower of Wisdom', the work of a certain *Magister Iohannes Metensis* or *Metlynsis*.

The whole of the tripartite chronicle was evidently compiled by a single writer writing apparently before 1413 and trying, not unsuccessfully, to combine local with general history.[2] Further, this writer, it can hardly be doubted, was a monk of Dieulacres, the composition of whose work was determined by the nature of his materials, viz. the standard histories for Part I; an earlier, thirteenth-century chronicle of Dieulacres for

the volume and is written on slightly larger parchment; it is also separately paged.

[1] On f. 137 is a list of the earls of Chester headed *Comites Cestrie fundatores de Deulencres*.

[2] It is written in two hands, the first from f. 129 to f. 132, the second from this point to the end. The *Speculum* was, perhaps, written in the second of these hands.

Part II; for Part III another chronicle the composition of which is examined below. It is obvious that the plan of the chronicle was governed by the compiler's possession of the earlier account of the Abbey.[1]

The ascription of the whole volume to Dieulacres is confirmed by the fact that it belongs to a group of manuscripts, one of which (MS. No. 10) was the property of Ralph Egerton in the late sixteenth or early seventeenth century.[2] Ralph was the legitimate son of Sir Richard Egerton of Ridley, Cheshire; his bastard brother was Thomas Egerton, Lord Chancellor, 1596–1617,[3] the owner of the manor of Dodleston, some five miles south-west of Chester. As the property had formerly belonged

[1] Printed in *Monasticon* (v. 627). The chronicle is headed *Descripcio genealogice comitum Cestrie* and is anonymous, but the contents prove its provenance. The existence of the original MS. was unknown to the editors of Dugdale, who printed from an incomplete and extremely corrupt transcript. The identification of the MS. is of interest for the history of Staffordshire, and the chronicle might well be reprinted. It is worth noting that the name of the abbey is consistently written as *Deulencres*: but this can hardly be taken to settle the question of the correct spelling, since the still earlier charters of Ranulf Blundeville as consistently use the form *Deulacresse*. Cf. William Salt, *Arch. Soc.*, vol. ix, New Series, p. 293.

[2] About one-half of the extant MSS. of Gray's Inn have a definite Cheshire interest which suggests that they once formed a single private collection. Four of them (Nos. 1, 5, 11, 12) are known from notes in the volumes to have belonged to the Friars Minor of Chester, to whom it is probable, though not certain, that Nos. 2, 6, 7, 14, and 23 also belonged. Of the rest No. 8 is by 'Jehan de Souhabe' of the Order of Friars Preachers and may possibly have also belonged to the Minorites of Chester. No. 13 belonged to 'St. Mary de Cumba by Coventry' and No. 16 is by a Dominican of Dalmatia called Monaldus. No. 9 (the Dieulacres MS.) clearly belonged to this group, and we learn from the transcript in Harleian MS. 1989 (f. 403 or 39 according to the pencil number) that it was once in the custody of 'Mr. Bostock', doubtless Lawrence Bostock, a well-known Cheshire antiquary of the late sixteenth century (Ormerod, *History of Cheshire*, I. xxxix) There is an account of his historical collections in Dr. Foote Gower's tract published in 1771 proposing a new history of Cheshire. It is possible that this volume passed directly to the Inn from Bostock, or indirectly through the Randall Holmes or Challoner families. But on the whole the view set out in the text seems more likely, viz. that it belonged, together with the other Cheshire MSS., to the Egerton family, and passed from them to the library of Gray's Inn.

[3] Ormerod, *Cheshire*, ii. 301; Foss, *Judges of England*, pp. 228 ff.

to Dieulacres, it was probably in this way that the volume came into the hands of Ralph Egerton and so to the Gray's Inn Library.

In examining Part III of the MS. (ff. 141–7), we start from Horwood's acute discovery of its divided authorship. The writer of the portion 1337 to 1400, whom we may call A, was a strong partisan of Richard II, while his continuator to 1403, who may be called B, was an equally strong admirer of Henry IV. Now the whole of this section (1337–1403) is in a single script, and we may therefore conclude that the present MS. can only be a copy of the portion originally compiled by A. We may next ask whether Gray's Inn MS. No. 9 contains B's autograph or the original continuation of A. In other words, was B the compiler of the whole tripartite chronicle? The answer is that he was not, but that the compiler of the existing MS. had before him a chronicle, already composite, extending to 1403. The proof of this is apparently slight but really conclusive. The hexameter

'Contra naturam tauri dispergere curam'

incorporated in the account of Henry Bolingbroke's landing in Yorkshire must have been a marginal gloss in an earlier MS. Similarly the words

'Quia nondum venerat tempus eius sed adhuc "Renovabuntur castra Veneris",'

which are wholly contrary to the tone of what precedes and follows, must have been ignorantly transferred into the text from the margin of another MS. It is not difficult to see what has happened. The original MS. of A was continued by B from 1400 to 1403. Then some sympathizer with Richard II, not A,[1] scribbled in the margin these two prophecies, one of which (*Renovabuntur castra Veneris*) he had already written at the head of Richard II's reign and which has been duly copied by

[1] Since A believed that Richard had died at Pontefract in 1400. *Bulletin of the John Rylands Library*, xiv. 52.

the scribe of Gray's Inn MS. 9.[1] We must therefore conclude that the compiler of the existing MS., whom we may call C, was merely copying a composite chronicle whose separate authors have yet to be discovered. That this conclusion is substantially correct is borne out by the frequent passages abruptly terminated by the words &c.[2] C was not only copying the whole chronicle but abbreviating it in places.

The possibility, it may be said, remains that Gray's Inn MS. 9 is a later transcript or fair copy of the original tripartite chronicle, of which B was in fact the compiler. But this is rendered unlikely by the fact that the present MS. was apparently written before the death of Henry IV, while the excisions and deletions in the early folios of the MS., the striking difference between the various hands in which it is written, and the frequent blanks between the entries on the last three folios, as though to leave room for fresh matter, prove fairly conclusively that we are dealing with an archetype which has 'grown' and not with a later transcript.

The provenance of the original compilation from 1337 to 1403 is thus not so certain as that of the surviving MS. It would seem natural to assume that it was written at Dieulacres, but against this we may set the common assumption of historians who used the printed fragment,[3] that the early portion was written at Chester. At first sight the loyalty of A to Richard, together with the reference to de Vere and Bolingbroke in Chester, the account of the Cheshire Guard, and of the coming of Harry Percy to the county, suggest that A was a religious living permanently in the town itself. But it seems inconceivable that the account of the Peasants' Revolt

[1] It is possible that the same hand is responsible for the inconsistent comment (*Bulletin of the John Rylands Library*, xiv. 54), 'Sed quampluribus discretis videbatur quod causa dictarum tempestatum principaliter fuit quia predicti iustum titulum contra eos non habuerunt.' Cf. ibid., p. 59, n. 2.

[2] Ibid., pp. 45, 50, 53–4, 56, 59.

[3] e.g. Professor Tait in *D.N.B.*, sub 'Richard II'.

should have been written by a Chester monk without the slightest reference to the rising in the Wirral of the bondmen of St. Werburg's Abbey:

'in contemptum domini regis et affraiam et perturbacionem pacis sue manifestum et terrorem populi sui tam civitatis Cestrie quam totius comitatus predicti et ad nullacionem et destruccionem predicti abbatis et conuentus sui ac bonorum et catallorum domus et ecclesie sue predicte.'[1]

The Chester references, though frequent and of great interest, are never in the first person and have a certain detachment as (of Henry's entry)

'Deus scit quo animo a civibus receptus.'

In fact the whole tone of these references suggests a writer whose Cheshire news came to him intermittently, exactly the way in which we can imagine news coming to Dieulacres. The Chartulary shows that the Abbey held fishing rights in the Dee, one *liberum batellum in aqua Cestrense*, a garden at the bridge head, and lands at Pulford, Poulton, and Dodleston, less than six miles south of the city. Care of this property must have made frequent visits necessary, at least as often as once a year for the audit of the reeves' accounts. Now Dieulacres was as much a Cheshire as a Staffordshire house; it was originally at Poulton on the Dee, and in 1214 it was refounded by Ranulf, sixth earl of Chester, on the county border, within a few miles of Newcastle-under-Lyme. It held salt-pans in the Wiches, lands and fishing rights along the Dee, and property in Chester itself. Closely in touch with Cheshire and royalist interests, it also lay on the northern frontier of Lancastrian influence in Staffordshire. It is in just such a house we should expect to find both knowledge of events in Cheshire and Shropshire and clash of opinion over the rival claims of Plantagenet and Lancaster.

This conclusion, it must be admitted, is not more than

[1] Trevelyan and Powell, *The Peasants' Rising and the Lollards*, pp. 15–16.

an hypothesis. It is, however, supported by the fact that all three writers, A, B, and C, follow one another so closely in point of time. Thus A wrote either after February 1408, if we accept the MS. reading of *comitem*, or after 1403, which seems more likely, if we amend the MS. and read *comitis*.[1] Again B states in effect that he finished his chronicle before the death of Edmund Mortimer (Dec. 1408–Feb. 1409),[2] and the MS. as we have it was apparently finished before the death of Henry IV. These dates give but little time for circulation of MSS. and suggest strongly the personal connexion of common membership of the same house.

The narrative of A, of which only the portion 1381–1400 is printed, probably began in 1337.[3] As far as the death of Edward III he used a meagre continuation of the Polychronicon, which is of no special interest. With the accession of Richard II there is a marked change of style: he ceases to transcribe and becomes himself the author. The first entry describes the coronation of the *nobilis et excellentissimus rex regum omnium terrenorum Ricardus secundus*. This is followed by a column of prophecies and verses ending with the note

'plura de laude et nobilitate istius regis, dicti albi[4] regis et nobilis possent hic interseri secundum diversorum scripturas, sed quia estimo quod prolixitas scriptur(arum) quosdam invidos non modicum tribueret tedium ideo ad presens hic multa omitto alibi ea inserere proponendo.'[5]

The rest of the column is left blank, the continuous history of the reign beginning on the next folio with an

[1] *Bulletin of the John Rylands Library*, xiv. 52.

[2] *Bulletin of the John Rylands Library*, xiv. 55: 'et in operacione istius cronice in eodem errore perseveravit'.

[3] An early entry (f. 19) suggests that the Edward III portion, as well as what follows, formed a part of A's work. About the Feast of St. Nicholas (1337), it says there occurred an eight weeks' frost 'ita ut in dissumpcione gelicidii multi pontes caderent et maxime apud Cestriam'.

[4] Cf. Adam of Usk's Chronicle, ed. E. M. Thompson (1904), 28, 179.

[5] f. 142^{v}.

account of the Peasants' Revolt. The chronicle has little direct historical importance until the writer reaches the events of 1399, which he knew at first hand. For the earlier portion he had, clearly, neither special information nor even good books to draw on. His fondness for the metrical prophecies of Merlin and John of Bridlington suggests that he relied chiefly upon the popular versified histories of the time, all written from the Lancastrian point of view.[1] The interest thus lies in the interpretation a royalist writer puts on facts well known and by his sources construed to the king's discredit.

Apart from a few incidents of church history—a papal indulgence, Bishop Spenser's crusade—the chronicle is concerned only with the struggle of the 'just' and 'innocent' king with his 'rebel' and 'perjured' barons. There are occasional references to the king's council, but parliament is mentioned only once in the year 1399 (when it could hardly be omitted)—and the Commons not at all. The unlimited nature of the royal power is summarized in his comment on the Appellants' rising.

> 'Sed absurdum est servum vel subditum contra suum dominum esse rebellem.'

This unqualified belief in the rightness of the king colours the interpretation of every crisis of the reign. The arrest of the Appellants, for example, in 1397 he regards as a just retribution for their rebellion ten years before.

> 'Sed quia nullum malum erit impunitum deus cor regis illustravit ut predictos rebelles quodammodo puniret unde . . . arestavit &c.'

The murder of the Duke of Gloucester is described as a mystery, but since the king can do no wrong, it is at least certain that he was not responsible,

> 'obiit qua morte deus scit justo rege non consenciente.'

[1] e.g. Wright, *Political Poems and Songs* (Rolls Series), i. 417–54. The verses were accompanied by notes, which were in effect a chronicle. The dates make it unlikely that the writer actually saw Gower's *Tripartite Chronicle*.

In the same spirit he mentions the closing incidents of Richard's autocracy—the 'blank' charters and the banishment of Henry of Lancaster—as matters of hearsay only (*ut quidam dixerunt*) and seems to suggest that the blame lies with the Council.

For the return of Henry of Lancaster and his movements in and about Chester the chronicle is an authority, as valuable for the facts he gives as for the construction he puts upon them. The revolution of 1399 had its sordid side, and no other chronicle brings this out with such force and brevity. In a few gloomy pages he describes how Henry's banner attracted all kinds of rogues and robbers who were in exile, the pillage of the county of Chester ('*Havok*' *super eam proclamato*), and the final surrender to Henry IV.

The continuation of B begins with the protest against A, referred to above.

> 'Iste commentator in locis quampluribus vituperat commendanda et commendat vituperanda et hoc est magnum vicium in scripturis et maxime in strenuis personis quando aliquis scribit de eis enormia per aliorum loquelam et non per veram noticiam sicut in copia multa fuerunt scripta minus vera et hoc scio pro certo quia in multis locis interfui et vidi et propterea veritatem novi.'[1]

We are justified in supposing that the writer of this protest was the compiler of the continuation of the chronicle to 1403, and that he was a monk of Dieulacres Abbey. The patron of the abbey was Henry IV and it is perhaps not going too far to suggest that the original compiler of the continuation was a clerk in the service of Henry IV who entered Dieulacres Abbey after the revolution. The chronicle, so far as it goes, is consistent with this view. It is largely confined to Welsh border affairs, culminating in the battle of Shrewsbury—matters of close interest to the monks of Dieulacres. And that the writer knew the king at first hand is likely enough from the vivid description of his heroic conduct at the battle of

[1] *Bulletin of the John Rylands Library*, xiv. 52.

Shrewsbury. He knows, too, the name of the king's confessor—Robert Mascal, a detail preserved in none of the other chronicles. It has been thought that the name of the compiler is preserved. The last folios of the MS. describe, with a number of diagrams, a 'Tower of Wisdom', the author of which was a Master John Metensis or Metlynsis. The seventeenth-century transcriber of the chronicle in Harley MS. 1989 assumed that this was the compiler of the continuation, but although this is possible there is really no proof or even indication that he wrote it.

B's work, it will be seen, lacks the personal interest of A's chronicle. This defect, however, is more than counterbalanced by an excellent account of the battle of Shrewsbury and in particular of the obscure negotiations between Henry IV and Hotspur which immediately preceded it. It is apparently independent of all the other chronicles and mentions a number of facts found in none of them. At the same time it is in general agreement with the best extant authority—the *Annales Henrici Quarti*, while many matters of detail, when not supported by the *Annales*, are borne out by one or other of the narratives of the battle. Still other statements are substantiated by the official sources such as the Patent Rolls and the Privy Council Proceedings. Where so much can be verified it is tempting to accept the account of the negotiations between Percy and Henry IV on the day of the battle. The question is one of real importance, but in the nature of things is likely to remain more or less a matter of conjecture. Which side was finally responsible for the battle? The royalists blamed the earl of Worcester, the Lancastrians the Scottish earl of Dunbar: while the judicious chronicler, whose work was printed by Giles, divides the blame equally between the two.[1] The Dieulacres writer, who does not even mention the earl of Dunbar, boldly lays upon Henry IV the direct responsibility for joining battle, though only after he had offered

[1] *Chronicon incerti auctoris*, ed. Giles, 1848, p. 32.

the rebels every possible concession. The king, he explains, was loth to fight and offered either a free parliament or even to meet Percy in single combat. Part at least of his statement is confirmed by Bower's *Scotichronicon*.[1]

'Cui (Percy) rex subdolo nuncium misit exhortans eum ut parceret effusioni sanguinis; et si sibi videbatur quod iniuste coronam usurpasset convocato parliamento ad insinuacionem prelatorum et procerum coronam deponeret et debenti eam tradi consentiret.'

Bower adds that Percy accepted these terms and ordered his men to bivouac for the night: whereupon the king, waiting until his enemies had dispersed, suddenly attacked them. The important point in this account is that so hostile a witness as Bower admits that Henry made an offer to summon a free parliament, though he holds that the offer was not made in good faith. The *Annales* and the *Eulogium Historiarum* agree that it was the king who eventually broke off negotiations, but while the first says Percy's archers actually began the fight, the *Eulogium* states, almost in the words of the Dieulacres writer, that the king gave the signal to advance.

'"Precor dominum," dixit rex, "quod tu habeas respondere pro sanguine hic hodie effundendo et non ego. Procede signifer," quod est dictu, "anauant baner."'[2]

But the Dieulacres writer is rather more explicit at this critical point, and attributes to Henry IV a remarkable outburst not elsewhere recorded. Losing all patience, he says, the king, when his offers were refused, cried out to Hotspur's ambassadors,

'Divulgatum mihi esse vestrum nequam consilium. Profiteor quod me vivente in eternum non fiet. Disponitis siquidem filios comitis Marchie spurios et Edmundum de Mortuo mari proditorem approbare; sicque Henricum Percy vel filium eius iure hereditario uxoris sue in regem coronare.'[3]

[1] *Scotichronicon*, ed. W. Goodall (1759), ii. 438.

[2] *Eulogium Historiarum*, iii. 397. *Bulletin of the John Rylands Library*, xiv. 57: 'Precedat vexillum in nomine domini.'

[3] Ibid. 57.

We can well believe that this was precisely what was in Henry IV's mind; nor is it unlikely that Hotspur may have had dreams of the throne or even designs upon it. Two incidental statements in other chronicles point in this direction. The chronicle, printed by Giles,[1] says that Worcester hoped for the king's death in the battle 'ut ipso extincto, sub suo consanguineo melius valeret dominari'; while, according to the *Annales*, Hotspur's troops, at the critical moment in the battle, cried out (*clamabant ingeminantes*), 'Henry Percy Kyng.'[2] He had disappeared, we are told, and his followers were hoping against hope that he had captured Henry IV—and thus that no obstacle remained in his way. Here again casual references in other chronicles seem to confirm a remarkable statement of B. Is there, one may ask, any other explanation as simple and as likely of Hotspur's inconsistent actions in this half-unexplained revolt?

If Bower, the *Eulogium*, and the *Annales* support the Dieulacres writer's account of the negotiations before the battle, he in turn goes far to substantiate a most curious document preserved only by the chronicler Hardyng. This is the proclamation made by Percy and his friends in which they accuse Henry IV of having murdered Richard II. The proclamation mentions:

> 'Quod quando tu post exilium tuum Angliam intrasti, apud Doncastre tu jurasti nobis supra sacra evangelia corporaliter per te tacta et osculata iuxta clamare regnum, seu regium statum, nisi solummodo hereditatem tuam propriam et hereditatem uxoris tue in Anglia, et quod Ricardus dominus noster rex ad tunc regnaret ad terminum vite sue gubernatus per bonum consilium dominorum spiritualium et temporalium.'[3]

The oath is duly mentioned below, though with slight variations.

> 'Henricus dux juravit aliis duobus Henricis super reliquias de Bridlynton quod coronam nunquam affectaret.'

[1] p. 33; the authorship of this chronicle is discussed below, pp. 78 seqq.
[2] *Annales Henrici Quarti* (Rolls Series in 'Trokelowe'), p. 368.
[3] *The Chronicle of John Hardyng* (1812), p. 352.

Hardyng is one whose testimony, other things being equal, one would more readily reject than believe, but so confirmed, the genuineness of this proclamation which has a real bearing on the question of Richard's deposition, must be accepted.

The value of this unusual little chronicle, compounded of two such different elements, is greater than perhaps might be gathered by a casual reading. In the early part we feel the impact of great events upon that part of England that was most attached to Richard II: it was written close to these events, and it is the unique and pathetic statement of the case of those who believed in him. Yet whoever feels that Richard has been hardly used by historians, will scarcely claim to revise the general verdict of contemporaries on the strength of this Dieulacres chronicle. It does indeed suggest that Richard had a party in 1399 had he known how to use it; but it illumines no dark place in the reign before the year 1399, and the writer in his abuse of Henry IV shows a malice at least as great as that with which he credits his opponents. But if it helps Richard but little, it does much, it will be seen, to blacken the character of his enemies, and to discredit the official version on the Rolls of Parliament of the actual process of deposition.

The work of the continuator leaves no such direct impression as that of the original writer: but it is at least plain, from his own statement, that he had a sound conception of truth in historical writing. He had grasped how much evil is spoken in current gossip of men who hold great positions, and in his account of the battle of Shrewsbury there is every reason to think he lived up to his own standard, writing *per veram noticiam et non per aliorum loquelam.*

II

The Revolution of 1399 is perhaps as fully documented as any event of equal importance in medieval history, yet the main trend of events remains in obscurity, overshadowed not by a cloud of witnesses but from their alinement into two hostile camps. The contemporary authorities have been ranged against each other as Lancastrian propagandists or as French royalists—English testimony versus French, one man's word against another's. On the whole, orthodox historians have accepted the English version. They follow the lead of Stubbs who dismissed the crucial problem of the place and terms of Richard's abdication in two sentences. 'He saw at once that all was over, and made no attempt to stem the tide of desertion and ingratitude. After a conference held at Conway . . . he offered to resign the crown.' This rapid slurring over the decisive moment in the revolution reflects the attitude of the official Lancastrian apologists, the St. Albans Chroniclers, and Adam of Usk. Behind them is the weighty testimony of the Parliament Roll, and to challenge it is to challenge the orthodox interpretation of the whole cause and course of the revolution.

Stubbs dismissed the main French authority, Creton, as containing 'so much else that is at variance with our other authorities that it cannot be relied on implicitly', but as far back as 1824 Creton's editor, Webb, rejected the official version and maintained that the decisive point of variance was the place and terms of Richard's abdication. Was it at Conway, at Flint, or in the Tower, and on what conditions? Accepting Creton's story in detail, he concluded: 'I am reluctantly compelled to look upon the ground of Richard's retirement . . . given in the Roll of Resignation to be a gross fabrication by Henry IV for purposes of state. . . .'[1]

In 1846 Benjamin Williams, the editor of the *Traison et Mort*, put forward the view that the Parliament Roll must be 'branded with fabrication' because it was contradicted by 'the testimony of two foreign and independent

[1] *Archaeologia*, xx. 138.

chroniclers'.[1] This judgement was adopted by Wallon in *Richard II: Épisode de la Rivalité de la France et de l'Angleterre* (1864).[2] He accepted the whole French version and concluded that 'la fausseté de l'abdication de Richard à Conway est prouvée'.

Webb, Williams, and Wallon came to the same conclusion for reasons that were substantially the same. They believed that Creton's *Histoire du roy d'Angleterre Richard* and the *Traison et Mort* were independent of each other, and they accepted Creton's picture of himself as an eyewitness at Conway. The French authorities name only Northumberland as Henry's envoy, and this, a matter on which an eyewitness could not err, is made a test of English veracity. The English official version emphasizes the presence of Archbishop Arundel; therefore, they argue, it must be false. They also point out the improbability of abdication at Conway, where Richard was free, rather than at Flint, where he was a prisoner.

All these arguments, except the last, rest on premisses which do not bear close examination. The two French authorities are not independent, but interdependent. The author of the *Traison* began his narrative at 1397 and apparently wrote with special knowledge until Richard's departure for Ireland in May 1399. For the critical months of June to September he obviously borrowed from Creton, adding no detail of his own and merely swelling his text by putting into Richard's mouth much tearful complaining and rhetorical appeals to the king and princes of France. As an independent witness he must be put out of court. We are left with Creton, on his own showing an eyewitness from Richard's sailing for Ireland until his imprisonment in Chester Castle. The exact and realistic detail of much of his narrative bears out the claim, but it has been too hastily assumed that because he was an eyewitness for part of the time that

[1] *Chronique de la Traison et Mort de Richard Deux* (Eng. Hist. Soc., 1846), p. 202, note.

[2] Vol. ii, p. 247.

he was an eyewitness all the time. This is exactly what he wished his readers to believe, but in his double anxiety to convince and to make a pathetic appeal for Richard he overreached himself. He admits that he did not sail with Richard from Ireland; 'for the sake of song and merriment', he went with Salisbury's contingent to Conway. At the point when he describes Salisbury's advance to the Cheshire border his style becomes inflated and the sequence of events confused. There is no longer anything in his narrative to suggest personal observation and much that can be explained only as a misunderstanding of the tales of others. He reports with equal fullness Richard's conclaves at Conway and Henry's at Chester, and has a more convincing account of the surrender of Holt than of anything that was happening in Wales at the same time. His chronology will not work. He says that Richard first heard of Henry's landing through news of the executions at Bristol which we know took place on 29 July.[1] He then describes how Richard was hindered by Aumarle's treachery from sailing until eighteen days after Salisbury had left. Even if Salisbury could have got under way as soon as 1 August, Richard could not have reached South Wales before 19 August. Yet he gives the date of Richard's coming to Chester as 22 August, making no allowance for the journey north and even saying that eight days were spent in waiting for a reply to a message sent to Henry. To fill in the time, he describes aimless wanderings from Conway to Beaumaris, to Carnarvon and back again, castles which the king had really visited on his hurried march north from Milford. In fact, he plainly had no personal knowledge of Richard's plans or movements and cannot be accepted as an eyewitness. Probably Salisbury left him with the garrison at Flint when he withdrew on Conway, an explanation which would account for the reappearance of convincing detail from the point when Northumber-

[1] *Rot. Parl.* iii. 656. Petition of Rauf Grene.

land brought Richard to Flint. It would also account for his failure to mention Archbishop Arundel's mission to Conway, a fact on which all other authorities are agreed, and for the false and hollow ring in Richard's lamentations. This forlorn and weeping king, railing against ingratitude, is a propagandist legend; the Richard Creton saw with his own eyes was 'pale with anger'.

If we thus reduce the French authorities to one and dismiss Creton's claim to be heard as an eyewitness, it must be granted that Webb and his followers have failed to prove their case. The value of their work lies in the attention they draw to the inherent improbabilities of the story on the Parliament Roll. We are asked to believe that Richard abdicated at Conway when he was free and in a strong castle with shipping in the bay which could have brought him to Dublin or to Bordeaux, and that he confirmed his abdication in the Tower with joyful face (*hilari vultu*), and without any protest of his right to confront Parliament or to have some form of trial. These difficulties, first stated over a century ago, have never been resolved nor the real value of the French narratives estimated. The discovery of new chronicle material and the examination of official documents makes it possible to open the whole question again and to attempt to find an answer.

In the first place it is necessary to fix the chronology of events. Stubbs, Ramsay, Tait, and Tout accept the dates of the *Annales*, Evesham, Creton, and the *Traison* in so far as they place the critical days of negotiation and surrender in the third full week of August, but some juggling with figures was necessary before they reached the conclusion that Richard surrendered at Conway on the seventeenth, saw Henry at Flint on the eighteenth, rode to Chester on the nineteenth, and set out for London on the following day.[1] They had no warrant for

[1] *Traison* dates the surrender 18 Aug., *Annales Ricardi Secundi* (Rolls Series), 20 Aug., and Creton gives 22 Aug. as the day when Henry brought

putting the Conway interview on the seventeenth, but it was necessary to push everything back one day to account for the issue of writs for a parliament at Chester on the nineteenth. Even then they made little allowance for the time and fatigue of the fifty miles' hard riding between Conway and Chester or for the march of some thousands of Henry's army to Flint and back again. They would have been wiser to adopt the chronology of Usk, who was certainly among the Lancastrian camp-followers. He shifts all events a week earlier and his dates are confirmed by official records. Henry was at Chester on 9 August, and there letters patent were issued by Richard on 16 and 17 August.[1] It is true that the Regent, York, was attesting royal letters at exactly the same time, but these are dated at Wallingford. The letters dated at Chester are the first that can be connected with the king's itinerary since his departure for Ireland in May, and we must accept them as proof of Richard's presence. We may assume, therefore, that he was in Chester on 16 August, and place the critical days of negotiation and surrender in the preceding week.

This change in chronology is not without significance. It brings order into the hitherto meaningless manœuvres of Lancastrian and royalist armies, and it throws into strong relief the relentless pressure of Henry's strategy and his full knowledge of the movements of the king. Henry was still at Bristol when he heard of Richard's landing in South Wales;[2] at once he guessed that the enemy's objective was Chester and made a rapid march north to forestall him. At Shrewsbury he had news from

Richard to Chester. Evesham makes the envoys set out on Sunday the seventeenth to go to Richard, *abierunt ad regem*. They could not have reached Conway before the eighteenth, and he definitely dates the surrender *tertia die post haec, id est die Martis* (19 Aug.).

[1] On 10 Aug. Henry issued a safe conduct to the prior of Beauval, tested at Chester, Madox, *Formulare Anglicanum*, p. 327. Usk and the Dieulacres chronicler agree that he reached Chester on the previous day. For the letters patent see *Cal. Pat. Rolls*, pp. 591, 592.

[2] *Annales*, p. 247.

the deserters, Scales and Bardolf, and at Chester Thomas Percy and Aumarle came in, running the gauntlet of the Welsh of the Towy valley to join his banner.[1] Salisbury's army, which had advanced to the Cheshire border, scattered in a panic, hearing that the king was dead; its commander, after this pitiful display of incompetence, withdrew to Conway, with barely a hundred men.[2] All this took place in the second full week of August. In the same week Richard, who had sailed from Ireland about 24 July,[3] had lost his first army at Haverford West[4] through the treachery of Percy and Aumarle. He then travelled hard 160 miles along the Welsh coast to join the second army which he had sent with Salisbury to Conway, no doubt with orders to raise North Wales and Cheshire on his behalf; he found that it had dispersed on the eve of his coming. The chronology shows that Richard and Henry must both have been hurrying north at exactly the same time, only Henry, moving on the interior lines of the Wye and the Dee, was naturally far quicker. He reached Chester on 9 August, and at once sent his envoys to Conway. Richard's messengers to him arrived just after Northumberland and the archbishop had set out. Even if Richard took three days to deliberate, as the *Dieulacres Chronicle* suggests, he could still have left Conway on 14 August (the date given by Usk), reached Flint on the fifteenth, and on the sixteenth, when Henry's army had deployed before the castle, gone as a prisoner to Chester. We thus shorten by a week the time of Richard's wanderings in Wales, which historians have taken as a sign of crazy panic. Even with favouring

[1] Evesham, p. 154; Creton, pp. 104–5. [2] Creton, p. 71.

[3] P.R.O., T.R.E. Enrolled Accounts, 364/34. *Annales*, p. 248. [This note and the date in the text have both been changed to meet criticism kindly given us by Mr. H. G. Wright and J. W. H. Redfearn.]

[4] Richard's personal baggage, plate, and chapel furniture were seized at Haverford West, where he probably abandoned it before his march north. Palgrave, *Antient Kalendars and Inventories of the Treasury of the Exchequer*, iii. 358.

winds from Ireland, only a bare fortnight can have passed before he heard that Henry was in Cheshire. He had lost two armies in as many weeks because Percy and Aumarle were knaves and Salisbury was a fool, but he had still his liberty and the self-confidence of an anointed king. He had not yet time to distrust his native ingenuity or to understand the terrible danger of his position. By cornering Richard in North Wales, Henry had isolated him from his supporters and cut him off from all authentic news. Bold in his ignorance, he took the risk of staying at Conway instead of withdrawing by sea. Is it probable that he should have promised to abdicate at the first message from his enemy?

In what may fairly be called the official Lancastrian Chronicles there is agreement over a plain tale of Richard's abdication at Conway. The *Annales* describe how Richard, when he saw no hope of escape, sent Exeter to Chester and how Archbishop Arundel and Northumberland came back to him as Bolingbroke's envoys. Then he told them 'that he wished to resign and to be relieved of the trouble of governing, provided his life were spared . . . and that he had security for eight companions'. When this security was granted he went to Flint to speak with Bolingbroke, and the cousins rode together, *bonum vultum invicem*, to Chester. Walsingham tells the same story in a shortened form and Usk repeats it, slightly amplified and with a change of dates. That we have here the official narrative is made clear by the definite statement on the roll of the Deposition Parliament: 'idem rex . . . apud Conewey in North Wallia in sua libertate existens promisit Domino Thome Archiepiscopo Cantuariensi et dicto Comiti Northumbr' se velle cedere et renunciare Corone Anglie et Francie et sue Regie Magestati. . . .'[1]

To this Creton's narrative is a flat contradiction. Northumberland offered Richard fair terms at Conway.

[1] *Rot. Parl.* iii. 416.

If he would agree to refer to Parliament Henry's claim to be hereditary seneschal and to permit the trial of five of his councillors, he should be *couronnez haultement, roi et seigniur*. 'Duke Henry . . . wisheth for nothing but his land, and that which appertaineth to him; neither would have anything that is yours, for you are his immediate rightful king.' After some privy consultation, Richard decided to feign agreement in hope of finding a way to his revenge; 'There are some of them', he said, 'whom I will flay alive.' When Northumberland was told his decision he replied—'Sire, let the body of our Lord be consecrated. I will swear that there is no deceit in this affair and that the duke will observe the whole as you have heard me relate it here.' Each of them then heard mass and the earl 'made oath upon the body of our Lord'. The *Traison* is merely a redaction of the same story and, as Creton was not an eyewitness, we cannot reject the official narrative on his bare word. It is only by the help of other contemporary sources that we can decide between witnesses so sharply divergent.

We cannot fairly deduce anything from silence, even from partisans like Gower and *Richard the Redeless*. But the Monk of Evesham deserves close consideration as a Lancastrian contemporary chronicler who gives us more exact topographical detail about Henry's movements than any other writer. He borrowed freely from St. Albans for the earlier part of his work and probably had access to the official *cedula* of the deposition parliament, as he quotes with verbal accuracy Richard's formal act of resignation. His story is that Richard interviewed the archbishop and Northumberland at Flint and was then taken to Conway where Henry came to him with all reverence and said he had returned to enjoy his life, lands, and inheritance. There is no mention of abdication, but the transposition of Flint and Conway discredits the whole story. It cannot be imagined that Richard was carried forty miles back into Wales before Henry came to him. It may be explained away as a mere slip of the pen, but is it not possible that the confusion arose out of conflict between what Evesham had heard in the west and what he had read in the official *cedula*?

The first part of the *Dieulacres Chronicle*, now that we can be reasonably sure of its date and provenance, appears to us to decide the issue against the Parliament Roll. Though clearly independent in origin, it dovetails into Creton's story at point after point. A false adviser delayed Richard's sailing; Creton names him as Aumarle. Only fifteen remained in the royal suite; Creton says at one time thirteen and at another sixteen were faithful to the king. Richard lodged at Harlech, Carnarvon, and Beaumaris; Creton mentions, though in great confusion, visits to Beaumaris and Carnarvon. Apart from Creton's omission of Archbishop Arundel, the Dieulacres story of what happened at Conway is the French version, shorn of its rhetoric and propaganda. Henry's envoys claimed for him the hereditary stewardship of England and a free parliament; they swore on the host that Richard *staret in suo regali potestate et dominio*. After three days Richard accepted these terms, and yet at Flint he was treated as a captive and a slave. There can be no doubt that the French version of the surrender and that current in Cheshire are essentially the same.

Further confirmation comes from a continuation of the *Polychronicon*, one manuscript of which belonged to the Cistercian abbey of Whalley, Lancashire.[1] The monks of Whalley, like those of Dieulacres, had migrated from a Cheshire site to Lancastrian territory and, through their estates round Stanlaw, they retained a close connexion with the Palatinate.[2] The Chronicle breaks off at 1430 and, from the treatment of the French war, it

[1] Harleian MS. 3600; identical with Cotton Dom. A. XII for Henry IV's reign. Kingsford, *English Historical Literature*, pp. 279 ff., prints the fifteenth-century portion under the title 'A Northern Chronicle. 1399–1430.'

[2] *Coucher Book of Whalley Abbey*, ed. W. A. Hulton, Cheetham Society, 1847.

may be assumed that it was written not long after that date. The account of Richard's reign takes the same general line as the *Dieulacres Chronicle*.

f. 232^{v}. 'Postmodum prefatus dux cum complicibus suis ivit Cestriam ubi dominus Ricardus rex securitate sibi facta per sacramentum domini Thome Arundel et comitis Northumbrie venit Cestriam ad colloquium, sed prefatus dux Herfordie contra iuramentum predictum cepit ibidem eundem Ricardum rege[m] et ducens London, posuit in turri London' in custodia donec resignaret sibi coronam regni cum omni iure sibi pertinente.

'. . . Postmodum Ricardus quondam rex translatus est de turri London' usque ad castrum de Pomfret ubi diu ante mortem pane et aqua ut dicebatur sustentatus tandem fame necatus est secundum communem famam et sepultus apud Langley; deinde tempore Henrici quinti translatus est London' et ibi in ecclesia Westmon' honorifice tumulatur.'[1]

It will be noted that Richard is said to have gone to Chester *ad colloquium* on security given on oath by Arundel and Northumberland. Though the whole story is contracted into a sentence, it is remarkable that the essential facts have been retained.

When we consider that the narrative of Creton is confirmed at the critical point by the Chronicles of Dieulacres and Whalley, and when we weigh this evidence against the significant confusion of Evesham and the smooth improbabilities of the official version, it is impossible to halt any longer between two opinions. The account on the Parliament Roll of the place and time of Richard's abdication must be false, deliberately concocted to gloss over the capture and coercion of the reigning king.

If we reject the story of free resignation at Conway confidence is naturally shaken in the account on the Parliament Roll of the true abdication in the Tower. It has often been noted that there is something strange in

[1] There follows a remarkable passage about a deposition of Richard in 1388, printed and discussed in Note B. Below, pp. 91–5.

the description of Richard as showing a glad countenance (*hilari vultu*) to the commissioners who visited him in prison and in his insistence in reading his own renunciation, 'Idem tamen Rex gratanter, ut apparuit, ac hillari vultu, cedulam . . . tenens, dixit semetipsum velle legere, et distincte perlegit eandem.'[1] Webb remarked on 'an overstrained affectation of cheerful acquiescence . . . which defeats itself. The parties are all very courteous and happy in each other's society while it lasts. . . . The whole is curious; and, I fear, in many particulars, a piece of deliberately recorded falsehood.' Ramsay drew exactly the opposite conclusion; he took Richard's good humour to prove that he had security for his personal safety: 'There is', he says, 'a naif simplicity about it that inspires confidence.'

Examination of other contemporary sources appears to us once more to decide the question against the official record. In the first place Usk, a strong Lancastrian witness, makes no mention of Richard's cheerfulness in the abdication scene; it would have accorded ill with his account of a visit to the Tower a week earlier when, he says, he heard the king 'discoursing sorrowfully . . . musing on his ancient and wonted glory and on the fickle fortune of the world'.[2] Evesham is again just different enough to arouse suspicion. He represents Richard as causing the renunciation to be written out and merely saying, *Ego Ricardus, Rex praedictus, me subscribo*.[3] The *Traison*, a better authority than Creton for events in London, omits all reference to the renunciation and records as the king's last speech before deposition a demand to be brought before Parliament for trial.[4] The brief account in the *Dieulacres Chronicle* is a convincing compromise between the French and English versions.

[1] *Rot. Parl.* iii. 416. Cf. *Annales*, 255.

[2] Usk, p. 30.

[3] Evesham, p. 159, with the addition that Richard reserved for himself certain lands and revenues which he intended to bequeath for his soul to Westminster.

[4] *Traison*, p. 218.

'Unde ne parliamentum intraret humiliter, ut dictum est, rogavit; et corona regni super humo posita Deo ius suum resignavit.' Resignation to God instead of to Bolingbroke is a last gesture characteristic of Richard. There is no contemporary confirmation for the fatuous scene of smiles and cordiality rehearsed for us on the Parliament Roll, and there seems no alternative but to reject it altogether.

A third and last issue is raised by the reference in the *Dieulacres Chronicle* and in the *Traison* to Richard's demand to be given a hearing in Parliament. There is no mention of any such demand in the official version, where it is implied that Richard was thoroughly satisfied with agreements reached in Conway or in the Tower. New light is thrown on the subject by examination of the unpublished portion of the work known as *Giles' Chronicle*,[1] which follows Evesham closely from 1377 to 1402 and extends to 1455. It is extant in two manuscripts, Sloane 1776 and the Royal MS. 13, C. 1. We may dismiss the Sloane MS. as a later copy, as it gives the four reigns continuously, while the Royal MS. has the reigns out of order as follows: Henry V, Henry VI, Richard II, and Henry IV. The part dealing with Henry V's reign is the *Gesta Henrici Quinti* of Thomas Elmham. We have, therefore, three distinct chronicles, one of which is a variant of Evesham.

The Royal MS. contains two versions of the events of 30 September, the second day of the deposition parliament; one is scored out and reads at first sight like a rough draft of the other. A closer examination shows that the whole passage was partly copied and partly condensed from the Parliament Roll, with the addition of new matter describing a debate on the justice of deposing Richard without a hearing. Its significance cannot be understood except by verbal comparison with the Parliament Roll.

[1] *Chronicon incerti auctoris*, ed. Giles, 1848.

Rot. Parl. iii. 417.

'In crastino autem, videlicet die martis in festo Sancti Jeronimi, in magna aula apud Westm' in loco ad parliamentum tenendum honorifice preparato, dictis Archiepiscopis Cantuarien' et Eboracen', ac duce Lancastrie, aliisque ducibus ac dominis . . . presentibus . . . supradictus archiepiscopus Eboracen' suo et dicti Hereforden' episcopi nomine . . . eandem . . . cessionem et renunciationem per alium, primo in Latinis verbis, et postea in Anglicis, legi fecit ibidem. Et statim ut fuerat interrogatum a statibus et populo tunc ibidem presentibus, primo videlicet ab archiepiscopo Cantuarien' predicto, cui ratione dignitatis et prerogative ecclesie sue Cantuarien' metropolitice in hac parte competit primam vocem habere inter ceteros prelatos et proceres regni, si pro eorum interesse, et utilitate regni vellent renunciationem et cessionem eandem admittere? Status iidem et populus reputantes, ex causis per ipsum regem in sua renunciatione et cessione predictis specificatis, hoc fore multum expediens, renunciationem et cessionem hujusmodi singuli singillatim, et in communi cum populo, unanimiter et concorditer admiserunt. Postquam quidem admissionem fuerat publice tunc ibidem expositum, quod ultra cessionem et renunciationem hujusmodi, ut prefertur, admissam, valde foret expediens ac utile regno predicto, pro omni scrupulo et sinistra suspicione tollendis, quod plura crimina et defectus per dictum regem circa malum regimen regni sui frequentius perpetrata, per modum articulorum in scriptis redacta.'

Royal MS. 13, C. 1, ff. 115–v, excerpt A.

'Et perlecta cedula renunciacionis omnes ad hospicia redierunt et in crastino die viz. in festo Ieronimi apud Westmonasterium fuerat ista renunciacio coram omnibus dominis tam spiritualibus quam temporalibus primo in Latinis verbis secundo in Anglicis [perlecta]. Et statim ut fuerat interrogatum a stantibus et populo tunc ibidem presentibus primo viz. ab archiepiscopo Cantuar' cui racione dignitatis et prerogative ecclesie sue Cantuar' metropolitece in hac parte competit primam vocem habere inter ceteros prelatos et proceres regni, si pro eorum interesse et utilitate regni vellent renunciacionem eamdem et cessionem admittere, cui idem archiepiscopus et quam plures alii domini affirmant illam renunciacionem et cessionem regno fore utile et expediens. Sed quidam alii opinantur quod ista renunciacio licet fuerat ore regio proclamata verumtamen dummodo fuerat in carceribus a libertate proprie voluntatis impeditus non penitus agnoscitur an huius resignacio fuerat ex plenaria et sinsera cordis affectione aut mortis timore incussus omnia facere et dicere que libenter detentores offerebant. Et cum regia dignitas maiorem privilegii libertatem quam alii inferiores persone, postulat ex racione hinc est quod ipse idem rex quemadmodum alii persone tamen inferiores poterint publice, sic ipse in persona propria coram iudice aut sui imperii populo iuxta sui intencionis arbitrium suam plenariam voluntatem intimare quia sic nostra regni statuta et privilegia vendicant discernendum pro omni suspicione evitanda. Tamen pro huiusmodi suspicione tollenda alia pars adversa allegebat plura crimina et defectus per regem perpetrata in maximum dedecus et detrimentum toto regno.' [A summary of the 'Articles' against Richard follows.]

Royal MS. 13, C. 1, f. 122, excerpt B. A scored-out passage.

'Sed aliqui affirmant absentem et impeditum a libertate sui iuris quod equali libra esset omnibus regni incolis concedenda hoc ab ipso rege non fore deneganda viz. pro declaracione sue voluntatis in persona propria coram regni statibus et plebeis saltem in parliamento compareret quia quamvis ista renunciacio fuerat sine reclamacione oretenus prununciata tamen quia in carcerali tedio tentus poterit a quibusdam personis estimari quod cicius timore quam sincera cordis intencione omnia ista fecit, attamen cum maior numerus dominorum et eciam comitatum p[ro] tunc favebant duci Lancastrie affirmabant prefatam resignacionem fore et esse utile et expediens, unde pro maiori suspicione tollenda alligabant plura crimina per dictum regem in magnum detrimentium proceribus regni et eciam omni communitati perpetrata.'

At first glance comparison of the three passages suggests that we have before us an excised portion of the Parliament Roll, but the wording and the repetition in two forms make it impossible to put forward so simple an explanation. We have either two passages from the same author, or else an excerpt from some other source has been copied in as an afterthought. Farther on in the Royal MS. the same trick of writing in a second or even a third and fourth passage on the same subject recurs.[1] We have three versions of the burning of Richard Wick and two of the death of the duchess of Clarence: they are not verbally identical and in each case the information varies slightly. There are also three accounts of the disgrace of the duchess of Gloucester; they differ considerably in detail and in treatment: two are cautiously worded but the third and most severe mentions her death sixteen years later at Flint. Finally there are four accounts of events overseas in 1441–3 which deal with the appointment of Somerset as Captain-General in France over the head of the duke of York. This appointment was a provoking cause of the Wars of the Roses, and it is significant that two variants are Lancastrian and two Yorkist in sympathy. In short, differences in matter, style, and point of view make it impossible to believe that they were all composed by the same writer, and we may reasonably conclude that they are extracts from various sources collected by the compiler. This hypothesis coincides with what we know of William Worcester from whose papers the manuscript was probably put together.[2] His *Itinerarium* shows that he was a disorderly and tireless copyist of chronicles; he refers to no less than ten, more than half of which have not been traced.[3] We conclude, therefore, that we have excerpts from two chronicles, one from an unknown source and the other from an

[1] The later variants are not in Giles's edition, but are printed by Kingsford, *English Historical Literature*, pp. 339–41, as 'Brief Notes, 1441–3.'

[2] British Museum Catalogue of Royal MSS. describes the whole volume as 'Historical Collections made, wholly or in part, by William Worcester (†1482?), secretary to Sir John Fastolf'.

[3] Chronicles of Wells, friars of Norwich, St. John's, Bristol, St. Thomas's, Bristol, Dominicans of Thetford and Augustinians of Yarmouth; excerpts from the *Brut*; notes from Gildas, Giraldus Cambrensis, and Marianus Scotus. See *Itinerarium*, ed. Jas. Nasmyth, Cambridge, 1778.

earlier portion of that printed by Giles. To estimate their historical value it is necessary to come to at least a tentative conclusion as to their date, provenance, and authorship.

Analysis of *Giles' Chronicle*, to which excerpt A belongs, brings out some puzzling facts. It breaks off abruptly with a reference to the Parliament of 1411, and its general treatment of Henry IV and the Prince of Wales is that of a cautious contemporary, yet it cannot be earlier than 1421, as the marriage of the duke of Clarence, who died in that year, is described as barren. Analysis of the subject matter shows that it has been made up from several sources. Down to 1402 Evesham is followed closely, though with interesting emendations or omissions and the interpolation of a long complaint of fortune, ascribed to W. Feruby. References to events in London are often in substance the same as those in the *London Chronicles*, *Gregory's Chronicle*, and the *English Chronicle*;[1] Kingsford therefore concluded that they had a common original, the work of a London writer. But this London source and Evesham are only a part—and the most commonplace part—of the compilation. It has two more remarkable characteristics; one the steady citation of official documents, the other special knowledge of events in the North. The parliament or statute rolls are used for six out of the nine parliaments of Henry IV;[2] sometimes the text is copied verbatim, sometimes it is neatly contracted. Only a clerk in the Chancery could have had access so continuously to official records. For the North we have a unique explanation of Hotspur's reason for revolt, the sole text of the tripartite convention between Northumberland, Glendower, and Mortimer, and an account, with a good deal of local detail, of

[1] Ed. Davies (Camden Society).

[2] 1399, Giles, pp. 3–7, *Rot. Parl.* iii. 452, 453. 1401, Giles, pp. 22–3, Stat. 2, Hen. IV, cap. xv. 1402, Giles, pp. 34–5, *Rot. Parl.* iii. 487. 1404, Giles, pp. 35–9, *Rot. Parl.* iii. 526–7, 528. 1406, Giles, pp. 49–52, *Rot. Parl.* iii. 571–2, 574–6. 1411, Giles, p. 63, *Rot. Parl.* iii. 658.

Archbishop Scrope's execution. If the writer was a Chancery clerk he must have had a strong northern connexion.

The chronicle is, in fact, a patchwork, rather clumsily cobbled together, but at the same time the whole work bears the stamp of a clearly defined personality. The writer has a guarded but steady sympathy for Richard II. He cuts out the blackest charges in Evesham and, writing of the starvation of the heir to the Scottish throne, he slips in *quemadmodum Anglici Ricardum regem suum interemerunt.* His attitude to Henry IV is correct but grudging. He omits Evesham's praise of him as *pius et misericors et generosus* and emphasizes the disasters of the Welsh campaigns. Though careful to preserve the forms of loyal speech, his sympathies were plainly with the northern rebels. He gives a shrewd and convincing picture of Thomas Percy as *causa principalis* of the battle of Shrewsbury, sets out Archbishop Scrope's manifesto with obvious satisfaction, and skilfully tells the story of his execution as the passion of a saint. He names no northern lord, not even Westmorland or Fitzhugh, as having a share in the *execrabile opus.* We have the impression of a man who had friends on both sides or whose personal opinions ran counter to his professional interests.

Now the only personal excursus in the chronicle is a long lament on the death of Richard, beginning *de hujus mundi fortuna et mutatione subita scribit W. Feruby in hunc modum.* Kingsford identifies this Feruby with the William Feriby who was taken prisoner at Conway and executed immediately after the Holland rising early in 1400; as he was certainly dead before Richard's death was announced he cannot have written the lament. But the Feribys were a great Yorkshire family of officials, connected with, if not related to, the Thoresby-Ravenser-Waltham clan, and several of them at this time were called William.[1] A William Feriby, notary public, went

[1] Tout, *Chapters in Mediaeval Administrative History,* iii. 215–16.

to the Tower with the commission to hear Richard's renunciation; he was probably the William Feriby who was the Chancellor of the Prince of Wales in 1403 and master of St. Leonard's Hospital, York, from 1409 to 1415.[1] St. Leonard's Hospital was a typical Chancery benefice, held throughout the fourteenth century by king's clerks, like Gilbert de Stapleton and Richard de Ravenser. It is tempting to find in this William Feriby the Chancery clerk of northern connexions who wrote *Giles' Chronicle*, especially as William Worcester in his *Annales* has a reference to *Chronicam Wi. Feriby* which he borrowed from the bishop of Ely.[2] But this Feriby died in 1415, six years before the earliest date when *Giles' Chronicle* can have been written. He cannot have been the author, but he may have collected the official documents and excerpts from the Parliament Roll which, with his lament, were used by some one who had access to his material. It is possible that excerpt B may come from a lost chronicle begun by William Feriby, afterwards carried on to Henry VI's reign by some one who wrote certain of the additions to *Giles' Chronicle* printed by Kingsford.

Assuming that Feriby collected much of the material, we may hazard a suggestion that the author was one of his successors at St. Leonard's. Robert Fitzhugh, master from 1415 to 1431, was a northern clerk, the son of Henry V's chamberlain, the nephew of Archbishop

[1] *Rot. Parl.* iii. 416; Nicolas, *Proceedings of Privy Council*, i. 206; *Cal. Pat. Rolls, 1408–13*, p. 88; *1413–16*, p. 283. I should like to thank Professor A. Hamilton Thompson for his help in unravelling the intricacies of the Feriby family, a subject which is peculiarly his own.

[2] Published in *Letters and Papers illustrative of the wars of the English in France*, ed. Joseph Stevenson, 1864. The note, sub anno 1446, vol. ii, part ii, p. 764, is as follows: 'Nota folia duo immediate praecedentia bene, et latus sequens, et pro temporibus regis Ricardi Secundi, Henrici etiam V et Henrici regis VI nota chronicam Wi. Feriby, ut in libro domini Nicholai, prioris Sancte Margarete de Lyne, quem accomodavit domino meo Johanni Alkok, episcopo Eliensi. Nota etiam chronica Ranulphi monachi Cistercensis' (sic).

Scrope, and the first cousin of Sir William Plumpton, executed in 1405. His sympathies may well have been divided between his uncle, the rebel and martyr, and his father who tricked him into surrender,[1] but there is nothing else in his career to carry the suggestion of his authorship farther. The next master of St. Leonard's was William Scrope (1431–56), another nephew of Archbishop Scrope, this time on the father's side.[2] He was king's clerk at the time of his appointment and held several other preferments in the North with a papal indulgence because 'by both parents he is of a race of barons'.[3] Raine suggests that he resigned because 'the wish to suppress the honours that were paid to Archbishop Scrope would destroy William Scrope's chance of holding preferment in York Minster'.[4] He had no other preferment before his death in 1463. It is remarkable that first one and then another nephew of the archbishop should have succeeded Feriby at St. Leonard's; either of them may have worked up his material into the form in which we find it in the Royal MS.

If we accept either of these Scropes as having a share in putting together Feriby's material, we have a clue to the way in which the manuscript came into the hands of William Worcester. Sir John Fastolf, Worcester's patron, was the stepfather of Stephen Scrope, the 'Master Stephen' of the Paston letters. He was the son of another Stephen Scrope, who was taken prisoner with the other Feriby at Conway in 1399, and his uncle was the earl of Wiltshire, beheaded at Bristol in the same year. His

[1] *Annales*, 407; *Historians of Church of York*, iii. 289. Fitzhugh was afterwards bishop of London, 1431–6.

[2] See Scrope pedigree, Note A, below, p. 90.

[3] *Cal. Pat. Rolls, 1431*, p. 181; *Cal. Papal Letters, 1417–31*, pp. 338–9.

[4] *Testamenta Eboracensia*, iii. 36. Raine cites from Torre MS. 224 his epitaph in York Minster: 'Hic jacet Magister Willelmus le Scrope, Archidiaconus Dunelm', et Residentarius in ecclesiis collegiatis beate Johannis Beverlac' et Sancti Wilfridi Rypon, qui obiit xii° die mensis Mai anno domini M.cccc.lxiii, cuius anime propitietur deus.'

mother, the heiress of Castlecombe, married Fastolf in 1409, and he spent much of his life at Caistor where Worcester was secretary. Fastolf treated his stepson badly and sold his wardship to Sir William Gascoigne: 'thorugh the wiche sale,' Stephen writes, 'I took sekenesses that kept me a XII or XIII yere swyng: whereby I am disfigured in my persone and shall be whilest I lyve. . . .'[1] He lived a sickly, studious life, translating from Christine de Pisan *The Boke of Knyghthode*; *The Boke of Noblesse*, also from Christine, was probably translated by him in collaboration with Worcester.[2] In Worcester, who 'said that he wold be as glad and as feyn of a good boke of Frensh or of poetre as my Mastr Fastolf wold be to purchase a faire manoir',[3] he must have found a congenial companion, and it is possible that he possessed or procured for his friend the chronicle which tells so much of his family's history and which may have been put together by one of his cousins of Masham.

Thus several converging lines of evidence, no one of which we can defend as strong in itself, leads us to the opinion that excerpts A and B are both derived from material collected by the Chancery clerk William Feriby, some of which was later worked up into *Giles' Chronicle* by a master of St. Leonard's, York. We are therefore inclined to treat the accounts of the deposition parliament as having the value of contemporary evidence. It is even possible that Feriby was an eyewitness. Confirmation of the whole story comes from the much-disputed passage in the *Traison* where the bishop of Carlisle spoke in Richard's defence:

'My lords, consider well before you give judgment upon what my lord the Duke has set forth, for I maintain that there is not one present who is competent and fit to judge such a sovereign as my lord the King whom we have acknowledged

[1] G. P. Scrope, *History of the Manor and Barony of Castle Combe*, p. 274.

[2] *The Epistle of Othea to Hector, or the Boke of Knyghthode*, ed. G. F. Warner, Roxburghe Club, 1904.

[3] *Paston Letters*, ed. Gairdner, i. 431.

our (liege) lord for the space of twenty years and more, and I will give you my reasons; there never was, nor is in this world, any false traitor nor wicked murderer, who, if he be taken prisoner by the hands of justice, is not, at the least, brought before the judge to hear his sentence. My lords, you have well and truly heard the accusations that my lord the Duke has made against King Richard; and it appears to me that you are about to give judgment, and to condemn King Richard, without hearing what he has to answer, or even his being present. . . .'[1]

The speech is in content almost identical with our excerpts, but the *Traison* places it not on 30 September, but on the following day, when Parliament did not meet. The *Eulogium* preserves the tradition of the bishop's presence at the deposition scene,[2] and it is much more probable that he made his protest then instead of waiting until after the coronation. The same charge of deposition by coercion and without a fair trial was brought against Henry again and again by the northern rebels,[3] and it was made as early as 1402 to the king himself. Certain friars were accused of plotting treason. Their leader, Robert Frisby, warden of the convent at Leicester, maintained before Henry in the Tower that Richard was 'veray king' of England. 'The king saide, "He resigned." The maister ansuerde, "He resigned ayens his wil in prison, the whiche is nought in the lawe. . . . He wolde not haue resigned . . . yf he hadde be at his fredoum; and a resignacion maad in prisoun is not fre. . . ."' The juries of London and Holbourne twice refused to

[1] *Traison*, pp. 221–2.

[2] *Eulogium*, iii. 383, Bolingbroke sat in his father's place *iuxta episcopum Carleoli*. The position cannot be correct as the spiritual and temporal peers already sat on opposite sides. This is illustrated in the miniature of the deposition scene, the earliest picture of a parliamentary session, B.M. Harl. MS. 1319, reproduced in *Archaeologia*, xx, Pl. XVI.

[3] e.g. the manifesto ascribed to Archbishop Scrope, but probably issued by Northumberland in 1407, *Historians of Church of York*, ii. 297; Hardyng, 349, says Northumberland told him that Richard made resignation 'under dures of prison in the Toure of London in fere of his life'. Cf. Hotspur's defiance before Shrewsbury, ibid., pp. 351 ff.

convict these friars, and they were finally sentenced to death on the verdict of jurors from the villages of Islington and Highgate.[1]

Holinshed knew the *Traison* through Hall, and from him Shakespeare drew the material for the speech he put into the mouth of Carlisle at the deposition parliament:

> What subject can give sentence on his king?
> And who sits here that is not Richard's subject?
> Thieves are not judged but they are by to hear,
> Although apparent guilt be seen in them;
> And shall the figure of God's majesty,
> His captain, steward, deputy-elect,
> Anointed, crowned, planted many years,
> Be judged by subject and inferior breath,
> And he himself not present? . . .

These lines are like a poet's echo, not only of the *Traison*, but of the clumsy Latin of the Royal MS. They are in harmony with the stiff legalism of the age and are confirmed by a long tradition of anti-Lancastrian disaffection. The first protest against the usurpation of Henry of Lancaster was made in the deposition parliament; the procedure of deposition as well as the act itself was a cause of the 'disorder, horror, fear, and mutiny' of the fifteenth century.

Thus collation of the official story of Richard's deposition with other sources of the early fifteenth century has led us to conclude that on three points the Parliament Roll has either distorted or suppressed the truth. The free resignation at Conway and the account of Richard's cheerful bearing in the Tower are soothing falsehoods which probably no one at the time believed or was expected to believe; silence about Richard's demand to confront Parliament and about a public protest on his behalf are deliberate suppressions of the truth. The statement in the Royal MS. that the articles of deposition

[1] *English Chronicle*, ed. Davies (Camden Society), pp. 25–6; *Eulogium*, pp. 393–4; *Cal. Cl. Rolls*, 1 June 1402, p. 528.

were drawn up as a substitute for the trial of Richard draws attention to their hasty composition and *ex parte* character. But it is on these articles that Stubbs and other constitutional historians have based their discussion of Richard's tyranny and his theory of absolutism. If, as we think, the authority of the Parliament Roll has been shaken, it will be necessary to go over all the ground again and to treat the official story of the revolution as carrying no more weight than any other tainted and partisan contemporary evidence.

NOTE A

SCROPE PEDIGREE

(N. H. Nicholas, *Scrope and Grosvenor Controversy*, vol. ii)

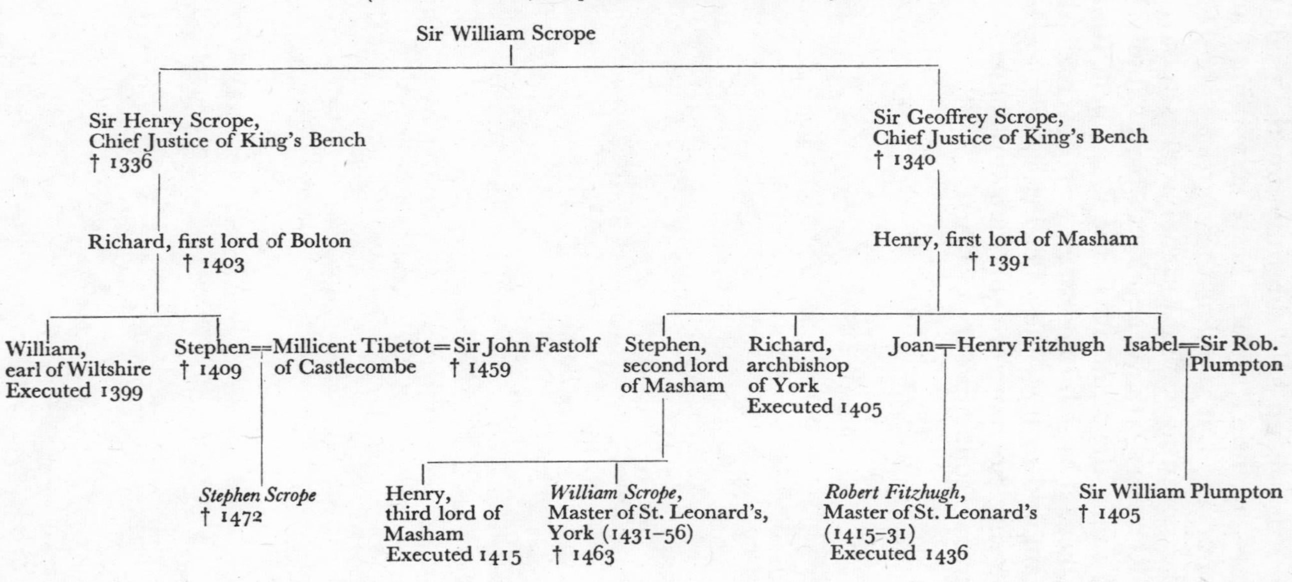

NOTE B

ANOTHER DEPOSITION OF RICHARD II?

Harleian MS. 3600.[1]

f. 232v. 'Hic intercerere disposui quod in tempore suo pretermissum fuit. Nam cum Thomas Wodstok comes de Bokyngham,[2] comes de Arundel, comes Warwyc' cum ceteris magnatibus consurrexissent adversus quosdam consiliarios regis et Symonem de Burlay decapitassent ac ducem Hibernie apud Ratcotebrige profugassent et Thomam de Molenewes cum aliis multis ibidem occidissent, adierunt regem Ricardum et eum de solio regali deposuerunt et sic per triduum mansit discoronatus; sed ill(is) de successione concertantibus, communibus volentibus exaltari in regem Thomam Wodstok sed e contra Henrico duce Herfordie[3] se de seniori fratre progenitum protestante ac per hoc regem se fore debere vendicante, videntes magnates et timentes ne illi duo inter se discordarent et illi quasi proditores notarentur concilium iniunt et regem Ricardum iterato recoronant ammoventes omnes familiares suos et consiliarios a maiori usque ad minimum, eidem alios assignantes ad quorum concilium rex regeretur, sed qualiter rex se de hiis vindicaverit supra patet.'

At first sight this story of a deposition of Richard II seems preposterous and directly counter to all contemporary evidence. A closer examination of the authorities shows that, while there is no direct confirmation of the deposition itself, there was one short period when it might have taken place.[4] After the defeat at Radcot Bridge (20 December), Richard shut himself up in the Tower. He knew that his plight was desperate, as by allowing de Vere to bring an army from Chester and by plotting

[1] See p. 75.

[2] Thomas of Woodstock had been duke of Gloucester since 1385.

[3] Henry was still only earl of Derby; he was not duke of Hereford until 1397.

[4] The detailed chronicles for the period 1387–8 are Walsingham, Knighton, the Anonymous of Westminster, and the short account of the Merciless Parliament and events immediately preceding it by Favent, *Camden Miscellany*, vol. xiv. Knighton is the least useful, except for official documents; Walsingham has a fair account of events in London; Westminster and Favent, one inclined to favour Richard and the other the official defence of the Appellants, are both of great value.

with the Londoners he had broken the protection, ratified on oath, which he had issued to the appellants on 18 November. By 27 December the army of the appellants was encamped at Clerkenwell, and the leaders had won over the citizens of London. The king was blockaded in the Tower and the Thames was guarded to prevent his escape by water. A parley was arranged by Archbishop Courtenay and Northumberland. Taking elaborate precautions against treachery, the appellants entered the Tower with 500 men and the gates were closed and guarded by their supporters. The uproar in the inner ward was so great that the king and the leaders withdrew into the chapel for quiet. What happened at the interview is obscure. Knighton and Favent represent Richard as agreeing at once to all that was demanded of him. Walsingham says that he promised in tears and confusion to hold a council at Westminster on the following day; the same evening he changed his mind, but was forced to yield by the threat of the appellants *quod eligerent alium sibi Regem.*[1] The Anonymous of Westminster describes a much more prolonged crisis. The appellants spoke sternly to Richard, rehearsed his misdeeds, and reminded him that *suum heredem fore indubie perfectae aetatis.*[2] Richard, *stupefactus*, swore to govern by their council, saving his crown and royal dignity. The barons then left him with a rough warning that if he wished to enjoy his crown and regality in the future he must keep faith with them.

Unfortunately authorities differ as to the date on which this interview was held. Knighton says 27 December; Favent and Walsingham, 28 December. The Anonymous of Westminster's chronology is confused at this point; he describes the whole of 28 December as spent in preliminary negotiations, implies that the interview took place on 29 December, and then names 30 December as the actual day. On the whole, the evidence suggests either 28 or 29 December. The point is of crucial importance if we are to find three days of deposition. A council was held on 1 January[3] at which new writs were issued for the

[1] This Council did not meet until 1 January; Walsingham is running events together too quickly.

[2] The earl of March, who was heir presumptive, was still a minor, and this ambiguous phrase may refer to Gloucester or to Derby.

[3] *Cal. Cl. Rolls*, p. 460; *Anon. Westminster*, p. 115.

coming parliament, and from that time onwards there can be no possible doubt that Richard was acknowledged as king by the appellants. If they ever deposed him, it must have been between 28 or 29 December and New Year's Day. It is, perhaps, significant that there is not a single entry on the close or patent rolls bearing the dates of the last three days of December.

Certain facts, which have not hitherto been emphasized, must also come under consideration. Gloucester's confession, exacted at Calais on the eve of his death (8 Sept. 1397), contains some important admissions.[1] In spite of the circumstances of its drafting, the document has a convincing ring. The saving clause, the ambiguity of the wording at the crucial point, and the poignant closing appeal for 'compassion and pytee' show that it could not have been dictated by Rickhill or concocted after the murder. He acknowledged:

> '. . . in that tyme (1387–8) that I came armed into my Lordes presence, and into his Palais, howsoever that I dede it for drede of my lyf, I knowleche for certain that I dede evyll, and azeyns his Regalie and his Estate. . . .'

He put forward as the final plea for mercy:

> '. . . It was never myn entent, ne my wyll, ne my thoght, for to do thynge that schuld have been distresse or harmyng azeyns the salvation of my lyege Loordys persone, as I wyll answer to for Godd at the day of Jugement. . . .'

He admitted:

> ' . . . that I among other communed for feer of my lyf to zyve up myn hommage to my Lord, I knowlech wel, that for certain that I among other communed and asked of certeins Clercs, whethir that we myght zyve up our homage for drede of our lyves, or non; and whethir that we assentyed therto for to do it, trewlich and by my trowth I ne have now none full mynde therof, bot I trowe rather ze than nay: Wherfor I submett me heygh and lowe evermore in his grace.'

The crucial paragraph concerns the deposition of the king, and we give it in full, transcribed from a copy of the confession, sewn as a schedule to the Parliament Roll of 1397.[2]

'Also in that I was in place ther it was communod and

[1] *Rot. Parl.* iii. 379. Cf. *E.H.R.*, 1923, xxxviii. 249–51.

[2] The original sealed confession is attached to *Parl. and Council Proceedings (Chancery) Roll 4*.

spoken in manere of deposail of my lyege loord trewly I knowlech wel that we wer assented ther to for two dayes or thre and than we for to have done oure homage and our oothes and putt hym as heyly in his estate as ever he was bot for sothe ther I knolech that I dede untruly and unkyndely as to hym that is my lyege loord and hath bene so gode and kynd loord to me wherfor I beseche to hym naght wyth stondyng myn unkyndenesse I beseche hym evermore of his mercy and of his grace as lowly as any creature may beseche it unto his lyege loord.' (Parliament Roll 61, m. 3, schedule.)

The avowal of armed coercion, the emphatic declaration that no personal injury to Richard was intended, and the guarded references to renunciation of allegiance and to deposition bear out and carry farther the story in the chronicles. In the deposition paragraph the phrase *We wer assented ther to for two dayes or thre* might be read as an independent confirmation of the Harleian MS.

The account of Gloucester and Derby contending over the succession also falls into line with what we know of the factions of the time. It is not always remembered that the five appellants belonged to two clearly marked parties. The original appeal, issued at Waltham Cross on 14 November and repeated before the king at Westminster on 17 November, was in the names of Gloucester, Arundel, and Warwick. They were the recognized leaders of the baronial opposition, and the muster of the army at Haringay was their work.[1] Derby and Nottingham, representing the Lancastrian faction, did not join them until de Vere's army was on the march. It was at this point that the project of deposition was first brought forward and opposed by Warwick, who may have held an intermediate position between the two groups. Furthermore, Knighton says that Richard detained Derby and Nottingham to sup with him after the interview in the Tower, and Walsingham tells the same story, omitting Nottingham. Later, Favent and Walsingham tell how Derby and Nottingham joined in the plea for Burley's life.[2] It

[1] *Rot. Parl.* iii. 248–9.

[2] Ibid. 431. Gloucester was said to have admitted to Rickhill at Calais that 'le Roy parla a luy de Monsieur Simond de Burley, et le dit Duk respondi a Roy, et disoit a luy, que s'il voloit estre Roy covient estre perfourne et fait.'

may therefore be granted that, if there was a dispute about Richard's successor, it must have followed the lines indicated by the Harleian MS.

Certain proceedings in the Merciless Parliament are not incompatible with the story of a deposition. Business was begun by a solemn declaration by the appellants that they had never imagined or consented to the death of the king. Favent represents Gloucester as demanding, through Speaker Plessington, an opportunity to clear himself of the charge of treason. The Chancellor's reply to him is strangely worded: 'Domine dux, ex quo oriundus excuteras de tam digna stirpe regali et ita proximus reperimini ei in linea collaterali non suspicabatur de vobis talia ymaginari.' The concluding scene of the parliamentary session is still more significant. After a solemn mass and sermon in Westminster Abbey, in the presence of the lords and commons, the king renewed his coronation oath and the lords spiritual and temporal 'ea quae domino regi solebant in sua coronatione praestare cum omni subjectione ac grato animo sibi exhibuerunt.'[1] Favent explains this remarkable procedure by saying it was done partly because the king had taken the oath *in minori etate* and partly 'propter cordium scrupulas et titubaciones tam penes regem quam penes proceres evellendas et evitandas . . . '. It may be that the repetition of the coronation oath was itself the cause of a later legend of deposition. If this be so, it is remarkable that it should have dropped almost out of knowledge only to be discovered again in a form that fits neatly into place with other evidence. But if, as we think, the story be true, it is easy to understand that both Richard and his enemies—he for his prestige and they from fear—would combine to check its circulation and force it into oblivion.

NOTE C

NEPHANDUS CULPEPER DE CANCIA NOMINATUS JAK STRAWE

JAK STRAWE is obviously a 'masonic' name, like Piers Plowman, and it is possible that we have here a clue to the family and social standing of Wat Tyler. Culpeper or Colepepir is a well-known Kentish name; the family had estates on the Medway,

[1] Higden, ix. 183; Favent, p. 24. Cf. Harleian MS. *iterato recoronant.*

where a fourteenth-century bridge crosses the river at Aylesford between Rochester and Maidstone. One Walter Colepepir died in 1326–7, seised of lands in Aylesford, East and West Farleigh, and other villages on the Medway, both north and south of Maidstone (Hasted, *Kent*, iii. 174). His descendants, Thomas and John, sat on various commissions in Kent in Richard II's reign; a John Colepepir served Gaunt as constable of Pevensey Castle and master forester of Ashdown Chase (*Register*, 279, 701). An entry on the close rolls (*Cal. Cl. Rolls*, p. 778, 8 Feb. 1381) names a Walter Colepepere as witness, with John Colepepir of Farleigh, to a charter quit claiming the manor of Cobham. The patent roll at almost exactly the same time (*Cal. Pat. Rolls*, p. 629, 15 Feb. 1381) records the appointment of Walter Colepepere as one of nine commissioners appointed to survey all ports in the hundreds of Hoo, Shamele, and Totyngtrowe, Kent, where galleys, barges, or other vessels might enter, and to guard against invasion by repair and construction of piles and trenches. The hundred of Hoo lies north of Rochester in the dreary, almost empty peninsula between the Thames and the Medway; it is opposite Canvey Island and the marsh villages of Fobbing and Corringham where the revolt in Essex began. No later reference to Walter Colepepere can be traced in the official records.

It is, perhaps, fanciful to connect this seemingly respectable Walter Colepepere with Wat Tyler, though the coincidence of his Christian name, the association of the Culpepper family with the district round Maidstone where Tyler first appeared, and his own association with the district which could most easily communicate with the Essex rebels are remarkable enough to deserve attention. It should also be noted that the jurors of three Kentish hundreds later declared that Tyler was born in Essex; this runs counter to all other evidence, and it may be that his connexion with the no man's land opposite Fobbing was the cause of the confusion. According to the *Anonimalle Chronicle*, a valet at Smithfield recognized Tyler as the greatest thief of Kent, and Froissart, who had some detailed knowledge of the revolt, describes how he was identified as a disbanded soldier by Sir John Newton, constable of Rochester Castle. The little we know of Tyler is not incompatible with the suggestion that he was an unruly cadet or hanger-on of the

Culpepper family. The information might have come to Dieulacres through Matthew de Swettenham, a Cheshire yeoman of the king's chamber who was granted maintenance for life at the abbey in January 1383 (*Cal. Pat. Rolls*, p. 418). If the suggestion is rejected, we are confronted with a Culpepper leader of the rebels whose name does not appear in any narrative, indictment, or pardon.

NOTE D

THE CHESHIRE GUARD

THESE squires have Cheshire names and their history can be traced in the entries on the close and patent rolls and in Reports 31 and 36 of the Deputy Keeper. Nearly all were officials in Cheshire and in 1397–8 they were drawn more closely to the king by special gifts and grants. John de Leigh del Bothes submitted to Henry at Shrewsbury (Evesham, p. 154; Report 36, p. 292) and John Downe a fortnight later in Cheshire (Report 36, p. 154). Henry evidently tried to win the Guard over to his side. In his first parliament the Commons petitioned that the great sums of gold and silver delivered by Richard to 'Esquiers Maestres del Wache de Chestreshire' should be repaid, and he replied that they could not make repayment but would serve him for a certain time at their own expense (Oct. 1399, *Rot. Parl.* iii. 439). Bostock, Beston, Cholmondeley, Halford, and Leigh probably took part in the disturbances in Cheshire early in 1400, as they were exempted from a general pardon in May of that year (*Cal. Pat. Rolls*, 286). Cholmondeley drops out of the records at this point. All the others, except Davenport and including Downe, were out with Hotspur in 1403 and either were killed at Shrewsbury or forfeited their estates.

Peter or Perkin de Leigh was not an officer in the Cheshire Guard, but he was the kinsman of one of them and was evidently regarded as the leader of the king's party in the county. His estates lay round Macclesfield, not far from Dieulacres (Ormerod, *Cheshire*, iii. 671 ff.), and he held various important appointments in the Palatinate. He was bailiff of the manor of Macclesfield in 1382 (Report 36, p. 286) and almost until the end of the reign justice in eyre for Macclesfield. His great prestige in the county and with the *vernaculos* of the Guard is illustrated by a passage from the Kenilworth Chronicle compiled by John Strecche (Add. MS. 35295):

f. 260. 'Verumtamen Rex Ricardus anno regni sui XIX°. proceres et valectos de comitatu Cestrie sibi sic adstiuit [*sic*] et ut confidentissimos et carissimos in custodiam sui corporis deputauit pre omnibus aliis regni sui per vigilias diurnas atque nocturnas ita ut sub eorum tutela securius ac quiescius ut putauit ubique respiraret: quos sue salutis conseruatores veresimiliter existimauit. Hii namque in curia regis Ricardi pre ceteris tantum favebantur ita quod nullus officiarius ausus fuerat quod petebant in aliquo denegare. Et in tantam familiaritatem domino regi annectebantur ut eidem in materna lingua audacter confabularentur "Dycun, slep sicury quile we wake, and dreed nouzt quile we lyve sestow: ffor zif thow haddest weddet Perkyn douzter of Lye thow mun well halde a love day with any man in Chester schire in ffaith.'[1] Ecce quomodo nimia familiaritas parit contemptum maxime in populo stulto et insipienti.'

A local tradition supporting the Dieulacres attitude to his death and opposing that of Usk (p. 27) is preserved in the church of St. Michael, Macclesfield. A brass in the Leigh Chapel is inscribed:

Here lyeth the bodie of Perkin a Leigh
That for King Richard the dethe did die,
Betrayed for righteousnesse;
And the bones of Sr.Peers his sonne,
That with King Henry the Fifth did wonne,
In Paris.[2]

[1] Cf. *Traison*, p. 293, n. 1.
[2] D. and S. Lysons, *Magna Britannia*, 1810, p. 728.

IV

THE KIRKSTALL CHRONICLE, 1355–1400[1]

THE direct historical value of the Chronicle is limited almost entirely to that portion which was written at Kirkstall at the end of the fourteenth and the beginning of the fifteenth centuries. The author's interest is concentrated on two periods of Richard II's reign, 1387–8 and 1397–9, and his original idea was probably to balance the story of Richard's revenge against the victory of the Appellants. Although his account of the years 1387–8 is brief, he has used his material skilfully to emphasize his conclusion. He must have been aware of the action of Parliament in 1386 when de la Pole was impeached and the Commission Council was set up, but he chose the Council of Nottingham as his point of departure in order to set out Richard's theory of government through the questions put to the judges. He describes how the baronial leaders at once recognized that they were, by implication, accused of treason and how by defeating the royalist army at Radcot Bridge they were able to force submission to the judgements of the Merciless Parliament. More space is given up to the fate of the judges than in any other chronicle, and emphasis is laid more than once on Richard's resistance to the sentences of exile and death.[2] The conclusion is moderate; the Parliament was an instrument for the torture of

[1] This essay was written as the second half of the Introduction to an edition of the Chronicle (from Bodleian MS. Dodsworth 140) prepared by Miss Clarke and Mr. N. Denholm-Young, now of Magdalen College, Oxford, for the *Bulletin of the John Rylands Library*, vol. xv, no. 1, Jan. 1931. We wish to thank Mr. Denholm-Young and the editor of the *Bulletin* for permission to reprint this portion of the work.

[2] 'The Kirkstall Chronicle', ed. M. V. Clarke and N. Denholm-Young, *Bulletin of the John Rylands Library*, vol. xv, no. 1, p. 29, '. . . de assensu regis spontaneo non prodierat . . .'; p. 31, the death of Burley was *contra voluntatem regis*.

some who deserved it and of others who were innocent.[1] Then after a short interval follows the account of the Revenge Parliament of 1397–8, and again the writer's interpretation of events is clearly outlined. Richard, with marvellous and long-lasting patience (*admirabilis et diutiurna paciencia*), was determined to avenge the wrongs done in 1388 and to bring England under his own control. His vengeance is shown as no sudden impulse nor as the frenzy of a madman, as some modern historians suggest, but as a calculated plan deliberately acted upon when the time was ripe. The chronicler has no pity for the victims. Arundel fitly perished on the very spot where Burley had suffered, and of Gloucester it is grimly said that he could not appear in Parliament because he had gone to a higher court before the Supreme Judge. He concludes with a grandiloquent sentence comparing Richard to the sun in splendour rejoicing to run his course; at last he has dispersed his clouds of enemies and has let his light shine forth.

At this point the narrative is broken, the chronology becomes confused and after a fresh start, going back to Arundel's translation from York to Canterbury in 1396, the events of the last few years are told with a new reticence. There is no marked change in style. The same writer was at work, but he now knew the end of the story and walked delicately in fear of those in high places. Henry of Lancaster, Archbishop Arundel, and his brother are styled *venerabilis*, an epithet of honour applied hitherto only to the Black Prince and to Percy, Norfolk becomes *horrificus*, and Warwick the 'noble earl'. The sequence of events is skilfully set out with scarcely a single comment, though the adjective *admirabilem* is let slip for Richard's renunciation of the crown. At the end,

[1] *Kirkstall Chronicle*, p. 31. The passage is marked in the margin by C, for *cave*. The moderation was, perhaps, partly because Derby was one of the Appellants. Kirkstall lay in the Lancastrian honour of Pontefract and Gaunt was a patron of the abbey, e.g. *Cal. Papal Letters*, v. 16.

accounting for the revolution, he tries to sum up on the winning side, but he can do no better than bring out the trite comparison of Richard to Rehoboam, who forsook the counsel of the old men and consulted with the young men who had grown up with him.[1] The repercussion of events on the Monastic scriptorium is plainly illustrated. As in other houses, notably at Dieulacres, St. Albans, and at Leicester,[2] the Monks of Kirkstall found it hard to trim their prejudices quickly enough to meet the shifting fortunes of the age. Their clumsy efforts are so patent that the date of composition becomes clear. We cannot doubt that the *Kirkstall Chronicle* was written in two sections: the first shortly before Richard's fall and the second within a year or two of Henry's Coronation.

The chronicler's attention was turned to the general history of his time, but he was too far away from London and the court to have detailed knowledge of affairs, and his emphasis has more value than his information. Archbishop Arundel, twice styled *principalis regis consiliarius*, was accused at his trial of revealing the king's privy counsel to his brother.[3] When Richard rode to Plesshy to arrest Gloucester he first commended London to the custody of the mayor and citizens.[4] Deserters swarmed from Bristol castle through doors and windows and down ropes from the walls.[5] Bolingbroke's northern itinerary after the landing at Ravenspur is clearly outlined; though

[1] Cf. the same comparison in the chronicle of Louth Park, another Cistercian house (edited by Rev. Edm. Venables, Lincolnshire Record Society, 1891), p. 41, sub anno 1377.

[2] In the *Dieulacres Chronicle* the break comes in 1399; two writers were at work, and the second blames his predecessor because 'vituperat commendanda et commendat vituperanda' (published *Bulletin of the John Rylands Library*, vol. xiv, no. 1, Jan. 1930). At St. Albans the *Chronicon Angliæ* was drastically revised before it was incorporated into the *Historia Anglicana* of Walsingham. The continuator of *Knighton's Chronicle* wrote with enthusiasm for the king's opponents in 1386–7, but, suddenly changing his tone, he became reticent and commonplace when Gaunt, the patron of Leicester Abbey, returned from Spain in 1389.

[3] *Kirkstall Chronicle*, p. 30.

[4] Ibid., p. 32.

[5] Ibid., p. 36.

this has long been in print from Dodsworth's transcript it is satisfactory to know from what source it was derived.[1] There is disappointingly little further detail for Yorkshire history. No doubt the writer had knowledge of what befell Richard when Bucton brought him to the county, but beyond the fact that a month was spent at Knaresborough before the removal to Pontefract he is too cautious to write more than 'in quadam turre castelli . . . solitare inclusi et qualiter ibidem mortui deus novit. . . .'[2]

The sentences that precede the account of Bolingbroke's landing are, perhaps, of greater interest than any other passage in the chronicle,[3] for they throw a light back on the last and most dangerous phase of Richard's new policy. We are told that the Regency Council, acting on royal authority, proclaimed throughout England certain statutes of the last Parliament and the sentences of banishment passed on Hereford and Norfolk. Up to that time these statutes had not been generally known.[4] Also, all men of property, both clerk and lay, were compelled to pledge their goods and their bodies in defence of the statutes and to ratify the oath under their seals. While this business was pending and before it was fully carried out, Bolingbroke landed at Ravenspur. Here we have definite information about the special activities of the Regency, a matter hitherto obscure. Though we cannot accept it exactly as it stands, with its help it becomes possible to trace the final stages of Richard's subtle manœuvres for security and power. Essentially the same story appears in the *Dieulacres Chronicle* with significant variations.[5] When Richard sailed for Ireland Bolingbroke's perpetual banishment

[1] *Vide Kirkstall Chronicle*, n. 3, p. 35. [2] Ibid., p. 38. [3] Ibid., p. 35.

[4] Cf. ibid., p. 34, 'statuta fuerunt ordinata set minime promulgata'. As we shall see, there can be no doubt that the statutes were already generally known.

[5] *Ut supra*, p. 12. As in the *Kirkstall Chronicle*, the passage immediately follows the statement that Richard sailed to Ireland.

was proclaimed,[1] and all laymen and clerks were forced to set their seals to blank charters and to swear to keep what would be written on them.[2] Hence ill rumours of hard bondage in days to come spread among the people. These two passages from independent, though kindred, writers are enough to show that up to the very day of Henry's landing the king's ministers were busying themselves in enforcing a policy which roused suspicion and alarm throughout the realm. It remains to discover what this policy was and to give a meaning to the tangled stories of blank charters and forced oaths.

The elaborate and various devices which Richard used to secure his victory were probably far more unpopular than the victory itself. Oath after oath was imposed upon his subjects, binding them to maintain the statutes and judgements of the Parliament of 1397–8. The first oaths were sworn on 30 September 1397. Prelates and lords swore one by one on the shrine of St. Edward at Westminster, and the knights of the shire gave their promises together, holding up their right hands as a sign of consent. Before the high altar sentence of excommunication was passed against contrariants.[3] At the Shrewsbury session the prelates and lords renewed their oaths, this time on the cross of Canterbury; the Commons, clerical proctors, and knights standing round the king swore with right hands raised;[4] the king gave notice

[1] This, no doubt, was the popular, and not unnatural, interpretation of the revocation of the letters of attorney (cf. *Annales Ricardi Secundi*, Rolls Series, p. 232).

[2] *Dieulacres Chron.*, p. 48, '. . . feceruntque albas cartas per omnes comitatus regni sigillari . . . et omnes iurare fideliter observare que in eis scribenda forent. . . .'

[3] *Rot. Parl.* iii. 355–6.

[4] Ibid., p. 359, 30 Jan. 1398. The earl of March, at the request of the Commons, took the oath on 28 Jan., probably because he had not sworn at Westminster. The second series of oaths was imposed after an inquiry into the best means by which the statutes and judgements of Parliament might be secured. The king asked the advice of *toutz l'estatz du Parlement*. The judges and king's sergeants answered that 'le pluis greindre seuretee que poet estre, est ceo q'est establiz, ordeinez et affermez par Parlement', but they also advised the renewal of oaths.

that he was writing to Italy to procure papal sanction for the decree of excommunication.[1] When the parliamentary committee met in March 1398, the form of oath was enlarged to include a pledge to maintain the statutes and ordinances 'made after the Parliament by its authority'.[2] Finally, when a year later the letters of attorney granted to Hereford and Norfolk were revoked, eighteen prelates, sixteen peers, and four commoners renewed their oaths on the cross of Canterbury, with an addition covering the sentences of banishment and other acts of the committee.[3] Not content with these public and official acts of obligation, the king issued writs demanding special pledges from all his subjects. At least one copy of the writ is extant.[4] It is addressed to the bishop of Norwich, and enjoins him to assemble all the clergy of his diocese, and have them swear to maintain the statutes and judgements of the last Parliament and of its committee; in proof of their undertaking their seals were to be set to a form of oath set out in a schedule annexed. The imposition of this oath was denounced in the articles of Deposition as 'juramenta . . . odiosa . . . verisimiliter causare possent destructionem finalem populi'.[5]

More formidable than these enforced oaths was the wholesale proscription subtly concealed in the general pardon issued on the last day of the Shrewsbury session. The Commons had asked the king for a general pardon in return for a grant of supply.[6] The pardon was issued

[1] *Rot. Parl.* iii. 359-60. The statement that the Commons accepted this proposal with acclamation occurs only on that copy of the parliament roll (57) which Mr. Edwards has shown was 'an altered version drawn up at some date (probably soon after) 18 March, 1399' (*E.H.R.*, xl, July 1925, pp. 324-5). The message to the Pope was the basis of the tenth article of deposition (*Rot. Parl.* iii. 419). [2] Ibid., p. 372.

[3] Ibid., pp. 372-3, 18 Mar. 1399. The Commons present, other than those who had already sworn, assented by raising their right hands.

[4] Register of William Curteys, abbot of Bury St. Edmund's, 1429-46. British Museum, Add. MS. 7096, ff. 165^{v}-6. Cf. the transcript in Bodley MS., Tanner 342, f. 193. Printed in Note A, *infra*, pp. 111-12. [5] *Rot. Parl.* iii. 421.

[6] Ibid., p. 359. At the opening of Parliament, Sept. 1397, a general

with a specific exception of all who 'chivacherent et soy leverent forciblement encontre le Roy' with the Appellants in 1387–8. Such persons must seek for special charters of pardon before 24 June 1398.[1] An entry on the Close Rolls, dated 27 February 1399, shows that, though the general pardon was renewed, those who had followed the Appellants at Haringey and Radcot Bridge were still reserved for special treatment.[2] It is startling to discover that the exception was interpreted to cover the seventeen counties who had supported his enemies in 1387. More than half the population of England was thus proscribed merely for failure to show 'constant good affection'[3] to the king.

The charge was plainly put in the twenty-first article of deposition.[4] The king had forced the people of seventeen counties to submit themselves to him like traitors (*tanquam proditores*), and by this means he extorted great fines to recover his pleasure. Though he restored the letters of submission, their proctors, who had been given plenary powers to act for them, were constrained to bind themselves under their seals in the name of the people. The substantial accuracy of the accusation is established by a remarkable document, which has not hitherto been printed.[5] It is a servile petition to the king from London and the counties of south-eastern England from Norfolk to Wiltshire—seventeen in all, if London is included. They acknowledge the misdeeds and evil imaginings of certain of their number, admit that they have deserved

pardon had been promised to all subjects except fifty persons, named by the king, and those impeached in Parliament (ibid., p. 347).

[1] Ibid., p. 369.

[2] Ibid., p. 410; from the Close Roll. The excepted persons are styled 'illos qui in comitiva dominorum nuper apud Haringey et Rodcotbrig contra eorum ligeancium ad invicem congregatorum extiterunt'. Cf. *Annales*, p. 225.

[3] The phrase was used to justify the Cromwellian plantation of Ireland.

[4] *Rot. Parl.* iii. 420.

[5] Letter Book, All Souls Library, MS. 182, ff. 193^{v}–4. The full text of the petition is printed in Note B, *infra*, pp. 112 seqq.

punissement assez cruel and promise to do, endure, and obey whatsoever the king may impose upon them. To this end sufficient persons were appointed from London and from each shire to go before the king to take the oath and to do whatever else was necessary on their behalf. That each of the seventeen groups negotiated separately is shown by an English version of the same petition drawn up for London only.[1] The 'sufficient persons' of the petition are obviously the same as the proctors of the article of deposition. The price they paid for buying back the royal pleasure is said to have been £1,000 or 1,000 marks for each shire.[2] The legal basis for the whole proceedings was probably an assumption that in 1387 the petitioners had concealed knowledge of treasonable intent.[3] Such knowledge was a species of contempt, punishable at law; it could be purged by confession and making fine with the king.[4] Reviving and developing the policy expressed in his questions to the judges at Nottingham, Richard was stretching the statute of treason to coerce his subjects wholesale.

So far all is reasonably clear. The difficulty arises over the charters, blank and sealed (*albae cartae*), to which many of the chroniclers refer, though always in some confusion. On the face of it they were not either the oaths sworn and ratified under seal or the sealed confessions and petitions for pardon carried by the proctors or

[1] *Chronicle of London, 1089–1483*, ed. Nicolas, London, 1827, Note X, pp. 155–6. From Cotton MS. Julius, B 1, ff. 32^{v}–3^{v}. The printed text is corrupt in parts. The names of the counties are not given, and the only additions are the names of the persons appointed to act for the city—Walden, archbishop of Canterbury, Braybroke, bishop of London, and Richard Whittington, mayor—and the names of some of those who sealed the petition—the archbishop, Braybroke, Whittington, William Askeham, and John Wodcok.

[2] Evesham, p. 147; *Annales*, p. 235. London paid £1,000, *Chronicle of London*, p. 83. The fines were known as *le Plesaunce*, because they bought back the king's pleasure.

[3] The four points of treason defined in Parliament on 20 Sept. 1397 were: to compass and design to slay the king, to depose him, to withdraw homage from him, to raise his subjects and ride against him in war (*Rot. Parl.* iii. 351).

[4] Holdsworth, *History of English Law*, iii. 373, 388–93.

'sufficient persons' to the king. Yet they were obviously confused and associated with both these classes of documents. In the Bury Register the royal letter to the bishop of Norwich has a title of a later date: 'Breve regis Ricardi secundi transmissum episcopo Norwicensis precipiens sibi quatinus oneraret omnes prelatos sue diocesis iureiurando et quod sigillarent quasdam cartas albas que postmodum fuerunt causa destrucionis ipsius regis.'[1] This description cannot be correct because the document ordered to be sealed was not *alba* or blank, but 'quandam cedulam formam sacramenti'. Again, in the *London Chronicle* it is said that 'be selyng of blank chartres the citee of London paied to the kyng a M[l] livres and othere schires as they myghte beren'.[2] Here the reference is plainly to the confessions and petitions with which fines were paid. That *alba* or *blank* does not bear a peculiar meaning is made clear by the use of the phrase *cartas non scriptas* in one version of the *Evesham Chronicle*.[3]

In the continuation of the *Eulogium* we have the definite statement that, after the imposition of the oaths was ordained, the king and the parliamentary committee (*cum compromisso parliamento*) decreed that prelates, lords, and all the Commons in cities and towns should set their seals to blank charters. It was said that the king intended to write on them this sentence: 'because in time past we have grievously offended your majesty we give up ourselves and all our goods to your pleasure' (*ad libitum vestrae voluntatis*).[4] By itself this evidence is not decisive, as the continuation is frequently inaccurate and bears signs of later interpolation.[5] However, the treatment of

[1] Note A, p. 111. [2] *Chronicle of London* p. 83. [3] Sloane MS. 1776, f. 26.

[4] *Eulogium Historianum*, iii. 378. An English version of the same story appears in *Chronicle*, ed. Davies, Camden Society, pp. 13-14. It was also rumoured that, by means of the blank charters, Richard intended to convince the king of France that he had the consent of his subjects for the sale of Calais and other lands in France (*Annales*, p. 236).

[5] For example, the statement that Richard recognized the earl of March as his heir in 1385, which was obviously inserted under Yorkist influence (*Eulogium*, iii. 361).

blank charters in a separate category is confirmed by the official records. In the first Parliament of Henry IV, at the request of the Commons, the blank charters and miscellaneous documents which Richard had exacted from London and seventeen counties were declared null and void.[1] In the following month orders were issued for their public destruction, and a distinction was clearly drawn between the pledges for the keeping of statutes and ordinances and the *raggemans* or *blaunk chatres* by which London and divers counties, cities, and boroughs acknowledged their guilt and submitted to the king's grace.[2] It is still not absolutely clear that the blank charters were distinct from the confessions and petitions of grace, as the same description of the contents would apply to both sets of documents. This last difficulty is resolved in the twenty-first article of deposition by the statement that the king gave back the letters of submission presented by the seventeen counties, but he coerced the proctors to bind themselves under their seals in the name of the people.[3] In the *Annales*, which for the last years of the reign is a running commentary on the articles of deposition, we are told that the letters of submission were returned when Richard was setting out for Ireland because he wished to placate the counties. The fact that the confessions or letters of submission were returned explains why there was no order for their destruction. We cannot, therefore, doubt that Richard exacted three

[1] '. . . diverses escriptz et blanches chartres' (*Rot. Parl.* iii. 426, 15 Oct. 1399).

[2] 30 Nov. 1399. Rymer, viii. 109; *Cal. Cl. Rolls*, p. 57. Ramsay (*Genesis of Lancaster*, ii. 344, n. 3) says that a bundle of these blank charters is preserved in the Record Office, Treasury of Receipts, Miscell. 15/7. Tout (*Chapters in Mediaeval Administrative History*, iv. 48, n. 3) points out that the bundle, in the modern classification *Exchequer, Treasury of Receipt, E. 34/1: Privy Seals and Letters Patent for Loans*, contains no 'blank' charters but 'numerous indentures between individuals and royal agents . . . covenanting to lend the king money'. These loans from individuals were exacted in 1397 and 1398. Tout seems to confound them with the fines for pardon paid by London and the shires.

[3] *Rot. Parl.* iii. 420.

distinct categories of bond from his subjects in the last years of his reign: the oath to maintain the statutes and judgements of the last Parliament and its committee; the confessions of treasonable intent and petitions for pardon; the blank charters sealed by the proctors of the counties in which no man knew for certain what was to be written.[1]

In order to understand the cumulative effect of this policy, it is necessary to set out the order of events. According to the chronicles, the decision to exact oaths and to terrorize the counties into submission was taken either at a Council at Nottingham on 24 June 1398,[2] or in the autumn after the dukes had been banished.[3] Probably the matter was discussed at more than one session.[4] 24 June was the last day for those excepted from the general pardon to ask for special terms, and it may have been found at the Council of Nottingham that few persons or districts recognized that they were required to take special action.[5] About this time Richard is said to have complained that he was afraid to travel in the seventeen counties round London because of the sympathy there for the Appellants; his itinerary shows that throughout 1398 he spent nearly all his time in the Midlands and the West.[6] The final decision to terrorize

[1] *Annales*, p. 235. 'Expost vero, profecturus in Hiberniam, placere volens personis eorundem comitatum, fecit illis restitui litteras suas obligatorias, vel submissorias; non tamen eo pacto ut liberarentur ab obligationibus quibus se obligaverant; quia coegit ipsius populi procuratores, habentes plenam potestatem eis concessam per communitates dictorum comitatuum, se obligare, et haeredes suos, sibi, sub sigillis eorundem, nomine et auctoritate populi supradicti.'

[2] *Eulogium*, iii. 378. A note in the minutes of the Council of 4 June states that a Council meeting would be held at Nottingham on 24 June. Nicholas, *Proceedings*, i. 81.

[3] Evesham, pp. 146–7.

[4] Essex and Hertfordshire evidently had special treatment as they began to compound for pardon as early as the end of 1397. A commission to treat with them and to accept a fine of £2,000 was issued on 20 Dec. 1397 (*Cal. Pat. Rolls*, pp. 311–12; *Continuation of Croyland*, p. 413). Cf. the forced loans described by Tout, *Chapters in Administrative History*, iv. 47.

[5] Evesham, p. 147; *Eulogium*, iii. 378.

[6] Tout, *ut supra*, iv. 33–5. Cf. Evesham, p. 145.

London and the shires may have been taken at the end of September, soon after the banishment of Hereford and Norfolk. Neither the general petition nor that of London bears a date, but Whittington's title of mayor shows that the London document must have been drawn up before 13 October 1398, when he ceased to hold office.[1] Probably the policy was enforced only by degrees. The reiterated exclusion of the Appellants' supporters from the general pardon may have been issued on 27 February 1398, in order to force all who were holding back to make submission. In the same month (8 February), the letter demanding oaths from the clergy of Norwich was sent to the bishop, and we may assume that like orders were sent to other districts at the same time.[2] On 18 March the parliamentary committee revoked the letters of attorney granted to the banished dukes and new oaths were exacted.[3] In Easter week (27 April–3 May) papal letters ratifying the excommunication of contrariants were published at St. Pauls and St. Mary Spittal.[4] By this time the preparations for the Irish expedition were well under way and the letters of submission were given back to those who had sued and made fine for pardon. Richard sailed for Ireland at the end of May,[5] leaving the Regency in the feeble hands of York. By combining the narratives of Kirkstall and Dieulacres we find that he left orders that the revocation of the duke's letters of attorney should be proclaimed, that new oaths should be exacted and that the proctors of the counties

[1] *Calendar of the Letter Book H*, p. 444.

[2] The Norwich letter refers to oaths already taken by Drugo Barentyn, mayor of London, and the aldermen of citizens. Barentyn succeeded Whittington as mayor on 13 Oct. 1398 (*Cal. Letter Book H, ut supra*).

[3] *Rot. Parl.* iii. 372-3.

[4] *Chronicle of London*, pp. 82-3. The papal letters were dated 16 Jan. 1399: they confirmed the excommunication issued by the king 'with the consent of the prelates, nobles, magnates, cities and other commons of the realm in royal parliaments and other congregations held at London, Shrewsbury and Coventry' (*Cal. Papal Letters*, v. 259).

[5] He was at Milford Haven on 27 May, *Cal. Pat. Rolls*, p. 574.

should be compelled to seal blank charters. His last actions in England as unchallenged king confirm the harsh judgement of the *Annales* that he was always thinking by what bargain he could ensnare his subjects so that they would never again return to their former liberty.[1] It is possible that he left England when he did partly to avoid a storm of resentment and that he meant to use the curialists Scrope, Bushey, Bagot, and Grene as his scapegoats. The demand in Parliament for the destruction of the charters proves that they had begun to come into Chancery before the beginning of July, and suggests that the king's instructions were carried out with zeal. Henry landed on 4 July, just at the time when alarm and anger at a long-drawn-out policy of harrying had reached its height. It is not surprising that his army grew from day to day like the sand of the sea[2] and that throughout all the south-eastern counties none were loyal to Richard. The oaths, the crooked pardon, the forced confession, and the blank charters must have drawn far more recruits to Bolingbroke than his own wrongs or fear of a theoretical absolutism.

NOTE A

JURAMENTA ODIOSA

[f. 165] Breve regis Ricardi secundi transmissum episcopo Norwicensis precipiens sibi quatinus oneraret omnes prelatos sue diocesis iureiurando et quod sigillarent quasdam cartas albas que postmodum fuerunt causa destrucionis ipsius regis.

Ricardus dei gratia rex Anglie et Francie et dominus Hibernie venerabili in Christo patri H. eadem gratia episcopo Norwicensis salutem. Cum Drugo Barentyn maior civitatis nostre Londonii ac aldermanni et cives necnon ceteri omnes eiusdem civitatis ad omnia et singula statuta, ordinaciones et stabilimenta, in ultimo parliamento nostro apud Westmonasterium tento et usque Salopiam adiornato, edita ordinata et

[1] *Annales*, p. 235.

[2] *Dieulacres Chronicle*, p. 49, '. . . exercitus velut arena maris in dies crescebat'.

stabilita una cum omnibus iudiciis et ordinacionibus apud Coventre virtute et auctoritate eiusdem parliamenti redditis, editis atque factis, ac cum omnibus dependenciis et omnibus aliis que inde sequi possunt pro se et successoribus suis singulariter et generaliter bene et fideliter observandum in perpetuum, sacramenta super sacra dei evangelia prestiterint corporalia et pro maiori securitati et veritatis premissorum testimonio ad quandam cedulam formam sacramenti predicte continentem cuius transcriptum vobis mittimus presentibus inclusam sigilla sua apposuerunt. Nos consimilia sacramenta et securitatem de universis et singulis ligiis nostri regni nostri Anglie de statu reputatis habere volentes, vobis mandamus quod [f. 166] statim visis presentibus et inspecto transcripto predicto omnes et singulos abbates priores decanos et archidiaconos de vestra diocese et alias personas ecclesiasticas eiusdem diocesis coram vobis ad certos dies et loca quos ad hoc provideretis infra eandem diocesem cum omnis celeritate et festinacione qua poteritis venire facere et sacramenta huiusmodi ab eisdem abbatibus prioribus decanis archidiaconis et aliis personis ecclesiasticis predictis quod ipsi ac successores sui premissa, modo et forma quibus in dicto breve transcripto sit mentio, conformiter pro parte sua observabunt recipiatis et eiusdem sacramenti formam in cedulam consimilem redigatis prefatosque abbates priores decanos archidiaconos ac alias personas ecclesiasticas eandem cedulam sigillis suis consignari faceretis et cedulam illam, cum sic consignata, fuerit una cum certificacione tocius facti vestri in hac parte nobis in cancellariam nostram sub sigillo vestro distincto et aperto sine dilacione mittatis et hoc breve. Teste me ipso apud Westmonasterium viij die Februarii anno regni nostri XXII. (Add. MS. 7096, f. 165^{v}–6.)

NOTE B

THE SUBMISSION OF LONDON AND SIXTEEN COUNTIES

[f. 193, col. 2] A nostre tresexcellent tresredoubte tressouverein seigneur le Roy treshumblement supplient voz treshumbles liges espirituelx et temporels gentils et communes de voz citee de Loundres countees de Kent Sussex' Surry Suth' Wilts' Oxon' Berk' Bokyngham Bedf' Huntyngdon' Cantabr' Nortff'

Suff' Essex' Hertf' et Midd' que come tresgrandes et dolerouses malices mesprisions et malveises coniecturacions dascuns malfaisours de voz ditz citee et contees eient estez procurees faites et perpetres a vostre mageste roiale a tresgrand et perpetuele confusioun et reproef des ditz malfaisours et grand vergoine et vilenie de touz les inhabitantz des ditz citee et contees sibien innocentz come des autres, lesquelx malfaisours pur leur demerites ount deserviz punissement assez cruel si la treshaute benignite de vous nostre tresredoubte seigneur, replenis de toute grace, vorroit proceder envers eux selonc lour demeritez, que serroit destruccioun de grande multitude de vostre poeple: y plese a vostre tresexcellente et tresredoubte mageste roiale la tresgrande repentance de les ditz malfaisours et lour tresardant desir qils ount damender, redrescer et en toute manere selonc lour [f. 194, col. 1] petitz poers reformer, de tant comme ce purra ascunement estre possible, lour excesses folies et defautes desuznomez, lour resceivere a mercie et grace et de la habundante fontaigne de grace dount vous ad endowez lui tout puissant Roy, exemplair de toute mercie et grace, pardonner entierment et de coer tout qanque devers les ditz malfaisours en lour defaute et les inhabitantz de mesme les citee et countees par cause de eux ad conceu vostre tresexcellente mageste avantdite. Et lour vuillent voz ditz treshumbles lieges souzmettre et lour souzmettent de fet; de fere porter et obeier tout quanque purra ascunement plere vostre mageste roiale susdite. Et en oultre supplient treshumblement voz ditz treshumbles liges que certaines sufficiantz gentz de chescune des ditz citee et contees, qore sont presentz devant vostre dite mageste roiale et eslitz et ordeinez par les ditz citee et contees, dount leur nouns severalment desoubz sont escriptz, sufficiantement enformez de lour voluntees et aiantz pleine auctoritee et poair depar trestouz voz ditz treshumbles[1] liges, purront estre receux en noun de eux et de chacun de eux et pur lour mesmes, a iurer destre toutdis voz loialx et obeissantz liges a vostre dite mageste et de tenir loialment, garder, observer, loer et maintenir a trestoutz leur poers, sanz fraude ou mal engin toutz les estatutz establissementz et juggementz faitz ou renduz en vostre treshaute parlement [f. 194, col. 2] somonz et commencez a Westm' lundy proschein apres la feste de la exaltacioun de la seinte croice lan de vostre

[1] MS. *treshumblement.*

tresgracious regne vintisme primer et de illoeque aiournez a Salop' tanque al quinzisme de saint Hillaire alors proschein suyant et illoeque terminez et touz les autres estatutes ordenances et establissementz puis encea faitz par auctoritee de vostre dit parlement sanz iammais venir fere ou procurer rien a lencontre en ascun manere a vivre et morir au fyn qils purront estre mys parmy vostre treshabundante grace, hors de toute suspicioun et estre tenuz come ils desirent sur toute rien voz loialx liges pur dieu et en oevre de charitee. En tesmoignance de quele chose et pur icelle bien et loialment garder tenir[1] observer et mainteiner pur touz iours a trestouz lour poers a viver et morir en maner comme desus est dit voz ditz treshumbles liges si bien en noun de touz voz ditz Citee et Countees come de lour mesmes, a i ceste supplicacoun ount mys lour sealx. Cestassavoir R. par la grace de dieu ercevesque de Cant', etc.[2]

[1] Altered by the scribe to read *tenir garder*.

[2] All Souls College, Oxford, MS. 182, ff. 193^{v}-4. The preface to the *Register of Archbishop Peckham* (ed. C. Trice Martin, 1882) contains a description of the MS., which is a fifteenth-century formulary book. My thanks are due to the Warden and Fellows of All Souls College for leave to publish the document, and to Miss M. K. Pope and Miss D. M. Legge, of Somerville College, for help with the text.

V

FORFEITURES AND TREASON IN 1388[1]

MY interest in the forfeitures of 1388 was first roused by an examination of the printed inventories of the reign of Richard II, undertaken in the hope of finding references to pictures painted for the king. The examination was necessarily brief, as there is little in print except Gloucester's great inventory of 1397, a few wills, some short lists in the calendars of Close Rolls, and the inventories, chiefly of forfeitures, published in Palgrave's *Kalendars and Inventories of the Treasury*. Palgrave naturally suggested a search in the Record Office, and I soon became aware of a considerable body of material there, relating to the forfeitures of 1388. Though none of it turned out to be directly useful for my original inquiry,[2] it seemed to have sufficient historical interest to deserve discussion.

The chief source of evidence is the volume entitled *Liber forisfacturarum ducis Hibernie et diversarum personarum in parliamento tento apud Westmonasterium anno regni Ricardi secundi undecimo adiudicatarum*,[3] a book of twenty-nine folios, with some blank spaces. Except for two writs issued under the privy seal to the Treasurer and Chamberlain of the Exchequer, it consists of inventories of the plate, garments, and household stuff which belonged to seven persons condemned by the Merciless Parliament —Robert de Vere, duke of Ireland; Michael de la Pole, earl of Suffolk; Alexander Neville, archbishop of York; Robert Tressilian, Chief Justice; Robert Belknappe,

[1] A paper read before the Royal Historical Society on 23 April 1931. We wish to thank the President and Council of the Society for permission to reprint it from their *Proceedings*.

[2] The results of the original inquiry are stated in an article on the Wilton diptych, *Burlington Magazine*, June 1931. *Infra*, pp. 272 seqq.

[3] P.R.O., *Miscellaneous Books*, No. 66.

Chief Justice of the Common Pleas; Simon Burley and John Salisbury, knights of the royal household. In addition to these inventories in the *Book of Forfeitures*, there are a number of others on separate parchments or in small rolls, preserved in bundles in the classifications known as K.R. *Various Accounts* and *Inventories of Goods*. There are also entries on the rolls of L.T.R. Foreign Accounts (*Forfeited Goods*), which sometimes repeat the inventories in the bundles or in the *Book of Forfeitures*. Though there are some unique lists in each class, many of them are duplicated, and in one or two cases there are three copies of what is substantially the same inventory.

It is clear that the inventories are by no means complete. This can be seen, not only by comparison of different versions of the same list, but by noting omissions of various kinds. For some of the victims of 1388—certain of the judges, for example—no inventories have come to light. Those that we have refer only to goods seized in particular places; all de Vere's inventories belong to Chester, all Archbishop Neville's to York, and all de la Pole's to London, though these persons must have had many valuable possessions in other castles and manors. No doubt when they fled they carried off what money, jewels, and bonds they could, but much must have been hidden away by kinsfolk or appropriated by dishonest officials. It is also difficult to accept certain of the valuations as genuine, as variations in price seem altogether capricious. The most striking example occurs in the archbishop's inventories. Two lists of the same goods are extant; the valuations in the *Book of Forfeitures* for all except the cheapest articles are much higher than those on the separate list which the sheriff of Lincoln handed in when he conveyed the stuff in seven sacks from the north.[1] A bed of baudekyn valued at £4 on the separate list appears as worth £13 13*s.* 4*d.* in the *Book*, and the

[1] P.R.O., *Liber Forisfacturarum*, ff. 17–19; E. 154/1/24.

value of a violet surcoat, furred and with a hat to match, goes up in the same way from 13*s*. 4*d*. to 50*s*. These variations may represent the difference between the genuine value and the sale price, though we would then expect all the values to be scaled up together.

In spite of these and other drawbacks, the historical interest of the inventories is considerable. We notice, for example, that beds with rich hangings and coverlets were the most valuable secular articles in a great man's house. One of Burley's beds was of green tartarine, embroidered with ships and birds; it came into the hands of the bishop of Salisbury and in 1392 the king bought it from him for £13 6*s*. 8*d*.[1] This was cheap compared to de Vere's bed of blue camoca, embroidered in gold with owls and fleur-de-lis and valued at £68 13*s*. 4*d*.[2] Other costly articles in the household were chapel furnishings: both de Vere and the archbishop possessed *vestements* valued at £80, and every great personage seems to have several sets, embroidered in various colours and designs. The long lists of expensive garments, especially those of Burley, Salisbury, and de Vere, illustrate the splendour of the court, condemned by monastic writers as luxurious and unprofitably gay. In no list, however, is there any imitation of the special refinement of the king, who just before this time bought from his tailor handkerchiefs—'parvis peciis factis ad liberandum domino regi ad portandum in manu suo pro naso suo tergendo et mundando'.[3] Another more significant omission is the absence

[1] Devon, *Issues*, p. 250.

[2] These valuations do not include the mattresses, blankets, sheets, and pillows, which are always valued separately. The linen nearly always came from France or the Low Countries, e.g. 'un peire de lyncheaux de Reynes, pris XVIs. VIIId.; IIII naps de Parys pour la table le seignur contenant LXIII verges, (pris) XLIIIs.; deux napes de Dynant molt usez, (pris) VIs. VIIId'.

[3] 'Rotulus expensarum diversarum in officio magne Garderobe domini regis . . .' 9–11 Ric. II, P.R.O., E. 101/401/15. Account of Walter Rauf, king's tailor. The entry quoted comes at the end of a bill for sheets. The elaborate description indicates a special order and it is evident that there

of all reference to livery collars or badges. The only liveries mentioned are de Vere's: 'VI liverez pur valletz, IIII liverez pur ministrales, VI liverez pur gromes.'[1] Great men, it seems, did not wear collars of livery until a later date in the reign.

The inventories throughout contain information useful for the social detail of the period, but they are often of little further value. Those of de Vere and of Burley are exceptional in that they contribute considerable evidence bearing a wider interest. De Vere's inventories, so far as they have been preserved, all relate to the goods that were brought to London from Chester.[2] The valuation of the larger part was estimated at £435 6*s.* 2*d.*, and they show beyond all doubt that he had made Chester the head-quarters of his splendid housekeeping, a fact which is nowhere recorded in the chronicles. Among the articles inventoried are two saddles for *damoiselles* of Bohemia and one old saddle of the Bohemian fashion.[3] We may suppose that they were used by Agnes Lancecrona, the queen's maid, whom de Vere abducted from the court and brought to Chester.[4] He may have moved his household to Chester as a preliminary to crossing to Ireland,[5] but it seems more probable that he took up residence there in order to organize the army which he afterwards led to Radcot Bridge. One of the separate

was still no word to describe what the king required. I have not found any other reference to handkerchiefs used for this purpose in England before the sixteenth century.

[1] P.R.O., Liber Forisfacturarum, f. 20.

[2] *Ibid.*, ff. 5–8; 20–1; 25–6. E. 101/334/23. E. 101/335/1.

[3] *Ibid.*, f. 7. 'Item, ii celles novelles pour damoiselles de Boeme, pris iiii livres. Item, i veille celle a guyse de Boeme, pris XXs.'

[4] Walsingham, ii. 160; Higden, ix. 95; *Dieulacres Chronicle*, p. 45 (*Bulletin of the John Rylands Library*, Jan. 1930). Cf. *Cal. Pat. Rolls, 1389–92*, p. 20.

[5] De Vere had been given custody of the Lordship of Ireland when he was made marquis of Dublin, 1 Dec. 1385 (*Rot. Parl.* iii. 209–10), but entries on the close and patent rolls suggest that he abandoned the idea of going there soon after the parliament of 1386. On 8 Sept. 1387 he was appointed justice of Chester on the surrender of the office by the duke of York (Chester Recognizance Rolls, Appendix, 31st Report of Deputy Keeper of the Public Records, p. 254).

lists of de Vere's goods has the names of persons to whom they were delivered or sold scribbled in the margin.[1] They were distributed between Gloucester, Derby, Edmund de la Pole, the bishop of Durham, and a group of London merchants. The most valuable pieces went to Gloucester and Derby, and in the inventory of Gloucester's forfeitures, drawn up in 1397, we can trace two of de Vere's beds and a set of his chapel furnishings.[2] *In lordshipe is no sikerness.*

The entries of Burley's goods in the *Book of Forfeitures* are surprisingly meagre. The total value amounts only to £73 9*s.* 10*d.* The lists are disordered and the objects seem hardly fine or numerous enough for the courtier who had no peer in the splendour of his apparel and who excelled other great men in his horses and in all pomp.[3] There is, however, a separate roll of Burley's goods which seems to have been drawn up at the time of an official inquiry into the disposal of his property.[4] It consists of a series of inventories and other documents, none of which appear in the *Book of Forfeitures*. It contains miscellaneous information of great interest, but is too long for a full discussion here.

The first document on the roll is an inventory of the goods in Burley's two London houses, drawn up at his own order before the seizure by the escheator.[5] We may therefore assume that it is fairly complete. The objects listed are household stuff, clothing, furs, armour, and

[1] P.R.O., E. 101/335/1.

[2] 'Inventory of the goods and chattels belonging to Thomas, duke of Gloucester, and seized in his castle at Pleshy, Co. Essex, 21 Richard II. . . .' *Archæological Journal*, liv, 1897. My thanks are due to Professor A. Hamilton Thompson for drawing my attention to this inventory and for much other help in examining the *Book of Forfeitures*.

[3] *Kirkstall Chronicle*, p. 31 (*Bulletin of the John Rylands Library*, Jan. 1931).

[4] P.R.O., E. 154/1/19.

[5] The heading runs: 'Conuz soit a toutz gentz que monsieur Simond de Burley ordeina affaire son inventore le VIII iour de Novembre lan XIe. de toutz les biens que le dit monsieur Simond avoit a le Meawes come a Baynardes Castell in Loundres, les queux biens sont contenuz en y cest rolle.'

books. The plate was dealt with separately and the jewels were not inventoried at all. There is no valuation of the articles, but the description of them shows that they were at least as splendid and as costly as de Vere's. Probably the most valuable pieces were the two 'halls' or sets of hangings—one for Baynard's Castle and one for Dover—and nine beds with all their equipment. The list of clothing certainly leaves an impression of richness and splendour—eight fur cloaks or gowns, seven tabards, five long and six short gowns, not to speak of doublets, hats, and sleeves. There were, for example, a tabard of scarlet with a sleeve (*ele*), embroidered with the sun and letters of gold and lined with white tartarine; a tabard of cloth of gold with roses on a red ground, lined with green tartarine; a coat of white leather, embroidered with stakes and with fifty-four gilt buttons; and a fur of pure minever for a royal mantle, with a cape of ermine. The armour is nearly all classified as 'armour for jousts'. The plates and helmets were gilded or painted with stakes and the surcoats were embroidered with the same badge. There are thirty-one items on this list and only half a dozen on another, headed 'armour for war'; but the roll is damaged at this point and something may have been left out.

The most interesting items are the books, unfortunately not fully described. Nine were French Romances and the only English book was also a romance, the Romance of the Forester and the Wild Boar.[1] In almost the same class were the Chronicle of the Brut and the Prophecies of Merlin. The rest were more serious works: a paper book of diverse words in diverse languages, which sounds like a traveller's dictionary; a book of the government of kings and princes;[2] a battered book of philosophy, which

[1] 'i livre de Englys del Forster et del Sengler.' I have been unable to trace this book.

[2] Henri de Gauchi's translation of the *De Regimine Principum* by Egidio Colonna. The duchess of Gloucester left in her will 'i livre de Giles de regimine principum', possibly Burley's book (J. Nichols, *Royal Wills*, p. 181).

perhaps once belonged to Walter of Burley; two books of the Ten Commandments, one new; and 'un graunt livre de la Bible ove les histoires escolastre'.[1] All these, except the English romance, were in French. Only one volume was certainly in Latin; it is described merely as a Latin book covered in black. Another, a book beginning 'Miserere mei Deus', is in fact a French poem.[2] That Burley had other books than these is shown by the confession of his servant that he had in keeping a volume called 'livre de songes de Panyell'.

There are two other fourteenth-century inventories of laymen's libraries, which it is interesting to compare with Burley's. One belonged to Guy de Beauchamp, son and heir of the earl of Warwick: he died in 1360 and left forty-two books to Bordesley Abbey, Worcestershire.[3] Nineteen of these books were romances—about the same proportion as Burley's—and the rest were mainly devotional works. There was no Bible. The other inventory is that of Gloucester.[4] He had eighty-three books at Pleshey: only nineteen were romances: of the rest twenty-one were devotional works, five law books, six philosophy, and nine chronicles. There were also two English Gospels and an English Bible in two great volumes. Among the chapel furnishings were thirty-nine service books and two Bibles. Beauchamp was the heir of a great noble and Gloucester was a prince of the blood; both, especially Gloucester, probably received many books as presents, and we cannot be sure that their collections were the result of their own interests. Burley's library is more likely to represent his own personal taste. Certain of the

[1] Guyart des Moulins' translation of Comestor's *Biblia Scholastica*.

[2] A long religious poem in French beginning 'Miserere mei Deus, trop me sui longement teus', by Renches de Moiliens or Molliens. My thanks are due to Miss K. Chesney for much help in tracing these books.

[3] Henry S. Todd, *Illustrations of Chaucer and Gower*, 1810, pp. 161–2.

[4] *Inventory*, loc. cit., pp. 300–3. Gloucester's wife bequeathed in her will eleven books—a Bible, five works of devotion, two chronicles, a law book, a book of philosophy, and a romance. *Royal Wills*, loc. cit., pp. 181–3, 9 Aug. 1399.

volumes may have been procured when he was tutor to Richard. It is possible that the king's interest in books may have been due, in part at least, to Burley's influence. Though no inventory of the royal library has come to light, we know from entries in the accounts that books were bought for the king from the beginning of the reign[1] and that he kept a considerable number of them in his private chamber.[2] It is, however, disappointing that no work of Chaucer's appears on the inventory, as he and Burley sat on the same commission of the peace in 1385.[3]

Another point of interest in Burley's roll is its revelation of his desperate financial straits on the eve of the attack on the king's advisers by the Appellants. The inventory was drawn up on 8 November 1387, hardly a week before the barons mustered their forces and published the appeal. A damaged note on the roll states that when the inventory was made Burley pawned the goods described in it to certain creditors because he had no money to pay his debts. No names are given, but some of the articles in the inventory appear in the *Book of Forfeitures* among goods found in the hands of a group of six London citizens: Gilbert Prince, painter; Thomas Prudance; John Grocer; John Hayne, tailor; John Gest, pelterer; and William But, draper.[4] It is also stated on the roll that the escheator of London seized certain parcels of these goods, apparently before the creditors were able to secure them; these are probably the articles

[1] Devon, *Issues*, p. 213; a French Bible, the Romance of the Rose, and the Romances of Percival and Gawain were bought for £28, 12 Sept. 1379.

[2] P.R.O., 'Rotulus expensarum . . .' 9–11 Ric. II, loc. cit.—'pro emendacione et ligacione unius libri de closett domini regis vi s viii d: et pro factura et garnistura xiiii coopertoriorum de satyn pale blu et albo, liniatorum cum satyn rubeo, garnitato cum serico blu et botonatorum de auro de cipre et tassellis de serico pro xiiii libris de closett domici regis; et iiii coopertoriis de panno adaurato liniatis cum satyn, garnitatis cum serico et botonatis de auro et tassellis pro iiii aliis libris; ac pro consutura et garnistura diversarum bagarum de tel', de Reyns et tel' lini Brabancie pro eisdem libris imponendis, xxxv s id.

[3] *Cal. Pat. Rolls*, 1385–9, p. 84, 12 Oct. 1385.

[4] Liber, loc. cit., f. 10.

in the *Book of Forfeitures*. Two coffers of plate were pledged to other creditors, Sir John Devereux and Richard Whittington, on 25 November, that is, after the king had promised that the appeal should be heard in Parliament and when de Vere was gathering his army in Cheshire. The amount of Burley's debts is nowhere stated, but the plate was valued at 560 marks, 16½ ounces. The story in *Knighton's Chronicle* that Burley, having no more than twenty marks as a patrimony, amassed a fortune which brought in 3,000 marks a year,[1] cannot stand against this evidence. It is also probable that these pressing debts have political significance, as, after de Vere, Burley was the king's closest personal friend. They illustrate the practical effect of the action of the Commission Council in cutting off supplies from Richard and his household when, as Tout shows, 'the great and privy seals were in hostile hands' and 'the signet was pushed aside as unconstitutional'.[2] We have thus a compelling motive for the court party's determination to prevent at all costs the renewal of the commission when its term expired on 20 November 1387.

The forfeitures lead naturally to a consideration of the trials and punishment of their owners, the victims of the Merciless Parliament. Though the material for a detailed study is abundant, it is by no means easy to follow the sequence of events or to understand their significance. The main body of evidence comes from the Parliament Roll, which embodies a separate record of the appeal and of the process against the parties accused.[3] Evidently an attempt was made to secure general support by circulating part of this document, as the questions put to the judges and the articles of appeal are preserved in

[1] *Chronicon*, ii. 294.

[2] *Chapters in Mediaeval Administrative History*, iii. 418.

[3] *Rot. Parl.* iii. 228–52. Cf. the *Placita Corone* of 1397, where the hearing of the appeals is recorded separately.

several chronicles. Another attempt at propaganda was Favent's history of the Parliament,[1] a contemporary pamphlet, written, as its editor says, in 'a lively partisan spirit'. More valuable, because less biased, is the French pamphlet preserved in the Chronicle of Westminster, probably also written for immediate circulation. It follows the chronicler's account of the opening of Parliament and consists of the articles of appeal, the articles of the impeachment of Burley and the other knights, a narrative of the trials, and a few common petitions.[2] The official documents are obviously taken from the Parliament Roll, but the narrative has some important additions. The formal detail of the roll is very much cut down and in its place a full account of Brembre's trial is inserted. There is also fresh matter for the later trials. When the Westminster Chronicler had copied out the pamphlet he went back to his own narrative and told again the story of the Parliament, adding new details about the trials of Tressilian, Brembre, Blake, and Usk. The other chronicles are all greatly inferior in value, and hardly require consideration. We have, however, four records, all virtually contemporary—the Parliament Roll, Favent, the French or Westminster pamphlet, and the Chronicle of Westminster. When these are compared it becomes clear that the narrative on the roll is silent just where there is something discreditable to record, and it is therefore necessary to use it with great caution. The Westminster pamphlet, on the other hand, is confirmed on essential points by the others, and it is probably the best narrative we have of proceedings.

A more serious obstacle in the way of the interpretation of events lies in the legal theory behind the whole procedure. To understand this difficulty the political conditions of the time must be recalled. Hatred of royal favourites had turned the king's enemies back to the

[1] Edited by M. McKisack, *Camden Miscellany*, vol. xiv, 1926.
[2] Higden, ix. 119–65.

policy and catchwords of the reign of Edward II, but they had to reckon with the rapid growth of Parliament in the interval. It is true that in 1388 Parliament was almost entirely under their control and that a great claim to parliamentary supremacy was therefore put forward. But the solution could not be so simple, for the monarchy had also strengthened its defences, perhaps as much by a statutory definition of treason as by the prestige politics of Edward III. When the Appellants sought to justify their whole course of action by raising the cry of 'Traitors', they were confronted by the great treason statute of 1352. It was by no means suited to their purpose, yet they did not dare to propose its repeal or suspension. They were thus forced into the illogical position of setting past events and common law precedents above statute law just at the time when they proclaimed the supremacy of Parliament.

The claim to supremacy was larger and more specific than any before the defence of the Militia Ordinance issued in 1642. The lords, with the king's consent, declared that high crimes could not be tried elsewhere than in Parliament, nor by any other law than the law and procedure of Parliament; the lower courts were merely the executors of the laws and customs of the realm and of the decrees of Parliament.[1] At a later stage it was further declared that 'the law of the land is made in Parliament by the king, the lords spiritual and temporal, and all the commonalty of the realm'.[2] These great claims are usually related to the Treason statute of 1352, which assigned to the king in Parliament the right and duty of declaring what was treason and what felony, when doubt arose in lower courts.[3] An examination of what actually happened shows that in several different ways the facts do not correspond with this explanation.

[1] *Rot. Parl.* iii. 236. [2] Ibid. 243.

[3] For example, Professor S. Rezneck, 'The Early History of the Parliamentary Declaration of Treason', *E.H.R.*, 1927, p. 503.

Not only was the statute never mentioned during the trials, but there are unmistakable signs that it was deliberately shelved and that Parliament, though claiming to be above all other courts, was really following, closely though irregularly, the principles and procedure of common law. The question is of considerable importance; it raises the problem of the authority of the most famous fourteenth-century statute, and also the wider issue of the powers and practice of Parliament.

In the first place, it is necessary to examine the purpose and antecedents of the statute itself. In addition to definitions of the points of treason, it enacted that doubtful cases arising in lower courts should be reserved for judgement in Parliament. It was also specifically denied that *chivaucer* or private war was anything more than felony or trespass. It is usually assumed that the direct cause of the statute lay in two common petitions presented in 1348 and 1352, complaining that judges were defining new treason unknown to the Commons.[1] The case of Sir John Gerberge obviously provoked the petition of 1348. He had attacked one William de Botesford with a drawn sword and on the king's highway, and had detained him prisoner until he paid £90 ransom. For these offences he was indicted and condemned for usurping the royal power, against his allegiance, to the prejudice of the king and crown and as open treason.[2] Other evidence suggests that Gerberge's case was merely a pretext and that the real issue was the charge of accroaching the royal power.

The charge takes us back to the stormy years of 1321 to 1331, when it had brought the greatest families in England under a cloud of forfeiture and disgrace. Sentences of treason were, for the most part, given and executed in the heat of reprisals or of civil war and with little or no attempt to conform to recognized legal proce-

[1] *Rot. Parl.* ii. 166, 239. Cf. Professor Rezneck, loc. cit., p. 449.
[2] Hales, *Hist. Plac. Coronæ*, pp. 80–1.

dure. Historians have, perhaps, not emphasized enough the shock and dismay caused by these irregular trials and judicial murders. The contemporary attitude may be illustrated by a document, written about 1334 and copied into the Register of Newenham Abbey.[1] It is entitled *Mirabilia facta tempore regis Edwardi secundi*. The marvels are the deposition of the king and the death by violence of eight earls and two bishops between 1322 and 1330. It was inevitable that these events should raise the whole issue of the meaning of treason, how it should be defined and by what process it should be tried.

The question was kept alive by a long series of petitions to Parliament, presented by the injured parties or their heirs and demanding the reversal of unjust sentences. In 1321 the first sentence on the Despencers was reversed;[2] in 1327 the sentences on Lancaster, the Mortimers, and Badlesmere were annulled as erroneous.[3] In 1331 the heir of Edmund of Kent recovered his inheritance and it was declared that the judgement on his father was to be as if it had never been given.[4] In the same Parliament the titles and estates of Arundel were restored to his heir, but it was distinctly stated that the restitution was of grace, not of right, as the judgement had been ratified by statute in 1327.[5] Thus Arundel was left with a grievance. He and Mortimer's heir soon came to stand high in royal favour and were not inclined to drop their claims for rehabilitation.

Apart from individual grievances, the precedents of the years of disorder concerned all the barons, and it was natural that in 1341 they should seize the opportunity of Archbishop Stratford's claim to a parliamentary inquiry to define the privileges of the whole order. The attack on the archbishop in the *libellus famosus* had con-

[1] British Museum, Arundel MS. 17, ff. 40–40^{v}.

[2] *Cal. Cl. Rolls, 1318–23*, pp. 541–6.

[3] Printed in full by Vernon Harcourt, *His Grace the Steward*, pp. 327–34.

[4] *Rot. Parl.* ii. 33, 55.

[5] Ibid., p. 56.

cluded with a general charge of treason—many acts done 'in status nostri detrimentum et dignitatis regie laesionem'.[1] In his reply the archbishop denied that he had aroused 'seditionem in populo proditorie', and he reminded the king 'quia premissa proditionis crimen in caput nostrum retorquere videntur, quo casu rex nullus vel dominus temporalis judex noster competens esse potest'. Saving the privilege of his order, he maintained his right to answer the charges against him 'in pleno parliamento coram proceribus et paribus vestri regni'.[2] Edward III, we may suspect, never intended to press the charge of treason, but the archbishop was quick to grasp the opportunity it offered to win support for himself among the barons. He appealed to Magna Carta and linked together the three issues underlying the *mirabilia* of 1321 to 1330—ecclesiastical immunity, privilege of peerage, and the law of treason.

In the parliamentary crisis of April and May 1341, Arundel stands out as a leader of the baronage. He sat on both committees set up to report on the trial of peers[3] and was one of the six appointed to hear the archbishop's answers.[4] He and his uncle, Earl Warenne, protested, probably in Council, against the treatment of the archbishop. Warenne maintained that only *peres de la terre* should aid and counsel the king in great matters; Arundel demanded that the archbishop should have a hearing and, if he could not excuse himself, that the peers should ordain what ought to be done.[5] Arundel's father and Warenne himself had been deeply implicated in the charges and counter-charges of treason so fatal under

[1] Rymer, v. 228. Cf. the report made to the Pope of the king's words: 'I believe that the archbishop wished me, by lack of money, to be betrayed and killed.' *Cal. Papal Letters*, ii. 585. The charge of treason was repeated in two other royal letters, Rymer, v. 236, 240.

[2] Birchington, *Anglia Sacra*, i. 31, 34.

[3] *Rot. Parl.* ii. 127, 129.

[4] Ibid. 131.

[5] *French Chronicle of London*, p. 90. Cf. *E.H.R.*, April 1931, for a full discussion of the protest of the earls by Dr. B. Wilkinson.

Edward II, and it was natural that they should at once recognize the gravity of the issue.[1] The fact that king and barons were in general agreement over the war made the time seem propitious for a permanent settlement which would protect their order in the future. The archbishop had appealed to clause thirty-nine of Magna Carta, claiming for all free men immunity from punishment, 'nisi per legale judicium parium suorum vel per legem terrae Anglicanae'.[2] By stressing the term peer, a catchword of the time, he shifted the emphasis from the protection guaranteed to the way in which it was secured. Attention was thus directed not so much to the charges brought against great men or royal officers as to the form of trial to which they were entitled. When the committees made their reports[3] the findings, obviously based on the memory of recent events, were embodied in a statute:

'Because in times past peers of the land have been arrested and imprisoned, and their temporalities, lands and tenements, goods and chattels seized into the hands of kings, and some put to death, without judgement of peers: it is accorded and assented that no peer of the land . . . shall be brought to judgement to lose his temporalities . . . or be arrested, imprisoned, outlawed, exiled or forejudged, or made to answer or be judged except by the award of the said peers in Parliament.'[4]

The king in Council revoked his consent to this statute after the dissolution of Parliament.[5] In the Parliament of 1343 the statute was repealed as prejudicial and contrary to the laws and usages of the realm and the rights and prerogatives of the crown. At the same time it was promised that such points in the statute as were

[1] Warenne did not sit on any committee, and his name does not occur elsewhere in the records. It is therefore probable that his nephew, Arundel, was the real leader of the barons.

[2] Sentence of excommunication against violators of Magna Carta, Walsingham, i. 238. Cf. ibid., pp. 235, 236; Birchington, p. 32.

[3] *Rot. Parl.* ii. 127, 130.

[4] 15 Ed. III, stat. 1, § 2; *Rot. Parl.* ii. 132.

[5] 1 Oct. 1341. Rymer, v. 282.

conformable to law and reason should be re-enacted, on the advice of the judges and those learned in the law.[1]

No further legislation on the subject was proposed. The magnates had met with defeat and had failed to secure a precise definition of the form of trial to which they were entitled. They left the question in abeyance for nine years. When it was reopened they had come to understand the need to put their case in more general terms: not the procedure of the trial, but the substantive law of treason became the main point at issue. It is possible that Arundel was again the chief mover in the business.[2] He was then involved in litigation with Kent's descendants, who claimed lands forfeited by his father. In 1351 the restitution of 1331 was reaffirmed by Parliament, with the rider that Kent's heirs had no grounds for action against him by reason of his father's sentence.[3] Even this did not content him, and on his petition in 1354 the statute by which his father had been condemned was examined in full Parliament and reversed.[4] At the same time, on petition of Roger Mortimer, the sentence of the Parliament of 1331 was reversed and he was fully restored to the lands and titles of his grandfather.[5] A third treason case was decided in 1352. John Maltravers, who had been condemned by Parliament in 1331 for traitorously encompassing the death of Kent, was granted a full pardon, confirmed in Parliament by the assent of the king, prelates, earls, and barons.[6]

Arundel, Mortimer, and Maltravers had all been sentenced in Parliament as traitors—the two earls for accroaching the royal power and Maltravers for procuring

[1] 15 Ed. III, stat. 2; *Rot. Parl.* ii. 139.

[2] He was then high in royal favour. In 1345 he had married Eleanor, sister of Henry of Lancaster, and in the same year he was appointed sheriff of Shropshire for life. His brother-in-law, Henry, was made duke of Lancaster in 1351. Tout, iii. 188, 191.

[3] *Rot. Parl.* ii. 226–7.

[4] Ibid. 256–7.

[5] Ibid. 255–6.

[6] Ibid. ii. 53, 243–4. The pardon, which was at first temporary, was issued as a reward for services in Flanders, 28 Dec. 1347. Rymer, v. 600–1.

the death of the king's uncle. These offences were not treasons by the statute of 1352, passed in the Parliament that affirmed Maltravers's pardon and only two years before the reversal of the judgement on Arundel and Mortimer. The coincidence of time can hardly be accidental. It suggests that the statute was less the result of common petition than of an agitation by certain powerful persons to redeem their family honour and to secure full restitution of rights. Though the grievances were personal, the form of the demand ensured general support. The immediate gain to the monarchy was obvious; nearly all the *mirabilia* had been directed against the chosen servants of the Crown, and the charge of 'accroaching the royal power' was devised to deprive the king of ministers who had roused the jealous hatred of the magnates. The Commons included on their roll of petitions a request that the points of treason might be declared. The Church was propitiated by the statute *Pro Clero*, which explicitly denied secular jurisdiction over clerks for all felonies and treasons 'touchantes autres persones qe le Roi meismes ou sa roiale majeste'.[1] The connexion with the treason statute is underlined by the clause postponed until the next Parliament: 'all clerks convicted of having falsified or counterfeited our money or our great or privy seals ought to enjoy the privilege of Holy Church. . . .'[2] There was plainly no difficulty in winning general baronial support. Great landlords had most to lose by judgements on traitors, and they gladly supported a statute which confined treason within narrow bounds, secured their franchise rights, and tacitly confirmed the protection of lands entailed, established by *De Donis*

[1] 25 Ed. III, stat. 6, § 4. Cf. Leona C. Gabel, *Benefit of Clergy in the Later Middle Ages*, pp. 35–6, 59.

[2] *Statutes of the Realm*, i. 328. This article is written on the dorse of the statute roll after the *Ordinatio pro Clero*. The reference was plainly to the third definition in the treason statute. It was provided that, in the meantime, no clerk should be executed on such a charge. Cf. Wilkins, iii. 28–9.

Condicionalibus.[1] This protection had been overridden in 1321–31, in accordance with the standard of punishment set by Common Law.[2] It seems, then, that the main purpose of the statute of 1352 was, by means of statutory definition, to prevent the recurrence of the reckless charges and arbitrary punishments which had ruined so many noble families in the reign of Edward II. Hard cases, the lawyers say, make bad laws; the narrow definitions and the limited penalties of the treason statute were the direct cause of the ambiguities of judicial construction and of the frank injustice of attainder.

If the main purpose of the statute were indeed to secure a certain immunity both for contrariants and for the king's servants, its value could not be tested until the next grave political crisis. For over thirty years the cry of treason was never raised in political controversy. In the impeachments of 1376 and at the trial of the bishop of Norwich in 1383 the term seems to be carefully avoided,[3] and it was not even used in the charges brought against de la Pole in 1386. For this reason the punishments were moderate and the fatal craving for reprisals was not roused. It was the king himself who broke the tacit bargain reached between Crown and subjects in 1352. By the question put to the judges at Nottingham in August 1387, he extracted from them definitions of new treasons outside the statute; chief of these was impeding the king in the exercise of his prerogative, a definition stretched by further questions to cover the whole policy of the baronial opposition.[4] It was, in fact, a plot to destroy the Commission Councillors as traitors. When it failed Richard was helpless before angry barons, who saw their lives and heritages threatened by interpretations of the law made expressly to destroy them. It

[1] Coke, iii, *Institutes*, p. 19; Hale, loc. cit., p. 240.

[2] Bracton, ii. 261 (Rolls Series).

[3] The negotiations of the bishop's captains with the French were termed treason, but this was not a political charge (*Rot. Parl.* iii. 153, 158).

[4] Ibid., pp. 233–4.

is not surprising that in the Merciless Parliament they jettisoned the statute of 1352 and declared that the law of their own making was supreme. It may be that they did not wish to use the powers given them by the statute because they would then raise the whole question of the definitions of treason contained therein. Arundel, at least, must have clearly understood the importance of the issue, as his own father had been fully reinstated under the definitions of 1352. It seemed more expedient to claim for Parliament full supremacy and to revert to the evil precedents of the reign of Edward II.

The logical result of the claim to be above the law was the short cut of attainder, and in the next century this procedure would certainly have been followed. But the time was not yet ripe for the bold injustice of judgement by bill. Parliament was still at least as much a court as a legislature, and its members were strongly influenced by legal tradition. The compromise adopted was characteristic. Parliament was determined not to judge but to punish, yet the forms of law were maintained in so far as they served; failing them, Parliament fell back on its own authority. This attitude of compromise, hesitating between common law precedents and parliamentary authority, does not become clear without an examination of what actually happened.

The first move of the baronial opposition, once they realized the danger of the new judge-made treason, was to raise an army and to bring an appeal of treason against the king's chief advisers. The appeal was published by Gloucester, Arundel, and Warwick to the Commission Council; three days later it was affirmed before the king himself.[1] The appellants declared that they were ready to maintain their charges and for this to find security. Richard accepted the appeal and undertook that the parties should have full justice in Parliament.

[1] 14 and 17 Nov. 1387. *Rot. Parl.* iii. 229. Derby and Nottingham did not join the other appellants until they marched against de Vere.

The legality of this appeal raises an interesting preliminary question, as it was altogether different from a criminal appeal at common law.[1] The nearest precedent was probably the covenant of Lancaster and the Marchers against the Despencers in 1321.[2] The apology and defence of the confederates are set out in the official pardon which they procured for themselves;[3] the peers of the land, earls, and barons, in order to pursue and to attaint the evil deeds of the Despencers, who could not be attainted by process of law because they had accroached the royal power, allied themselves together and marched with banners displayed against the traitors. Though the 'contrariants' of 1321 had been forced to admit that they had no legal redress, the appellants of 1387 found an ingenious way out of the difficulty. Their leader, Gloucester, was Constable of England, and his tract on the order of battle in the Court of Chivalry shows that he took his official position seriously.[4] Suits in the Court of the Constable and Marshal were begun by appeal, and it was before this court that the appellants probably intended their charges to come.

The chroniclers are not in agreement as to this intention. The Westminster chronicler states that the appellants demanded that the persons accused should be kept in custody until Parliament met and there be prosecuted according to common law.[5] Other evidence, however, suggests that the writer has confused the barons' demand

[1] Stephens, *Hist. Crim. Law*, i. 245.

[2] The indenture was drawn up at the 'Parliament' of Shirburn in Elmet, 28 June 1321. An English translation of it is printed in Robert Brady's *Continuation of the Complete History of England* (1700), p. 128, taken from a French document in a register of Christ Church, Canterbury. Cf. a transcript in Bodley, MS. Tanner 12, xii, f. 50. What appears to be the Latin preamble to the indenture appears in a volume of Ashmole's transcripts, Bodley, MS. Ashmole 860, ff. 375–6.

[3] *Cal. Cl. Rolls, 1318–23*, pp. 492–5.

[4] *Black Book of the Admiralty*, i. 300 seq. Gloucester may also have been influenced by the *Modus Tenendi Parliamentum* and the Lancastrian tract on the Steward, Vernon Harcourt, loc. cit., pp. 164–7.

[5] Higden, ix. 108. Cf. p. 106.

with the royal answer. There is no reference to Parliament in the appeal itself; Favent, Knighton's continuator, and Walsingham all ascribe the promise of a parliamentary inquiry to the king, and Walsingham adds that in the royal presence the appellants flung down their gloves as a challenge to the duellum.[1] When Parliament met the lawyers reported that the appeal was not in order either by common or by civil law. The law of the Constable's court was civil law, and this specific reference to it proves that the appeal had raised the question of its authority.[2] The Lords, 'par assent du Roi', declared that 'the realm of England . . . never was and never shall be ruled nor governed by the civil law'.[3] It seems, then, that Gloucester was using his office of Constable to give a legal form to the appeal. Richard's transfer of the hearing to Parliament may have been intended as a counter move, partly to gain time and partly in the hope of winning support in the country. If Radcot Bridge had been a royalist victory—like Boroughbridge—the Parliament of 1388 would have paralleled the Parliament of York. As it was, the king lost everything by defeat in the field and was bound by his own decision to allow the hearing of the appeal in Parliament.

The preliminary procedure has, therefore, a threefold interest. It shows that the great hereditary offices could still be used to justify proceedings which were, in fact if not in name, against the Crown. It illustrates the arbitrary way in which the appellants manipulated procedure according to circumstances, readily giving up their appeal to the Constable's court when they understood that Parliament was better suited for their purpose. It also explains the origin of those parliamentary appeals for treason, which are a peculiarity of the period. They were

[1] Favent, p. 10; Knighton, ii. 248–9; Walsingham, ii. 166.

[2] Gloucester's library contained: 'II larges livres de ley cyvill en Latyne, lun appellez Digeste veil et lautre Code, pris VIs. VIIId.', Inventory, loc. cit., p. 301.

[3] *Rot. Parl.* iii. 236.

employed again under a royal direction in 1397; Hereford appealed Norfolk in 1398; in the first Parliament of Henry IV there were so many appeals and cross challenges and such a rain of gloves and gages on the floor of the parliament chamber that the danger to public peace was clearly evident and the procedure was abolished by statute.[1] In Richard II's reign, however, it had twice served the purpose of arraigning unpopular persons in Parliament without the elaborate preliminaries of an impeachment.

When Parliament assembled on 3 February 1388, the appeal with its thirty-nine charges was read and the persons appealed were solemnly summoned. De Vere, de la Pole, and the archbishop of York had already fled over sea; Tressilian was in hiding; only Brembre was a prisoner in the Tower. The summons was repeated twice and then the Lords examined the articles of accusation. Their deliberations lasted for over a week (4–13 February), and apparently included both the law of treason and the guilt of the accused. Finally, they found all four absentees guilty and declared fourteen out of the thirty-nine charges to be treason. The charges were a miscellaneous jumble, really an indictment of the whole policy of the king's advisers. Articles 29 to 32, accusations of treasonable negotiations with France, may have been brought under the statute as giving aid and comfort to the king's enemies.[2] The other specific charges were overt acts, proving the general charge of accroaching the

[1] *Rot. Parl.* iii. 442; Stat. 1 Hen. IV, c. 14; *Annales Ricardi secundi et Henrici quarti*, pp. 309–10, 313–14; MS. Bodley 596, ff. 82–5, translated *Archaeologia*, xx. 278–81. For example, when Fitz Walter appealed Aumarle of treason 'getta avant soun chaperoun. Et XX autres seigneurs et barouns getterount auxi lour gages pur mesme la querele devers Damerle. . . .' Aumarle also 'getta avant soun chaperoun sur la terre encountre Fitz Walter, les queux gades furont lyveres a Constable et le Marchal dengleterre et les parties arestez. . . .' Bodley 596, ff. 83–83v.

[2] It is possible that the accusation of raising armed forces on the king's behalf—articles 22, 37–9—may have been stretched to cover levying war against the king, even though *chivaucer* was excluded under the statute.

royal power expressed in the first article. This was a deliberate reversion to the precedents of Edward II, a reversion which it is difficult to defend on constitutional grounds. It was not the creation of a new statutory treason, as there is no record of the consent of king and Commons; nor is there either evidence or probability that the statute of treason was stretched so far. The pronouncement was, therefore, neither legislative nor judicial. It could have no other justification than as an act of public necessity, based on old precedents like the exile of the Despencers in 1321.

The four absentees were then sentenced as traitors. Six days later Tressilian was captured and brought to Parliament for judgement. Only the Westminster Chronicle records his protest against the sentence.[1] He pleaded, first the privilege of sanctuary and then that the process against him was erroneous, invalid, and ought to be annulled: this he offered to prove *per jura sua*. He was answered that the act or judgement of Parliament (*factum sive judicium parliamenti*) was irrevocable, and was ordered forthwith to be drawn to the gallows at Tyburn. It was, perhaps, argued that Tressilian had been sentenced already and was in the position of an outlawed man. The chronicler must have had his sentence in mind when he wrote: 'And tho v lordis were quyt before the justicez of alle thyng that was put ayens thaym [yet there was] made a lawe and an ordenaunce, that yf the parlement appelid or enpechid eny man of eny cryme, he sholde be dampned withoute ansuer, for with the parlement he mygte not figte. . . .'[2]

Tressilian's capture and execution broke into the middle of Brembre's trial. He alone of the five appealed was in custody and, with the king's aid, he made a bold fight for life. The trial lasted for four days, and in order

[1] Higden, ix. 167–8.

[2] Davies's *Chronicle*, pp. 5–6 (Camden Society); cf. *Eulogium Contin.* iii. 366, for the same statement in Latin.

to understand its significance it is necessary to follow it in some detail. When brought before Parliament (17 February) Brembre at once asked for counsel: this was refused to him—'by the law of Parliament' it was said, though such refusal was a practice well established at Common Law.[1] Then he asked for a copy of the articles of appeal and time to prepare his answer.[2] This was also denied, and he was forced to plead to each article as it was read to him. He entered a plea of not guilty to all, whereupon the appellants repeated their appeal, and offered to prove it in any way chosen by Parliament.[3] It was probably at this point that the Commons declared that if Brembre had not been appealed that they would have impeached him.[4] Brembre then offered to submit to the ordeal of battle, hoping, Favent says, to meet death in the lists rather than on the gallows.[5] His plea was denied on the grounds that trial by battle lay only when there were no witnesses. On the following day (18 February) the king himself opened the proceedings by a defence of Brembre, declaring that he had never known him to be a traitor nor guilty of any of the charges in the appeal.[6] This speech at once roused a storm of anger. The five appellants threw down their gloves at the king's feet, and 'like a fall of snow' from every side lords, knights, esquires, and commons threw their gloves and shouted that they would prove the appeal true with their bodies.[7] The Westminster chronicler reckons the number of gloves at 305.[8] Apparently the uproar was so great

[1] Holdsworth, ii. 107; v. 192.

[2] It was not until 1695 that a prisoner was allowed a copy of the indictment. [3] Higden, ix. 148–9. [4] *Rot. Parl.* iii. 238.

[5] Favent, p. 16. [6] Higden, ix. 166. [7] Favent, loc. cit.

[8] Higden, ix. 149, '. . . touz les seignurs appellantz devant le roy en plein parlement ont ewages les gaunz et toutz les seignurs piers du roiaume et plusours chevaliers et esquiers illoeqes gageront ensi lour gauntes et getteront devant le roy a nombre de CCC gauntz et V . . .' Cf. ibid., p. 166. The figure 305 offers a clue to the number of persons present 'en plein parlement'. Fifty-seven temporal peers had been summoned (Report on Dignity of Peers, iii, pp. 724 seq.): of these we may count out at least de Vere, de

that the king withdrew hurriedly from the assembly. Battle was still refused, and twelve peers, including York, Kent, Salisbury, and Northumberland, were appointed to investigate the truth of the charges. The next day the committee reported that they found Brembre guilty of nothing worthy of death. The appellants were so indignant at the verdict that only the interruption caused by the capture of Tressilian prevented serious disorder.[1]

The short shrift given to Tressilian probably hardened their resolution not to let Brembre escape, but, as he had been acquitted of treason by the lords, judgement against him was sought in a new quarter. Two members of each London trade gild were sent for and asked if Brembre were guilty under the articles of appeal. We have no record of their answers. Favent refers to the summons, but only in general terms.[2] The Westminster chronicler says that they merely wasted time in 'superfluous words'.[3] However, it is to this occasion that we must assign eleven petitions from sixteen non-victualling gilds; two are printed after the Parliament Roll of 1386, another in *Select Cases before the King's Council*, and the rest are still unpublished.[4] They are all directed against Brembre and apply the charge of accroaching the royal power—evidently the catchword of the day—to his manipulations of municipal elections and other measures undertaken

la Pole, and probably the 12 lords on the judicial committee, leaving 42 as the largest number of peers who offered battle. The rest, 263, may represent roughly the size of the Commons. Cf. the statement in *Anonimalle Chronicle*, p. 80, that 280 'chivalers et esquiers et citisayns et burgies' attended the Good Parliament.

[1] Favent, loc. cit.; Higden, ix. 149, 167.

[2] Favent, p. 17.

[3] Higden, ix. 168.

[4] *Rot. Parl.* iii. 225–7; *Select Cases*, pp. cvii–cviii, 74–6. P.R.O., Parliamentary Petitions, S.C. 8, File 20, 999–1000; File 21, 1001–6. Hitherto these petitions have been assigned to the Parliament of 1386, though they were obviously drafted after the royal prohibition of seeking pardons for Northampton and his followers, 7 Oct. 1387 (*Cal. Letter Book H*, p. 317), while Parliament was sitting and before Brembre's execution, 20 Feb. 1388. The charge of accroaching the royal power is plainly borrowed from the articles of appeal.

against John of Northampton's party. Probably these petitions were countered by those of the stronger victuallers and the evidence from the gilds thus cancelled out. Then the mayor, aldermen, and the recorder were summoned and asked if they believed that Brembre had knowledge of the treasons contained in the appeal. They replied that he was more likely to know of them than to be ignorant, and the recorder was asked, 'What does your law say in such a case?' He replied that the man who knows of and conceals treason deserves the punishment of death. This opinion was taken as decisive and Brembre was sentenced as a traitor and executed.[1]

The general interest of these proceedings lies partly in the evidence they supply of a neutral party among the Lords with the courage to declare Brembre guiltless of treason and partly in the summons of the London gilds in order to use the factions of the city against the accused. From the constitutional point of view the procedure is indeed remarkable. In the first place, the fierce casting of gloves by Lords and Commons shows that Parliament had little of the judicial decorum of a high court and that the original appeal to the court of chivalry was more than a mere technical device. The difficulty found in securing a conviction is also surprising, as it was obviously not due to any hesitation of the majority about the prisoner's deserts. The evidence suggests that the finding of the committee was accepted in so far as the original charge was concerned. Baulked by legal technicalities yet determined on punishment, Brembre's enemies found themselves in an impasse comparable to that of Strafford's accusers in 1641. They were not bold enough to make a parliamentary declaration of treason, though they had not hesitated to go behind the statute of 1352 in giving judgement on the articles of the appeal. Apparently they altered the charge to misprision of

[1] Higden, ix. 168.

treason and, refusing to act on the powers claimed for Parliament, sought and accepted the opinion of the recorder of London. He gave a ruling recognizable at common law,[1] which served as a justification of the sentence. The verdict recorded on the parliament roll, making no specific reference to these preliminaries, runs: 'les ditz seigneurs temporels avoient trove par deue et diligent examinacion pris par bone deliberation et deue proove et information, que le dit Nichol [Brembre] estoit coupable de haute treson contenu en les ditz articles. . . .'[2] Thus misprision was identified with high treason, and we have an example of a return to Common Law, directly contrary to the view that it was superseded by the statute.[3] Lack of courage among the leaders and lack of tradition in the assembly had made it impossible to maintain the full claim to parliamentary supremacy.

The proceedings under the appeal had cleared the ground for the trials of the judges and others of the court party who were in custody. The form of impeachment was adopted in order to associate the commons with the accusations. The prisoners were allowed to speak in their own defence. There is no evidence that any witnesses were called or examined, but this was in accordance with the practice in the lower courts.[4] The judges and the bishop of Chichester were accused of abetting traitors and of misprision of treason, without any sign of opposition to making these offences treason. Blake and Usk were impeached for counselling and aiding traitors. All

[1] Bracton (R.S.) ii. 260, 'Quod autem si ad tempus dissimulaverit et subticuerit, quasi consentiens et assentiens, erit seductor domini regis manifestus . . .' Cf. Holdsworth, iii. 389, n. 1.

[2] *Rot. Parl.* iii. 238.

[3] The view, put forward in another connexion by Miss Thornley (*E.H.R.* xxxii. 556–7), that the treason statute did not supersede the common law is rejected by Sir William Holdsworth (iii. 293, n. 5) as 'contrary to the whole history of the law of treason since the statute, and a wholly unnecessary supposition in view of the wording of the statute'.

[4] It was not until the sixteenth century that proof came to depend mainly on the sworn testimony of witnesses. Holdsworth, i. 334.

were sentenced to the full penalties for treason, but only Blake and Usk were executed. Then sixteen articles of impeachment were put forward against Burley and three other knights of the royal household.[1] No one was found guilty on more than two counts. It was declared that Burley had plotted the death of those who had assented to the Commission Council in 1386; Beauchamp and Berners had taken advantage of the king's youth to make him hate magnates who were his faithful subjects; Salisbury had conspired to hand over Calais and other strongholds in France to Charles VI in return for help in treasonable designs. Each of these charges was declared to be treason and all the knights were sentenced and executed.

As soon as they had destroyed their enemies the victors hoped to put the clock back and to avoid the inevitable consequence of tampering with the law. It seems as if they neither believed in nor understood their own declaration of parliamentary supremacy, since they failed to recognize that what one supreme Parliament could do another could as easily undo. One last treason was made on a common petition: it was enacted that all who sought to reverse the judgements of this Parliament should be condemned and punished as traitors and enemies of the king and kingdom.[2] Also, at the request of the Commons, a statute was passed declaring that all 'assemblies, appeals, pursuits, accusations, processes, judgements, and executions' of this Parliament would not be treated as precedents in time to come. Then followed a clause which proves that the irregularity of the whole proceedings was understood. It provided that, since divers points had been declared to be treason which were not in the statute, no judges in future should have power to give judgements in cases of treason beyond what they had before the meeting of parliament.[3]

[1] *Rot. Parl.* iii. 241–3.
[2] 11 Ric. II, c. 1.
[3] *Rot. Parl.* iii. 250; 11 Ric. II, c. 1.

The penalties in the parliamentary judgements of treason must have seemed a precedent of great danger. The treatment of forfeitures had overridden the law of entail, established by *de donis condicionalibus* and confirmed, implicitly, by the statute of 1352. Before 1534 forfeitures for treason did not extend to entailed property and a traitor forfeited only what he could dispose of freely.[1] Yet in every sentence given by this Parliament the forfeiture clause is explicit: the traitor and his heirs are disinherited for ever and their lands, goods, and chattels escheat to the king.[2] It is here, perhaps, that we come nearest to the fifteenth-century bill of attainder, which always contained a clause covering the forfeiture of entailed estates and was probably devised partly for that very purpose.[3]

Before Parliament dissolved an attempt was made to reverse or to modify the judgements on forfeitures. Following a statute appropriating all forfeitures to the king, it was enacted: 'It is not the intent of the king nor of the lords and commons of the parliament that by force of this statute the issues in tail, or they in reversion or in remainder, or women of their heritage or jointure . . . of gifts, grants, and feoffments made before the said time limited of forfeiture shall be barred or foreclosed of their right when their time shall come according to the common law.'[4] This reads as if the judgements were in fact to go no further than statute law allowed, but an examination of the history of the properties concerned shows that they were strictly enforced. It is true that Aubrey de Vere succeeded to the lands and title of his nephew Robert,

[1] 26 Hen. VIII, c. 22; I. D. Thornley, 'Treason Legislation of Henry VIII', *Transactions of Royal Historical Society*, 3rd series, xi. 116.

[2] *Rot. Parl.* iii. 237, 240, 241, 243.

[3] The treason statute of 1397, repealed in 1399, declared that the traitor 'forface de luy et de ces heires queconqes toutz ses terres, tenementz et possessions et libertees et toutz autres enheritementz queux il ad . . . si bien en fee taille, come en fee simple. . . .' Ibid. 351.

[4] 11 Ric. II, c. 5. An addition to a common petition, *Rot. Parl.* iii. 246, § 24.

but his right derived from his father and therefore was not barred by the judgement. On the other hand, Robert's wife, Philippa, was apparently deprived of everything and as late as 1401 she was still petitioning for her dower.[1] A series of petitions were presented in Lancastrian Parliaments by the judges and their sons, asking for the reversal of the sentences of 1388, especially that they, their heirs and their blood might be able to sue at common law for their rights by descent.[2] A similar petition was presented by the heir of Simon Burley.[3] The clearest case is the forfeiture of the lands and title of Michael de la Pole, which were specifically granted to him and to the heirs male of his body.[4] The Parliament of 1388 made his wife a compassionate grant of lands, which, it was expressly stated, she had held before the forfeiture of her husband; the title of earl was not restored until 1397.[5]

There seems, then, no doubt that the statute protecting dower and estates tail was inoperative and that it was probably inserted only to avoid a dangerous precedent. It affords an example of a different kind of the contempt shown by Parliament for its own law-making. Both in judgement and in execution the Parliament of 1388 went behind *de donis* and the treason statute; it is still more surprising that they should go behind a statute of their own making. It is clear that statute law was not yet strong enough to bear a heavy strain and that the magnates discarded it when it suited their purpose. In their whole policy they had reverted to the old common law rule expressed by Bracton: The traitor 'shall sustain the last punishment with aggravation of bodily pain, the

[1] *Rot. Parl.* iii. 460–1.

[2] Ibid. 442, 461; iv. 38, § 19; v. 393. For example, Hamond Bealknap petitioned 'q'il poet estre persone able al commune ley, et il, et son issu, et son sank, ables a demander par discent de lour auncestres . . . nient contre esteant ascun juggement ou estatut fait a contraire . . .' (iv. 38, § 19).

[3] Ibid. 464.

[4] Ibid. 668.

[5] Ibid. 245.

loss of all his goods and the perpetual disinheritance of his heirs, so that they be admitted neither to the paternal nor to the maternal inheritance. For that crime is so grave that it is scarcely permissible for the heirs to live.'[1]

[1] Bracton, ii. 261; cf. Coke, *Hist.* iii. 211, 'Corruption of blood, and that the children of a traitor should not inherit appeareth also by holy Scripture' (Psalm cix. 9–13).

VI

WILLIAM OF WINDSOR IN IRELAND, 1369–76[1]

I

NO scholar can deny that, through the destruction of the records in the Four Courts (1922), many social and legal problems of Anglo-Irish history must remain unsolved. Though the disaster is irreparable—no less than 'wisdom at one entrance quite shut out'—yet it is not 'total eclipse without all hope of day'. Anglo-Irish government was never self-contained; behind the authority of Irish officials and institutions lay the paramount authority of the English King, Council, and Parliament. Therefore, we are never lost on an uncharted sea of darkness. In the constant interchange of news, complaints, and commands it was inevitable that the pull of the stronger tide should gradually deposit a mass of documents on the English side of the Channel. It might even be maintained that the records in Dublin had a value mainly for the routine of government, and that the significant evidence for conflict and change was irresistibly drawn across the water. Certainly ever since the Conquest Anglo-Irish documents have been slowly silting up in English official repositories. Many of these have found permanent security in the English Public Record Office, and it is there that the scholar must look in the first place for solution of Irish problems of medieval colonial government.

The documents relating to William of Windsor's government of Ireland illustrate—perhaps to an exceptional extent—the value to the Irish historian of records which have always been in English custody. The main evidence is contained in two rolls embodying the charges

[1] A paper read before the Royal Irish Academy on 11 April 1932, and printed in the *Proceedings* of the Academy in August 1932. It is here reprinted by kind permission of the President and Council.

brought against the Irish administration between 1373 and 1376.[1] One, endorsed *Les copies des accusements*, is a roll of eighty-five articles of complaint, or impeachment; the other has been given at a much later date the title of *De Gestu ministrorum regis Edwardi tertii in Hibernia diversorum annorum.*[2] A note on the close roll of 1376 explains how these documents came to England.[3] When Windsor and other officials were indicted before royal commissioners in Ireland eight[4] inquisitions were taken and sent over to England. They were delivered to John de Freton, clerk, together with 'a great long roll containing many articles . . . brought from Ireland by Richard Deer and William Stapolyn'. The clerk, by order of the Council, made copies of the roll and the inquisitions; these were deposited in the English Treasury, and the originals were returned to Ireland for further inquiry. To the inquisitions are stitched, so as to form one roll, a number of miscellaneous documents relating to the inquiry, which were probably deposited in the Treasury at the same time. They may be classified in three parts: writs summoning the Irish commons to Westminster in February 1376, with the returns; inquisitions taken at Dublin and Drogheda in 1373; documents relating to proceedings in the English Council.

This substantial addition to our knowledge of Ireland in the fourteenth century has hitherto received slight attention or emphasis from historians.[5] Its value appears

[1] P.R.O. Parliament and Council Proceedings, Chancery, 47-50 Ed. III, Rolls 2 and 3.

[2] This is the title given in the Bodley MS., Rawlinson, B. 491, a volume of transcripts made early in the eighteenth century which includes six documents taken from this roll in a collection of forty writs relating to Ireland, Edward I-Henry VI, pp. 1-86.

[3] *Cal. Cl. Rolls, 1374-7*, p. 368.

[4] Only six of these inquisitions are now extant.

[5] Cf. Sir W. Betham, *Origin and History of the Constitution of England and of the Early Parliaments of Ireland* (1834), pp. 305-10, and J. T. Gilbert, *Viceroys of Ireland* (1865), pp. 230-41. Three plates (XIX, 1-3), with a full printed text of one writ and returns relating to the summons to Westminster in 1376, were published by Gilbert in *Facsimiles of National MSS. of Ireland*, Part III, 1879.

to be threefold. It supplies a mass of vivid and detailed information about Anglo-Irish administration at the close of Edward III's reign. Further, it enables us to reconstruct a narrative of the attacks made on Windsor and other ministers between 1373 and 1376, attacks which were in effect proceedings against the Crown. Lastly, the evidence for Windsor's system of government and the resistance he provoked warrants the claim that under his rule the Irish Parliament acquired the shape, coherence, and functions which it retained until the Reformation. The value of the material for Irish administrative history must be left to the consideration of experts. Here it is possible to deal only with the proceedings against the Crown and with the reshaping of the Irish Parliament.

II

In the spring of 1376 two distinct movements in opposition to the Crown converged in the Good Parliament: an English movement of resistance to the inner circle of household officers and financiers who were dominant at the court, and an Irish movement against the government of William of Windsor. The two movements were linked together by personal attachments and enmities. The natural leader of the Anglo-Irish was Edmund Mortimer, the young earl of March; he was the greatest absentee landlord of Ireland and had married the eldest grandchild of the king. Already his political importance was recognized; in 1373 the Kilkenny Parliament requested that he should be sent to Ireland, and in the same year he served on an English parliamentary committee of magnates appointed to advise the Commons.[1] At the centre of the court circle was Alice Perrers, the king's mistress; as she was the wife[2] of Windsor, any movement

[1] *Rot. Parl.* ii. 316.

[2] The date of the marriage, which was secret, is unknown; it may have taken place after Windsor's first recall from Ireland (1372-3). Edward III maintained in the Parliament of 1376 that he had not known of it when the

against the Irish administration was a direct challenge to her influence. In short, the Irish grievances provided an English opportunity, which March and his following were able to turn entirely to their own advantage.

As soon as Windsor came to Ireland as Lieutenant (22 June 1369) he had shown a determination to increase the royal revenue drawn from subjects. There was little in the experience of the colony to prepare it for a fiscal policy of Thorough. Complaints against it, probably supported by March, began to reach England in 1371. The first sign of their effect was a royal command to stay the levy of certain imposts, alleged to be unlawful, which Windsor had laid on the men of Dublin and Drogheda.[1] This order was issued under the privy seal in September 1371. It was followed a month later by a general command forbidding all undue tallages and exactions. It was also stated that the king had heard, by complaint of a great number of his lieges in Ireland, that Windsor was laying upon the people new and unheard-of imposts, and that it seemed to the Council, after due deliberation, that by such burdens peril of the loss of Ireland was likely to arise.[2] The petitions embodying these grievances have not yet been traced;[3] as the Irish also complained that Windsor had hindered them from repairing to the king for redress, it is possible that they had been unable to present any formal statement of wrongs to the Council.

Windsor's party was not yet in the ascendant in the English Council. He evidently failed to justify his fiscal policy, and he was recalled in the spring of 1372.[4] A clamour for an inquiry into his administration at once

fact was discovered by diligent inquiry. Cf. *Rot. Parl.* iii. 41; *Chronicon Angliae*, p. 97.

[1] *Cal. Cl. Rolls*, p. 246, 10 Sept. 1371. Repeated on 8 and 10 Dec., ibid., pp. 265–6.

[2] Ibid., pp. 256–7, 20 Oct. 1371. Cf. p. 259 for repeated order on 12 Nov.

[3] At a date later than 7 June 1371 the commons of Meath sent Stephen Gray to complain on their behalf to the king and council in England (Inquisitions, Meath County, ii, cap. 6, below).

[4] He left Ireland on 21 March 1372.

broke out, and, for a time at least, the English Council gave it full attention. Sir Robert Ashton was sent to Ireland as Justiciar. He was a man well qualified for the work of investigation, as he had served as Chancellor under Clarence from 1364 to 1367.[1] He was instructed to stay the levy of unlawful taxes and to bring the whole matter before the prelates, lords, and commons in the Irish Parliament.[2] He and the bishop of Lismore and Waterford were also commissioned to find by inquisition what had been the profits and expenditure of Windsor's government and to examine the accounts of the Irish treasurer.[3] These instructions and commissions, issued in May and July 1372, indicate an intention to undertake a thorough inquiry into the Irish administration.

Ashton seems to have carried out his instructions conscientiously, though slowly. At a Parliament held in January 1373, when the government of Windsor was brought under review, it was decided to send an embassy to the king and council in England. The envoys chosen were the Chancellor, the Treasurer, the Chief Baron of the Exchequer, and the bishop of Cloyne. Official interests and sympathy naturally lay with Windsor, and afterwards the Treasurer and the Chief Baron were accused of giving a message contrary to that with which they had been charged. The true message was a statement of the abuses of the Irish administration, accompanied by requests that March should be sent to Ireland with sufficient power and that more suitable persons should be appointed judges.[4] This embassy does not seem to have appeared before the English Council until September 1373.[5] The delay was due, perhaps, to obstruction either in England or by the messengers themselves.

[1] He had also some connexion with Alice Perrers, as he gave certain lands in Dorset to be held for her use, while sole, at some time before her marriage to Windsor, *Cal. Cl. Rolls, 1381–5*, pp. 354, 376.

[2] *Cal. Cl. Rolls*, p. 380, 28 May 1372.

[3] *Cal. Pat. Rolls*, p. 238, 28 July 1372.

[4] *Infra*, p. 203; pp. 213–15.

[5] Rymer, vii. 28.

It is also possible that the embassy waited for the findings of the inquisitions taken under the commission to inquire into the financial administration of Windsor and his treasurer. Records of six of these inquisitions are extant.[1] They were held in May and June 1373, before Ashton and Sir Robert Preston, Chief Justice of Common Pleas. Juries from Dublin city, Drogheda, and the county of Meath made a series of sworn statements, to which they affixed their seals, statements which were in effect an arraignment of the government of Ireland since the appointment of Windsor in 1369. That their accusations covered both local and general grievances may be illustrated by a few examples:

'The jurors (of Dublin) say on oath that on 10 July 1369 William of Windsor, by council of certain named persons, compelled the mayor and community of Dublin to send six men at arms and eighteen archers to Tassaggart for three weeks at their own expense, against their will and by extortion.'

'They say also that on 3 February 1371 Windsor commanded by royal writ eight citizens to go to Limerick and to dwell there, although they had no lands or goods in that city or county, which was a hundred leagues and more from Dublin. When the citizens understood the Lieutenant's malice they went to Cashel and there on 29 March 1371 made fine with him for twenty marks each.

(Dublin Inquisitions, § 1 and 8, 13 June, 1373.)

'The jurors (of Meath county) say that at the Parliament of Dublin, on 22 April 1370, James de la Hide and John Fitz John were present as knights of the shire: before they went to Dublin they were instructed by the faithful of the county at an assembly held at Trim not to consent to any subsidy or tallage, by reason of the losses borne by the county from Irish enemies. When they came to the Parliament they were forced by the Lieutenant and his council to agree to a tax of one mark

[1] *Infra*, pp. 220–32. There were originally eight inquisitions (*supra*, p. 147); the missing two probably were taken at Waterford and Cork. Complaints from these cities were answered at a later date by Stephen de Valle, bishop of Meath. [Memoranda rolls, Treasurer, 8 Ric. II, P.R.O., E. 368, 145.]

from each ploughland in the county. There are 520 ploughlands in the county and the tax was levied by the Lieutenant against the will of the community and by extortion.'

(Inq. Meath Co., 1, § 3, 20 May 1373.)

The six records of inquisitions contain in all fifty-one charges of the same kind as these examples. They often overlap and even resemble each other verbally, and there can be no doubt that they were the result of a carefully prepared questionnaire put before them by Ashton and Preston. They provided overwhelming evidence in support of the complaints, first made in 1371, that Windsor was imposing arbitrary taxes and tallages on the country.

The findings of the commission were probably sent to England in the summer of 1373. With them, we may suppose, went another small group of documents concerned with the accounts presented by Windsor and the Irish treasurer.[1] One document is a roll of certain moneys paid to Windsor by the treasurer between 1369 and 1371. The total sum amounts to £3,098 9*s.* 4½*d.*; there are eight articles of expenditure, and each of these is challenged. On the dorse there is a note stating that the auditors handed the account into the English Exchequer on 10 December 1373.[2] This record is supported by another and much longer roll, consisting of challenges to the accounts of the treasurer[3] during the period 1369 to September 1372. There are three groups of articles, with six items in the first, thirty-four in the second, and ten in the third. They repeat certain of the articles and challenges in Windsor's account, and include many other

[1] These documents were not preserved with the others, but appear in the collection of Irish Exchequer Accounts, P.R.O., E. 101, 244/12; 245/1–2.

[2] 'Hanc cedulam liberarunt hic Johannes de Appelton et Laurencius de Alrethorpe, auditores compoti hic in scaccario per manus suas proprias, X° die Decembris anno XLVII regis Edwardi III post conquestum.'

[3] Stephen de Valle, bishop of Limerick, 1360–9; bishop of Meath, 1369–79; Treasurer, 1369–74. See below, Article 38, Roll 2, for a reference to these accounts.

items of expenditure. The nature of this evidence may be illustrated by the following examples:

'£56 13*s*. 4*d*. paid to James de la Hyde, taken and imprisoned by Irish enemies in the king's wars, as a recompense for his ransome of 108 marks. Challenged, because the king is not bound to pay ransomes, nor have the Lieutenant and Treasurer power to pay ransomes from the royal revenue. (*Allowed*.)

'£86 6*s*. 8*d*. paid to Geoffrey de Vale and William of Scotland as divers rewards for divers causes. Challenged, because the rewards seem too great and given out of favour, since Geoffrey and William are the kinsmen and servants of the Treasurer. (*Allowed*.)

'£253 6*s*. 8*d*. paid to the Treasurer himself as a reward for divers causes. Challenged, because the Treasurer draws a double fee for his office in order that he should not draw further wages for men-at-arms, hobelers, and infantry of his retinue on pretext of war. (*Allowed*.)

'£255 paid to William of Windsor, Lieutenant, as the fee and wages of divers men-at-arms and archers in his retinue . . . over and above those specified in the indenture of his appointment, because the subsidy of a mark on the carucate, granted for their wages, was insufficient. Challenged, because the amount which the subsidy had brought in is not stated, nor how many men had been employed, nor for how long. . . . Further, even if the subsidy were not enough, there remained £2,144 15*s*. 11½*d*. levied by two other subsidies . . . from which the wages ought to have been drawn rather than from the revenue of the king. Lastly, the Treasurer has nothing in his account about the said three subsidies or any part of them. (*Allowed*.)

Marginal notes and erasures show that the Treasurer's roll was carefully examined, probably by the English Council.[1] It is significant that only two items were

[1] The words *alloc*. or *disalloc*. (*allowed* and *disallowed*) and other brief notes are scribbled against each item on the Treasurer's roll. These notes are too authoritative to be merely the work of auditors, as they sometimes refer to a writ or to a statement of the conditions under which the item was allowed. There are also many almost illegible erasures which seem to represent a change of opinion.

finally disallowed, and that they are almost the smallest sums in the account.[1] There is no record of date, beyond that of the deposit of Windsor's roll in the Exchequer on 10 December 1373. We know, however, that the embassy from the Kilkenny Parliament appeared before the English Council in September, and we may suppose that the findings of the commissions, that is, the inquisitions and the accounts, were examined at the same time. The decision reached was published in a letter patent issued on 20 September 1373. The Irish embassy, it was stated, had explained to the Council the perils of their country, and has asked for the help of the earl of March; the king promised that he would send the earl as soon as it was convenient, and in the meantime he appointed William of Windsor to be Governor and Keeper of the land.[2]

The Irish were thus completely defeated. Not only was William of Windsor sent back as their Governor, but in December an order was issued for the collection of the disputed subsidies. It seems plain that Windsor's faction recovered in 1373 the power that they had lost in 1372, and that all the evidence carefully collected to expose him was set aside.

Windsor returned to Ireland in 1374, and we hear nothing of open resistance to him until the autumn of the following year. In June 1375 Nicholas Dagworth was commissioned to go to Ireland on the king's behalf;[3] though the main purpose of his embassy was to persuade the Irish Parliament to make a grant of supply, it is possible that his appointment was a sign that the tide was again running against Windsor in the English Council. A year later Alice Perrers declared that Dagworth was her husband's enemy,[4] and it may be that he was

[1] Other items were first disallowed and then admitted.

[2] Rymer, vii. 28.

[3] *Cal. Pat. Rolls*, 18 and 19 June 1375, pp. 117 and 120.

[4] *Rot. Parl.* iii. 13.

sent to Ireland to check or even, to some extent at least, to supersede Windsor as governor. Dagworth left England at the end of July,[1] and on 6 October he addressed the Irish Parliament at Kilkenny.[2] When his request for a subsidy was answered by a point-blank refusal he produced letters under the privy seal commanding Windsor to summon representatives of the commons, elected as for a Parliament, to come before the English Council in February 1376. Here it is sufficient to notice that this extraordinary summons may not have had a purely fiscal purpose. It is significant that the commons were ordered to be at Westminster on 16 February, two days after the date originally fixed for the assembly of the English Parliament. It is even possible that the reason for postponing the opening of Parliament to 29 April was the delay caused by the Irish elections. Ashton, whom Windsor had superseded in 1373, had been appointed Treasurer of England in 1374, and it is possible that the project of reopening the Irish question may have originated with him. There can be no doubt that both he and March were fully informed about Irish affairs and likely to press for an inquiry.

Windsor, Holywood, the chief baron, and Carlill, the second baron of the Exchequer, were summoned to England in February 1376;[3] representatives of the Irish commons came over at an uncertain date.[4] Their affairs were thrust into the background by the excitement of English politics, and probably in Parliament interest in the matter did not go beyond the great roll of indictments which was presented to the English Council. The roll

[1] The account for Dagworth's Irish expenses is preserved in the P.R.O., Irish Exchequer Accounts, E. 101/317/3. He left London on 23 July and returned on 22 December 1375; the total cost for himself was £156 6*s.* 8*d.*, and for his clerk, William Tarent, £78; their travelling expenses were, respectively, £3 6*s.* 8*d.* and £2.

[2] *Infra*, pp. 232–3, for a narrative of Dagworth's proceedings at Kilkenny.

[3] *Cal. Pat. Rolls*, pp. 244–5. The summons was repeated for 27 April 1376, *Cal. Cl. Rolls*, p. 295.

[4] *Infra*, p. 158, n. 1.

was headed: 'These are the articles presented to the King's Council in England by Richard Deere and William Stapelyn touching the mischiefs, wrongs, and deceits done in Ireland by the king's ministers, to be examined by the Court and to be explained by those who have come to declare the truth on oath, according to their knowledge.'[1] The articles fall into five sections: thirty-six charges against William of Windsor; twenty-three against the treasurer, the bishop of Meath; eight against the Chancellor, William Tany; eleven against the chief baron of the Exchequer; and seven against the second baron, William Carlill. The accusations repeat and amplify the findings of the inquisitions taken in 1373. It is impossible to say when they were drafted, though we know that the messengers who brought them were paid £10 for their services at the end of May.[2] It is reasonable to assume that they were presented to the Council about the time when the Good Parliament assembled, and that they had the support of Ashton, the English Treasurer, and of March, the leader of the baronial opposition. It is even possible that the Irish indictments suggested to the English that startling change from procedure by petition to procedure by impeachment, by means of which the Good Parliament gave a new and political form to proceedings against the Crown.

We are not now concerned with the repercussion in England of events in Ireland, though it certainly served to deflect the attention of Parliament from Irish grievances. We can only guess at the date when the Irish officials were brought to trial. Both records and chronicles are silent about Irish affairs throughout the months of May and June, a sign that the whole business was shelved until after the dissolution of Parliament on

[1] *Infra*, p. 184, Roll 2. Many of the charges were taken from the inquisitions, see below.

[2] Devon, *Issues*, p. 199, 30 May 1376; £10 paid 'at the king's command for their trouble in lately coming from Ireland and residing in London to inform the king's Council of the defective government of the land aforesaid'.

10 July. The evidence suggests that the 'Continual Council', appointed by Parliament, dealt with the Irish indictments in July and August.[1] The result can be traced in a number of changes in the Irish administration. On 24 July Windsor was definitely superseded by Ormonde, and ordered to hand over the custody of Ireland to him.[2] Between 18 July and 12 August the Chancellor, the Treasurer, the chief and second baron of the Exchequer, two judges, and certain lesser officials were dismissed and replaced by others.[3] It was probably within these dates that Holywood and Carlill, the two barons of the Exchequer, were brought to trial before the Council.[4]

Knowledge of the trials is limited to the answers of Holywood and Carlill, preserved with the indictments sent from Ireland.[5] The procedure probably resembled that devised for impeachment in the Good Parliament. The Irish commons may have presented their accusations in person. Holywood certainly appealed to one of the knights from Meath to give evidence on his behalf,[6] and there are other signs that some at least of the commons

[1] March was a member of the Council, and Ashton, as Treasurer, would also be present.

[2] *Cal. Pat. Rolls*, p. 304.

[3] On 18 July 1376 the archbishop of Dublin was appointed Chancellor and the bishop of Ossory Treasurer, *Cal. Pat. Rolls*, pp. 300, 303. On 6 Aug. James de Boys was appointed Chamberlain of the Exchequer and John Tyrell was appointed Justice holding the pleas following the Justiciar, ibid., p. 303. On 8 Aug. Richard Plunket was made one of the Justices of the Common Bench, ibid. On 12 Aug. Stephen Bray was made Chief Baron of the Exchequer, John Pembroke second Baron, Thomas Bache Chancellor of the Exchequer, Richard Walsh Chamberlain of the Exchequer, and Robert Lughtburgh clerk of the Pipe, ibid., p. 335.

[4] Tout has already noticed that 'some sort of "great council"' was sitting in the summer of 1376, *Chapters in the Administrative History of Mediaeval England*, iii. 308, n. 3. Many of the appointments cited above were made by the Council or by the king and Council. Richard Whethill and other soldiers who had served under Windsor in Ireland presented a bill of complaint to the Council sitting in Black Friars on 11 Aug., *infra*, p. 219.

[5] *Infra*, pp. 207–19.

[6] Ibid., p. 213. Richard Plunket, appointed Justice of the Common Bench on 8 Aug.

were in England during the summer of 1376.[1] Both men put forward a vigorous defence. They claimed the protection of the statute of 1368, according to which no man might be put to answer without presentment before judges, or matter of record, or by due process and original writ, *solonc launcien leye de la terre*.[2] They also objected sharply to every charge which was expressed loosely or in general terms. Holywood several times vouched official records and asked for the testimony of particular witnesses, including those members of the Council who had heard his message from the Parliament of Kilkenny in 1373.[3] It is, however, certain that the defence was deemed insufficient, as both Holywood and Carlill were dismissed from office on or before 12 August.

The barons of the Exchequer served as scapegoats for the rest. There is no evidence that the three chief offenders were ever brought to trial in person. The Chancellor and Treasurer[4] were not even summoned from Ireland,

[1] On 25 July the Irish Justiciar and the Chancellor were ordered to see that the representatives of the Irish counties, cities, and boroughs who had come to the Council in England should have their reasonable expenses (*Report on the Dignity of a Peer*, iii. 669): a like order for John Droupe, citizen of Cork, was issued on 27 Aug. (ibid.). On 8 Aug. licences to ship grain to England were granted to Nicholas Howth and Richard White, knights elected for County Dublin; to Richard Plunket, knight for Meath, and to the Mayor and citizens of Dublin (*Cal. Pat. Rolls*, p. 303). Like licences were granted to the mayor and burgesses of Drogheda on 2 Aug., to John White, elected to represent Dublin city, on 26 July, and to William Lumbard, a citizen of Waterford, on 12 September. (Ibid., pp. 305, 309, 342.) The Latin comments on the articles of accusation, preserved on Roll 2, probably represent the evidence of Irish witnesses.

[2] Stat. 42 Ed. III, § 111. The statute was made on petition of the commons 'to eschew the mischiefs and damages done . . . by false accusers'; by their accusations, 'made more for revenge and for singular benefit than for the profit of the king; some have been arrested and others brought before the king's Council by writ and otherwise, under heavy penalty and against the law.' Alice Perrers pleaded the protection of the same statute in 1378, *Rot. Parl.* iii. 41.

[3] *Infra*, pp. 213–15.

[4] The Chancellor was William Tany, Prior of Kilmainham, and the Treasurer was Stephen de Valle, bishop of Meath. The Latin comments on the accusations brought against them suggest that witnesses against them

and were apparently dismissed without a hearing. The course of the proceedings against Windsor himself is very obscure, no doubt because strong influences were at work to protect him. On 16 August a writ was issued ordering the Mayor and Sheriffs of London to arrest him, because a quarrel had broken out between him and other persons in the king's presence at White Friars in Fleet Street.[1] Probably the Council was then sitting at White Friars, and an attempt to bring Windsor to trial had provoked a clash of factions in London.[2] Two days later he had surrendered himself at the Tower to stand his trial;[3] on 20 August he was released, on the surety of seven mainpernors that they would 'have him before the king and council when and as often as the king in council shall please, in order to answer touching whatever shall be laid against him, and to do and receive what shall be by the king and council appointed.[4] Once again the tide of fortune had turned in Windsor's favour, and perhaps we should date from this third week in August the revival of the Court party and the downfall of the 'Continual Council' appointed in Parliament.

The strength of the reaction was soon (November)

were examined by the Council. The accusations against Windsor, the comments suggest, were examined in the same way.

[1] *Calendar Letter Book H*, ed. R. Sharp, p. 44; H. T. Riley, *Memorials of London*, p. 402. Cf. *Cal. Cl. Rolls*, p. 443.

[2] A further indication of disturbance on 16 Aug. was the imprisonment on 18 Aug. of Henry le White, fishmonger, 'because he had been reported to the Mayor and Aldermen as having said publicly that the Mayor had knowledge of a cloak embroidered with pearls, which had been stolen from the house of Sir William de Wyndesore in Southwark the preceding Saturday' (16 Aug.). *Calendar of Plea and Memoranda Rolls, London, 1364–81*, p. 222. Windsor's house may have been plundered. The riots of 1377 show that London supported the party in opposition to the Court.

[3] *Calendar Letter Book H*, p. 44. A writ of *supersedeas* was issued to the Mayor and Sheriffs on 18 Aug.

[4] *Cal. Cl. Rolls*, 20 Aug. 1376, p. 443. The mainpernors were Ralph Basset of Drayton, Henry and Ralph de Ferrers, Guichard Dangle, Mathew de Redeman, Thomas de Rokeby and Lewis Clifford. They were all soldiers rather than politicians.

proved by the disgrace and trial of William of Wykeham[1] and the imprisonment of de la Mare, the Speaker of the Good Parliament. At the same time March, alarmed by Lancaster's hostility, resigned the marshalship of England, choosing, we are told, to lose his staff of office rather than his life.[2] The exact date of his resignation is unknown;[3] there are signs that until the end of November Windsor's enemies were pressing hard for a full inquiry and punishment. A new commission was issued to Dagworth, empowering him to bring back the original indictments to Ireland for further debate and determination.[4] This commission was revoked early in November, through the influence of Alice Perrers; against the argument that it had been ordained by Council, the king maintained that he was *sovereyn juge*, and that it was not reasonable that one enemy should judge another.[5] Windsor's enemies then made a final effort and procured another commission of inquiry (20 November), in which four Anglo-Irish officials and magnates were associated with Dagworth.[6] In little more than a fortnight the second commission was in turn superseded by an order sent to Ireland to stay any process against Windsor, as a day had been set for him to answer before the king and Council.[7] This appears to be the last document relevant to the inquiry. The day set for trial was a mere form of words drafted to pacify the Irish. Like so many other

[1] He was tried before Sir William Skipwith, who had been a judge in Ireland. Tout (loc. cit., iii. 311, n. 3) suggests that he was brought over from Ireland for the purpose.

[2] *Chronicon Angliae*, p. 108.

[3] Tout, loc. cit. iii. 313, n. 4, points out that his successor, Percy, was summoned to Parliament as Marshal on 1 Dec.

[4] *Cal. Cl. Rolls, 1374–7*, p. 368. The exact date of the commission is unknown, but it must have followed Windsor's release on 20 Aug.

[5] *Rot. Parl.* iii. 12–14.

[6] *Cal. Pat. Rolls*, 20 Nov. 1376, p. 416. The additional commissioners were Ormonde, the Justiciar; the earl of Kildare; John Keppok, who had held the pleas following the Justiciar in 1375; and Richard White, one of the knights elected to represent County Dublin in England.

[7] *Cal. Cl. Rolls*, 4 Dec. 1376, p. 469.

medieval attacks on the administration, the whole agitation ended[1] in a confused compromise. On the one hand, the chief offenders were protected from punishment; on the other, the great officers of the Crown were dismissed, and Windsor returned no more to Ireland.

III

During or immediately after the rule of William of Windsor the Irish Parliament changed fundamentally both in form and in function. The doctrine of taxation by the consent of elected representatives, given in Parliament, was accepted; two proctors from each diocese were added to the commons; the obligation imposed on lay magnates to attend Parliament became exclusively tenurial, and the issue of writs of summons was restricted to earls and barons. Each of these changes seems to date from the last decade of Edward III's reign and each is in some way connected with William of Windsor. It can hardly be a coincidence that each change brought the Irish Parliament nearer to the Parliament described in the *Modus tenendi Parliamentum*, the Irish version of which first appears early in the fifteenth century.[2]

In order to understand the significance of Windsor's parliamentary policy it is necessary to consider the stage reached by the Irish Parliament by 1369. Parliament, as a gathering of estates including representatives of the commons, cannot be traced further back than 1297, when the Justiciar summoned not only the magnates, but representatives of shires and liberties, to assemble at Dublin. By the end of Edward II's reign the practice of summoning citizens and burgesses had been established. The main work of Parliament seems to have been either

[1] The whole matter was reopened early in Richard II's reign, when Dagworth was given a new commission of inquiry. I hope at a later date to deal with the documents of this sequel.

[2] I hope to discuss the whole question of the Irish and English versions of the *Modus* in a special monograph. [This refers to Miss Clarke's *Medieval Representation and Consent*, published in 1936.]

judicial business or legislation and arbitration between factions. The idea of revenue based on parliamentary taxation did not appear until the succeeding reign, and even then it was received with surprise and anger. The ordinary revenue was derived from the profits of justice, the crown lands, escheats, wardship, the farm of shires, cities and boroughs, and the custom duties.[1] The clergy *inter Anglicos* contributed from time to time to the tenths granted to the king by the Pope.[2] Extraordinary aids were raised with the consent of particular persons or communities. In 1300, for example, Edward I demanded a subsidy for the war in Scotland, and sent a general writ to his earls, barons, knights and faithful subjects, and special writs to the cities and boroughs of Ireland. The Justiciar, John Wogan, summoned a Parliament; before it met he visited twenty-three towns in Leinster and Munster and extracted promises of contribution varying in amount from one to 260 marks. Parliament requested him to raise the rest of the subsidy by further piecemeal negotiation.[3] The counties, liberties, cross lands (ecclesiastical estates), and boroughs contributed in this way £2,361 6*s*. 8*d*.; the magnates served in person in the Scottish campaign of 1301.[4] The plan, which recalls the procedure described in the *Dialogus de Scaccario*,[5] shows an application of the doctrine of consent at its earliest stage. The method was well suited to Irish

[1] On 15 May 1275 the king ordered the Justiciar of Ireland to prevail upon the magnates, commonalty, and merchants of Ireland to grant the *Magna Custuma* as it had recently been granted in England. *Cal. Documents, Ireland*, vol. ii, no. 1117.

[2] These finally ceased at the beginning of Edward III's reign.

[3] *Early Statutes of Ireland*, pp. 229 seqq.

[4] G. H. Orpen, *Ireland under the Normans*, iv. 47–8. In 1292 the 'magnates and good men of the land' had granted the king a fifteenth, but there is no indication of how their consent was obtained. *Cal. Documents, Ireland*, vol. iii, no. 1090.

[5] *Dialogus*, ed. Hughes, Crump, and Johnson, 1902, p. 95: 'Fiunt interdum per comitatus communes assise a iustitiis errantibus . . . que ideo dicuntur communes quia, cognita summa que de comitatu requiritur, communiter ab hiis qui in comitatu fundos habent per hidas distribuitur. . . .'

particularism, and was only slowly and with difficulty replaced by consent in a representative assembly.

Edward III's need of money brought new demands for Irish subsidies. A general grant to the king was made in 1335, and at first sight it has the appearance of a parliamentary subsidy. In June 1336, Edward III thanked the prelates, magnates, clergy, and communities of cities, boroughs and towns of Ireland for *unum generale subsidium de redditibus, terris et bonis.*[1] The annalist Clyn records that in 1335 the king asked for two shillings from each carucate, a tenth from the clergy, and a competent subsidy from the cities and great towns.[2] However, the chronicles[3] and records agree that no Irish Parliament or Great Council was held between 1333 and 1337,[4] and it is also significant that the royal request for aid was sent, not only in a general writ, but separately, to the magnates, the prelates, and the city of Dublin.[5] From details of the accounts on the Pipe Rolls, it seems probable that, as in 1300, the money was granted locally. In the account of 11 Edward III for Cork city a number of separate payments are recorded as due from individuals or from communities in the county;[6] in a similar account for Tipperary (11–14 Edward III) it is noted that 'the community of county Tipperary, except the market towns, owes £54 7*s.* 6*d.* of the subsidy granted

[1] Rymer, ii, pt. ii, p. 939.

[2] *Annals of Ireland* by Friar John Clyn, edited by the Rev. Ric. Butler, Dublin, 1849, p. 26.

[3] The only Anglo-Irish chronicles of value for the reign of Edward III are Clyn's *Annals* and *Annals of Ireland, 1162–1360*; Bodley MS. Laud 526, printed in *Chartularies of St. Mary's Abbey, Dublin*, Rolls Series, vol. ii.

[4] Parliament at Dublin, June 1333; *Liber Munerum*, i, pt. iv, p. 12; and Parliament at Dublin, 1337, *Laud Annals*, loc. cit., p. 380.

[5] Rymer, iv. 641–5. Orders to come in person, with horses and arms, were sent to the prelates, the earls of Ormonde and Desmond, 54 knights, 109 esquires, and 14 Irish chiefs.

[6] *Report 45 of the Deputy Keeper of Public Records*, Ireland (1913), pp. 41–2. For example, 'William son of David de Barry owes £1; the community of Carictothell 6/8; of Castle Lyons 6/8; of Shandon 5/-; . . . of Buttevant 10/-.'

to the king for his war in Scotland'.[1] Numerous entries dealing with the tax on the clergy always refer to the grant made by particular dioceses, as, for example, 'for the twentieth granted by the bishop and clergy of Meath diocese £32 11*s.* 9¾*d.*'[2] or 'for arrears of 4*s.* 7*d.* owed on the twentieth granted by the diocese of Ossory'.[3] A special payment is recorded to the Chancellor of the Exchequer 'for his trouble, outlay and expenses in going by order of the king to Meath, and remaining there to stir up the clergy of the diocese to grant a tenth from their benefices . . . to speed certain arduous affairs of the king'.[4] At least for the ecclesiastics, the evidence points definitely to a subsidy raised by local bargains and varying from place to place in the amounts promised. Perhaps the fact that the magnates, as in 1301, were asked for personal service in the field turned attention away from Parliament as a general assembly with the power of consent.

The first true parliamentary subsidy was granted at the Parliament of Kilkenny in October 1346,[5] and it is significant that evidence for it should be derived from records of resistance to its collection. On the Plea Roll of 21 Edward III it is stated that the Parliament of Kilkenny had granted to the king for his Irish wars a subsidy of two shillings on every carucate, a shilling on every half carucate, and a shilling from all landless persons possessing goods worth sixty shillings; and that collectors had been appointed for eleven counties and for the liberty of Trim.[6] Before the end of the year commissioners were

[1] *Report 47 of the Deputy Keeper of Public Records*, Ireland (1915), p. 24.

[2] Ibid., R. 45, p. 50. The tax is usually described as a twentieth, not a tenth, as Clyn states; Cashel was in arrears on account of the tenth granted to the king by the diocese. Ibid., R. 47, p. 27.

[3] Ibid., p. 28, Account for the Cross lands of Kilkenny, 8–14 Ed. III.

[4] Ibid., p. 35, Account for Drogheda on the side of Meath, 12–13 Ed. III.

[5] The prior of Holy Trinity, Dublin, was returning from this Parliament on 25 Oct. 1346, *Account Roll of the Priory of Holy Trinity*, 1337–46, edited Jas. Mills (1891), p. 118.

[6] Quoted by Betham, loc. cit., p. 292. The counties were Dublin, Meath,

appointed to inquire into obstruction to the collection of the tax in the counties of Cork, Kerry, Limerick, Tipperary, and Waterford.[1] Probably as a result of the inquiry, proceedings were taken against the archbishop of Cashel and the bishops of Emly, Limerick, and Lismore. On 7 January 1347 they had decreed that any clerk of their province who paid the subsidy should be deprived of his benefice and stripped of his gown, and that any layman who contributed should be excommunicated with his children for three generations. On 8 February in the same year the bishop of Lismore went *in pontificalibus* to Clonmel, and in the middle of the town 'excommunicavit et excommunicatos pronunciavit omnes et singulos dictum subsidium concedentes, imponentes et procurantes, vel tallagium facientes, necnon scribentes dictantes, levantes, recipientes vel eisdem considentes [*sic*] auxilium vel favorem prestantes . . .'[2] We have no clue to the motives behind this vehement opposition, in marked contrast to the grants made freely in 1335. Edward III had then promised that the subsidy would not be drawn into a precedent,[3] and the tax of 1346 may have been taken as a breach of faith. It is more probable that the novelty of a parliamentary grant instead of a local bargain was resented; if the proctors were not summoned—and all the evidence suggests this—the clergy were being taxed without their consent.

For over ten years after 1346 no further effort was made to secure a parliamentary grant. A subsidy was granted in Munster, probably for local defence, between

Kildare, Carlow, Kilkenny, Wexford, Waterford, Tipperary, Limerick, Cork, and Kerry.

[1] *Cal. Pat. and Cl. Rolls, Ireland* (1828), p. 53, no. 81, 12 Dec. 1346.

[2] Betham, pp. 292–3, from the plea roll, 21 Ed. III. The bishop of Lismore was cast in damages of £1,000. The temporalities of the bishop of Ossory were seized for similar action against the collectors of the subsidy, ibid., p. 294.

[3] Rymer, iv. 641–2. Cf. Clyn, p. 26, 'sic ne in consequenciam vel consuetudinem duceretur'.

1350 and 1355, but no details of the levy are recorded.[1] Kildare and Ormonde, the Anglo-Irish Justiciars who ruled the country from 1356 to 1361, were more successful in raising money for the Irish wars. Entries on the patent rolls show that Leinster and Munster were taxed in 1358, though not on a uniform plan. The counties of Cork, Limerick, and Waterford and the cities of Limerick and Cork granted a tax of two shillings on the carucate.[2] The counties of Dublin, Kildare, and Kilkenny granted the wages of a fixed quota of soldiers to serve in the Irish wars.[3] In Kildare these wages were levied at the rate of forty pence on each carucate and on goods to the value of £6; a crannock of corn, a crannock of hay, and a fat cow were also taken from each carucate.[4] The variations in rate suggest that these taxes were the result of local bargains, and the suggestion is confirmed by the absence of all references to Parliaments or Great Councils between 1351 and 1359.[5] In 1359 an elaborate compromise between local bargains and parliamentary grants was attempted. Following very roughly the provincial divisions of Leinster and Munster, two assemblies were summoned, one to meet at Dublin on 1 April and the other at Waterford a week later (8 April).[6] The writs show that the commons of the counties, liberties, and boroughs were summoned as if for a Parliament,[7] though only the

[1] *Cal. Pat. and Cl. Rolls, Ireland*, p. 66, no. 31; the grant was made *tempore Thome Rokeby*, who was Justiciar from Dec. 1349 to Aug. 1355.

[2] Ibid., pp. 71–2, nos. 1–4, 10, 15. The county of Waterford had made the grant *spontanea sua*.

[3] Ibid., pp. 73–5, nos. 35–6, 55, 64–5, 92. Kilkenny County, for example, granted for a fixed period 12 men-at-arms with horses at 12 pence a day, 60 hobelers at 4 pence, and 200 foot soldiers at a penny halfpenny (no. 64).

[4] Ibid., p. 74, nos. 58–9.

[5] Great Council of Kilkenny, 31 Oct. 1351 (*Early Statutes*, p. 376), and Great Council at Dublin, 1 April 1359 (*infra*, n. 6).

[6] *Cal. Pat. and Cl. Rolls, Ireland*, p. 77, nos. 21–5. Cf. Edward I's double Parliaments at Northampton and York, 1283.

[7] There were summoned for Leinster representatives of the city of Dublin, of Drogheda, of the counties of Dublin, Louth, Kildare and Carlow, of the liberties of Meath (Trim), Kilkenny and Wexford, and of the cross lands of

more important lay magnates or bishops are named as specially cited.[1] Immediately after the dates of session orders were issued for the collection of subsidies in both provinces.[2] The subsidy imposed was forty pence on the carucate and sixpence on goods to the value of £1; it was apparently the same in Munster as in Leinster. Collectors are named for only two cities,[3] and it is possible that the others refused to make a grant.[4] The share of the clergy in this taxation is obscure. On 10 April the archbishop of Cashel was commanded to levy £10 recently granted by the clergy of his diocese; like orders were issued to the bishops of Lismore, Limerick, and Cloyne.[5] These four prelates had been summoned to the Waterford Council, and had probably consented in the name of the clergy of their dioceses. We have no evidence either that the money was paid or that the demand was resisted. The consent of the clergy was anticipated in a similar way at the Great Council of 1369.[6] Then the prelates granted two-tenths to be levied on benefices, on condition that the consent of the clergy was first obtained. The tax was to be collected within a year, but by April 1370 nothing had been done, and the archbishop of Armagh was ordered to call a convocation

Kilkenny and Wexford. For Munster like summonses were issued to the cities of Cork, Limerick, and Waterford, the towns of Kilkenny, Ross, Clonmel and Wexford, the counties of Kildare, Waterford, Limerick, and Cork, the liberty of Kilkenny and the liberty and cross lands of Tipperary. It is remarkable that the county towns of Kilkenny and Wexford were separated from Leinster, and that the county of Kildare and the liberty of Kilkenny were represented in both assemblies.

[1] Only 9 persons were specially summoned to Dublin and 12 to Waterford. The sheriff of Kildare and the seneschal of Kilkenny were instructed to return particular persons to the Waterford assembly.

[2] Ibid., p. 77, nos. 32–6, 41; p. 79, nos. 110, 111–14, Cl. Roll, 33 Ed. III. The letters are dated from 12 April to 16 May.

[3] Waterford and Kilkenny.

[4] Drogheda was ordered to send six burgesses to appear before the Council at Dublin, because their representatives at the last council had not carried out what they had been ordered to undertake. Ibid., p. 77, no. 42, 20 April.

[5] Ibid., nos. 29–30.

[6] Dublin, 22 April 1369. *Cal. of Archbishop Sweteman's Register*, p. 236.

or council of his clergy to secure their consent.[1] Though we do not know what line of action was taken by the lower clergy in 1359 and 1369, it is clear that the subsidy did not provoke resistance comparable to that in 1347. The experiment of seeking consent in provincial councils, whether deliberately undertaken for the purpose or not, brought the taxpayer a stage nearer to the practice of general consent in Parliament.

After 1359 there was another long interval without direct taxation. Even Lionel, duke of Clarence, seems to have made no attempt to secure a parliamentary grant. A sudden change came when William of Windsor was appointed the king's lieutenant in Ireland in 1369. His first term of office lasted until March 1372; though he was then recalled in disgrace, he returned after two years as governor and guardian of Ireland, and held office until early in 1376.[2] The detailed evidence of the inquiry into his administration shows him to have been a vigorous and greedy representative of the Crown.[3] In less than five years he held eight Parliaments and two Great Councils.[4] No legislation is associated with these sessions; all seem to be an essential part of a new fiscal policy, the purpose of which was to constrain the Irish, not only to bear the cost of their own wars, but also to contribute to the expense of the war with France. The methods and arguments employed and the resistance they provoked altered the form and increased knowledge of the functions of Parliament, to an extent which almost entitles William of Windsor to be styled the true founder of the Irish Parliament.

[1] *Cal. of Archbishop Sweteman's Register*, p. 236.

[2] He left Ireland on 21 March 1372, was appointed governor and guardian in Oct. 1373, and returned to Ireland on 18 April 1374.

[3] P.R.O. Council and Parliamentary Proceedings, 47–50 Ed. III, Rolls 2 and 3.

[4] Parliaments: Dublin, 6 Aug. 1369; Dublin, 22–5 April 1370; Kilkenny, 7 Jan. 1371; Ballyduagh, 4 June 1371; Kilkenny, 14 Jan. 1372; Dublin, 20 Jan. 1375; Kilkenny, 18 June 1375; Kilkenny, 6 Oct. 1375. Great Councils: Dublin, 25 Feb. 1372, and 27 May 1374.

Windsor's first Parliament (Dublin, August 1369) granted new custom duties and imposed on five counties a tax of half a mark on the carucate.[1] In the following spring (April 1370) the Parliament of Dublin appears to have doubled the tax on the carucate, but it is not clear over what area it was collected.[2] The Kilkenny Parliament, held in January 1371, granted a subsidy of £3,000, which the Parliament of Ballyduagh (8 June 1371) increased by £2,000.[3] Resistance to the collection of these grants was general and persistent. It was maintained that they were the result of illegal coercion, and no doubt it was to meet the complaints of the clergy that proctors of the clergy began to be summoned to Parliament in 1371. The Anglo-Irish had their connexions in England and, perhaps through Mortimer influence, the intervention of the home government was secured. In October 1371 Windsor was ordered to stay the levy of the £5,000 granted at Kilkenny and Ballyduagh,[4] and in May 1372 the king ordered the collection of the new custom duties to be suspended.[5] The Parliament held at Kilkenny in January 1372 and the Great Council in Dublin a month later were probably summoned by Windsor in a desperate attempt to secure confirmation of the earlier grants.[6] He was recalled in March, and an inquiry into his administration dragged on until the autumn of 1373. He was then reappointed as governor and guardian of Ireland, and orders were issued for the collection of the disputed subsidy.[7] He held three Parliaments in 1375. At the first (Dublin, 17 January) he secured grants from individuals for the maintenance of his retinue,[8] and at

[1] Roll 2, Articles 5 and 8, below, pp. 185–7.

[2] Ibid., Article 14, below, pp. 188–9. [3] Ibid., Article 8, below, pp. 186–7.

[4] *Cal. Cl. Rolls*, 20 Oct. 1371, pp. 256–7: cf. pp. 259, 262.

[5] Ibid., 28 May 1372, p. 380.

[6] The magnates and commons were forced to seal a letter to the king declaring that the tallage and subsidy had been granted freely and without coercion (Inquisition, Meath County, ii, cap. 7).

[7] *Cal. Cl. Rolls*, 20 Dec. 1373, p. 529.

[8] *Cal. Pat. and Cl. Rolls, Ireland*, p. 95, no. 200.

the second (Kilkenny, 18 June), the clergy and commons of Munster, Kilkenny, and Wexford made a grant of 400 marks.[1] At the autumn Parliament (Kilkenny, 6 October), Nicholas Dagworth, specially commissioned by Edward III, explained the king's heavy expenses and asked for a special subsidy.[2] The request was emphatically refused on the plea of poverty. An attempt to force consent by summoning two proctors from each diocese and two commoners from each county, city, and borough to meet the king's Council in England provoked a storm of resistance, and in February 1376 Windsor was recalled to meet new charges against his administration.[3]

The articles of impeachment, drafted in Ireland, charge William of Windsor and other high officials with tyrannical misconduct and embezzlement in every department of government, but the main emphasis throughout lies on unlawful taxation without the free consent of subjects. It was maintained that the custom duties were imposed by the Parliament of 1369 *contra assensum et voluntatem communium et mercatorum terre predicte*;[4] the tax of half a mark on the carucate was also imposed against the assent and will of the commons of Meath.[5] At the Parliament of Kilkenny in 1370 the knights of the shire for Meath, pledged when they were elected to refuse a subsidy, were coerced into assenting to a tax of a mark on the carucate;[6] they were terrorized by the imprisonment of the members for Louth who had refused consent.[7] The grants made in the Parliaments of 1371 were also contrary to the pledges of elected representatives. The members for Meath at the Parliament of Kilkenny re-

[1] *Cal. Pat. and Cl. Rolls, Ireland*, p. 98, no. 264. [2] *Infra*, p. 233.

[3] The earl of Kildare was appointed Justiciar of Ireland on 16 Feb. 1376, as Windsor and other officials were summoned to England. *Cal. Pat. Rolls*, p. 244. [4] Inquisition, iii, cap. 2, below, p. 223.

[5] Ibid., i, cap. 1, below, p. 222.

[6] Ibid., i, cap. 3; ii, cap. 3.

[7] Ibid. Cf. the coercion of the two members for Drogheda in Louth for refusing consent, ibid., iv, cap. 2, below, p. 225.

sisted for two or three days the demand for a subsidy of £3,000.[1] At Ballyduagh consent to an additional £2,000 was forced by the inconvenience of the place of session; it was three leagues from the city of Cashel, in a waste land, without houses or provisions.[2] Finally, the summons of clerical and lay representatives to appear before the English Council in February 1376 drew forth a series of returns which were almost certainly part of a concerted plan of action.

We have evidence that the governor and Dagworth made every effort to influence the elections. In Dublin county, perhaps regarded as a test case, the county court was assembled on no less than five separate occasions in the hope of securing favourable returns.[3] Feeling evidently ran high, as the elections were keenly contested, three separate parties putting forward candidates at one time and two at another. The differences were probably local or personal,[4] as all parties were agreed in resistance to taxation. In spite of the addresses of special messengers and threats of heavy amercements, each assembly refused to concede to their chosen representatives the power of consent to taxation. The general result of the elections throughout the country is equally significant. The counties of Dublin, Louth, Kildare, Meath, and Kilkenny protested that the summons was contrary to their rights and liberties; they agreed to elect representa-

[1] Inquisition, i, cap. 4, below, p. 221.

[2] Ibid., ii, cap. 6; iii, cap. 7; iv, cap. 5; vi, cap. 7, below, pp. 222, 224, 226, 230–1. The townland of Ballyduagh lies four miles south-east of Cashel, in the parish of Railstown.

[3] The county court met on the following dates:

13 November 1375 .	No agreement.
17 November 1375 .	No agreement.
18–19 November 1375 .	Two persons elected; protest by petition.
22 December 1375 .	Three separate elections by three distinct parties.
14 February 1376 .	Two separate elections by two parties.

The new elections of December and February were made by special order of the government (below, pp. 237–40).

[4] The local objection to the candidates first returned was that they were 'cousins germane and of one assent' (below, p. 237).

tives out of reverence for the king, but they refused to give them the power of consent to taxation. Like refusals were made by the city of Dublin, the town of Drogheda, and the clergy of Armagh, Kildare, Lismore, and Waterford. The counties of Waterford and Tipperary made elections, saving their liberties; a like reservation was made by the city of Kilkenny. Elections without reservations were made by the poor or remote counties of Wexford, Limerick, Cork, and Kerry;[1] by the cities or towns of Limerick, Cork, Ross, Wexford, and Youghal; and by the seven dioceses of Dublin, Ossory, Ferns, Limerick, Emly, Cloyne, and Kerry.[2] The returns made it clear that no subsidy would be granted by the prosperous areas of Leinster, and, probably for that reason, the whole project was abandoned, at least as far as taxation was concerned. The episode is important as the first struggle between the home government and the Anglo-Irish which can properly be called both political and constitutional. The main issue, it is clear, was the right of consent to taxation.

In maintaining for their defence the doctrine of consent, the Anglo-Irish were tacitly forced to admit the power of their own Parliament to impose taxation. By the addition of clerical proctors William of Windsor had made it fully representative, and from this time onward the parliamentary right of taxation does not seem to be disputed. None the less the idea of local consent died hard. The peculiar conditions of the country, with its incessant and half-isolated border wars, kept alive for a time the custom of local taxation for frontier defence, authorized by local representative assemblies. In August 1381, at a Great Council at Clonmel, the magnates and commons of seven southern counties agreed to provide the earl of March with 15 men-at-arms and 150 archers

[1] The county of Carlow refused to make an election, pleading poverty.

[2] The dioceses of Cashel and Meath elected only one proctor; Leighlin refused to elect on plea of poverty, and Tuam made no return.

for six months, and the clergy of the ten dioceses of the same area granted £78 6*s*. In 1388 the clergy and commons of county Dublin made a grant for the maintenance of 80 men-at-arms,[1] and we have evidence of a long series of similar local grants in the reign of Henry IV.[2] There is no record of the practice under Henry V, but it seems to have revived again in 1423, when the commons and clergy of Meath and Louth, in county or diocesan assemblies at Trim and Ardee, granted money for defence against Irish enemies.[3] From that time onwards no clear reference to the practice has been traced. In the second half of the century parliamentary consent to taxation was recognized as obligatory, and neglect to secure it was apparently deemed to be treason.[4] The evidence, therefore, suggests that the custom of local taxation through local assemblies finally gave way to taxation by Parliament in the first quarter of the fifteenth century, mainly as a result of Windsor's policy of Thorough and the resistance that it provoked.

IV

The other two changes in the Irish Parliament which are associated with William of Windsor relate less to function than to form and, therefore, require less detailed exposition. Clerical proctors were added to the commons, and the doctrine of barony by tenure replaced that of barony by writ. It is suggested that each of these changes came in under the influence of the *Modus tenendi Parliamentum*.

[1] *Cal. Pat. and Cl. Rolls, Ireland*, p. 141, no. 190.

[2] Ibid., p. 158, nos. 114–15, 119; p. 161, nos. 61–2; p. 166, nos. 242–3, 253, 14; p. 178, no. 77; p. 201, no. 113.

[3] Ibid., p. 230, nos. 112–15, 121–2. The commons of Meath granted 360 marks, the commons of Louth £40, the clergy of Meath 120 marks, and the clergy of Armagh 9 marks.

[4] This was secured by the so-called 'statute of assent and disassent', referred to in *Irish Statutes*, 7 & 8 Ed. IV, cap. 20; 16 & 17 Ed. IV, cap. 4; and 19 & 20 Ed. IV, cap. 34. The 'statute', as I hope to show elsewhere, was probably the Irish *Modus tenendi Parliamentum*. [Cf. *Medieval Representation and Consent*, chap. vi.]

The first reference to proctors in Parliament comes from the Register of the archbishop of Armagh, Miles Sweteman, 1360–80. Writs of summons are entered for the Parliament at Kilkenny, 7 January 1371, and for the Parliament at Ballyduagh, 8 June 1371; the archbishop was ordered to attend in person, together with proctors for the dean and chapter of Armagh and for the clergy of the diocese.[1] Writs of summons to the archbishop alone are entered for five earlier Parliaments and one Great Council,[2] and, though the Register is defective, it seems that 1371 was the first year that proctors were summoned. Proctors of the deans and chapters of cathedrals were summoned to a Great Council held at Dublin on 25 February 1372,[3] and proctors for the chapters and for the diocesan clergy were summoned to the Parliament of Kilkenny, 6 October 1375.[4] No returns to these writs are entered in the Register, but we have full returns, with names, from fourteen dioceses in reply to the extraordinary summons of two proctors from each diocese to appear before the Council in England in February 1376.[5] Writs summoning proctors are also extant for the Parliaments of 1378 and 1380.[6] These clerical proctors remained an integral part of the Irish Parliament until the Reformation. The later Registers of Armagh illustrated how closely proctorial representation was bound up with taxation and how a system of consent and supervision was worked out in diocesan convocations and rural deaneries. The line of development is that clearly indicated in the *Modus*, where the full burden of financial responsibility was laid upon the clerks and laymen elected by the commons.

[1] *Calendar of Archbishop Sweteman's Register*, edited by H. J. Lawlor, *Proceedings of the Royal Irish Academy*, xxix (1911), pp. 233, 248.

[2] Ibid., pp. 228, 229, 230–1, 250.

[3] Betham, loc. cit., p. 311.

[4] *Calendar of Archbishop Sweteman's Register*, p. 285.

[5] *Infra*, pp. 233–4.

[6] W. Lynch, *A View of the Legal Institutions, Honorary Hereditary Offices and Feudal Baronies established in Ireland* (1830), pp. 325, 328.

In contrast to the new power given to the clergy was the limitation of the attendance of lay magnates, brought about by the adoption of the doctrine of barony by tenure. The early writs of special summons to the Irish Parliament, as far back as they can be traced, were issued to all persons of importance whose presence was desired, irrespective of conditions of tenure. They were not even restricted to tenants-in-chief; in 1310, for example, eighty-eight secular persons were summoned to Parliament by special writ, and at least twenty-five of them were small land-owners, vassals of absentee lords like Roger Mortimer and the earl of Ulster.[1] This practice continued until the end of Edward III's reign, though the number of persons who received special writs declined. Then in 1372, the year after the first summons of proctors to Parliament, William of Windsor issued writs for a Great Council on a new principle.[2] The only lay peers who received a special summons were the earls of Kildare and Ormonde. In writs to the sheriffs or seneschals of Dublin, Meath, Louth, and Kildare, in addition to the usual formula for the election of two knights, a *premunire* clause was inserted, commanding the attendance of certain named persons under penalty of a fine of 100 marks.[3] The fifteen names of magnates usually summoned by special writ[4] appear in this way, together with the names of seventy-two other

[1] *Early Statutes*, p. 258. I have discussed these writs in 'Irish Parliaments in the reign of Edward II', *Proceedings of the Royal Historical Society*, 1925, pp. 35–7, 58–9 [*supra*, pp. 8–10, 31–2].

[2] The writs, taken from 'Chancery Roll, Dub., 46 E. 3', are printed by Lynch (op. cit., pp. 318 seqq.). Cf. *Cal. Pat. and Cl. Rolls, Ireland*, p. 82, nos. 110–18.

[3] For example, in the writ to the sheriff of Dublin (ibid., p. 320): '. . . et ulterius premunire facias Thomam Talbot, militem (and 15 others named) et quemlibet eorum in fide et ligeancia quibus nobis tenentur quacunque excusacione cessante et subpena C. marcarum nobis solvendum ibidem ad diem illum (25 Feb.) personaliter intersint. . . .'

[4] e.g. in the writs of summons to the Parliament at Dublin, Jan. 1375 (ibid., p. 323). Twenty-five others then received special writs whose names were not on the writs of 1372.

persons,[1] landed gentry of lesser degree. Lynch, who mistook this assembly for a Parliament, thought that Windsor's object was to secure a majority of lay magnates over the prelates.[2] In support of this explanation he cites Spenser's account of a tradition current in Ireland at the end of the sixteenth century:

'Edward III . . . being greatly bearded and crossed by the Lords of the Cleargie, they being there by reason of the Lords Abbots, and others, too many and too strong for him, so as hee could not for their frowardnesse order and reforme things as hee desired, was advised to direct out his writts to certaine Gentlemen of the best ability and trust, entitling them therein Barons, to serve and sitt as Barons in the next Parlament. By which meanes hee had so many Barons in his Parlament, as were able to weigh downe the Cleargy and their friends: The which Barons they say, were not afterwardes Lords, but onely Baronets, as sundry of them doe yet retayne the name. . . .'[3]

Spenser's statement has interest as a sign that the extraordinary summons of 1372[4] made a deep impression. There is, however, nothing in contemporary records to show that laymen were more favourable to Windsor's fiscal policy than the clergy. This Great Council, like the Parliament held at Kilkenny in the previous month, was probably summoned in a last desperate effort to secure ratification of the grants exacted from previous assemblies.[5] The writs of summons to the Council were issued only ten days before the date of meeting (15 Feb. for 25 Feb.), and the short notice no doubt explains why Windsor did not call a Parliament. Perhaps for a like

[1] Six named burgesses from Drogheda and the twenty-four jurats of the city of Dublin were also summoned. The only elected members were the representatives of the four counties and two citizens of Dublin.

[2] Loc. cit., p. 124.

[3] *A View of the State of Ireland*, 1596 (*Ancient Irish Histories*, Dublin, 1809, vol. i, p. 224).

[4] It is possible that the tradition may relate to the special summons of a large number of laymen to the Parliament of January 1375, *supra*, p. 169.

[5] *Supra*, pp. 169-70.

reason he summoned the magnates through the sheriffs, though it may be that he had observed the purely traditional system of issuing writs and hoped to turn it to advantage. By the new method he may have hoped at the same time to increase the revenue from fines[1] and to reduce the pride of the magnates by reminding them that their titles to the rank of baron were defective. Moreover, the omission from the sheriffs' writs of the earl of Desmond and twenty-two other persons summoned by special writ in 1375[2] indicates clearly enough a policy of deliberate selection or packing.

William of Windsor returned to England in March 1372, and no writs are extant for the Parliament summoned in his absence (January 1374). For the first Parliament held after his return, writs of special summons were issued to forty lay magnates in the usual way.[3] Two other Parliaments were summoned in the same year (June and October 1375), and, as they obstinately refused to grant supply, the extraordinary expedient was devised of summoning the commons only to meet the king and Council at Westminster in February 1376. This summons is in itself evidence that less resistance was expected from the commons than from the magnates. The list of lay magnates who received special summons to the first Parliament of Richard II contains twenty-six names, excluding five members of the Council; unfortunately it is defective, and we cannot tell how many names are missing.[4] In 1380 only twenty-one persons were summoned in this way,[5] and henceforth the number of lay peers remains fairly constant at or about this figure. In other words, not much more than half the lay magnates specially summoned to the first Parliament of 1375 remained permanently peers of Parliament.

[1] There is ample evidence that fines for absence were exacted from the time of Edward II. Cf. Lynch, pp. 53, 56, 57, and 58, and *Cal. Pat. and Cl. Rolls, Ireland, passim.*

[2] Lynch, pp. 321–5.

[3] Ibid. Parliament met on 17 Jan. 1375.

[4] Ibid., pp. 325–8.

[5] Ibid., pp. 328–31.

The explanation of this marked decline in numbers seems to be found in the case of Walter Lenfaunt, who in 1377 petitioned the Crown for a remission of fines imposed upon him for absence from the Parliaments of 1375 and 1377.[1] Lenfaunt pleaded that he had been summoned *tanquam tenens per baroniam*, although he had never held by that tenure. His petition was tried before the Treasurer and Barons of the Exchequer; it was found that he did not hold by barony, and the fine was remitted. At the same time a general principle was expressly stated: 'It does not belong to the law and custom hitherto used in this land, that any persons not holding by barony should be summoned to our Parliaments nor for their absence should the same be amerced.'[2] The same principle was applied in the case of Thomas Verneille, heard in the same year.[3] Verneille had petitioned for a remission of his fine for absence, on the grounds that he could not attend Parliament without the destruction of his lands by Irish enemies, and also that none of his ancestors were ever summoned before this time to Parliament except among the commons. The second plea was rejected altogether and, though the fine was remitted by reason of the Irish wars, it was found that Verneille's estates in Meath were sufficient to justify his summons as a baron.[4] A number of other persons were fined for absence in 1376 and 1377,[5] and it seems that these decisions were taken as test cases. Names like Power of Donhill, Calf of Norraghmore, Hussey of Galtrim, and Nangle of Navan disappear from the lists of lay tenants specially summoned to Parliament, though

[1] *Cal. Pat. and Cl. Rolls, Ireland*, p. 103, no. 89. The case is fully discussed by Lynch, pp. 62–3, 124–6.

[2] 'Non est iuris seu consuetudinis in dicta terra nostra hactenus usitatae, quod aliqui, qui per baroniam non tenuerunt ad parliamenta nostra summoneri seu occasione absenciae suae ab eisdem amerciari deberent.'

[3] Lynch, pp. 126–7.

[4] Verneille was summoned to the Parliaments of Richard II.

[5] Lynch, pp. 62–3.

the title of baron was retained in legal proceedings and in all official documents.[1]

It is, as Lynch writes, 'evident . . . that the feudal parliamentary dignitaries of Ireland were governed solely by the principle of tenure'.[2] The English doctrine of barony by writ was not accepted, even though it was in conformity with the practice followed until the end of Edward III's reign. The doctrine of tenure by barony was adopted as the sole qualification for parliamentary peerage, and this is identical with the doctrine of the *Modus*. 'Every earl and baron and their peers, that is, such as have lands or rents to the value of one whole earldom . . . or to the value of a whole barony . . . ought to be summoned and to come to Parliament; and no others of the laity or clergy[3] of lesser possessions ought, at their own costs, to appear on account of their tenures, unless the king should summon his counsellors or other wise men for some necessary cause. . . .'[4] It is certainly significant that this doctrine was suddenly applied and acted upon in Ireland in 1377.

The third sign of the influence of the *Modus* during the closing years of Edward III's reign was that the doctrine of parliamentary consent to taxation was definitely accepted by the Anglo-Irish. We have already seen how they were driven into this new position by the pressure to grant taxes put on them by William of Windsor, pressure culminating in the summons of representatives of the commons to Westminster. It has not hitherto been remarked that the extraordinary summons of the commons in 1375 was a particular application of a plan implicit in the *Modus* itself. The writs of summons were

[1] Lynch, pp. 132, 163–4. [2] Ibid., p. 131.

[3] The English version omits *vel clerici*.

[4] In the English version the phrase about counsellors appears in a slightly different form in the previous chapter. It is worth noting that writs of special summons to members of the Irish Council were issued for the Parliament of January 1375, and from that time an issue of this kind became a usual practice, Lynch, loc. cit.

directed to the bishops, sheriffs or seneschals, and mayors or sovereigns; they were commanded to send two proctors, two knights, and two citizens or burgesses from each diocese, county, and city or borough. No writs of special summons were issued, as the presence of spiritual and temporal lords was not desired. Though the summons roused vigorous opposition, no protest against the exclusion of the magnates is recorded. Emphasis throughout was laid either on the unprecedented citation to England or on the right of consent. Four dioceses, five counties, and the electors of Dublin and Drogheda clearly recognized the underlying purpose of the summons and refused to grant to their representatives any power to consent to taxation. It was, however, never asserted that the commons, without the lords, would be incompetent to grant a subsidy. Now this exactly conforms with the principle laid down in the *Modus*: 'All things which ought to be affirmed or abrogated, granted, denied or performed by Parliament ought to be granted by the commons, that is, by the three orders or estates thereof, the proctors of the clergy, the knights of the shires and the citizens and burgesses, who represent the whole community of England, and not by the magnates, since each of them is in Parliament for himself alone and for no one else.' The same principle is reiterated in the Irish version, with the significant addition, *communes . . . auxilii concessores vel negatores*. Thus the constitutional crisis of 1375 suggests that both parties, the English executive and the Anglo-Irish opposition, accepted the doctrine of the *Modus* that ultimate responsibility for taxation lies with the commons.

We have found that attendance of proctors, barony by tenure, and the consent of the commons to taxation were all established as part of Irish constitutional practice at the end of Edward III's reign. Each can be traced directly to the *Modus*, and the conclusion can hardly be avoided that each took its origin from the document itself. How it came to be known in Ireland at this time can only be conjectured. William of Windsor may have introduced it as part of his policy of forcing Parliament to undertake full financial responsibility. He was certainly acting in accordance with it when he caused proctors to be summoned and when he tried to compel the commons to grant taxes in 1375. At an early stage in the conflict between him and the Anglo-Irish, knowledge of the document must have passed to the opposition. Perhaps Sir Robert Preston, Chief Justice of Common Pleas, was the man who first understood its constitutional importance.[1] He was one of the commissioners who in 1373 inquired into the abuses of Windsor's rule, and he was summoned by special writ as a councillor to the Parliaments of 1375 (January), 1378, and 1380.[2] We may suppose then either that Windsor brought the *Modus* to Ireland in order to instruct the colonists and found them only too willing to use it as a defence,[3] or that Preston or some other Anglo-Irish official brought it forward and forced the executive to admit its authority.

The time of Windsor's rule in Ireland was one of those epochs of confused activity in which seeds are planted for growth during many generations. In Ireland periods of this kind have nearly always come when, for one reason or another, Irish affairs have troubled the main stream of English public life; some share in dramatic action on an English stage seems necessary to break down stiff colonial ideas and to make way for new concepts of government. In the last decade of Edward III's reign William of Windsor taught the Anglo-Irish the meaning of political control by using their Parliament as an instrument of power. The lesson was driven home when

[1] His son Christopher had in his possession the Irish version that was exemplified in 1419.

[2] Lynch, loc. cit., pp. 324, 327, 330.

[3] Another, less certain, example of the influence of the *Modus* may be seen in the protest made by the prelates, lords, and commons in June 1382, against the holding of Parliament in the absence of the Lieutenant, Roger Mortimer (cited in full by Steele, *Proclamations*, pp. cxxvi–cxxvii, n. 46, from *Report of Searchers*, 1806, no. 17).

Windsor's connexion with the entrenched favourites of the Court drew his Irish opponents into the struggle fought out at the English council board and in the Good Parliament. It was inevitable that they should learn from the conflict just those full-grown political ideas that in the mother country were almost out of fashion. In England the *Modus tenendi Parliamentum* was already ceasing to be a true description of the form and functions of Parliament, yet it served as the bridge over which English parliamentary traditions passed into Ireland. The Anglo-Irish soon adapted it to suit their own ends, and in their hands it became a Magna Carta of defence against the delegated prerogative of the Crown. The *Modus* was the seed for which Windsor, whether he knew it or not, prepared the soil; it was sown and quickened in the heat of faction on both sides of the Channel; the Anglo-Irish, finding at last the way to political life, reaped the increase in four broken centuries of parliamentary rule.

PARLIAMENT AND COUNCIL PROCEEDINGS—CHANCERY

47–50 Edward III, Rolls 2 and 3

LIST OF DOCUMENTS

Roll 2. Eighty-six articles presented to the Council in England by Richard Deere and William Stapelyn. Endorsed: 'les copies des accusementz.' Printed below, pp. 184–207.

Roll 3. A great bundle of rolls and smaller documents, which may be classified as follows:[1]

I. Numbers 1 to 13. Documents relating to the summons of the commons of Ireland to England, 16 February 1376:

(1) Writ from William of Windsor to Scurlag and Preston. Dated at Kilkenny, 23 January 1376. Endorsed: 'Executio istius commissionis et mandati patet in cedula huic commissioni consuta. Et sic respondet frater Scurlag, abbas domus sancti Thome Martiris iuxta Dublin., Thesaurius Hibernie.'

[1] The numeration of the documents is that of the Record Office classification; it refers to their order of arrangement, which has been determined by size rather than by chronology or subject-matter.

(2) Return of Scurlag to above writ.

(3) Writ of William of Windsor to the sheriff of Dublin. Dated at Clonmell, 29 November 1375. The sheriff's return is on the dorse.

(4) The names of the electors of Nicholas Houth and Richard White.

(5) The names of the electors of Nicholas Houth and William Fitz William.

(6) Return of Scurlag to the writ, below, no. 7.

(7) Writ of William of Windsor to Scurlag and Preston, Dated at Clonmell, 1 December 1375. Endorsed: 'Executio et responsio istius brevis patet in cedula huic brevi consuta. Et sic respondet frater Thomas Scurlag, abbas domus sancti Thome Martiris iuxta Dublin., Thesaurius Hibernie, et Robertus Preston, capitalis Justicia domini regis de communi banco Hibernie.'

(8) Damaged petition from certain freeholders of the county of Dublin to the lieutenant and his council. The wax of 28 seals is still attached and tags have been cut for 32 seals in all.

(9-13) A long roll of six membranes on to which the returns to the summons to England have been copied.

These documents have been summarized below, pp. 232-41.

II. Documents relating to the proceedings before the English Council:

(14) Two articles against the Treasurer of Ireland, repeated from articles 66 and 67, Roll 2.

(15) Seven articles against the Chancellor of Ireland, repeated from articles 59-66, Roll 2.

(16) Eight articles against the second Baron of the Exchequer (Carlill), repeated from articles 79-84, Roll 2. Two additional articles from this document are printed as articles 86 and 87 (p. 206).

(17) The answers of Holywood before the English Council. Printed pp. 207-12.

(18) The answers of Carlill before the English Council. Printed pp. 215-19.

(19) Additional answers of Holywood before the English Council. Printed pp. 212-15.

(26) A bill presented by Richard Whethill and others to the English Council, 11 August 1376. Printed p. 219.

(27) Notes of decisions relating to Ireland made in the English Council, 15 December 1376.[1]

(28) Twelve articles against the chief Baron of the Exchequer (Holywood), repeated from articles 58 and 68-78, Roll 2.

III. Inquisitions taken in Ireland in May and June, 1373. These documents have been summarized below, pp. 220-32.

(20) Inquisition taken at Drogheda in Meath, 1 June 1373.

(21) Inquisition taken at Drogheda in Meath, 20 May 1373.

(22) Inquisition taken at Drogheda in Louth, 31 May 1373.

(23) Inquisition taken at Drogheda in Meath, 9 June 1373.

(24) Inquisition taken at Drogheda in Meath, 20 May 1373.

(25) Inquisition taken at Dublin, 13 June 1373.

The documents summarized in English are those which contain much repetition either in subject-matter or in common form. Phrases of special significance are quoted in the original.

In the text of documents printed in full no attempt has been made to correct the defective and inconsistent grammar and spelling of the manuscripts. Modern punctuation and use of capitals have been adopted. My special thanks are due to Miss M. K. Pope, of Somerville College. Though she is in no way responsible for any errors, her help and advice have been invaluable to me in fixing the French text.

I. Roll 2

Ceux sont les articles mises a conseil nostre seigneur le roy en Engleterre par Richard Deere et William Stapelyn touchant les meschiefs, tortz et disceitez faitz en Irland par les ministres nostre dit seigneur le roy, illeoqes examinez par le court et par ceux qe sont venuz pur monstrer et declarer les tortz, meschiefs et desceitez faitez, esteantz en la dite terre et iurrez sur lour serement de dire la verite selonc lour conissance.

[1] Cf. *Cal. Cl. Rolls*, pp. 168, 171-2, 15 and 16 Dec. 1378. Though these notes are of great interest, both as early examples of Council minutes and for the last stages of the Windsor inquiry, they have not been printed, as they give rise to certain problems too intricate for discussion here.

1. Item, en primez, par la ou monsieur William de Wyndesore fuist ordeigne lieutenant d'Irland il envoya CCCC de ses gentz par une quarter dun aan devant sa venue, qe viveront sur les povres lieges sanz riens, ou poy paier ou profit faire, en grant damage des ditz lieges, et les gages de queux amontont $M^{l}M^{l}$ livrez et plus.
Inquiratur.

[22 June 1369.]
2. Item, le dit monsieur William arrivoist a Dyvillyn le IIIe iour devant la nativite de seint Jehan le Baptistre, lan le roy qore est XLIIIe, et ses gentz arriveront en diverses parties de la terre; et quant il avoit assetz soiournee a Dyvelyn il prist une prive counseil illeoqes et sen aloit a Carbry,[1] et desroba les tenantz del conte Dormonde et autres seigneurs, lieges peisibles nostre seigneur le roy, al mountance de CC marcz, de queux ils ne purroient avoir remedie.
Verum est, tamen ignorant de summa.

3. Item, le dit monsieur William, la qe les gentz de la marche pristeront pur lour travaille des enemys Irrez ascunz XII vaches, ascuns X, il fesoit denquerrer qi ceux furent et les fesoit enditer et areigner come larouns et prist de eux grant ransoun al mountance de CC marcz.
Dicunt quod verum est, tamen nesciunt de finibus neque de summa.

[July 1369.]
4. Item, le dit monsieur William, un moys apres sa venue en Irland, fesoit crier un parlement a Dyvelyn, et donqes le dit monsieur William monstroit sa commission et coment les terres des seigneurs en Engleterre furont forfaitz pur ceo qils ne furont presentez pur lour terres garder, qe lour terres et rentes devoient estre seisez en mayn de roy et dispenduz sur les guerres de la terre; et issint il prist des dites terres et rentes profit de $M^{l}M^{l}$ livrez et pluis.
Dicunt quod verum est de seisina, tamen nesciunt de summa nec ad cuius usum devenit.

5. Item, miz fuist sur les poverez lieges de roy encountre lour volunte de paier de chescun charue de terre en countees

1 The barony of Carbury, Co. Kildare.

de Dyvelyn, Mithe et Fryelle,[1] Kildare et Kathirlaugh[2] VI s. VIII d., par commandement du dit monsieur William, la somme de quele extorsion amonte CC livres et plus.

Dicunt quod verum est.

6. Item, apres sa premier venue il fesoit une false monstresoun ioust Dyvelyn, a quiele monstresoun il failloit de ses gentz CCIIIJ^{xx} et plus, nient contresteant qe touz ses garsounz del estable et autres gentz dapprest, al mountance de C et plus, furont arraiez pur faire grant route, en desceit nostre seigneur le roy, les gages des queux CCIIIJ^{xx} gentz amontont par an M^{l}VIII^{c} et XX livres, des queux CCIIIJ^{xx} gentz il falloit par toute laan entiere.

Dicunt quod verum est, ignorant tamen numerum hominum et summam defectus.

7. Item, le dit monsieur William donast une chartre de pardon a un George Telyng, qe avoit occiz felonousement Wauter, filz a soun eisne frere, pur avoir son heritage, qe heritage vault bien par aan C marcz; et de ce fuist le dit George attaynt et clerc convict al prisone levesque de Mithe, et les dites terres seisez en main de roy; le dit monsieur William resceut du dit George un fyn de C livrez et lui donast une chartre de pardon, et a monsieur James de Pikeryng[3] X^{l} livrez, et a Edmond [Laurence?][4] X^{l} marcz dune bribe, et en tiel manere est le roy desceu par la dite fyn, bribez donez de C marcz par aan touchantz les terres du dit Wauter.

Dicunt quod verum est, tamen nesciunt de summa bribarum nec de summa finis.

8. Item, le dit monsieur William prist de chescun last de heryng IIII s.; et de chescune C des grandez pessons XII d.; et de chescune C des meindres pessouns Vi d.; et de chescun tonelle de salmoun III s. ; et de chescune pipe de salmoun

[1] Uriel? (Co. Louth). [2] Co. Carlow.

[3] Pickering was afterwards twice Speaker of the English Commons (1378 and 1383) and one of Windsor's executors.

[4] Probably Edmund Laurence, Escheator of Ireland, 1374, *Liber Munerum*, i, pt. ii, p. 214.

II s.; et de chescun tonel de vyn VI s. VIII d.; et de chescune pipe de vyn III s. IIII d.; et de chescun livre de chares des boefs, porcz et berbiz VI d.; et de chescun weye de furment VI s. VIII d.; et de chescun weye de breez fevees et poys [orge], sigle et hastivelle V s.; et de chescun weye de seel VI s. VIII d.; et de chescun XX s. de peultz de chivalx, cervefs, affrerz, pilvelle, draps lienge et de layn, faldyngs et autres merchandies VI d.;[1] a grande damage et destruccion de ditz lieges, qe somme amonte CCCC marcz et plus.
Dicunt quod verum est, tamen nesciunt de summa et ignorant si ipse recepit an Thesaurius.

9. Item, en meisme le temps fuist Johan Strouppe clerk de gages du roy et un des chamberleyns del Escheqer de Carlaugh, et avoit II s. le iour de roy as gages, le dit monsieur William fesoit prendre le dit Johan, et lui fesoit mettre en prisone a chastel de Dyvelyn, et prist C livrez du dit Johan a fyn et uncore lessa en prisone le dit Johan tanqe il fuist mortz sanz iuggement, et prist toutz les roules nostre seigneur le roy qe le dit Johan avoit en sa garde, issint qe le roy ne puist estre certifie coment son tresore fuist despendu, a grant damage nostre seigneur le roy.
Moriebatur in carcere; inquiratur de aliis articulis.

10. Item, le dit William fesoit Robert de Iver[2] clerk des gages de roy en lieu de dit Johan Strouppe, prenant le iour du roy II s.; et aussi le dit Robert fuist un des chamberlayns de l'Escheqer de Carlaugh, prenant du roy par an XXV marcz, nouncontresteant qe le dit Robert fuist un des soudeors du dit monsieur William, prenant pour ses gages par an XL livrez.
Inquiratur.

[1] The Latin version of the last three items runs as follows: de qualibet weia brassei, fabarum, pisarum, ordei, siliginis et hastivell', v.s.; de qualibet weia salis vi s. viii d.; et de qualibet libra pellium equorum, cervorum, affrorum, pilfell' et pannorum laneorum et lineorum, et faldingorum, et aliarum mercandisarum, vi denarios. Order revoking the duties, Westminster, 28 May 1372, Rymer, iii, pt. ii, p. 940; inquisitions, *infra*, vi, cap. 2. Cf. *Early Statutes*, p. 478.

[2] Robert de Evere or Euer was second Chamberlain of the Exchequer, 1371–88, *Liber Munerum*, i, pt. ii, p. 215.

11. Item, le dit monsieur William fesoit Wauter,[1] frere du dit Robert, son controllour et issint fuist le roy desceu qar chescun falce monstresoun fuist fait par leur assent a damage de roy de M[l] livres et pluis.
Inquiratur.

12. Item, le dit monsieur William fesoit mettre sur les poveres lieges, encountre lour volunte, VII quarters de furment es countez de Urielle, Mithe et Dyvelyn, et fesoit une gernere a Tresteldormaugh,[2] qe toutz les bledz issint demandez des ditz lieges dussent estre avenez a dit gerner, a grant damage del poeple; qar ascuns qe porteront les ditz bledz illeoqes furont de loinz par cynkquant lieux; et le dit monsieur William ne paiast unqes riens pour les bledz qe tant come lui pleust; et quant pees fuist pris entre les enemys et la paiis le dit monsieur William vendoit les ditz bledz as ses soudeors, chescun buz' pour II s., et en tiel manere as enemyes Irrez, a grant damage nostre seigneur le roy et extorsioun de ses poverez lieges.
Dicunt quod de levacione bledarum verum est; de summa et aliis circumstanciis inquiratur.

13. Item, le dit monsieur William fesoit defendre qe nulle homme fuisse hardy de passer la meer vers Engleterre sanz coungie, pur quiel il covynt paier fyn de II s. pur le seel du dit monsieur William; et auxi qe nulle homme devoit achater coers, salvez les marchandes du dit monsieur William; et en meisme la manere il fesoit charger deux niefs ove X[xx] lastes de coers et avoit en les dites niefs les soudiours nostre seigneur le roy, plusqe XX, pur les salvement garder, et furont hors de la terre par demi an et plus as gages de roy al estimacion de IIIJ[xx] XII livres.
Dicunt quod misit duas naves corriis carcatas, cum quibus misit homines de retinencia sua; de numero nesciunt et nec si misit aliquos in locis eorum.

[25 April 1370.]
14. Item, a parlement tenuz a Dyvelyn le iour de Seint Mark lewangelist, lan de roy qor est XLIIII[e], mys fuist sur les

[1] Walter Eure or Euyr was Keeper of Writs, 1372–8, *Liber Munerum*, i, pt. ii, p. 209.

[2] Castledermot, Co. Carlow.

poveres lieges, encountre lour volente, par comandement du dit monsieur William davoir de chescune charue de terre XIII s. IIII d.; les queux deniers furont paiez tout entierement, a grant damage et destruccion des ditz poveres lieges.

Dicunt quod verum est.

15. Item, le dit monsieur William fesoit commissions de coiller bledz, vaches et autres vitailles des ditz poveres lieges sanz rienz paier; et il soiournast att Adare[1] sur les despens des ditz poveres lieges pour XXII septimasnez sanz iourneye faire, en grant destruction des lieges.

Dicunt quod verum est, et hoc per consilium episcopi Midensis et aliorum etc.

16. Item, le dit monsieur William fesoit coiller toutz les niefs et bateux d'Engleterre qui furont illoeqes, et aussi de la terre meisme, et les fesoit demurer illeoqes en lewe daler en Tomound[2] pur guerrer les enemys Irrez as costages de roy; et une falce pees fuist pris par le dit monsieur William et levesqe de Mithe[3] et autres, et toutz les costages de roy perduz, queux acomptont a roy une grande summe et rienz ou poy paieront en tut; et il avoit des contees de Cork et de Galweye[4] CCCC marcz et plus, tortuousement et encountre la volente des lieges et saunz null profit faire.

Dicunt quod verum est.

[13–20 Jan. 1371.]

17. Item, le dit monsieur William, apres sa venue de Adare, il vient a Kilkenny et tient un parlement en les octaves de seint Hillare et accordee fuist qe le dit monsieur William et ses soudiours sei retournerent a Casshell pur guerrer les enemys Irrez; et le dit monsieur William demourast a dit Casshell toute le iverne sanz nulle profit faire qi viveront toutz iours sur poverez communes de la terre sanz poy paier, a grande destruccion des ditz poverez lieges.

Dicunt quod male solvit; de aliis inquiratur.

[1] Adare, Co. Limerick. [2] Thomond or Co. Clare.

[3] Stephen de Valle, bishop of Meath, 1369–79, and Treasurer of Ireland, 1369–74.

[4] It is usually stated that Galway did not become a county until the reign of Elizabeth. Cf. Litton Falkiner, *Counties of Ireland*, p. 122, in *Illustrations of Irish History* (1904).

[7-13 June 1371.]

18. Item, en les octaves de la Trinite, lan susdite, il tient un parlement hors de Casshell trois lieux sur une tertre[1] appellee Balidoelle, nulle ville proschein, et illoeqes furont toutz les bones gentz de Urielle, Mithe et del conte de Dyvelyn, lercheveseqes, evesqes, chivalers, burgeois, et les bones gentz de Cork et de Kery, en grande meschief pur defaute de vitailles; et adonqes le dit monsieur William et autres de soun assent fesoient mettre sur les poverez lieges, encountre lour volente par extorsion, une subside de $M^{l}M^{l}$ livrez, et en meisme la manere devant a Kilkenny $M^{l}M^{l}M^{l}$, les quiels deniers furont paiez par toute Monster et ascune partie de Leynster, le premier demi aan.
Dicunt quod verum est.

19. Item, apres celle parlement le dit monsieur William fesoit monsieur William Skippwith[2] Justice seere sur les leis a Clonmell; et diverses hommes qe voilleit aver chartre de pardoun il purreit bien avoir pur XX s., celi qad fait a roy et ses poverez lieges damage de M^{l} marcz et damage nostre seigneur le roy et ses lieges de XX^{ml} livres et destruccion del poeple.
Dicunt quod verum est quod cepit fines; ignorant tamen de summa finum ad dampnum domini regis et fidelis populi sui.

[29 March 1371.]

20. Item, le dit monsieur William sen aloit a nief a Dyvelyn le VIII iour devant Pasque, lan de roy qore est XLVe, et lessa de ses gentz ove le conte de Kildare,[3] adonqes lieutenant de la terre departe monsieur William de Wyndesore, et sen aleront a Monestere et Casshell et Kilmallok qe viveront sur les poverez lieges de la terre, et poy paieront ou riens entre cy qe le tierce aan fuist pleinement accompliz, a damage de roy et ses lieges de VI^{c} livres et plus.

[1] The largest ordnance survey map marks four small hillocks (*tertre*) within a mile of Ballyduagh House, which is four miles south-east of Cashel.

[2] He was appointed Chief Justice of the King's Bench in Ireland on 15 Feb. 1370; in October 1376 he became Justice of the Common Pleas in England. He was the only judge who avoided answering the questions put by Richard II in 1387.

[3] Maurice FitzThomas, fourth earl of Kildare, 1318-90.

Dicunt quod verum est quod vixerunt super communes absque solucione etc.

21. Item, quant le dit monsieur William fuist att Adare et en autres lieuz de Monster illeoqes demureront par pestilence de sa retenue plusqe cent hommes, et il nullez retient en lour lieu tanqe a sa venue en Engleterre, les gages de queux amontont M[l] livrez et plus.
Dicunt quod verum est; nesciunt tamen de summa neque de numero etc.

22. Item, le dit monsieur William fesoit vendre vynes a Dyvelyn a retaille, les queles il avoit achatee des estraunges marchantz, le galoun plus chier par II d. qe autres gentz venderont, a grant damage nostre seigneur le roy et destruccion des liegez; et aussi en meisme la manere il fesoit vendre seel achatee des estraunges marchantz le buz' plus chier par I d. qe autres gentz venderont, a grant damage des lieges.
Dicunt quod verum est de vino. Item, verum est de sale quod emit. Nesciunt tamen an carius vendiderit.

23. Fait a remembrer del secounde venue de monsieur William de Wyndesore en Irland il avoit une skipisoun pur M[l] chivalx et plus, et ne vyndront en toutz accomptez que IIII[c], qar les viles soudiours furont en la terre plusqe la moite de son retenue, toutz iours de lui attendre pur lour viles gages non paiez, qui furont a dererz par un aan et demi. *Dicunt quod fuerunt in Hibernia in adventu ipsius Willelmi ibidem VIIJ[xx] et plus tam de Anglia quam de Hibernia nati, quos idem Willelmus retinuit penes se, qui nichil habuerunt de le skippesoun etc.*

24. Item, les gentz du dit monsieur William arriveront a Dyvelyn et a Waterford et autres lieux de la terre par XVI septimasnez devant sa venue, et touz iours viveront sur les poverez communes et lieges nostre seigneur le roy, et poy ou riens paieront pur lour costages, ou eider encountre les enemys Irrez.
Dicunt quod verum est et petunt solucionem pro amore Dei.

25. Item, en meisme le temps fuist le bon chastelle de Wikkelowe depesse et abateux, et touz les vitailles, armers et

autres eschoses dedeinz le dit chastiel pris et perduz par les enemys Irrez, quel chastelle est chiefe de tut Leynstre, qar si tout Leynstre fuisse perduz il purroit bien rescover par le dit chastelle.
Verum est; cuius culpa inquiratur.

[April 1374.]
26. Item, le dit monsieur William arrivoit a Waterford le tierce iour apres clusur de Pasqe, lan de roy qore est XLVIIe,[1] et en meisme le temps furont les Irrois de Monstere et ascunes de fauces Engleys a guerre; et les gentz de paiis supplient a dit monsieur William de eux socourer et eider, come homme qe fuist venuz en noune de roy; et le dit monsieur William ne voloit eux socourer, mes il ennaloit droitement a Kilkenny sanz plus faire.
Dicunt quod verum est.

[15 May-20 Aug. 1374.]
27. Item, le dit monsieur William tient un prive conseill ovesqe levesqe de Mithe et autres privez de son counseil a dit Kilkenny et accordee fuist daler droitement a Dyvelyn; et le dit monsieur William vient illeoqes le lundy devant le Pentecoste mesme laan et demurat illeoqes tanqe al dymenge proschein apres lassumpcion nostre dame; et il disoit tout outrement qil ne voloit unqes estre armee tanqe il fuisse paie pleinement del remenant de V mille livres pur lui meismes, mys sur les poverez communes, lieges nostre seigneur le roy, encountre lour volente, as parlementz tenuz a Balidoell et Kilkenny en Monstere par extorsion, soeffrant les enemys destruire la terre et les lieges, encountre sa ligeaunce; et tut fuist par counseill levesqe de Mithe.
Dicunt quod verum est.

28. Item, le dit monsieur William promist a paiis pur aver paie les viles soudiours del argent qe fuist en mains des bones gentz, issint a lever de paiis, queux soudiors furont adererez de lour gages par un an et demi, et tous iours viveront sur les poveres lieges de la terre et poy ou riens paieront pur lour costages ou profit faire.
Inquiratur de tempore et de summa.

[1] *Sic* for 48 Ed. III.

29. Item, en meisme le temps furont moultz bones gentz de la Marche ioust Dyvelyn pris et occiz, et grandz furont le rumour, cry et plente qe les lieges fesoient pur defaute deide et toutdiz le dit monsieur William gisoit en le chastelle de Dyvelyn sanz iourneye faire.
Dicunt quod verum est.

30. Item, en meisme le temps une ordenance et proclamacion fuist fait qe nulle homme, de quelqe qil feusse, mesneroit bledz hors de la terre sanz especial congie de roy, le dit monsieur William fesoit charger deux niefs ove VIIJ^c^ quarters de furmentz et de breez; et quant comenceit charger ses niefs homme purroit aver le buz' de bone furment pur VI d. et entre cy qe les niefs furont chargez le buz' vailloit bien XX d., a grant damage des ditz lieges et destruccion de tout le paiis.
Dicunt quod verum est; nesciunt tamen de summa crannoc et in quantum crevit caristiam etc.

31. Item, quant le dit monsieur William avoit chargee son niefs daler hors de la terre il prist VI bones gentz darmes et XII archers daler en soun niefs, pur les ditz bledz garder, queux deveient avoir serviz au roy en soun guerre, et furont hors de la terre par demi aan et plus, as gages de roy qe amontont par meisme le temps cent livres et plus.
Dicunt quod verum est quod misit homines de retinentia sua; nesciunt tamen de numero nec si substituit aliquos in loco eorum nec non.

32. Item, en meisme le temps le dit monsieur William fesoit une fauce moustresoun iouste Dyvelyn de ses gentz, et furent en toutz accomptez IIIJ^c^ et LX, de queles furont les gentz de lercevesqe de Dyvelyn, Chaunceller, Tresorer et garsouns del estable plus qe cent, et furont vestutz en cotes de la pye blank et noir pur faire grant rowte, en desceit nostre seigneur le roy et le povere poeple, des queux il failloit CC de son retenu, qe amonte IIIJ^ml^ livres et plus.
Dicunt quod verum est; ignorant tamen numerum hominum et summam defectus.

33. Item, quant le dit monsieur William avoit soiournee a

Dyvelyn et avoit le remenant de V mille livres sennaloit a Tresteldormauthe[1] sanz nulle profit faire.
Dicunt quod verum est.

34. Item, fait a remembrer qe, come le dit monsieur William vient come governour d'Irlande, il envoiast Nicholas Drwery[2] ove VI^{xx} gentz as chivalx a Kilmallok et illeoqes demourreront par un an entier et plus, qui viveront sur les poveres communes de paiis et poy ou riens paieront, a damage et empovrissement des ditz communes de CCC livres et plus.
Dicunt quod verum est; ignorant tamen de summa.

35. Item, le dit monsieur William et levesqe de Mithe envoieront a Balkahit et en les cantred de Mostredangan[3] Nicholas Loine ove IIIJ^{xx} archers et IIIJ^{xx} chivalx, et illeoqes demoureront par demi aan et plus sur les poveres communes sanz paiement faire, a grand damage et destruccion des dites communes de CCC livres dont ils prient paiement.
Dicunt quod verum est quod fuerunt ibidem, per cuius mandatum ignorant, et modicum vel nichil solverunt.

36. Item, le dit monsieur William a sa venue apres Pasqe il mandast a lercevesqe de Dyvelyn, le Chaunceller, priour de Kilmaynan, le Tresorer, deen de Dyvelyn et lour baillast CCCC marcz et plus del Tresore nostre seigneur le roy, pur enbeciler les tortz qils avoient faitz au roy, a damage du dit nostre seigneur le roy de M^{l}M^{l}M^{l} livres et plus.
Dicunt quod non venerit per communitatem, sed in preiudicium domini nostri regis et fidelis populi sui; ignorant tamen de dampno etc.

Evesqe de Mithe

37. Item, quant le dit evesqe fuist Tresorer d'Irland, lan de roy qore est XLIIe, fuist lan de guerre en la dite terre; et le roy avoit en son Tresorie a Carlaugh une grante some dor

[1] Castledermot, co. Carlow.
[2] On 3 Sept. 1375 Nicholas Drewry and Walter Padeley were empowered by Windsor to buy hawks and tercels in the counties of Tipperary and Waterford, *Cal. Pat. and Cl. Rolls, Ireland*, p. 94, no. 169.
[3] Ballykerwick, in the barony of Muskerry, East, co. Cork?

et argent; et le dit evesqe fesoit doner a contee de Desmound[1] VII^{c} marcz, et il meismes avoit du dit argent CC marcz et monsieur Robert Holiwode CC marcz, et sire William Carlille, chapellein, XL livres, et chescun autre officer de l'Escheqer XL marcz, en grante desceite nostre seigneur le roy et damage.

Dicunt quod tempore predicti episcopi, tunc Thesaurii, officiarii diviserunt inter se et suos de thesaurio domini regis, nomine reward, ad estimacionem M^{l}DCCCCLIIIJ libros et plus, ut plenius apparet in compoto predicti episcopi.

38. Item, quant le dit evesque veit qe le dit argent ne voilleit parfourner lour promessez il fesoit crier real service a Kilkenny pur paier les ditz promesses, a grant damage nostre seigneur le roy.
Dicunt quod verum est, quod per ipsum et alios de consilio etc.

39. Item, le dit evesque ad hoeu labbeie de Fowr[2] a ferme ses X aanz pur X marcz, qe vault par aan XL livres, en disceit nostre seigneur le roy.
Dicunt quod verum est; inquiratur per quot annos.

40. Item, le dit evesque ad hoeu a ferme les terres de seigneur Reccheford[3] III aans devant la venue monsieur Robert de Asshetoun pur riens, et vault bien par aan cent marcz et plus.
Dicunt quod verum est.

41. Item, le dit evesqe ad hoeu les terres de monsieur Bagotte ces VII aans pur riens paier, qe vaudront par an XL marcz et plus.
Dicunt quod verum est.

42. Item, le dit evesqe ad hoeu Fidemure[4] el counte de Limeryche pur rienz, qe vaudront par an XX marcz, a damage nostre seigneur le roy.
Inquiratur.

[1] Gerald FitzMaurice, fourth earl of Desmond, *ob.* 1390.
[2] Priory of Austin Canons at Fore, co. West Meath.
[3] Probably John Rocheford of Kildare, specially summoned to the Great Council, 1372, *Cal. Pat. and Cl. Rolls*, p. 84, no. 116.
[4] Fedamore, in the barony of Smallcounty, co. Limerick.

43. Item, le dit evesque ad hoeu les temporaltez levesqe de Kery,[1] qe vaudront par an XL livres et plus ces II ans et pur XL s.
Dicunt quod verum est et credunt quod valent C marcz.

44. Item, le dit evesque ad hoeu les temporaltez lerceveschee de Dyvelyn[2] qe vaudront par an VIII^c marcz; et il ad le countee de Weysford qe vaultz par aan C livres et plus.
Dicunt quod verum est de Dyvelyn. Item, verum est quod habet in comitatu Weysford; ignorant tamen extentam.

45. Item, il avoit hoeu le manoir de Jonestone,[3] qil purchaceit de Johan Grief par manace et extorsion encountre sa volunte, esteant en la service nostre seigneur le roy qe manoir vault bien par an XL livres.
Dicunt quod verum est.

46. Item, les fermes et autres eschoses qe le dit evesqe ad de roy vaudront par aan M^l marcz, sanz ceo qil ad par fauce suggestion C marcz de roy par an destre de son counseil.
Verum est quod habet C marcz; de suggestione tamen ignorant.

47. Item, ordene fuist par lassent du dit evesqe qe chescun officer du roy en la dite terre averoit doublez feez qils avoient devant la houre; et le dit evesqe fuist adonqes Tresorer, et cely qe averoit XL livres, averoit IIIJ^{xx} livres, a damage grante.

48. Item, le dit evesqe fait diverses gentz, soudiours, vivere sur les poveres communes, aucunes foitz CC hommes et ascunes foitz plusours, en les parties de Monstere, et poy ou riens paieront pur les dites costages, nouncontresteant qe le dit evesqe ad gages pur les dites gentz, soudiours, garder et paier, a damage de roy de M^l marcz et plus.
Dicunt quod verum est; ignorant tamen de vadiis.

[1] John de Valle was bishop of Kerry or Ardfert, 1348–72. He was probably a kinsman of Stephen de Valle, bishop of Meath.

[2] The last vacancy in the see of Dublin had been when John de St. Paul died in 1362.

[3] Probably Jonestown, co. Wexford. The owner may have been John Creef, who was sheriff of Carlow in 1372, *Cal. Pat. and Cl. Rolls, Ireland*, p. 84, no. 130.

49. Item, le dit evesqe fesoit deliverer certeinz clercz qi furont arestuz a Oxenford, filtz des enemys Irrois de Tamounde,[1] qe furont en le chastelle de Wyndesore par commission du roy, a damage de roy de CCC marcz et plus.
Dicunt quod verum est.

50. Item, le dit evesqe vient en countee de Tiperary et amenoist ovesqe lui Richard og Burke ove M^{l} hommes as chivalx, et illeoqes demoureraount par une quinzeine, qi viveront sur les poveres communes et poy ou riens paieront pur lour costages, a damage et oppression des communes susditz de CC livres et plus.
Inquiratur.

51. Item, apres celle temps le dit evesqe vient a Clomell ove XXX hommes as chivaux, et illeoqes soiourneront par oept iours et viveront sur les communes, a damage de X livres et pluis.
Inquiratur.

52. Item, le dit evesqe prist en countee de Kery $XIIIJ^{xx}$ vachez, encountre la volunte des communes, sanz rien paier pur ycelle, en grande damage et destruccion des ditz communes et preiudice nostre seigneur le roy; et auxi le dit evesqe fait de iour en autre plusours et grantz extorsions, destruccions et oppressiouns vers les lieges nostre seigneur le roy en le countee de Monstere.
Dicunt quod verum est.

53. Item, le dit evesqe fesoit mettre sur la clergie en la countee de Kery encountre lour volente LV marcz, les queles deniers furont paiez, a grant damage du dit clergie.
Dicunt quod verum est.

54. Item, le dit evesqe fesoit les communes de Monstere paier encountre lour eisnee degree a Richard og Burke diverses subsides, queles amontont $M^{l}CCCC$ marcz, a grandez damage des communes et destruccion dycellez, les queles deniers furont as diverses feitz paiez.
Dicunt quod verum est.

[1] Thomond.

55. Item, le dit evesqe la ou qe une femme qest appellee Mor M^c^chonmar[1] fuist prist en la citee de Limerich pur diverses trespas touchantz felonie, pur quele femme deliverer Thomas Fitz Johan, chivaler, voleit doner au roy VIIJ^c^ livres, le dit evesqe prist privement del dit Thomas Fitz Johan une grande bribe et le dit femme fesoit delivrer, en desceit nostre seigneur le roy.
Dicunt quod verum est quod capta fuit. Inquiratur qualiter deliberata extitit.

56. Item, la ou William Barette est notoire feloun et traitre a nostre seigneur le roy et ardist les suburbes del citee de Cork, le dit evesqe lui grauntast counge pur sauf conduit pur venir al dite citee de Cork et retourner a sa volente, pur recoverer vers voz lieges et avoir tut ceo qe au lui fuist due; et nulle de les lieges nostre seigneur le roy purroit avoir droit ne resoun de lui, qar le dit evesqe a lui fuist favorant et eidant en quanqe il purroit bonement.
Dicunt quod verum est.

57. Item, la ou Richard hoge Garette est feloun nostre seigneur le roy et notoire meyntenour des larons, et de ce fuist il enditee, le dit evesqe lui grauntast sa pees pur CC vaches et pur toutz de sa nacion et toutz ses gentz.
Dicunt quod verum est.

Note de les Messagers.

[7 Jan. 1373.]

58. Item, come grante fuist par les grantz et communes d'Irlande a parlement tenuz a Kilkenny adonqes monsieur Robert de Asshetone, Justice, as evesqes de Mithe et de Cloine[2] et frere William Tany, adonqes Chaunceller, et monsieur Robert Holiwode, chief Baroun de l'Escheqer illeoqes, CCC marcz pur faire lour messages et monstrer lour tortz et damages et meschiefs qils soeffrent de iour en autre, et pur remedie ent avoir, come plus pleinement en le dit parlement fuist monstreez et declarez as ditz messagers: les quels messagers fesoient lour message tut con-

[1] MacNamara. Laurence MacNamara was one of O'Brien's urraghts in 1395, Curtis, *Richard II in Ireland*, p. 180.

[2] John de Swafham, a Carmelite friar of Lynn, who was bishop of Cloyne, 1363-76.

trarie a lour escharge, en desceit nostre seigneur le roy et tres grande damage des ses poveres lieges.
Dicunt quod verum est.

Chaunceller

59. Item, fait a re[me]mbrer qe le Chaunceller d'Irlande ad a ferme de roy les terres qe homme appelle Lexlope, Chapelle Isowde,[1] qe terres vaudront par an CCXL livres, et les ad a ferme pur IIIJ^{xx} livres.
Inquiratur.

60. Item, le dit Chaunceller ad destruit le chastelle de Lexlope, et auxi coupe le bois appurtenant au dit chastelle, qe valoit CCC livres.
Inquiratur.

61. Item, le dit Chaunceller est priour de Kylmaynan et nostre seigneur le roy deveroit avoir en la dite priorie de Kilmaynan XII chapelleins pur chauntier pur lui et ses auncestres, et ore ne sont plusours qe sis ou cynqe.
Inquiratur.

62. Item, quant la fauce monstresoun fuist fait a Dyvelyn, le dit Chaunceller envoyast ascunz de ses gentz a dit monsieur William de Wyndesore, en desceit nostre seigneur le roy.
Verum est quod quidem de hominibus ipsius fuerunt ibidem; nesciunt tamen de numero.

63. Item, le dit Chaunceller par colour de soun office ad estoupe toutz les gurgez entre Lexslope et Dyvelyn, qest bien VI lieux, a damage de roy et ses poveres lieges de C marcz et plus.
Inquiratur.

Note de Chaunceller et Tresorer.

64. Item, la ou le Chaunceller et Tresorer furont ordeignez de surveere les monstresounz de monsieur William de Wyndesore et autres de sa retenue, les avantditz Chaunceller et Tresorer soeffrerount lours gentz ove autres daprester daler a dit monsieur William pur faire grante rowte, en desceit nostre seigneur le roy et grande damage de ses poverez liegez; et furent dassent de faire touz les faucez monstresounz qe furent faitz en la paiis en le temps du dit monsieur William, encountre lour escharge.

[1] Leixlip and Chapelizod, co. Dublin.

Dicunt quod verum est quod ipsi promiserunt et homines eorum erant in eisdem.

Note del Chaunceller, Tresorer, Monsieur Robert Holiwode et autres ministres.

65. Item, toutz les wardes et mariages, estentz et toutz les regardez qi furont grantez as diverses gentz par les ditz Chaunceller, et Tresorer, qe amonte une grante somme; les ditz Chaunceller, Tresorer et monsieur Robert Holiwode et autres ministres de court de roy furont dassent de les faire, et avoient lour profit, qe somme amonte plus qe $M^1M^1M^1$ livres et plus, sanz les faucez extentez, gardes, mariages, qe purront bien estre prove par laccompt del Tresorer en l'Escheqer nostre seigneur le roy en Engleterre: et soit enquis pur grant profit nostre seigneur le roy aussi bien par la paiis, come par les rolles del Escheqer touchantz les extentz et regardez.

Tresorer

66. Item, le Tresorer, haute Deen de Dyvelyn,[1] ad resceuz doublez feez par le temps qil ad este Tresorer, et ses genz hoeu les gages du roy pur lui garder en la ville de Carlaugh, a damage de roy de V^c marcz et plus.
Verum est quod recepit feodum duplicum; de aliis inquiratur.

Note de monsieur William Wyndesore, levesque de Mithe, Chaunceller, Tresorer, Chaunceller de verte ceire et de les Barons de l'Escheqer.

67. Item, la ou qe nostre seigneur le roy deveroit avoir wardes, mariages et extentz et autres diverses profitz en la dite terre d'Irlande, monsieur William de Wyndesore, governour de la terre, levesqe de Mithe, Chaunceller, et Tresorer, et le Chaunceller de verte sire, et les Barouns de l'Escheqer les extentent a lour oeps et disposicion desmesne, pur lour singuler profit et grantont et departont la greindre partie des issues de la terre entre eulx et lour amys, en noune[2] de regardez, a damages de roy de VI^{ml} livres et plus.
Dicunt quod verum est; inquiratur de summa etc.

[1] This Treasurer was not the bishop of Meath, but his successor, John Colton, who held office from 1374 to 1375. He was dean of St. Patrick's Cathedral, Dublin. I have found no other reference to the title *haute Deen de Dyvelyn*; the title *Dean of Dublin* was given to the Dean of St. Patrick's from time to time.

[2] *Sic*; read *noun*.

Holiwode

68. Fait a remembrer qe la ou qe aucunes terres soient tenuz en chief de roy, monsieur Robert Holiwode les fesoit extenter par viscontz et eschetours a sa volente; et en tiele manere il ad diverses terres; et monsieur Robert susdit est chief Baron del Escheqer nostre seigneur le roy.
Inquiratur.

69. Item, le dit monsieur Robert ad hoeu VII charues de terre, qe sont des demenez de roy, queux monsieur Elys d'Asshbourne[1] avoit du roy [iouxt] Dyvelyn a ferme; et le dit monsieur Robert les ad a ferme, lacre pur II d. ob.; et il ad les lessee a ferme as autres, lacre pur XVI d. par aan. Et aussi le dit monsieur Robert ad plus profit des dites terres, cest assavoir, de chescun beste qe porte busche ou grosse XVI d. par an a Dyvelyn, par extorsion, qe amonte par aan XL livres.
Dicunt quod verum est quod habet terras et plus recepit de predictis terris quam reddit domino regi; nesciunt tamen de summa.

70. Item, le dit monsieur Robert ad doublez fees de roy par aan, come piert, qar la ou qil naveroit qe XX livres, il ad XL livres, en desceit nostre seigneur le roy.
Dicunt quod verum est.

71. A counseil nostre seigneur le roy monstrount Richard Dere et William Stapelyn, qi ount longement pursuy pur droit et profit de roy touchant la terre d'Irland, la qe mestre Henri Ograde, archiedekne Macmathoun, archedeken de Fynabrance, mestre Douchud O Louchy, fitz a cheveteyn de sa nacion, mestre Donnyll O Dagl, fitz a cheveteyn de sa nacion, mestre Donat O Douchud[2] et un autre Irroys fecissian, Irrois enemys nostre seigneur le roy,

[1] Elias de Ashbourne was appointed Chief Justice, Ireland, in 1342, *Liber Munerum*, i, pt. ii, p. 206.

[2] Dr. Salter tells me that there are no such names in Oxford records. Three clerks probably came from co. Clare. The sept of O'Grady was in north-east Clare. O'Dagl may be the son of Cornelius O'Dea, and O'Louchy the son of Iriel O'Lochlin; both chieftains submitted to Richard II, as urraghts of O'Brien, in 1395 (Curtis, *Richard II in Ireland*, p. 180). It is also possible that O'Dagl was the Donnell O'Daly, called *bolg-an-lama*, or the budget of poetry, *Four Masters*, *sub anno* 1404. The archdeacons have not been traced.

qe furont bonz ostages en le counte de Lymerick et en tout le paiis de Monstere; et furont arestuz a Oxenford par commission de roy et mesnez a chastel de Wyndesore, et furont illeoqes as costages du roy par demi aan et plus; levesqe de Mithe et monsieur Robert de Holiwode fesoit suggestion a counseille, en desceit du roy, qe les ostages susditz ne furont qe poveres escolers; et prist de eux et de lour parentz une grant bribe et les fesoit deliverer, a damage de roy et as poveres lieges de M[1] marcz et plus, et sont gentz assetz cy de prover cest bille.

72. Item, le dit monsieur Robert vient a Carlaugh pur servir le roy chescun terme une septimasne ou deux, et toutz ses gentz sont as gages de roy pur lui garder, en grant desceit nostre dit seigneur le roy.

Quantum ad vadia scrutantur rotuli. Verum est tamen quod sepe est absens.

73. Item, par la ou monsieur William de Wyndesore mist sur le poeple en deux parlementz, lun a Kilkenny lautre a Balidowil tenuz, par imposicion et extorsioun V mille livres sur quel les communes de la cite de Dyvelyn, et de la ville de Droghda, et les communes des countez de Dyvelyn, Kildare, Mithe et Iriel pursuirent a nostre seigneur le roy, et avoient un *supersedeas*; et puis vous, sire Robert Holiwode, fauxement tesmuignates qe cel somme fuist resonablement graunte et par bone volunte, par quei le dit monsieur William avoit brief de lever ceo qe ne fut leve, en damage des ditz communes de VI mille livres.

Inquiratur.

74. Item, la ou qe nostre seigneur le roy donast soun chartre de pardoun as diverses gentz pur viles dettez, salvez viscontez [et] eschetours, le [dit] monsieur Robert lessa les ditz visconteez et eschetours davoir le benefice du dit pardoun auxi bien come autres, a damage de M[1] marcz.

75. Item, le dit monsieur Robert ad le manoir de Tirtayn en le countee de Dyvelyn, qest tenuz en chief de roy par le service destre latimer entre les Engleys et Irrois; et unqes il ne fesoit le dit service a roy; qe manoir vault par an XL marcz et plus.

Dicunt quod tenet de rege; ignorant tamen de servicio.

76. Item, la ou qe monsieur Johan Crophull,[1] chivaler, avoit certeinz terres en Irelande et furont seisez en mayn de roy, qe vaudront par aan IIIJ^{xx} livres, le dit monsieur Robert les ad a ferme pur XL livres, en desceit nostre seigneur le roy. *Verum est quod habuit predictas terras. Inquiratur quamodo.*

77. Item, par la ou George Telyn avoit occiz le fitz soun frere, le quiel tient de nostre seigneur le roy en chief C marchez de terre, la quele terre dust estre forfait a nostre seigneur le roy pur la dite felonie fait par le dit George, qar il fuist de ceo clerk convictz, le dit monsieur Robert avoit conissance du tute ceste matire et des profitz qe nostre seigneur le roy purroit ent avoir eu pleynement, et par la ou le dit monsieur Robert fuist chief Baroun de l'Escheqer et auxint de counseil nostre seigneur le roy en celles parties, il prist du dit George XL marcz pur estre a lui favorable et de ce, par assent du dit monsieur Robert, avoit chartre de pardoun, en desceit et a damage nostre seigneur le roy de mille livres.

[7 Jan. 1373.]

78. Item, par la ou monsieur Robert Asshetone, iadys Justice nostre seigneur le roy en Irland, tint un parlement a Kilkenny, lendemayne de la phiphanie lan du regne le roy qore est quarant septisme, en quiel parlement ordinee fuist par prelatz, seigneurs et communes, pur diverses meschiefs qe fuit en la terre de Irlande, de mander certeinz messagers a nostre seigneur le roy et son sage counseille pur declarer a sa seigneurie les ditz meschiefs et sur ceo prier et pursiure davoir le count de la Marche, come bien meschiefs avindrint et ce ove suffissant poer; et aussi pur avoir plus de suffissance al dit Justice que fuit en Irland, et qe pur nulle chose les ditz messagers ne duissent pursiure pur avoir monsieur William de Wyndesore, a cause qil avoit fait a tant de oppressions et extorsions sur le poeple en temps devant. De qeux messagers vous, sire Robert Holiwode, fuistes un et iure des ditz articles pursuir et, a contrarie des ditz articles, pursuitz la venue du dit monsieur William, en damage nostre seigneur le roy et de ses lieges illoeqes de CM^{l}. livres.

[1] Cf. *Cal. Pat. and Cl. Rolls, Ireland*, p. 90, no. 25.

Carlille

79. Fait a remembrer qe sire William Carlille, chapellein et Baroun del Escheqer de Carlaughe fesoit extenter les temporaltez levesqe de Osserie[1] a soun oeps propre pur XL ou L livres, qe valont le double et plus, en desceit nostre seigneur le roy.
Dicunt quod perquesivit temporalia Johanni fratre suo fraudulenter ad commodum suum proprium, que valent per annum duplicia, in preiudicum domini regis.

80. Item, la ou qe une nief fuist venuz hors d'Espaigne et fuist de Buskeye,[2] enemy a roy, et fuist chacee par tempeste en havene de Waterforde, et avoit diverses merchandies en la dite nief a value de M^1M^1 livres et plus, le dit sire William Car[l]ille, la ou la dit nief fuist arestuz, il resceut un grante bribe et lessa la dite nief aler en Flandres, en desceit nostre seigneur le roy.
Dicunt quod verum est quod deliberavit navem pro briba, sed de valore navis et bonorum in ea contentorum et summa bribe ignorant, etc.

81. Item, le dit sire William tient toutz les *nisi prius* qe sont envoiez hors del Escheqer en paiis de Monstere et les countez de Kilkenny de Weysforde, et il ad de roy le iour X s. Et ascun temps il est hors del Escheqer par VI simaignes et plus, et il ad tiels gages de roy nouncontresteant qil ad doublez fees, et en tiele manere est le roy desceu par les officers del Escheqer.
Dicunt quod verum est et nichilominus recepit finem inquisitionibus etc.

82. Item, le dit sire William, la ou Alisandre Balscote[3] fuist eliz evesqe d Osserie, il prist gentz darmes et archers de roy hors de lour garde et fesoit assercher les mesouns du dit Alisaundre pur li avoir pris et occiz; et en meisme le temps vindront les enemys Irrois et fesoient graunt damage as liegez nostre seigneur le roy de M^1 livres et plus.
Dicunt quod verum est quod insultum fiebat ad instanciam ipsius Willelmi [*et*] *Johannis fratris sui, sed de dampno facto per inimicos medio tempore ignorant.*

83. Item, la ou qe William Carlille fuist ordenee dextenter

[1] John of Tatenhale, bishop of Ossory, died in 1370; his successor, Alexander Balscot, was restored to the temporalities, 12 May 1371, Ware's *Bishops*, ed. Harris, i. 411. Cf. no. 82. [2] Biscay. [3] Cf. note on no. 80.

touz les esglises de Monstere et des countez de Kylkenny et Weysford, qe furont seisez en main de roy pur ce qe les parsones et vikers ne furent presentez pur la terre garder, le dit sire William fesoit extenter toutz les esglises pur son singuler profit, a damage de roy de M^l^ marcz et plus.

Dicunt quod verum est quod extendebat ecclesias et alias vendidebat ad minus quam earum verum valorem pro commodo suo singulari, in preiudicium domini regis, set de quantitate dampni ignorant. Inquiratur etc.

84. Item, la ou Morice Fitz Richard fuist tenuz a roy par certeines causes en CLX marcz, le dit sire William prist une grante bribe du dit Morice Fitz Richard et lessa une *nisi prius* passer encountre le roy, a damage de roy de M^l^ marcz et plus.

Dicunt quod verum est quod cepit inquisicionem falsam et ipsam contra regem promisit transire, sed de quantitate bribe et de dampnis ignorant. Inquiratur.

85. A sage counseille nostre seigneur le roy monstre Philippe Ray,[1] chapellein messager pur la clergie de Lessemore et Waterford d'Irland, la ou le tres reverent piere en Dieu, levesqe[2] de Lessemore et Waterford avantdit, avoit un brief selonc le purport de sa lettre qest appelle *significavit*, directe a viscount de Waterford de prendre Johan fit Geffrey Power, qestoit escomengee par longe temps par les sentences de seinte esglise, William Carlille, le seconde Baroun del Escheqer nostre dit seigneur le roy en Irlande, encountre la force et . . . del dit brief, ne veulleit seoffrer le dit Johan fitz Geffray estre pris selonc le ley, mes il donast a dit Johan . . . sauf aler et sauf revenire en contempt nostre dit seigneur le roy et preiudice de seinte esglise. Et le dit William Carlelle fesoit . . . meisme cely Johan fitz Geffrey viscount del counte de Waterford avantdit, nouncontresteant la sentence de escomengement, en preiudice de seinte esglise et a grant damage nostre seigneur le roy et destruccion de ses poveres lieges de la dit countee.

[1] Phillip Ray was one of the proctors elected by the clergy of Lismore and Waterford to go to England in 1376 (below, p. 234).

[2] Thomas le Reve was bishop of Lismore and Waterford, 1363 to 1393, Ware, loc. cit. i. 533.

Two additional articles against William Carlill, preserved separately.

[29 April 1370.]

86. Item, dicunt quod ubi ordinatum per statutum domini regis quod nullus homo perturbaret liberam elecionem, Willelmus de Carlhelle, clericus, die lune proxime post quindenam Pasche, anno domini regis nunc XLIIII^{to}, apud Dublin dedit predicto locum tenenti C marcas ad perturbandum et arestandum Alexandrum Balscot[1] libere electum ad episcopatum Ossoriensis, qui fuit apud Dublin super passagium versus curiam Romanam ad electionem suam prosequendum, qua quidem de causa idem Alexander perturbatus fuit de passagio suo per unam septimam tunc proximam sequentem etc.

[21 March 1370.]

87. Item, dicunt quod idem locum tenens per ordinationem et procuracionem Jacobi de Pykeryng, militis, Willelmi de Carlhelle clerici Baronis Scaccarii domini regis Hibernie et Simonis de Charweltoun,[2] clerici Remembratoris dicti Scaccarii, apud Dublin die Jovis proxime post festum sancti Patricii, anno XLIIII°, fecit dictum locum tenentem arrestare Johannem Scrope iniuste, et in castro Dublin imprisonare, et ibidem in prisona detinere quousque fecit finem cum dicto locum tenente per D marcas, unde solvit centum marcas et Jacobo Pykeryng X marcas et unum ciphum argenteum precii XL s.; et postea in prisona ibidem detinebat quousque, occasione oneris forisfacture et imprisonamenti predicti moriebatur etc.[3]

Si execucion et due punissement des choses susdites soient faitz et determinez selonc la ley, et les officers de la terre soient remuez hors de lour offices, issint qe le poeple neit doute de eux ne de lour meintenours pur dire la verite, les avantditz Richard et William serront prestz pur declarer a tantz des autres novels eschosez pur profit nostre seigneur le roy, come desus est escript.

[1] Cf. nos. 80 and 82.

[2] Simon de Charwelton was appointed Chief Remembrancer in 1370, *Liber Munerum*, i, pt. ii, p. 215.

[3] The additional articles are taken from document no. 16; they also occur in Dublin inquisitions, vi, caps. 9 and 11, below, pp. 231-2.

II. Documents relating to Proceedings before the English Council, 1376

[The answers of Holywood to the articles of accusation]

Quant as touz les articles dount Robert Holywode est accusez, il dist qil est accusez dacuns articles touchantz si bien tenementz et auxint des autres choses supposez estre faites hors du roialme d'Engleterre, et auxint, par estatut fait lan nostre seignur le roy qore est XLII,[1] et autres diverses estatutz, ordenee est qe nul homme par accusement serra mys a respondre devant le conseil nostre dit seigneur le roy naillours sanz presentement devant justicz, ou chose de recorde, ou due processe et brief original, et, si riens soit fait a lencontre, qil soit voide en leye et tenuz pur errour; et nentent mye qe par les causes suisditz es cestes accusementz veuilliez conustre. Et si la courte veulle agarder le dit Robert a respoundre, il pri qe ses accusours troevent sufficeant seurte a nostre dit seigneur le roi et a lui, selonc ce qe lestatutz ent faites demandent. Et le dit seurte troeve, le dit Robert dist en manere qensuyt severalment a checun article.

I. (68)[2] Quant al primer article qe Robert Holywod est chief Baroun del Escheqer nostre seigneur le roi et fait viscountz et eschetours extendre terres esteantz en la mayn le roi a sa volunte, et issint il ad divers terres. Le dit Robert respont qe depuis qe en celle article nest pas compris quelles terres ils sont, nen quel vile, nen quele counte en especiale, ne de queulle valieu, ne de quelle somme le roi est endamage, ou nyent responduz; ne qe lez terres atiendrent au roi, ne par queux viscountz et eschetours ils furront extenduz, ne ow, ne quant, ne quelle estate le dit Robert ad en les ditz terres; issint qe le dit Robert purra a ceo avoir response en certeyn, il entent qe a celle article en noun certeyn la ley ne luy mette pas a respondre etc. Et pur declarrer la fame le dit Robert et noun pas pur response, lacusement est faux, et ceo, sire, il prest aprover a quelle houre qil ad suffisantz matire monstre devers luy a quelle la ley luy mette a respondre, come la court agard, etc.

II. (69) Item, quant al secounde article des accusementz

[1] Stat. 42 Ed. III, cap. 3, 1368.

[2] The Arabic figures refer to the numeration of the articles of accusation printed above.

tuchant VII chareuz de terre queux furront a monsieur Elys de Asshebourne, le dit Robert respont nyent conissance qe les ditz terres sont de tiel valieu come lacusement suppose; et vous dit qe celles terres sont gissantz en la Marche de Otothils et Obrynnes[1] et autres Irreis a eux ioignantz, et graunt partie dicelles portantz jaun et grostes, et ascun partie de eux sont gastes terres, et ascun partie dicelles en temps de pees sont custifies et maynoveris, et en temps de guerre relinquis et desolates, sanz tenantz pur la greyndre partie, et en busoignent graunt costages et depense. Et qe monsieur Elys de Asshebourne en ascuns temps pursuy brief hors de la Chauncellerie d'Engleterre as ministres nostre seigneur le roi en Irelande pur enquerer, certifier et retrovere la valieu des ditz terres en la Chauncellerie avantdit, par quelle retourne feust certifie qe mesmes lez terres en temps de pees valuerent forsqe VI livres XV s. par an, et en temps de guerre rienz ne valuerent. Sour quei le dit monsieur Elys tant pursuy au roi pur mesmes les terres avoir pur lestent avauntdit, qe nostre dit seigneur le roi luy graunta mesmes les terres a terme de sa vie, rendant lextent avauntdit a soun Escheqer du Dyvelyn. Et puis apres nostre dit seigneur le roi graunta les terres avauntditz au dit monsieur Elys et a ses heirs a touz iours par sa chartre desoutz soun graunt seal d'Engleterre pur lextent avauntdit; et apres ceo autre foitz par sa chartre soun estate ratifia et confirma a luy et a sez heirs a touz iours pur le dit extent annuelment rendant al Escheqer avauntdit; le quelle monsieur Elys soun estate de mesme les terres apres graunta au dit Robert et de ceo luy enfeffa a luy et a ses heirs. Pur quei, apres ceo, pur ceo qe les ditz terres furront tenuz du roi en chief, le dit Robert fist fine au roi pur le dit purchase [about six words illegible . . .] du roi, de qei il vouche recorde. Et monsieur Thomas de Asshebourne, fitz et heire au dit monsieur Elys, tut soun droit luy relessa et quit clama. Et puis le dit Robert pursuy devers nostre seigneur le roi si en Engleterre, rehersant les matires avauntditz, tanqe nostre seigneur le roi lestate le dit Robert par fine fait en la Chauncellerie d'Engleterre ratifica et confirma, nyent obstant qil feust ministre le roi adonqes; et de ceo il ad la chartre nostre seigneur le roi dont il vouche recorde, et auxint des roules de la Chauncellerie ou la dit chartre est enroule etc. Et en tiel manere il tynt les terres

[1] O'Tooles and O'Byrnes, clans of North Wicklow.

avauntditz, sanz ceo qil tient nulles autres terres du Roi a ferme iouxt Dyvelyn, come lacusement suppose. Et ceo il est prest a faire come la court agarda et nentend my qe pur locupacioun de sa terre propre le roi luy voet empecher etc.

Et outre ceo quant al extorcioun compris en mesme le article, il dit qe ceo est soun frank tenement, come devaunt est dit, pur qel il porta rent au roi, et dit qe touz ceaux qont este seigneurs des ditz tenemenz et autres seigneurs semblable (?) en mesme la Marche qont tiels grostes jaun ou busch cressantz sour lour terres en la Marche puis la conqueste d'Irlande ount ewe et use, qe chascun persoun qe verroit voluntrefment venire et tiels profitez des grostes jaun ou busche enporter et encarier hors de lour terres illeoqes pur vendre et lour profit faire, repaieroit au seigneur, du soil IIII d. le quarter pur la maynovre en le soil le seigneur et issint le dit Robert, par soun seriant, prist en sa terre illeoqes, quelle profit ne amont pas par an a demi marz sanz ceo qil fist en autres manere, et ceo il tende daverer come la court agardera etc.

[1361-6.]

III. (70) Item, quant al article de doubles fees, le dit Robert vous dit qe quant l'Escheqer estoit a Dyvelyn il prist du Roi fors XX marcz de fee par an en soun office, mais quant monseigneur le duke de Clarence, qi Dieux assoile, lieutenant nostre seigneur le roi en Irlande, par avis de luy mesmes et du conseil le roi illeoqes, remua le dit Escheqer a la vile de Cathlow en relevement du dit vile et confort du pais envyroun, quelles vile et pais furront adonqes ars et destrutz par les enemis; et a cause qe les ministres du dit Escheqer furront faitz venire illeoqes, loigne de lour vivre propre, et nulle sustenaunce ne purroient avoir mais par purveantz en pais, et auxint lour coviensit a demuryr illeoqes afforcement et retenire gentz ovesqe eux en resistance des enemys autres qils ne purroient suffire sour lour offices et fees acustumez, par assent du dit lieutenant et conseil, ordine feust au dit Robert XX livres par an, en noune de regarde; auxint come ils fesoient as autres ministres outre soun fee acustume taunt come il demuroit illeoqes par la cause susdit, quele regarde puis encea ad este alowe as Thesorer d'Irlande sour lour acompte. Et vous dit outre qil despent de soun propre chascun an illoqes et aliours en service le roi C marcz et pluis outre le fee et regarde avauntditz, et nentent my qe nostre seigneur le roi luy voilent empecher encountre la matire alegge devant, et prie estre descharge etc.

IV. (72) Item, quant al article par quele est suppose qe le dit Robert deveroit rescevere gages le roi chascun terme par un septimanz ou dieux pur garder soun corps, le dit Robert respont qils nulles tiels gages resceut de roi par tiel causes, et de ceo il vouche recorde des Thesorer et Chaumberleyns illeoqes, et des roules del Escheqer illeoqes, ou autrement daverer come ceste court agardera etc.

V. (74) Item, quant a la pardoun des veils dettes nostre seigneur le roi, de queux le dit Robert lessa viscountz et eschetours avoir benefice du dit pardoun a damage du roi, le dit Robert respont qe depuis qe par lacusement nest pas sourmys au dit Robert quelle persoun ad ew tiel benefice a damage du roi, encountre la fourme du dit pardoun, ne des queux sommes le roi est par sa defence en celle partie perdaunt ou endamage, ne nad my declarre en especiale ou quant ne sovent nostre seigneur le roi par luy est endamage, issint qil purra a celle response en certeyn avoir etc. Et nentende my qe a celle article en noun certeyn la ley luy mette a respondre. Et pur declarrer la fame le dit Robert, si avis soit a la court qe lacusement soit suffisant a quei il doit respondre, il dit qe lacusement nest pas verroi; et ceo est il prest a prover par recorde ou en autre manere come le conseil nostre seigneur le roi agardra etc.

VI. (75) Item, quant al article tuchant le manoir de Tyrtayn, le dit Robert vous respont nyent conissaunt qil est tenant de frank tenement, ne que le dit manoir est tenuz par tiel service come lacusement suppose; mais il vous dit qe celle acusement tuche frank tenement quelle est en le counte de Dyvelyn en Irlande, come en le dit acusement est contenuz, et ne entende my qe de frank tenement, ou de chose qe tuche frank tenement, en Irlande par nule acusement sanz autre processe de ley qe la court cy voille conustre etc. Et, seigneurs, il vous dit outre qe depuis qe par mesme lacusement est suppose qil deveroit faire loffice de Latymer entre Engleis et Irrois et ne declare my quelle est loffice de Latymer et quelle chose il deveroit ou purroit faire par force de celle office de sa autorite propre sanz comandement du roi ou de soun conseil. Et auxint nest pas sourmys a luy qil feust charge par le roi ne soun conseil de faire chose appurtenant a mesme loffice et qil celle comandement refusa a faire, ne il ne fait pas mencioun en lacusement en certeyn en quei il ad trespase paront le roi est endamage, ne ow, quant ne coment, issint qe a ceo il purra avoir response en certeyn, par quei il prie que ceste mavois acusement soit tenuz pour nulle etc.; et nyent mayns pur attendre les acusours, il vous dit, hors de plee et nemy pur response, qe le dit manoir nest pas tenuz par le service come lacusement suppose, mais par seute real al counte de Dyvelyn, quele chose, quant mestre serra, serra prove par regarde des chartres de feffement de mesme le manoir des progenitours nostre seigneur le roi ou par avereyment come la court agardera etc.

VII. (76) Item, quant as terres Johan Crophulle, le dit Robert respont que par lacusement nest pas declarre quells terres ils sont, ne en quelles viles, ne countes ils sont, issint qe la ley luy mette a respondre; nyent meyns il dit qil ne les avoit unqes a ferme par commissioun le roi, ne en autre manere du lesse le roi etc., come larticle suppose; et ceo il est prest affaire com ceste court agardra etc.

VIII. (77) Item, quant a la deleverance des clerks Irrois hors du chastelle de Wyndesore, le dit Robert vous dit qe a la feste de Pentecoste (?), lan XLVII[e] nostre seigneur le roi qore est, [1373] il vint en message a nostre seigneur le roi et soun conseil en Engleterre de par les grantz et [communes] de la terre d'Irlande; et departie avant la feste de seiynt Michel procheyn ensuant et sen ala en Irlande, a quelle temps nulles dez ditz clerks Irrois estoient pris et punys, quelle temps encea il ne vynt unqes en Engleterre tanqe [two illegible words] qe il poet seute faire au conseil pur eux deliverer, ne tiel seute unqes fist pur eux. De quei il prie tesmoignantz de Chaunceller, Thesorer et Gardeyn du Prive Seal, qe a celle houre furront, ne rienz de eux resceut pur tiel seute faire, ne de eux avoit conissaunce a nule temps, ne unqore ad. Mais il vous dit qe le maire de Oxenforde et un mestre Johan Blake,[1] a la feste de la nativite nostre seigneur procheyn apres la dit feste de seynt Michel, les

[1] Dr. Salter has very kindly supplied the following note: 'John Blake I assume to be *cancellarius natus*, i.e. the senior theologian in residence; his duty was to act as Chancellor during a vacancy. From other evidence I had formed the opinion that the post of Chancellor was vacant about Christmas; Wilton was certainly elected between 25 December 1373 and 5 March 1374; Rimington resigned at or towards the end of 1373. A John Blake, prebendary of Lincoln, died in 1389.'

prist par comandement du roi, le dit Robert adonqes et tut temps depuis esteant en Irlande, et sanz ceo qil pursuy lour deliverance, come lacusement suppose. Et ceo est il prest affaire come la court agardera, et prie qe le dit mestre Johan soit examine et iurre sour le poynt pur saver ent la lealte et nentende my etc.

IX. (73) Item, quant a ceo qe monsieur William de Wyndesore avoit brief de lever V mille livres des communes des certeyns villes et countes, dount ils avoient brief de *supersedeas*, le dit Robert vous dit nyent conissaunz qe le dit monsieur William avoit brief de lever tiel somme etc. Mais il dit qe la dite subsidie feust graunte en les parlementz de Kilkenny et Baldoule [Jan. and June 1371], quelle parlementz et grauntz [sont] de recorde, et par mesmes lez recorde est prove qel es grauntz furrent faitz de lour bones voluntez, quelle recorde le dit Robert ne purroit dedire, s'il ust este ent appose; et coment qil ust dedit le recorde, ceo ne poet valoir ne profiter as ditz communes, ne il feust my appose par le conseil nostre dit seigneur le roi si la charge feust impose par volunte de ministres, sanz assent des communes, ou autrement par voluntrif graunte des communes, qare ceo qore luy est somys de la levee du dit subside par sa tesmoigne ne se [fait?] parcelle de soun message parount il serroit ent challenge, et ne fait my a supposer qe coment qil ust ceo tesmoigne come lacusement suppose qe le conseil verroit par soun tesmoignance sanz autre manere de recorde les avauntditz communes de si graunde somme encountre resoun charger. Et vous dit outre, pur la verite declarer, qe en tant come il poet il myst sa diligence en conseil pur les ditz communes excuser et eux del subsidie avauntdit descharger, pur quel chose il resceut graunt maugre du dit conseil, come mes seigneurs Chaunceller, Thesorer et Gardeyn du Prive Seal, qe adonqes furront presentz, purront bien, si lour plest, tesmoignere. Et auxint il dit en verite, en excuse de luy mesmes, que avaunt la feste de Seynt Michel apres lour message fait il passa en Irlande et avoit congé du conseil, a quelle temps nulle brief de lever la dit subsidie feust graunte au dit monsieur William longe temps apres le departire du dit Robert, come les dates des briefs ent faites purportont; mais le dit conseil luy graunta brifs en descharge du roi de paiement due al avauntdit monsieur William et [noun?] par soun tesmoignantz etc., en nentende my qe encountre la matire alegge le roi luy voet enpecher etc.

X. (77) Item, quant a ceo qe [half a line illegible . . .] le dit Robert resceut de lui [George Telyng] XL marcz pur luy aider daver sa chartre, le dit Robert respont qe unqes il nestoit en conseil ne du conseil a temps [de] graunte du dit chartre, ne par soun counseil ne assent estoit graunte, ne sachant du dit graunt tanqe longe temps apres. Mais, quant as XL marcz, il dit qe un Richard de Loundres longe temps passe, par ordinance, compasement et abette du dit George, vynt a Athcarus en la counte de Mithe ove graunt compaignie de gentz armes, et illeoqes derobba un Johan Stokis de ses bienz et chateux queux il avoit illeoqes, et sa mesoun entra et despoilla, et prist un Neste, adonqes la femme du dit Johan, adonque grose enseynt, (quelle est ore la femme le dit Robert), et ovesqe luy, tut nue forsqe qel estoit covert dun auncien faldyng, ovesqe luy amena tanqe el feust rescouz par gentz du pais. Par cause de quelle meschief la dit Neste resceut tiel maladie qe a graunde peyn exchapa la mort. Et vous dit outre qe les ditz Robert et Neste, par cause de celle trespas issint fait au dit Neste, suerint un bille de trespas en le chif place devaunt Johan Keppok,[1] Chief Justice a tenire les plees le roi, devers le dit George a Drogheda de la partie de Mithe, pendaunt quelle seute un acorde ceo prist par entre les avauntditz George, Robert et Neste, a la request et pursuyt de Richard Plunket,[2] Davy Telyng et autres amys le dit George, a fine qe lit dit George paieroit a les avauntditz Robert et Neste pur le trespas avauntdit XX livres dount le dit Richard devynt plegge, de queux XX livres la moite luy est unqore adirer. Et prie qe le dit Richard Plunket, qe si est present, soit charge par soun saerment de certifier au conseil ent la verite. Et dit outre par cause de luy aider davoir sa chartre ne autre cause, forprise ceste cause, come desoutz est dit, unqes largent avauntdit ne mise denere eut de luy resceut, come lacusement suppose; et de ceo il est prest affaire come la court vodra agarder etc.

XI. (78) Item, quant al article que les messagers avoient en charge qe Monsieur William de Wyndesore ne vendroit en Irlande come Justice ne Governour, come lacusement suppose, le dit Robert respont qe levesqe de Mithe, levesqe de Clone,

[1] John Keppok was appointed Chief Justice *ad placita* in 1371, *Liber Munerum*, i, pt. ii, p. 207. For his other judicial appointments see Ball, *Judges of Ireland*, pp. 36-9.

[2] Cf. *supra*, p. 157, n. 3.

le Priour del Hospitele d'Irlande, adonqes Chaunceller, et luy furront envoiez au roi et soun conseil cy, come messageres sour lesploit des busoignes de la terre d'Irlande. Les queux avoient lour message et charge en certeyn par endenture, quelle endenture ils mystrent avaunt et livererent au conseil cy; et pursuerint tant devers nostre seigneur le roi et soun conseil qe la venu del counte de la Marche[1] feust assentu, et ses endentures faitz par entre nostre seigneur le Roi et luy, et sez purveyours envoiez en Irlande ove commisions tesmoignantz sa venu. Et demanderent pur les terres nostre seigneur le roi garder un de fitz du roi et, si ceo ne poet estre, le seigneur de Latymer[2] ou autres seigneur covenable et suffisant pur la terre justisier et garder. A quelle temps de la pursuyt du dit message monsieur le duke de Loncastre[3] ove touz les grauntz seigneurs a poi de la terre estoient sour lour passage devers Fraunce ov graunt numbre de gentz; le count de Salesbury[4] estoit prest sour soun passage ov diverses seigneurs et autres pur rescover le chastelle et le vile de Brest; monsieur Nichol Tamworth[5] ove graunt numbre de gentz ordine de passer en Espaigne, issint qe poi de cheveteyns adonqe furront remys en la terre. Et coment qe le conseil nostre seigneur le Roi treta et parla ove ascuns seigneurs et chevaillers pur avoir ewe governance de la terre, ils ne purroient trover suffisant persoun qe la governance verroit emprendre, forpris le dit monsieur William qe, a graunt peyn et exitacoun du dit conseil, lemprist, come le seigneurs du conseil, qe adonqe furront, en saveront tesmoigner. Et depuis qe la noune venu le dit monsieur William ne feust pas forpris en lendenture, mais de pursuyr tiel governour come le Roi vodra assigner, et ils fesoient lour message en la manere solonc le purport de lour endenture bien et loialment quelle demert cy de recorde, dount il prie tes-

[1] Edmund Mortimer II, third earl of March, 1351–81; he had married Philippa, the de Burgh heiress and granddaughter of Edward III.

[2] William, fourth baron Latimer, 1329?–81; impeached in the Good Parliament.

[3] The expedition commanded by John of Gaunt, duke of Lancaster, began its march from Calais in July 1373.

[4] William de Montacute, second earl of Salisbury, 1328–97. He commanded an expedition to Brittany in the spring and summer of 1373.

[5] Nicholas de Tamworth had been Captain of Calais in 1370 (*Anonimalle Chronicle*, p. 65); on 16 June 1373 he witnessed two documents relating to a treaty with Portugal (Rymer, iii, pt. ii, pp. 984–5); on 3 June 1373 he was going beyond the seas on the king's service (*Cal. Pat. Rolls*, p. 295).

moignantz du dit conseil, et il ne fesoit rien al contrarie, le dit Robert prie destre descharge de celle acusement etc.

XII. (78) Item, quant al article en quelle est compris qe le dit Robert fesoit le contrarie de soun message, luy semble que celle acusement nest pas suffisant pur luy mettre a respondre, mais facent les acusours declaracoun en quei il fist le contrarie de soun message avauntdit, et il serra prest a respondre.

Answers of William Carlill

Quant as touz les articles dount William de Karlell est acusez, il dist qil est acusez des diverses articles supposez estre faites hors du roialme d'Engleterre, et auxint par estatut fait lan nostre seigneur le roi qore est XLII[1] et autres diverses estatuz, ordenee est qe nul homme par acusement serra mys a respoundre devant le conseil nostre dit seigneur le Roi naillours sanz presentement devant justicz, ou chose de recorde, ou due processe ou brief original, et si rien soit fait a lencontre qil soit voede en leye et tenuz pur errour; et nentent mye qe par les causes suisditz es cestes accusementz veulliez conustre. Et si le conseil nostre dit seigneur le roi veulle agarder le dit William a respoundre, il pri qe ses accusours troevent sufficeant seurte a nostre dit seigneur le roi et a lui, solonc ce qe les estatuz ent faites demandent; et meisme la seurte troevee il dist en manere qensuyt severalement a checun article.

I. (79) Item, quant al primere article, le dit William de Karlell dist qe par laccusement nest pas supposez en quel lieu les dites temporaltez sont, nen quele ville, et nest pas supposez qil les avoit au ferme, ne nest pas supposez qe les temporaltez feurent el main nostre seigneur le roi, et nentent point le dit William qa cest accusement noun certein et nient sufficeant la leye lui mettra a respoundre. Et outre pur declarer sa fame, il dist qil ne fesoit unqes extendre les dites temporaltez en deceit nostre seigneur le roi nen autre manere, et ce dist il en declaracion de la verite et nounpas pur respounce. Et si la courte agarde laccusement sufficeant, il est prest daverrer qil ne fist unqes extendre le dites temporaltez en deceit nostre seigneur le roi.

II. (80) Item, quant al seconde article, qe fait mencion de la niefe de Buskeye, le dist William dist que le haven de Waterforde se extende en longeure XVI lieus et pluis es diverses

[1] Stat. 42 Ed. III, cap. 3, 1368.

counteez, et par meisme laccusement nest pas supposez en quel lieu du dit havene la dite niefe feust arresteuz, ne quel iour, nen quele ville, nen quele countee, et il nentent mye qa cest accusement noun certein et nient sufficeant la leye lui mettra a respoundre. Et si la courte agarde le dit accusement sufficeant, le dit William dist qil y avoit une niefe de Portyngale, apellez seint Marie de Oliver, arrivez dedeinz le havene de Waterforde chargez des diverses marchandises, qe furent as marchandes de Loundres et Saresbiry; quele niefe feust arresteuz par le dit William par comandement monsieur Robert de Asshetoun, adonqes Justicer d'Irlande, et par commission de la chancellerie d'Irlande au dit William directe; et en areste demura la dite niefe et commys en garde des meir et baillyfs de la citete de Waterforde, tanqe brief nostre seigneur le roi vient hors d'Engleterre a monsieur William de Wyndesore, Governour d'Irlande, pur deliverer meisme la niefe ensemblement ove les mestre et mariners, biens et chatelx en ycelle contenuz; par force de quel brief, brief hors de la chancellerie d'Irlande issist as dites meir et baillifs de faire la liveree de meisme la niefe, sanz ce qe le dit William aucun niefe deliverast ou bribe prist pur la livere dicelle, come laccusement suppose. Et ce est il prest daverrer, si la courte voet agarder, come devant est dist.

III. (81) Item, quant al tierce article, le dit William dist qe la ou il deust avoir pris gages de nostre seigneur le Roi X s. le iour, nient contresteant qil ad fees doubles, il dist qil feust Baroun de l'Escheqer en Irlande et le fee de meisme loffice dauncien temps estoit XX marcz par an, et par cause qe l'Escheqer estoit assis a Cathirlaghe, qest en march de guerre bien pres enemys, meisme le fee estoit encreissez par X marcz par an, en temps monsieur le duc de Clarence, qe Dieu assoille, au temps qil estoit lieutenant d'Irlande [1361-6]; quele chose estoit ordenez par le conseil nostre seigneur le Roi celles parties, en quel lieu le dit Escheqer ad estee de tout temps puis tanqen cea; quele fee et encreisse, esteant le dit escheqer a Cathylaghe, il ad pris puis la dite ordenance pur le temps qil ad estee Baroun tanqen cea. Et quant le dit William ad estee assignez par commission nostre seigneur le roi de travailler es diverses counteez de prendre diverses inquisicions pur nostre seigneur le roi et de lever les deniers nostre dit seigneur le roi, travaillant par les parties de Mounester et Leynester ovesqe effoyable poair des gentz as grosses custages pur doubt des enemys, le conseil nostre dit seigneur le Roi, considerant les grantz custages et travalx, lui ont assignez aucun foitz gages, cestassavoir, demi marc le iour, come autres Barouns soleient prendre en cas semblable einz ces heures, et ala foitz regarde en certein selonc lavis du dit conseil quelx il prist come appiert par recorde, sanz ce qil prist X s. le iour en certein ou autres fees doublez ou la dite encreisse devant la dite ordenance, ou qil prist gages pur autres temps, qe nest avantdit, ou riens prist de nostre dit seigneur le roi pur *nisi prius* prendre; et la ou il est suppose par le dit accusement qil est hors de l'Escheqer aucun temps par VI symaignes ou pluis, il ad continuez son office illoeqes solonc ce qil deust faire, si noun qil estoit par resonable cause absent, cestassavoir, ala foitz assignez par commission de servir nostre dit seigneur le roi aillours, et aucun fotz attendant a Kilkenny davoir seur conduyt vers la courte pur pour de McMuragh[1] et autres Irreis enemys de Leynester. Et ce est il prest de prover come la courte agarde et nentent point de ce qil prist par liveree des Tresorer et Chamberleins par ordenance et avis du conseil en la fourme et par les causes avantditz que de cest accusement par la leye il est empeschable.

IV. (82) Item, quant al quart article, le dit William dist qe par ceste accusement il nest pas suppose en quele ville il deust avoir enserchez les mesouns du dit Alisandre de lui avoir pris et occis, ne quel iour ne quel an, ne nest pas suppose par le dit accusement en quel lieu les enemys fesoient damage as lieges nostre seigneur le roi, ne as quelx persouns, et nentent point qa cest accusement noun certein et nient sufficeant la leye lui mettra a respoundre. Et outre pur declarer sa fame, le dit accusement est fause et de riens veritable; et si la courte agarde le dit accusement sufficeant, il est prest daverrer, come la courte agarde, qil nest pas coupable.

V. (83) Item, quant al quint article, le dit William dist qe par ceste accusement il nest pas supposez en queles villes les eglises sont, ne come bien en un, ne come bien en autre, ne de quele value, ne quel an, ne quel iour il les fesoit extendre, ne a

[1] Art Og Mac Murrough Kavanagh, who claimed to be *Ri Laighen* or king of Leinster, succeeded his father in 1376; his supremacy included much of the modern county of Wicklow, north Wexford, and part of co. Carlow (Curtis, loc. cit., p. 22).

quel value, ne nest supposez qil les avoit au ferme, en quel cas ne poet mye estre entenduz qil avoit profit dycelles, ne nest supposez en quel manere il purroit profit prendre dycelles, et nentent point qa cest accusement noun certein et nient sufficeant la leye lui mettra a respoundre. Et si la courte lagarde sufficeant, il dist qil extendist nulles eglises come laccusement suppose, mes pur declarer sa fame et de monstrer la verite, le dit William dist que briefs istrent hors de la Chauncellerie d'Irlande as evesqes de Mounester et des counteez en cest article contenuz, denquere de touz parsouns et vicairs et autres gentz de seint eglise eantz benfices dedeinz leur diocises et reseantz hors d'Irlande, checun evesqe en sa diocise, et de retournir la value dycelles en l'Escheqer illoeques; et puis meisme les extentes faitez et certefiez par les dites evesqes en l'Escheqer, commission issist hors de la chauncellerie d'Irlande au dit William de vendre les fruytz des ditz benfices et meismes les fruytz vendist, solonc sa discrecioun, et final acont ad ent renduz, et quietz est, come appiert par recorde en le dit Escheqer; et nentent mye qe de cella nostre seigneur le Roi lui voet empescher.

VI. (84) Item, quant al sisme article, le dit William dist qe par ceste accusement nest pas supposez en quel lieu il deust la bribe prendre, ne quei il prist de Morice fitz Richard, ne quel an, ne quel iour ou le dit *nisi prius* feust pris, et issint le dit accusement nient sufficeant et noun certein; nientmains, si la courte agarde qil soit sufficeant, le dit William dist ce qil fist, il fist come iugge par commission a lui fait hors de l'Escheqer d'Irlande de prendre le dist enquest, sanz ce qil prist riens du dit Moricz pur la prise dycelle, come larticle suppose; et al remenant qest compris en lacusement nulle leye lui mettra a respoundre, pur le noun certeinte, et nentent mye qe de ce qil fist come iugge nostre seigneur le Roi lui voet empescher.

VII. (86) Item, quant al septisme article, le dit William dist qe par ceste accusement nest pas supposez a qi les C marcz feurent donez, ne par qi Alisandre Balscote feust aresteuz ou destourbez, ne quel iour, ne quel an, ne quel lieu, et nentent mye qa cest accusement noun certein la leye lui mettra a respoundre; nientmains pur declarer sa fame et la verite, il dist qil est de rien coupable et ce est il prest daverrer, en cas qe la courte agarde laccusement sufficeant.

VIII. (88) Item, quant al octisme article, le dit William dist qe Johan Scrope estoit Chamberlein de l'Escheqer en Irlande, et pur diverses deceites et fausetez troevez en lui touchantz son office en l'Escheqer il estoit convictz devant monsieur William de Skippewych, adonqes Justicz du Bank le roi, au quel temps le dit William de Karlelle estoit Baroun de l'Escheqer; et les deceites et fausines le dit William de Karlelle et autres ministres du dit Escheqer feirent monstrer au lieutenant d'Irlande et au conseil nostre seigneur le roi; sur qei le dit Johan feust arresteuz et mys a respoundre as dites deceites et fausines, et convicte devant le dit monsieur William come Justicz, et aiugges au prison par la cause susdit tanqil fait fine a nostre seigneur le roi, sanz ce qil feust emprisonez autrement qe devant est dist par le dit William, et nentent mye qe de cest accusement par la leye il est empechable.

[11 Aug. 1376.]

IX. (26) Memoire qe ceste bille estoit baillee au counseil nostre seigneur le roy a les freres prechours de Londres, lendemain Seint Laurence lan L^{me}, par Robert Whethille, esquier, et autres gentz darmes et archers, nadgairs soldeours del dit monsieur William en la terre d'Irlande, etc.

Et en temps qe monsieur William de Wyndesore fuist lieutenant en Irlande, il faillast de soun retenue, dedeinz le primer an, LV; et le second aan, des tant ou des plusours; et le tierz aan de IIIJ^{xx} et plusours, de quele dit retenuz furont mortz et occiz dedeinz les deux primer aanz IIIJ^{xx}.

Et del temps qe le dit monsieur William fuist gouvernour, ils estoient en sa compaignie, par nostre enquere entre nous soudeours, le primer aan IIIJ^{xx} et IIIJ gentz darmes et CCCXX archers, des queux furont XVI hommes darmes et XLII archers de la terre d'Irlande neez; et del second an XI^{xx} des gentz darmes et archers, les queux pristront lour departer de le dit monsieur William a le demi aan et tierz quarter de le second aan.[1]

[1] The implications of this bill are made clear when the figures contained in it are compared with Windsor's account as Governor (preserved in P.R.O. Foreign Accounts, E. 364, 13), in which he claims wages for 200 men-at-arms and 400 archers of his retinue maintained in Ireland under the terms of his indenture with the king.

III. Calendar of Inquisitions taken at Drogheda and Dublin, May and June 1373.[1]

[Parliamentary and Council Proceedings, Chancery, 47-50 Edward III, Roll 3, nos. 20-5

I. *Meath County.*

Inquisition taken at Drogheda on the side of Meath, before Robert de Ashton, Justiciar of Ireland, and Robert de Preston, appointed by letters patent to inquire into certain matters set forth therein, which letters are attached to this inquisition.[2] The inquisition was taken on the Friday before Ascension Day [20 May 1373] in the forty-seventh year of Edward III's reign as king of England and his thirty-third year as king of France, by the following:—

Christopher Petyt. Laurence Waryng. Walter Meset. Adam Rath. John Jancok. Walter Gerard. Adam Galwey. John Meonys. John Feypowe. William Lynham. Robert Kerduf. Robert Loghken.

1. The jurors say on oath that William of Windsor, lately lieutenant, with the counsel of Thomas, archbishop of Dublin, Stephen, bishop of Meath and lately Treasurer, James Pickering, knight, and Edmund Laurence, in Dublin on 10 December 1369, imposed on the commons of Meath a certain tallage of half a mark on every carucate of cultivated land in the county. They say that there are 520 such carucates in the county and that the tallage was levied 'absque assensu et contra voluntatem comitatus predicti in extorcionem fidelis populi eiusdem comitatus'.

2. They say that William of Windsor, with the counsel of the archbishop etc., *ut supra*, at Tamelyn [Timolin] on 2 February 1370, imposed on the commons of Meath a further tallage of a crannock of corn and a crannock of hay on each carucate. When these crannocks were delivered to the lieutenant at Naas he paid for the corn 5*s.* 4*d.* a crannock and for the hay 3*s.* 4*d.*, though the market price in Meath was 9*s.* 4*d.* and 5*s.* They say that there are 520 carucates of cultivated land in the county

[1] The text of the inquisitions here numbered II, IV, and V is printed in Rymer, iii, pt. ii, pp. 977-80.

[2] No letters patent are attached to the inquisition; they may be merely copies, as they bear no marks of seals.

and that the tallage was levied without their consent. Further, John Hoke and other officers appointed by the lieutenant used false measures and paid nothing for carriage to Naas. They rejected, as unclean, grain in which peas were mixed and demanded other grain instead of it.

3. They say that at the Parliament at Dublin [22 April 1370], James de la Hide, knight, and John Fitz John of Delvin, knights elected for the county, were coerced by the lieutenant, by counsel of the archbishop etc., *ut supra*, to grant one mark from each carucate of cultivated land in the county. They had promised when they had been elected at Trim to refuse their consent to any subsidy or tallage, because of the losses of the faithful commons in the Irish wars.

4. They say that at the Parliament at Kilkenny [7 January 1371], Simon Cusak, knight, and John Rothwelle, elected knights for the county and pledged not to consent to any subsidy, consented to a tax of 6*d*. on every pound of goods in the county. The lieutenant, with the counsel of the archbishop etc., *ut supra*, had asked the prelates, magnates, and commons assembled in Parliament to grant him £3,000; though the knights from Meath resisted for two or three days, at length they consented to the above tax, as part of the levy of £3,000. They do not know if the knights consented by coercion or not, but the tax was levied *contra voluntatem communitatis comitatus*.

5. They say that when George Telyng was indicted and put in prison for divers felonies he gave his manor of Cremartyn to his brother Thomas to procure for him *cartam pacis domini regis generalem*. Before the lieutenant and others of his Council, Thomas offered to make a fine of 100 marks with the king for the charter. Before the charter was granted, George, through Thomas, on 23 May 1370 paid 50 marks to the lieutenant, 10 marks to James Pickering (then Chief Justice of the pleas following the lieutenant and the principal person *de secreto consilio ipsius locum tenentis*), and 100*s*. to Edmund Laurence. These sums were paid in addition to the fine made with the king.

6. They say that John Justice was indicted for certain felonies, tried before the lieutenant at Trim, found guilty and sentenced to be hanged. James Pickering, Chief Justice, took 10 marks from Justice, through certain of his friends whose names are unknown, and deferred the execution from Friday,

15 March 1370, until the Wednesday following [20 March]. In the interval Pickering procured from the lieutenant a general pardon for Justice on payment of a fine of £20; they do not know if this were for the king or for the lieutenant. They say that Justice paid Edmund Laurence, who was of the lieutenant's secret council, 100*s*. for his assistance.

As testimony to the above, the jurors set their seals to this inquisition.

II. *Meath County.*

Inquisition[1] taken at Drogheda, as above, on 20 May 1373, by the following:

Robert Cadell. Reginald de la Felde. Richard Mann. Robert Saresfeld. William Hamelyn. Nicholas Dodenham. John Herdeman. John Prout. William de la Pull. George Telyng. Richard Moure. Thomas Kent.

1. As above, I, cap. 1.

2. As above, I, cap. 2, with the additions that the grain from the baronies of Slane and Margalyn [Morgallion] was brought to Drogheda.

3. As above, I, cap. 3. It is stated that the knights yielded to coercion because they saw that the knights elected for Louth, Roger Gernoun and Richard [Vernoun], had been imprisoned for refusing to agree to a subsidy.

4. As above, I, cap. 4.

5. As above, I, cap. 5, in a shortened form. [George Telyng was one of the jurors.]

6. They say that by the assent of the lieutenant, in the octave of the Trinity [1-8 June 1371], a Parliament was held at Ballyduagh. In that place there were no buildings nor provision for hospitality. The lieutenant demanded a subsidy of £2,000 from the prelates, magnates, and commons. Though the commons refused to agree for two or three days, at length *de mora sua ibidem ex causis predictis tedio effectus*, they consented. Since the commons of Meath were unable to bear this burden, their share being £500, they sent Stephen Gray as their messenger to seek a remedy from the king and council in England.

7. They say that at the Parliament at Kilkenny [14 January 1372], John Prout, elected for the county, was forced by coer-

[1] This document is badly rubbed and illegible on the outside margin.

cion to seal a letter to the king, stating that the subsidies and tallages levied by the lieutenant had been granted *de mera et spontanea voluntate*.

8. They say that when James Pickering was appointed to hold pleas at Trim [18 March 1370], he took for his own use from John Drak 10 marks in return for a charter exempting him from taking up knighthood against his will.

9. As above, I, cap. 6.

10. They say that John Northampton, deputy of Henry Covyntre, then Marshall, during the sessions of the lieutenant's court at Trim, on 13 March 1370, took 10 marks from John Huse, knight, by duress of prison. He also took by the same means 20 cows from Adam de la Mare and from divers other persons he extorted money during the same session.

As testimony to the above the jurors set their seals to this inquisition.

III. *Meath County*.

Inquisition taken at Drogheda, as above, on 9 June 1373, by the following:

Francis Wyot. John Gellons. Adam Panteney. Adam White de Dinshaghlyn [Dunshaughlin]. Adam Callan. James Whiteacre. John Boys. Adam Fulpot. Thomas Waffre. Richard Daundey. Walter Galmole. Adam Bron de Ryngereston.

1. The jurors say on oath that at the Parliament of Dublin [30 July 1369], William of Windsor, the lieutenant, with the counsel of Thomas, archbishop of Dublin, Stephen, bishop of Meath and Treasurer, James Pickering, knight, Edmund Laurence, and John Duket, imposed certain customs on the commons and merchants of Ireland. On each last of herrings he imposed 3*s*.; on each 100 of great fish 12*d*.; on each 100 of lesser fish 6*d*.; on each *dolium* of salmon 4*s*.; on each pipe of salmon 2*s*.; on each *dolium* of wine 6*s*. 8*d*.; on each pipe of wine 3*s*. 4*d*.; on each *weia* of corn 6*s*. 8*d*.; on each *weia* of malt, beans, peas, barley, wheat, and *hastivell*[1] 5*s*.; on each *weia* of salt 6*s*. 8*d*.; on every pound of other merchandise 6*d*. These customs were levied on goods exported from all the harbours of Ireland 'contra assensum et voluntatem communium et mercatorum terre predicte'.

[1] *Hastivell* appears to mean any early crop.

2. As above, I, cap. 1.[1]

3. As above, I, cap. 2, though different prices are given—4*s*. 6*d*. for a crannock of corn and 3*s*. for a crannock of hay, when the market price was 6*s*. 8*d*. and 5*s*.

4. As above, I, cap. 3. (Shortened.)

5. As above, I, cap. 4. (Shortened.)

6. As above, I, cap. 5. It is stated that the crime for which George Telyng was indicted was the murder of Walter Telyng, captain of his nation. Before Windsor came to Ireland as lieutenant he had been charged by the Council in England to refuse a charter of pardon to George. The lieutenant took 50 marks from George on 18 March 1370; Pickering received £20 and Laurence 20 marks for their help in procuring the charter.

7. As above, II, cap. 6. (Shortened.) The amount of the £2,000 subsidy assessed on the county of Meath was £660.

8. As above, I, cap. 6. The court sat at Trim on 18 March 1370.

As testimony to the above, the jurors set their seals to this inquisition.

IV. *Drogheda in Louth.*

Inquisition taken at Drogheda on the side of Louth, as above, on 31 May 1373, by the following:

William Roth. John Fulpot. William Hobbesoun. Thomas Asshe. John Jordan. Henry Gernoun. Walter Lymford. Robert Dover. John Frombold. Nicholas FitzHugh. Henry Simond. Adam Simond.

1. As above, III, cap. 1.[2] The jurors also stated that Walter Myles was elected by the mayor and community of Drogheda on the side of Louth to go to this Parliament. Roger Leonys was appointed *custumarius* in Drogheda and John White was his *contrarotulator*, and they collected the new customs from 8 August 1369 until 2 February 1371. During this time Leonys took 16*s*. on 4 *dolia* of fish exported by John Walsh, 6*s*. 8*d*. from Robert Forest, 30*s*. from Roger Heyn, and divers sums of money from other merchants exporting goods.

[1] In this and in the three following articles John Duket is named among the counsellors of the lieutenant.

[2] An additional charge of 6*d*. on each pound of the flesh of oxen, pigs, and sheep is mentioned.

2. They say that John Fulpot and Walter Milys were *electi milites pro communitate ville de Drogheda ex parte Uriel* to attend the Parliament at Dublin (15 April 1370). The lieutenant demanded a subsidy from their town, which they refused because of the heavy burden of the new customs. Whereupon the lieutenant by royal writs commanded the mayor, seneschal, and bailiffs of Drogheda *ex utraque parte aque* to come to him in person together with 12 of the better burgesses on 20 May 1370. When they had come he refused to allow them to leave the city until they had paid him £40. They paid 40*s*. to James Pickering, who was of his secret council, for his assistance, and later they paid £40 to Simon Charweltone and Roger Leonys, whom the lieutenant had appointed to receive it.

3. They say that the lieutenant sent letters to Robert Babe, Richard Mole, William Roth, John Frombold, and others of the town demanding either that they should lend him £200 or else, under penalty of full forfeiture, should come to him in person, together with 30 men-at-arms, to serve for three months with his retinue in the district about Adare. Because for various reasons they did not obey, the lieutenant by royal writ ordered the mayor and six burgesses from Drogheda in Louth to come to him at Kilkenny on 3 May 1371. When John Frombold, the mayor, with Robert Dover, Nicholas FitzHugh, Thomas Skynner, Robert Forster, Adam Maule, and Adam FitzSimond came to Kilkenny, the lieutenant asked why they had disobeyed the writ ordering them to go to Adare; he forbade them to leave the town without his special licence, notwithstanding their answer that no such writ had come to them. Therefore, considering the inconvenience to them of a long stay in Kilkenny, the mayor and burgesses agreed against their will to pay the lieutenant £100 for the community of Drogheda *ex utraque parte aque*. Frombold, the mayor of Drogheda in Louth, paid into the Exchequer at Carlow £50 for himself and the town, which was taken by extortion.

4. They say that at the Parliament of Kilkenny [7 January 1371] the lieutenant asked for a subsidy of £3,000 from the commons of the land; of this subsidy the mayor and community of Drogheda in Louth, against their assent and will, paid £42 1*s*. 9*d*. Roger Leonys and Robert Loghteburgh collected it from them.

5. As above, II, cap. 6, omitting the reference to Gray's message. The jurors stated that Adam FitzSymond and other persons representing the mayor, seneschal, and community of Drogheda *ex utraque parte aque* refused to agree to the subsidy, whereupon the lieutenant forbade them to go away from Ballyduagh. They and others elected by the cities, boroughs, towns, and counties, considering that Ballyduagh was *locum vastatum* and worn out by their tedious sojourn there, at length agreed to grant the subsidy.

6. They say that the mayor, Frombold, was summoned by writ to appear before the Treasurer and Barons of the Exchequer on 13 October 1371, to render account of divers debts and to pay 100 marks which the writ supposed had been granted by the mayor and community at Kilkenny, though that grant had been made under coercion and by extortion. When Frombold came to the Exchequer he was arrested for payment of £50 out of the said 100 marks. The mayor pleaded in defence that the king, by *supersedeas* sent from England, had ordered the lieutenant to stay the levy of the subsidy imposed upon Drogheda. Though the lieutenant received this writ at Limerick on 20 October 1371, he kept the mayor under arrest until he paid £50 into the Exchequer, by extortion and against the king's command.

7. They say that on 4 February 1370 the lieutenant sent a writ to Richard Mole, Thomas Asshe, Henry Gernone, Roger Heyn, and others of Drogheda, commanding them to be in their own persons at Limerick by the following Easter and to dwell in that city. Another writ was sent to John Duket (a member of Windsor's household) and to the mayor and seneschal of Drogheda ordering the arrest of the above-named should they refuse to go to Limerick. Asshe made a fine of 20 marks for his release from the command; Richard Mole in like manner made a fine of £20, of which he paid £10, etc.

8. They say that two ships laden with salt touched at Dalkey on 6 May 1370, and John Frombold, Henry Rath, Henry Asshewell, and Robert Sextoun, merchants of Drogheda, bought the cargo. At the command of the lieutenant, James Pickering seized the ships and the salt. Afterwards the lieutenant took the salt for his own use, selling it again, against the will and to the heavy loss of the merchants who first bought it.

9. They say that Robert Dover and Thomas Asshe, merchants of Drogheda, on 29 October 1369, freighted with hides in the port of Drogheda a ship belonging to Walter Stamen to bring them to the king's staple. By command of the lieutenant, and for his use, Robert Leonys and Robert Thorpe arrested the ship; they loaded it and another vessel which belonged to the lieutenant with 60 lasts of his hides, upon which no custom duty was paid. This was done to the prejudice of the king and to the heavy loss of Dover and Asshe.

10. They say that John Leonys, deputy of the Admiral Roger Leonys, on 1 July 1370, took from John Walsh and Thomas Jordan one mark for himself for his leave to carry 4 *dolia* of fish from the port of Drogheda to England; and he took 20*s*. from William Staffetone, ship master, for leave to carry overseas in his ship more than 20 *runilotes*, taking for each runlet 2*s*. by extortion.

As testimony to the above, the jurors set their seals to this inquisition.

V. *Drogheda in Meath.*

Inquisition taken at Drogheda on the side of Meath, as above, on 1 June 1373, by the following:

John Asshewell. John Dowe. Simon Owre. Henry Russell. William Symkok. Richard Spes. Ralph Drewer. Ralph Beynagh. Simon Tirry. Thomas Rath. John Dleyn. Michael Rodypak.

1. As above, III, cap. 1.[1] They say also that John Leonys, deputy for Roger Leonys, was appointed by the lieutenant to collect the customs in Drogheda and other neighbouring ports. He took from Richard Malyn 3*s*. for one last of herrings exported, from Simon Owre 5*s*. 6*d*. for 11 pounds of linen cloth, faldings, and fur, and divers other sums from other merchants. They say that foreign merchants, by reason of the customs aforesaid, have altogether given up (*totaliter retraxerunt*) coming to Ireland as they were wont to come, to the great impoverishment of the land.

2. They say that the lieutenant issued writs ordering the seneschal and bailiffs of Drogheda to compel, by distraint of

[1] Brother Thomas de Burley, prior of the hospital of the order of St. John of Jerusalem, Ireland, is mentioned as an additional adviser.

their lands and goods, Thomas Rath, senior, and Richard Rath, clerk, to be at Limerick by Easter, 1371, to dwell there. Wherefore Thomas and Richard went to Kilkenny to treat with the lieutenant for his grace. They were told that the lieutenant had threatened to imprison them if they should come before him and so from fear they crossed to England. There they remained, not daring to return for a long time, at a cost to each of them of £13.

3. They say that at the Parliament of Dublin [6 August 1369] the lieutenant imposed on the burgesses of Drogheda *ex utraque parte aque* £20, without their assent and against their will; by his command they paid James Pickering of Trim 100*s.* by extortion.

4. They say that at the Parliament of Dublin [25 April 1370] John Asshewell, seneschal of Drogheda in Meath, and John Stamen, burgess, were arrested and kept in detention until they agreed under coercion to grant 20 marks from the community of the town. Afterwards Roger Leonys was appointed to receive the money, but whether it was for the lieutenant himself or for the king they do not know.

5. They say that at the Parliament of Kilkenny [7 January 1371] the lieutenant imposed on the burgesses of Drogheda in Meath a tallage of 6*d.* on every pound of goods, without their assent and against their will. Roger Leonys was appointed to collect it, and he took £7 and more, etc., by extortion, etc.[1]

6. They say that John Asshewell, seneschal of Drogheda in Meath, was summoned by writ to come before the lieutenant at Naas on 29 July 1370. There he was compelled to grant in the name of the town five archers to go in the retinue of the lieutenant to Limerick. The archers were dispatched and, after some service with the retinue, they were sent back again. Then on 3 March 1371 the lieutenant caused Simony Tyrry and Richard Spes, burgesses, to be arrested at Kilkenny, because the archers had not been provided. They protested that the archers had been duly dispatched and had served in the lieutenant's retinue. Notwithstanding this defence, they were detained under arrest until they made a fine for themselves and for the community of 25 marks, in part payment of 100 marks

[1] Cf. I, cap. 4.

which the lieutenant imposed on Drogheda *ex utraque parte aque* for the reason aforesaid.

7. They say that when two ships laden with salt touched Dalkey on 1 May 1371, merchants from the ship came to Drogheda and sold the whole cargo to John Stamen, John White, and other merchants of the town at 4*s*. 9*d*. for each crannock. The lieutenant, by the counsel of James Pickering, arrested the ships and would not suffer the merchants to bring their salt from the harbour unless they paid 6*d*. on every pound as a tallage or custom. Whereupon the merchants, at the instigation of Pickering, sold the salt to the lieutenant at the price of 4*s*. 6*d*. for each crannock. They say that the lieutenant caused the salt to be brought to Dublin and there it was offered for sale by his officers.

As testimony to the above, the jurors set their seals to this inquisition.

VI. *The city of Dublin.*[1]

Inquisition taken at Dublin, as above, on 13 June 1373, by the following:

Robert Walsh. Roger Gyffard. Godfrey Leycestre. John Hyncley. Maurice Yonge. Richard Badelond. Simon Neill. John Cornwalshe. Robert FitzLeonys. Wolfrand Drover. William Orchard. William Drandewod.

1. The jurors say on oath that on 10 July 1369 the lieutenant, by counsel taken at Dublin with Thomas, archbishop of Dublin, Stephen, bishop of Meath, James Pickering, knight, Edmund Laurence, William de Carlhell, clerk, and John Duket, caused the mayor and community of Dublin to maintain 6 men-at-arms and 18 archers at Tassagard [Saggard] for three weeks at their own expense, against their will and by extortion, etc.

2. As above, III, cap. 1.[2] They say also that on 1 October 1369 the lieutenant took from John Taillour 6*d*. on each pound

[1] This document is rubbed on the outside margin, and the outside bottom corner is torn and partly illegible.

[2] As in IV, cap. 1, an additional charge of 6*d*. on each pound of the flesh of oxen, pigs, and sheep is mentioned; also, here alone, a like charge on the skins of horses, deer, and farm beasts, and on *pilfell*, linen and woollen cloth, faldings, and all other merchandise. Cf. articles of accusation, cap. 8 and note.

of faldings and levied the said customs on merchandise going from Dublin both to other parts of Ireland and elsewhere.

3. They say that the lieutenant, at a certain Council held in Dublin on 7 January 1370, by the advice of the archbishop, etc., *ut supra*, imposed [a tallage of] £40 on the mayor and community and levied it by extortion, etc.

4. They say that by the advice of the archbishop, etc., *ut supra*, the lieutenant at the Parliament of Kilkenny on 22 April 1370 imposed [a tallage of] 100 marks on the mayor and community, which was levied against their will and by extortion.

5. They say that at the Parliament of Kilkenny [7 January 1371] the lieutenant, by the advice of the archbishop, etc., *ut supra*, imposed on the king's faithful subjects [a tallage of] £3,000; towards this the community of Dublin were compelled to pay 6*d*. on every pound of their goods, against their will and by extortion.

6. They say that on 24 September 1370 the lieutenant, on the advice of the archbishop, etc., *ut supra*, sent letters to John Taillour, David Tyrell, and other citizens commanding them either to lend him 50 marks or else to come themselves with 60 armed men to join his retinue at Adare for three months, at their own expense and on penalty of forfeiture of life and limb. Some of those to whom the letters were sent were abroad (*extra patriam*), others were dead, others dying, and others insufficient [for the burden]. The lieutenant, therefore, on 25 February 1371 summoned the mayor and bailiffs of the city to come with 12 of the better citizens to him at Kilkenny on 3 March. On this day John Passevaunt, then mayor of the city, with William Tyrell, [John?] Bokeford, Roger Falyagh, Hugh Callan, Maurice Yong, Stephen Flemyng, Robert Piers, John Elys, William Blakeney, Roger Giffard, Thomas Foill, and John Hull came to Kilkenny and were examined as to why they had not obeyed the said letters. Notwithstanding that they maintained that no writ nor other letters had been sent to the mayor and 12 citizens or to the community, they were forbidden to leave Kilkenny without the lieutenant's special licence; there they were forced to remain until they made a fine with him of 100 marks.

7. They say that at the Parliament of Ballyduagh [7 June 1371] the lieutenant, on the advice of the archbishop, etc. (*ut*

supra, except James Pickering), imposed £2,000 on the king's faithful subjects, the share of the mayor and community of Dublin being £134 4*s*.

8. They say that the lieutenant, on the advice of the archbishop, etc., *ut supra*,[1] on 3 February 1371 sent writs to 8 citizens—Edmund Serle, Nicholas Seriantz, William Seriaunt, John Foill, Richard Chaumberleyn, John Bokelond, Godfrey Gallan, and Walter Passavant, senior, commanding them to be at Limerick by Easter and to dwell there. These citizens had no tenements or goods in the city and county of Limerick, which is a hundred leagues and more from Dublin. When they understood the lieutenant's malicious intent, they went to him at Cashel on the vigil of Palm Sunday [29 March] and there made fines as follows: Serle £20, paid at once; Nicholas Seriantz 20 marks, which he did not pay; William Seriaunt 20 marks, of which he paid 100*s*.; Foill 20 marks [which he did not pay?]; Chaumberleyn £20, which he did not pay; and Bokeland 20 marks, which he did not pay. Gallan and Passavant [remained there and ?] made no fine.

9. They say that, though it is ordained by statute that no one should disturb a free election, William de Carlhell, clerk, on 29 April 1370 gave the lieutenant 100 marks to disturb and arrest the free election of Alexander Balscot to the See of Ossory. Balscot was in Dublin on his way to the Roman Curia to pursue his election, and he was delayed in his journey for the week following.

10. They say that the lieutenant, on the advice of the archbishop, etc., *ut supra*, between 5 February 1369[2] and ——— 1372, arrested the wine and salt brought both by foreign merchants coming to the city ——— and in ships. By this means he forced them to sell their merchandise to him. [In this way], on —— after Pentecost, 1370, he seized one *dolium* of wine from John Wydoun, from Roger Mar———, from William de Drandewod 2 *dolia* of wine, from John de Beke 6 *dolia* of wine, from William Seriaunt 2 *dolia* of wine, and other merchandise from divers other citizens. After 1 May 1370, he arrested at Dublin

[1] William Skipwith, knight, is added to the list of councillors: cf. above, IV, cap. 1.

[2] According to the articles of accusation, cap. 2, Windsor did not come to Ireland until 22 June 1369. Probably the date should be *1370*.

two ships from Brittany laden with salt. 800 crannocks of the salt [were bought by other merchants?], but the lieutenant kept the ships in arrest until the cargo was sold to him *ad voluntatem suam*. Afterwards, like a merchant, he [sold] the salt in Dublin ———— and sold the wine in taverns [*tabernavit*]. This wine and much more he sold and retailed [*vendidit et tabernavit*] in the city at 12*d*. a flagon [*lagena*]; and no other merchant dared. . . .[1]

11. They say that the lieutenant, by the ordinance and procurement of James Pickering, knight, William de Carlhell, clerk and Baron of the Exchequer, and Simon de Charwelton, clerk of the Remembrancer [of the Exchequer] at Dublin, on 21 March 1370 unjustly arrested John Scroup and imprisoned him in Dublin Castle to remain there until he made a fine of 500 marks to the lieutenant. He paid 100 marks and gave James Pickering 10 marks and a silver cup worth 40*s*., but was detained in prison until he died, burdened by forfeiture and by duress.

As testimony to the above, the jurors set their seals to this inquisition.

IV. Calendar of Documents relating to the Summons of the Commons of Ireland to England, 16 February 1376

[Parliamentary and Council Proceedings, Chancery, 47–50 Edward III, Roll 3, nos. 1–13]

In the Calendar the documents are divided as follows: A, the returns to the writs of summons throughout Ireland, and B, documents relating to the elections in the county court of Dublin.

A. *The returns to the writs of summons throughout Ireland* (*nos*. 9–13).

The returns are preceded by a short narrative describing the refusal of the Parliament of Kilkenny (6 October 1375) to grant an aid to the king. Whereupon Nicholas Dagworth showed a commission from Edward III commanding that two proctors from each diocese, two knights from each county, and two citizens or burgesses from each city or borough should come to England to consult with the king and council about the govern-

[1] This article is badly damaged, and the ends of the lines are illegible.

ment of Ireland and about an aid for the king. Writs were issued by William of Windsor ordering the election of representatives, with sufficient power to act for themselves and their communities, to go to England 'ad tractandum, consulendum et concordandum nobiscum tam super gubernacione dicte terre, quam super auxilio et sustentatione guerre nostre'. The writs bear the date of Kilkenny, 25 October 1375; returns were to be sent in by 25 November; the representatives were to be with the king on or about 16 February 1376.

Returns of the archbishops and bishops.

1. The archbishop of Armagh.

The clergy of his diocese reply that they are not bound to send proctors to England, yet, out of reverence for the king and on account of the urgency of the business, they elect as proctors John Cusack and William FitzAdam. They save all their rights and liberties and do not grant to their proctors any power to agree to a subsidy from the clergy.

2. The keepers of the spiritualities of the archbishop of Dublin, William de Gayles, canon of St. Patrick's, Dublin, and John FitzElys, archdeacon of Glendalough.

John FitzElys and Thomas Athelard, vicar of Donabate, elected proctors, with full powers. Dated Dublin, 12 November 1375.

3. The archbishop of Cashel.

The clergy have elected John Giffard, canon of the monastery of Osserry and rector of Kiltewenan [Kiltenan?] with power to act for them as the writ requires. They cannot afford to send two proctors.

4. The archbishop of Tuam.

No return.

5. The Bishop of Meath.

The clergy of Meath granted an aid to the king in the Parliament of Kilkenny and have sent 100 marks to the king and council in England by Nicholas Dagworth. They are not bound to send proctors to England, yet, out of reverence for the king and saving their liberties, they have elected master Bartholemew Dullard, rector of St. Mary's, Drogheda.

6. The bishop of Kildare.

The clergy have elected as proctors William White, dean of

the cathedral of Kildare, and Richard White, rector of Donaghda [Donadea], without power to agree to any subsidy. The Prior of Kilmainham refused to attend the convocation of the clergy, though the greater part of the churches of the diocese are impropriated to him.

7. The bishop of Leighlin.

The clergy unanimously refuse to elect proctors by reason of the poverty of the diocese, only 14 carucates of land being 'extra manus Hibernicorum inimicorum'.

8. The bishop of Ossory.

Proctors: Alexander, bishop of Ossory, and John de Acres, clerk.

9. The bishop of Lismore and Waterford.

Proctors: Thomas, bishop of Waterford and Lismore, and master Philip Raye, clerk. They are elected saving the liberties of the clergy and without power to grant any subsidy.

10. The bishop of Ferns.

The clergy, saving their liberties, have elected master William de St. John, dean of Ferns, and Richard Whittey, clerk.

11. The bishop of Limerick.

Proctors: master John Fox and John Route, clerk.

12. The bishop of Emly.

The clergy are too poor to send proctors; they authorize the proctors for the clergy of Lismore to act for them.

13. The bishop of Cork.

Proctors: master Thomas Rys and master John White, clerks and canons of the cathedral of Cork.

14. The bishop of Cloyne.

Proctors: Thomas, prior of Ville Pontis [Bridgetown] and John Sandy, chaplain. They shall act with the other proctors of the province of Cashel as the writ requires.

15. The bishop of Kerry [Ardfert].

Proctors: master Gilbert O'Conylle and John FitzJohn, canons of the cathedral of Ardfert.

Returns of sheriffs and seneschals.

1. The sheriff of Dublin (Reginald Talbot) (see below, pp. 237 seqq., nos. 1, 2).

2. The sheriff of Louth.

The magnates and commons of the county declared, *una voce*, that they were not bound to send any one to Parliaments and Councils in England, yet, out of reverence for the king and saving their privileges and liberties, they have elected Roger Gernoun and Richard Verdoun. They have granted to them no power to agree to a subsidy.

3. The sheriff of Kildare.

John Rocheforde and Peter Rowe have been elected, with the same protests and reservations as in Louth.

4. The sheriff of Carlow.

The commons of the county unanimously refused to send any one to England, by reason of their poverty, only 14 carucates of land being 'in manibus ligeorum domini regis'. Their inability was explained to the Governor and to Dagworth in the Parliament of Kilkenny by Godfrey de Valle and Philip de Valle, knights representing the county.

5. The sheriff of Waterford.

Richard Botiller and David Cogan elected, saving the liberties of Ireland.

6. The sheriff of Wexford.

Richard Whittey and William de St. John elected.

7. The sheriff of Limerick.

Henry Berclay and Thomas Kildare elected.

8. The sheriff of Cork.

Richard de Wynchedoun and Philip, son of Robert White, elected, with a pledge to pay their expenses.

9. The seneschal of the liberty of Meath and the sheriff of the crosslands there.

William de Londoun, knight, and Richard Plunket elected, without power to agree to any subsidy.

10. The seneschal of the liberty of Kilkenny and the sheriff of the crosslands there.

Alexander, bishop of Ossory, and Godfrey Forstall elected, without power to agree to any subsidy. Because they had not given full powers to the persons elected and because laymen and not ecclesiastics were required by the writ, the Governor and Council ordered that another election should be held. Instead of the bishop, Walter, son of William Coterelle of Kenlys, was elected. No additional powers were granted.

11. The seneschal of the liberty of Tipperary and the sheriff of the crosslands there.

William Neghbore (?) and William Yong elected, saving the liberties of Ireland.

12. The seneschal of the liberty of Kerry and the sheriff of the crosslands there.

Gilbert FitzWalter and Thomas FitzDaniell of Rathlaici elected.

Returns of mayors and sovereigns.

1. The mayor and bailiffs of Dublin.

The citizens and commons declared, *una voce*, that they were not bound to send any one to Parliaments and Councils in England, yet, out of reverence for the king and saving their privileges and liberties, they have elected John Blakhorn and John White. They have granted to them no power to agree to a subsidy.

2. The mayor, seneschal, and bailiffs of Drogheda (*ex utraque parte aque*).

William White and Nicholas Starkey elected on the same terms as in the city of Dublin.

3. The mayor and bailiffs of Waterford.

William Shaundhull (?) and Godfrey Forstall[1] elected as above.

4. The mayor and bailiffs of Limerick.

Henry Bercley[2] and Thomas Kildare[2] elected.

5. The mayor and bailiffs of Cork.

William Dalton and John Droupe elected.

6. The sovereign and reeve (*superior et prepositus*) of Kilkenny.

Robert Flode and John Ledrede elected.

7. The sovereign and bailiffs of Ross.

William Rykyll and William Seymor elected.

8. The sovereign and bailiffs of Wexford.

James Freynsshe and Laurence Broun elected.

9. The sovereign and bailiffs of Youghal.

Bernard Baret and Richard Cristofre elected.

Note at the end of the returns:

Et quia prefato Gubernatori et Custodi ac Consilio Hibernie predicto videbatur maius autenticum esse ad negotia predicta versus dominum regem et dictum consilium suum in Anglia

[1] Also elected by the liberty of Kilkenny.

[2] Also elected for the county of Limerick.

sub magno sigillo dicti domini regis in Hibernia quam aliquo alio modo transmittendum, de avisamento et ordinacione dictorum Gubernatoris et Custodis et Consilii regis in Hibernia, magnum sigillum domini regis in Hibernia predictum presentibus in premissorum testimonium est appositum. Datum apud Cassell XX die Marcii anno regis Edwardi tercii post conquestum regni sue Anglie quinquagesimo et Francie tricesimo septimo [20 March 1376].

B. *Documents relating to the elections in the county court of Dublin, 1375–6.*

1. Writ to the sheriff of Dublin ordering the election of two lay persons with full powers to represent the county in England. Dated at Kilkenny, 25 October 1375.[1]

2. Return of the sheriff.[1]

Nicholas Houth and Richard White have been elected by the magnates and commons of the county, without power to agree to a subsidy.

3. (No. 8.) Petition addressed to the Governor, Chancellor, and others of the Council by many sufficient persons of the county of Dublin. The petition is badly stained and is almost illegible. It bears the wax of twenty-eight seals and the tags for four others. The document is evidently a protest against the election of Houth and White on the grounds that they 'sount cosines germaynes et de une assente'; the petitioners wish to substitute William FitzWilliam for Richard White. The Governor made use of the petition to order a new election (cf. 8 below).

4. (No. 3.) Writ to the sheriff of Dublin ordering a new election to be held in the presence of Thomas Scurlag, abbot of the house of St. Thomas the Martyr, Dublin, and Robert Preston, Chief Justice de Banco. The persons to be elected shall be given full powers and their names shall be returned to the Chancery by 7 January (1376). Should the magnates and commons refuse to make a proper election, the sheriff shall distrain the lands and goods of each of them of 100 shillings and shall have them in the Chancery on 7 January. He shall act speedily and make a return of the names of the magnates and commons with this

[1] Documents 1 and 2 are included in the general returns of writs (nos. 9–13 on the roll). The numbers of the other documents are given in brackets.

writ. Tested by William of Windsor, Governor and Keeper, at Clonmel, 29 November 1375.[1]

5. (No. 7.) Writ to Thomas Scurlag and Robert Preston, as above. They are ordered to be present at the election to inform the magnates and commons of their duty, and to make returns to the Chancery of the names of the persons elected, and whether they were chosen by common assent or by a majority. Dated at Clonmel, 1 December 1375. *Per ipsum Gubernatorem et Consilium.*

6. (No. 3.) Return of Reginald Talbot, sheriff of Dublin, to the writ of 29 November.[2] He had assembled the magnates and commons of the county on 13 November to elect two persons in accordance with the writ of 25 October. They were unable to agree, and he summoned a second meeting on 17 November. Again no agreement was reached, and a third assembly was held on 18 November, when, in the presence of Nicholas Dagworth, envoy of the king, it was proclaimed that all free holders of the county should come to Dublin on the following day (19 November). On that day many of the better sort (*de melioribus*) came; others who were absent were amerced. Those of the better sort elected Nicholas Houth and Richard Whyte in the presence of Dagworth.

Then, in obedience to the second writ, the sheriff summoned the magnates and commons to come to Dublin on 22 December to make a new election in the presence of Scurlag and Preston. With one voice they declared that they were not bound to send any one to Parliaments and Councils in England, yet, out of reverence for the king and on account of the urgent necessities of the land, the majority of the better sort elected Houth and Whyte. They would not concede to them power to agree to any subsidy, and stipulated that the election should not be prejudicial to the rights and liberties of Ireland.

7. (No. 6.) Return of Scurlag and Preston to the writ dated 1 December. On 22 December they addressed the magnates and commons of Dublin on the necessity of making a proper election, but they were unable to persuade them to be of one accord. In the presence of Scurlag, Preston, and the sheriff, brother William Youglon (the proctor for the abbot of St.

[1] Reproduced and printed in *Facsimiles of National MSS. of Ireland*, iii, Pl. XIX and text.

[2] Printed in *Facsimiles*, loc. cit.

Mary's, Dublin), the prior of Holmpatrick, Robert Holywod, knight, and others (whose names are on the schedule annexed) elected Nicholas Houth and William FitzWilliam. They would not grant them power to agree to any subsidy. Also, on the same day, before Scurlag, Preston, and the sheriff, the prior of Holy Trinity, Dublin, Nicholas Houth, John Fynglas and others (whose names are on the schedule annexed) elected Nicholas Houth and Richard White of Kyllestyr [Killester], without power, as above. Further, Thomas Mawreward and John FitzRery elected Richard White and William FitzWilliam, without power, as above. In no other way would the said magnates and commons agree to make elections.

8. (No. 5.) Schedule with the names of the forty-four electors of Nicholas Houth and William FitzWilliam:[1]

William Youglon, procurator abbatis beati Marie.
Prior de Holmpatrick.
Robertus Holywod.
Nicholas Cowlok.
Willelmus White de Borondistone.
Patricius Carmardyn.
Johannes Walsche.
Ricardus Milys.
Michael Darcy.
Ricardus Tyrrelle.
Willelmus FitzWilliam.
Nicholas Snyterby.
Nicholas Lympt.
Reginaldus Bernevalle.
Johannes Beg.
Johannes Belynges de Belynges.
Hugo Byrmyngham.
Willelmus Boltham.
Reginaldus Blakebourne.
Robertus Cadell.
Ricardus Bernard.
Radulphus Prodom.
Thomas Stauntone.
Henricus Michelle.
Willelmus FitzEustace.
Willelmus Rodiard.
Johannes Gerveys.
Johannes Haselbery.
Ricardus Glandhary.
Robertus Kysshok.
Walterus Rath.
Johannes FitzWilliam.
Rogerus Belynges de Rogerestoun.
Hugo FitzWilliam.
Rogerus Tyrell.
Johannes Belynges de Balyloghe.
Thomas Tyiell.
Robertus Gale.
Ricardus Venerous.
Johannes Kedy.
Ricardus Forneys.
Johannes Bristow.
Reginaldus Lovelle.
Robertus Bernevalle.

[1] Many of these names occur on the petition for a new election, 3, above, p. 237.

9. (No. 4.) Schedule with the names of the twenty electors of Nicholas Houth and Richard White:[1]

Prior Sancte Trinitatis, Dublin.
Nicholas Houthe.
Johannes Fynglas.
Ricardus White de Kyllestyr.
Ricardus Cruys de Kylsalghan.
Johannes Cruys.
Laurencius Wodeloke.
Ricardus FitzRoberti Cruys.
Willelmus Seriaunt.
Robertus Geffrey.
Nicholas White.
Johannes Tryveus.
Thomas Botyller.
Robertus Wellys.
Johannes Houthe.
Thomas Houthe.
Johannes Talbot de Mayn.
Ricardus Talbot.
Ricardus Netervyll.
Ricardus Cruys, junior.

10. (No. 1.) Writ from William of Windsor to Scurlag and Preston, reciting the return made by Scurlag above, and ordering that Nicholas Houth and William FitzWilliam, whom the majority had elected, should be sent to England with sufficient powers. Scurlag and Preston are commanded to summon the magnates and commons, and to demand that they shall give Houth and FitzWilliam 'potestatem sufficientem ac racionabiles sumptus pro eorum expensis'. All who offer resistance either to the election of Houth and FitzWilliam or to the concession of powers shall be amerced. A return shall be made to the Chancery by 16 February. Dated at Kilkenny, 22 January 1376. *Per Consilium.*

11. (No. 2.) The return of Scurlag to the above writ. On 14 February 1376 Scurlag and the sheriff met the electors of Houth and FitzWilliam[2] and many other magnates and commons, and informed them of the orders contained in the writ. The supporters of Houth and FitzWilliam refused to grant them power to agree to any subsidy, tallage, or other burdens, since they were reduced to great poverty by the slayings and oppressions of English malefactors and Irish enemies; they agreed to grant 80 marks for the expenses of their representatives. But the other party (*alia pars*) of the magnates and commons, the Prior of Holy Trinity and the rest, presented a document called 'le respounce dez communes suditz queux ount esluz Nicholl

[1] Reproduced in *Facsimiles*, loc. cit., Plate XIX a.

[2] The names of Will. Youglon, John Belynges of Belyngs, John Belynges of Balylogh and Hugh Bermyngham are omitted.

Houthe et Richard White', in which they styled themselves 'la greyndre partie dez communes gavellers du dit countee', declared that they would pay for the expenses of their representatives, and refused to bear any share in the expenses of FitzWilliam. Scurlag informed them that they would be amerced for these expenses, but he left the enforcement of the amercements to the discretion of the Governor and Council. In the presence of the magnates and commons, he delivered the king's writ of summons to Houth and FitzWilliam, and they protested that they were ready to go to England, to do what pertained to them there, as soon as they were paid their reasonable expenses.

12. (Nos. 9–13.) In the general returns of the writ all the preceding matter is briefly summarized, with this conclusion: 'Et pro eo quod dicti magnates et communes in discensione et altercacione, ut predicitur, perseverant, ne negocia regia in hac parte expediendum propter huius singularem discencionem sive altercacionem diucius retardentur, tam litere et brevia predicta quam retorna eorumdem modis quibus fuerint, de avisamento dictorum Gubernatoris et Consilii, coram domino rege in Anglia transmittantur.'

VII

THE ORIGIN OF IMPEACHMENT[1]

THE word *empeschement* originally meant a hindrance or an embarrassment and it acquired its special legal significance very slowly. Its vogue as a technical or semi-technical term seems to have begun in the reign of Edward II. The pardon granted to the Marchers in 1321 declared that they were not to be 'impeached, aggrieved, or molested' for felonies or trespasses committed in the attack on the Despensers.[2] Another pardon, granted to the men of Chester in 1324, promised that they should not be *empeschez* for acts done on the king's service in 1322.[3] This is the first appearance of the word on the Parliament Roll and it already bears the technical meaning of an accusation in a court of law.[4] Under Edward III it was used frequently, sometimes in the technical sense and sometimes with the original meaning of a hindrance or an annoyance. It is clear that the two meanings were at first closely allied; the more technical use as accusation carried with it an idea of malice and it was employed only by persons *empeschez*, as a term of complaint or abuse. That it was not deemed equivalent to a normal accusation in a court of law is shown by a complaint, made in the Parliament of 1362, that men were being *empeschez*, arrested, and imprisoned without indictment or other legal process.[5] It had not then a neutral and technical sense as a term for a particular kind of procedure. One of the earliest examples of such a use occurs in 1376, on the roll of the Good Parliament,[6] yet, in spite of the official sanction of the roll, we may

[1] This essay is reprinted, with the kind permission of the editor, Professor Powicke, from *Oxford Essays in Medieval History presented to H. E. Salter*.

[2] *Cal. Cl. Rolls, 1321*, p. 495.

[3] *Rot. Parl.* i. 438.

[4] Cf. *acculpavit* in the Segrave case, 1304, ibid. i. 172.

[5] *Rot. Parl.* ii. 270.

[6] Ibid. ii. 321–60 passim.

suspect that the neutral meaning was not contemporary and that impeachment, as a term descriptive of a particular kind of parliamentary procedure, came in, like Whig or Tory, as a catchword of partisan abuse. From 1376 onwards, though the word retained other meanings and implications, it is possible to isolate a special use to describe a criminal accusation brought forward in Parliament by the Commons, acting as a whole. To inquire into the origin of impeachment, defined in this way, is the purpose of this essay.

That the impeachments of 1376 were a daring novelty the detailed records on the Parliament Roll and the long narratives in two chronicles[1] leave no doubt. The Commons, through their Speaker, laid before Parliament a series of charges against eight or nine[2] persons, all in some way concerned in the king's business. It is impossible to examine in detail the whole course of proceedings in Parliament. The charges themselves require thorough investigation before it can be determined how much the drafters were moved by political venom rather than by zeal for honest government. Much in the procedure remains obscure. What part of the trials was held in Parliament is by no means certain[3] and the exact share of the Commons in the prosecution remains undefined.[4] We know, however, that after an inquiry, held partly in Parliament and partly in the Council, judgement was given by the Lords, at least in Latimer's case, *en plein Parlement*, against all who had been accused. The legality of the proceedings was challenged in later Parliaments

[1] *Chronicon Angliae*, Rolls Series, pp. 68–87 and *Anonimalle Chronicle*, ed. V. H. Galbraith, pp. 79–92.

[2] It is doubtful whether Alice Perrers was accused in the same way as the others.

[3] The Commons, for example, heard Latimer's answer, but he made his defence *si bien en plein Parlement come autrement devaunt les prelatz et seigneurs soulement* (*Rot. Parl.* ii. 326). It seems that the trials were held partly before the Council.

[4] William Elys was examined by the Commons in the Chapter-house, ibid. ii. 327.

and certain sentences were reversed.[1] Ten years later (1386) the procedure of the Good Parliament was revived again in the charges brought by the Commons 'together and of one accord' against Michael de la Pole;[2] the same procedure was followed in 1388.[3] In scarcely more than a decade impeachment had become a recognized part of parliamentary practice and a recognized form for the expression of hostility to royal officials and servants. How this form was adopted, and why for a time the whole procedure was regarded as irregular, can be understood only by a review of legal ideas and practice in the reign of Edward III.

Apart from grants of supply, law-making was the chief business of the frequent Parliaments of Edward III. How strong was the demand for legislation may be seen in the long lists of common petitions and in the numerous statutes entered on the rolls during the period 1327 to 1377. It has been pointed out that the demand of the Commons for written answers to their petitions led to the 'series of repetitive and ill-digested statutes which are characteristic of the reign'.[4] Pressure, either political or fiscal, drove the king and his advisers into hurried and even contradictory legislation; assent was given to petitions without sufficient scrutiny of their merits or examination of their relation to laws already enacted. For this reason the hugger-mugger jumble of Edward III's statutes became a rich quarry for seventeenth-century lawyers opposed to the Crown, and Coke was able to speak gratefully of the reign as 'a most happy time'.[5] The immediate result was equally important. An array of statutes and precedents was assembled, drafted, or accepted, in accordance with popular demand; by the end of the reign the king, his ministers, and Parliament

[1] *Infra*, pp. 182–3. [2] *Rot. Parl.* iii. 216. [3] Ibid. iii. 238 seqq.

[4] G. Sayles and H. G. Richardson, 'Parliaments of Edward III', *Bulletin of the Institute of Historical Research*, ix (June 1931), 12–13.

[5] *Journals of the Commons*, i. 531.

itself were so confined by an encirclement of prohibitions that almost any new policy of action was bound to take an illegal and violent form. Two distinct and ultimately inconsistent tendencies may be traced, each having its origin in suspicion of the Crown. On the one hand the rights at common law of all the king's subjects were defined by a series of statutes in such a way as to limit the jurisdiction of Council and Parliament and to infringe upon the discretionary power of the monarch; on the other, a steadily increasing demand for satisfaction of wrongs done by the king's servants led to recognition of means of redress which were in fact proceedings against the Crown, outside the sphere of common law. No one clearly understood that the conservation of ancient forms was, in fact, incompatible with the demand for an honest and efficient administration. To understand the *impasse* reached in 1376 it is necessary to consider briefly the pull of these tendencies against each other.

Magna Carta was the main defence against encroachments on the rights of subjects at common law. It was probably more prominent in Parliament under Edward III than in the reign of any other king; again and again it was confirmed, cited in statutes, and made the subject of petitions. The famous thirty-ninth chapter, which protected the free man from arbitrary punishment, was paraphrased, glossed, and affirmed in such a way as to leave no doubt as to its meaning. Every subject, *nul homme de quel estate ou condicion il soit*,[1] was entitled to a civil or criminal trial, by indictment or presentment of neighbours, or by process made by original writ at common law. Only the more outstanding statutes of the series need be recalled. In 1331 the principle was affirmed which later legislation merely reiterated or

[1] 28 Ed. III, c. 3. Vinogradoff compares this phrase with the use of *homme* without the limiting adjective (*libre*) in the similar statute of 1331 and comments, 'the omission . . . is not likely to have been accidental' (*Magna Carta Commemoration Essays*, p. 82).

amplified. 'No man from henceforth shall be attached by any accusation, nor forejudged of life or limb, nor his lands, tenements, goods nor chattels seised into the king's hand, against the form of the Great Charter and the law of the land.'[1] Among the statutes of 1341, which the king afterwards revoked, two explicitly claimed for peers of the realm, clerks, and other free men the protection of chapter thirty-nine and ordained that those who broke Magna Carta and other statutes or laws should answer for it in Parliament.[2] In 1351 the first of a group of statutes against petitions or suggestions to the king and Council was passed; it asserted the right of persons accused to trial by the procedure of common law and secured the same protection for all freehold property.[3] A statute of 1368 was more exact in detail: 'no man be put to answer without presentment before justices, or matter of record, or by due process and writ original, according to the old law of the land; and if anything from henceforth be done to the contrary, it shall be void in the law and holden for error'.[4] At the same time it was also enacted that 'the Great Charter and the Charter of the Forest be holden and kept in all points, and if any statute be made to the contrary, that shall be holden for none'.[5]

The purpose of thus exalting Magna Carta was plainly to defend common law jurisdiction and procedure from the less formal, quicker, and more efficient action of Council and of Parliament. Stubbs assigned to the year 1351 the beginning of the movement against the jurisdiction of the Council,[6] though to understand the significance of the later statutes it is necessary to look back at least as far as the fall of Mortimer. In 1330 the reaction began against the ugly sequence of reprisals and counter-

[1] 5 Ed. III, c. 9.

[2] 15 Ed. III, I, cc. 2 and 3.

[3] 25 Ed. III, V, c. 4. Cf. 37 Ed. III, c. 18, and 38 Ed. III, c. 9.

[4] 42 Ed. III, c. 3. Cf. 28 Ed. III, c. 3.

[5] 42 Ed. III. c. 1.

[6] *Constitutional History*, ii. 637.

reprisals which had followed the death of Gaveston. It was recognized that summary trials and judicial murders lacked the permanent sanction necessary for public order. The most remarkable outcome of the new attitude was the attempt to define treason by the statute of 1352, and it was probably the result of direct pressure by the heirs of those who had suffered under the general charge of 'accroaching the royal power'.[1] The first sign of change may be seen in the rider attached to the sentences on Mortimer and his accomplices when the magnates declared for a return to normal procedure: in future the peers should not be bound or charged to give judgement on those who were not peers, which was contrary to the law of the land.[2] The principle is the same as that asserted in the statute of 1331 and it was clearly intended, not as a self-denying ordinance, but as a declaration of the right, secured by Magna Carta, that each man should be tried by his peers. In spite of this significant declaration, the strong accord between king and magnates might have neutralized the movement back to Magna Carta and the common law, if it had not been for the crisis of 1340–1 and the vigorous action of Archbishop Stratford.

The crisis was the result of the second tendency, working for administrative efficiency, but, paradoxically, it was provoked by Edward III himself. His need of money, as Tout has shown,[3] led him to embark on the policy of 'thorough', set out in the Walton Ordinances[4] (July 1338). The Ordinances gave a new unity to the great departments of State and, chiefly through privy seal warrants, brought them under 'the severe executive control' of the king and his personal advisers. At the same time an attempt was made to establish public

[1] See my paper on 'Forfeitures and Treason in 1388' (*Proceedings of the Royal Historical Society*, 1931) for a discussion of the origin of the statute of treason [*supra*, pp. 115–45]. [2] *Rot. Parl.* ii. 54.

[3] *Chapters in Administrative History*, iii. 66. [4] Ibid., pp. 143–50.

responsibility for local officials by provision for their popular election.[1] The governing motive behind the Ordinances was increase of revenue, and the new co-ordination of departments was coupled with drastic changes in fiscal policy. All exemptions from customs, tallages, tenths, fifteenths, and other taxes were cancelled and both respite of debts and payment by instalments were forbidden.[2] The threat of a new efficiency and the challenge to vested interests roused hostility on all sides; even before the Ordinances were enforced, the Council at Northampton (26 July 1338) complained that *estallementz* of royal debts could not be suspended without the consent of Parliament.[3] As it became clear that the campaigns abroad were failing for lack of funds, an explosion of some kind was inevitable. On the one hand the ordinary tax-payers obstinately opposed all attempts to increase the revenue or even to expedite its collection; they had support from the magnates and from those officials who were alarmed by the curialist monopoly of control. On the other, the king's wrath against dilatory or dishonest servants was mounting fast and he was in no mood to observe legal forms in pursuit of those who thwarted his plans. He was too impatient and, perhaps, too much under the influence of foreign allies[4] to understand that in England the argument of necessity and an imposed efficiency stood second to the financial interests of his subjects and to their rights at common law.

The use of *droit administratif*, in a form which would

[1] *Chapters in Administrative History*, iii. 71; cf. Ordinance 2. Mr. J. G. Edwards has pointed out to me that, according to the wording of the ordinances, the intention was that the shires and towns should 'answer at their peril' for the officials elected by them. This is not 'public responsibility *of* local officials', as Tout suggests.

[2] Ibid., p. 147.

[3] D. Hughes, *Early Years of Edward III*, p. 241; Tout, op. cit. iii. 79, 92.

[4] In May 1339 William, Marquis of Jülich, Edward's brother-in-law, had been appointed 'priue et tres especial souuerain secretaire de nostre conseill et de toutz nos bosoignes qui nous touchent, tant par dela mer comme par decha' and in 1340 he was made Earl of Cambridge and *parem regni*, Tout, op. cit., pp. 99–101, 137.

coerce officials rather than protect them, followed logically from the design of a strong executive, as outlined in the Walton Ordinances. As early as 1339 the Council in England advised Edward to appoint commissioners for every port and every county, who would have power to arrest careless and disobedient sheriffs and to report on them to the Council.[1] In the autumn of 1340 a special Council had been summoned 'for the punishment of false ministers'; sheriffs, mayors, bailiffs, and representative men of the chief ports, collectors of customs, and sixteen eminent merchants were ordered to appear before it.[2] This inquiry was apparently never held, but the intention behind it helps to explain how the king himself precipitated the crisis by his violent onslaught on those whom he blamed for failure to remit supplies. After the humiliating treaty of Esplechin (25 September 1340), he suddenly returned to London (29 November), bent on vengeance for the 'anguish and peril' into which lack of money had plunged him. In his anger he struck out in all directions. The Chancellor and Treasurer were dismissed. About twenty prominent persons were thrown into prison; the list included the Chief Justice and four other judges, four chancery clerks, and three leading merchants.[3] Special animus was shown towards ecclesiastical ministers, as the king probably hoped to stir up the laity against them. Archbishop Stratford, who in 1339 had been *dux regis et eius concilarius principalis*,[4] took sanctuary with his monks. He was first cited to answer for the king's debts and later, when he put himself forward as leader of the opposition, he was denounced

[1] Answers of the Council to various points suggested by the king, 26 July 1339, cc. 5 and 7 (J. F. Baldwin, *The King's Council*, Appendix I, p. 479).

[2] Hughes, op. cit., p. 95, referring to *Cal. Cl. Rolls, 1339–41*, pp. 626–7, and *Rep. Dig. Peer.* iv. 527–8.

[3] *Cal. Pat. Rolls, 1340–3*, pp. 110–11; cf. Tout, op. cit. iii. 121–2; *French Chronicle of London*, pp. 85–6; G. Lapsley, 'Archbishop Stratford and the Parliamentary Crisis of 1341', *E.H.R.* xxx (1915), 9.

[4] *Historia Roffensis*, p. 375.

as a traitor.[1] All over England officials were dismissed. In the opening months of 1341 six escheators and twelve sheriffs were deprived of office and writs were sent out for the election of new coroners in every shire.[2] Elaborate preparations were made for inquiry and punishment. On 10 December sixteen separate commissions of trailbaston were issued to inquire into wrongs done by justices and other ministers of the king;[3] a special tribunal was set up (13 January) to try the judges and the merchants under arrest;[4] a general inquest was ordered into the activity of almost every official throughout the realm.

We may suppose that eyres on so large a scale and with the ultimate purpose of extorting revenue must have caused widespread alarm and thus destroyed any chance the king had of securing popular support.[5] In this way the country was prepared for the great political agitation in Parliament (April 1341), when the constitutional principles which guided the rest of the reign were formulated. At first it was not obvious either how far Edward III had gone directly against the law or what line political agitation was to follow. The king's right to dismiss and to appoint ministers at his pleasure could not be explicitly denied. Eyres of trailbaston had been authorized by the statute of Northampton (1328),[6] as Parliament virtually admitted afterwards.[7] There were, however, technical grounds upon which the king might be challenged. The arrest and detention of clerks ran counter to *privilegium fori*; summary arrest of free men, without presentment of neighbours and formal indictment, was illegal; special tribunals set up to try prelates

[1] Hughes, op. cit., p. 125; Lapsley, op. cit., p. 14.

[2] *Cal. Cl. Rolls, 1339–41*, p. 607.

[3] *Cal. Pat. Rolls*, op. cit., pp. 111–13.

[4] Ibid., pp. 110–11.

[5] At first the attack on the clergy was probably popular. Cf. Lapsley, op. cit., pp. 9, 198; *French Chronicle*, p. 86.

[6] 2 Ed. III, c. 2.

[7] The Londoners were able to challenge the commission on the ground that it was contrary to the franchise of the city. *Cal. Letter Book F*, pp. 59–60; *Cal. Plea and Memoranda Rolls, 1323–64*, pp. 133–4.

or lay magnates deprived them of their right to judgement by peers. All these technicalities might be comprehended in Magna Carta, an advantage that was almost at once understood by Archbishop Stratford.

If Stratford had been no more than a turbulent prelate, who saw himself as another Becket, he would certainly have gone no farther than the first clause of the charter. *Ecclesia libera sit* covered the whole range of wrongs done to himself and his order; by maintaining benefit of clergy he could secure immunity for himself, his kinsmen, and the other clerks detained in prison. No doubt he saw that to isolate the injuries of ecclesiastics would merely fan the fire of anticlericalism which Edward III sought to kindle. By taking his stand on the Charter as a whole he was able to state the whole issue in a popular form and to hurl back the thunderbolts of excommunication as a counterblast to royal authority.

It must be granted that victory lay altogether with the archbishop.[1] When Parliament met in April 1341, public attention, held by Stratford's series of able letters and pronouncements, had altogether turned away from administrative reform or the misdeeds of dismissed officials. The petitions of magnates and commons alike were grounded upon the archbishop's manifestoes; Magna Carta must be maintained at all points and the rights of subjects at common law must be secured.[2] To these demands the king's necessity forced him to give a grudging assent. Though he soon revoked the statutes as 'contrary to English law and the royal prerogative',[3] much of the ground thus lost was recovered in the next few years. The famous statutes of Treason and *Pro Clero*, passed in 1352, covered two major issues raised in 1341 and the long succession of Acts already referred to re-

[1] The importance of Stratford's action has been questioned by Mr. Wilkinson, *E.H.R.* xlvi (1931), 177 seqq. Cf. Stubbs, ii. 408.

[2] *Rot. Parl.* ii. 128–30.

[3] Revocation of 15 Ed. III, Stat. I, *Statutes of the Realm*, i. 297.

iterated the right of subjects to be tried 'by due process of law'. Thus the general principle was maintained that, apart from benefit of clergy and the privilege of peerage, which were not further defined, criminal jurisdiction was vested exclusively in the courts of common law.

Events soon showed that the exceptions were not adequate and that neither the king nor his subjects were prepared to act consistently upon the principle laid down. Both were drawn in the opposite direction by the second tendency towards administrative reform. The procedure of the courts was, in fact, too clumsy and too deeply embedded in the ritual of a more barbarous age to serve all the growing needs of a highly organized society. As common law recognized no essential distinction between a criminal trial and private litigation, the rules about arrest and the forms of accusation put the Crown at a disadvantage and offered many opportunities for obstruction. It was dangerous to arrest a suspect before he was indicted, as, if the case against him broke down, those who made the arrest could be sued for false imprisonment.[1] Normally, only those presented by a jury of neighbours or appealed by individuals were arrested; both for presentment and for appeal, the Crown was dependent upon local knowledge and goodwill. Rules about venue or the area of jurisdiction were so strict that, later, eighteen statutory exceptions were necessary. For the indictment, or written statement informing the king of the facts upon which the prosecution was based, 'formality, certainty, and verbal precision' were obligatory. These requisites were derived partly from the old rules about verbal accuracy in the appeal and partly from the learning and dialectical subtlety of lawyers trained in the more complicated procedure of civil cases. Every material fact must be stated finally and with certainty, and it was necessary to prove each averment as it was laid. Omission or variance in minute detail—

[1] Stephen, *History of Criminal Law*, i. 278–97.

as an error in a Christian name or the misspelling *murderavit* for *murdravit*—was fatal; like the 'broken' oath in Anglo-Saxon pleading, a technical slip in the indictment entitled the accused to acquittal. As Stephen says, 'the law relating to indictments was much as if some small proportion of the prisoners convicted had been allowed to toss up for their liberty'.

A procedure which seemed designed to give even the notorious local malefactor a fighting chance of life and liberty was ill suited to punish crimes which required special knowledge to detect. It was natural that both king and Parliament should grow impatient of a system which served to shelter offenders who were either highly placed or guilty of offences beyond the plain man's understanding. Characteristically, a remedy was sought, not in reform of existing conditions, but in drawing exceptional cases before special tribunals. Even in 1341, when the common lawyers seemed to hold the field, a statute was passed providing that offences against Magna Carta should be declared in Parliament and that offenders of any condition whatsoever should be judged by the peers in Parliament.[1] Thus Parliament made exception out of its statutes even more readily than contemporary judges[2] and, no doubt, with the same defence; neither authority nor precedent could be set against reason or natural justice.[3] At least in fact, it was an easy transition from reason to political expediency.

Here it is necessary to recall briefly the form taken by proceedings against the Crown in the fourteenth century. The Crown enjoyed the protection of the rule that

[1] *Rot. Parl.* ii. 132.

[2] Cf. T. F. T. Plucknett, *Statutes and their Interpretation in the first half of the Fourteenth Century*, pt. ii, chaps. iii and iv.

[3] 'Nulle ensaumple est si fort come resoun', Sharshulle, J., *Year Book, 18–19 Ed. III* (Rolls Ser.), pp. 376–7. Cf. ibid., pp. 378–9, for an interesting dialogue: 'R. Thorpe (pleader): You will do as others have done, otherwise we shall not know what the law is. Hill: Law is *volunte des Justices*. Stonor: *Nanyl—ley est resoun*'.

no writ ran against the king, or that he could not be sued in his own court, and it was therefore difficult to recover property from or to establish rights against him or his officers. The common law principle that officers of the Crown could be sued in the ordinary way was evolved only very slowly and its growth was due at least as much to the king's wish to secure efficient administration as to pressure from his subjects. He consented to a long series of statutes regulating the conduct of sheriffs, escheators, and purveyors, and he waived his privilege of protection from suit in allowing proceedings against them to be heard in the Court of Exchequer.[1] The courts of common law were already too far withdrawn from royal control to be entrusted with new business touching upon prerogative right. The development of the petition of right as a remedy against the Crown was mainly the work of the Chancellor.[2] Though issues which required the verdict of a jury were heard in the King's Bench, suits brought by means of the traverse or the monstrance of right went to Chancery.[3] The great ministers of State and the more intimate servants of the king remained under the direct protection of the prerogative, but they themselves were devising ways in which the Crown might provide remedies outside the common law. In the middle years of Edward III's reign the writs of *premunire* and *quibusdam certis de causis* were evolved to bring cases before the Chancellor and Council;[4] they contained no mention of the charges to be brought and compelled attendance by such threats as *sub periculo quod incumbet* or *sub gravi indignatione*. Though these develop-

[1] Ehrlich, *Proceedings against the Crown (1216–1377)*, pp. 28–9.

[2] Holdsworth, *History of English Law*, ix. 13 seq. Cf. Ehrlich, op. cit., pp. 168 seqq.

[3] Use of these technical legal instruments was facilitated by the statutes of 1360 and 1362, 34 Ed. III, c. 14, and 36 Ed. III, c. 13.

[4] Thus they showed the characteristics of the *sub pena* writ developed under Richard II. For a valuable discussion of these writs see Alice Beardwood, *Alien Merchants in England, 1350–77* (Cambridge, Mass., 1931), chap. vi.

ments were mainly on the civil side, they were, in fact, an encroachment upon the sphere of common law and they endangered that monopoly in criminal procedure which contemporary statutes were seeking to maintain.

Even a cursory examination of the cases brought before Council in the second half of Edward III's reign shows that indictment by jury of neighbours was not always essential in a criminal prosecution. From the end of the thirteenth century proceedings on 'suggestion' or 'information' are recorded,[1] and they become much more frequent under Edward III. Alien merchants laid criminal information by means of petitions to the Council;[2] officers of the Crown were accused of abuse of power either directly by private persons[3] or on suggestion made to the king;[4] individuals denounced each other for open violence or for flagrant breaches of the law.[5] Two examples will suffice to illustrate the procedure. In or about 1364 Richard Spinke of Norwich was tried before the king and Council on the charge, brought by John Rodeland, of procuring by false suggestion the release of four burgesses of Amiens, held in Dover Castle for ransom. After a long inquiry Spinke was acquitted and Rodeland was imprisoned under the statute of false accusers.[6] The case of *Brantingham and Piriton* v. *Chesterfield* throws a little more light upon procedure. Brantingham and Piriton were the two chamberlains of the exchequer and in 1364 they brought twenty-four charges against Chesterfield, the treasurer's clerk in the receipt. The roll on which the charges were drawn up was en-

[1] Pollock and Maitland, *History of English Law*, 2nd ed., ii. 658.

[2] e.g. *Rex* v. *Rouceby and Avenel*, 1355, and *Lombards* v. *Mercers*, 1359, *Select Cases before the King's Council*, pp. 37 seqq., 42 seqq. Cf. Beardwood, loc. cit.

[3] e.g. *Ughtred and others* v. *Musgrave, Sheriff of Yorkshire*, 1366, *Select Cases*, pp. 54 seqq.

[4] e.g. *Rex* v. *Middleton, escheator of Norfolk and Suffolk*, 1353, ibid., pp. 35 seqq.

[5] e.g. *Abbot and convent of Burton* v. *Meynell*, 1355, ibid., pp. 41 seqq.

[6] *Cal. Cl. Rolls, 1364–8*, p. 179. i. Cf. Selden, *Judicature of Parliament*, *Works*, 1726, iii. 1591–2.

trusted by the king to a strong committee of the Council, who after due deliberation declared Chesterfield to be innocent. The accusers agitated for a second inquiry, accusing the Council of 'fraud, favour, and wrong-doing'; they presented another roll of charges implicating another clerk in the treasury, Chesterfield's cousin. The case was then heard before the whole Council. The judgement of the committee was confirmed and the chamberlains were dismissed in disgrace.[1] Uneasiness roused by this form of conciliar jurisdiction is reflected in the frequent passing of statutes requiring accusers to find security that they would establish their suggestions in court[2] or by the more general acts upholding procedure by indictment.

The jurisdiction and procedure of the Council were closely involved in that of Parliament, though the difference in composition led to a different line of development. Whatever we may mean by 'Parliament' at an earlier date, by the reign of Edward III it was certainly a council of estates or orders representing the whole realm. Not all these estates inherited the full authority of the original Council; no doubt, as much for reasons of convenience as of prestige, the Commons, in fact if not in theory,[3] were excluded from the judicial functions of the magnates.[4] As soon as a judgement in Parliament began to gain political value, this exclusion reacted upon parlia-

[1] *Cal. Cl. Rolls, 1364–8*, pp. 124–5; Tout, *Chapters*, iii. 248–50.

[2] 37 Ed. III, c. 18.

[3] Cf. *Modus tenendi Parliamentum*, cap. 23, 'Omnes pares sunt judices et justiciarii'. In the *Modus*, *par* signifies any member of Parliament.

[4] Edward II was deposed by Parliament as a whole, through a committee of estates on which the Commons were represented (see my paper on 'Committees of Estates and the Deposition of Edward II' in *Historical Essays in Honour of James Tait* [now incorporated in *Medieval Representation and Consent* as Chapter IX]). In 1399, however, the Commons made a formal declaration that the judgements of Parliament belonged to the king and to the Lords and in no way to themselves. They were answered, on behalf of Henry IV, that they came to Parliament as *petitioners et demandours* and that the king and Lords always had and should have the right of judgement (*Rot. Parl.* iii. 427).

mentary procedure. It was the business of the Commons to grant supply and to present petitions; by means of the petition they were able to lay information or to make suggestions upon which the magnates could act with authority. If Lords and Commons were agreed upon a common policy,[1] a double advantage was secured; the right to withhold supply could be used to force a judgement on the Crown and, by division of function with the Commons, the Lords avoided the appearance of acting as judges in their own suit.[2] Though the advantage was inherent in the structure of Parliament, it was understood only by slow degrees.

The delay was due mainly to the popularity of the French war with the secular magnates. As long as Edward III was able to pursue a vigorous military policy there was little danger of a combination of estates against him. It was not until the war languished at the end of the reign that men like Percy, March, and Arundel found in domestic disorder the reason for disaster abroad and began to look for allies in a campaign for reform. In the meantime the Commons had greatly strengthened their position; they had not only maintained and increased their control over taxation, but on two occasions, at least, they had made use of the common petition to initiate criminal proceedings. In 1347 they had presented three general petitions against the extortions of certain farmers of the customs.[3] They gave no names, but the charges were so plainly directed against particular persons that two farmers, Wesenham and Chiryton, at once presented a counter-petition. They prayed for an inquiry by the Council, since they had heard that the Commons had made complaint of them by divers Bills in Parliament.[4] The endorsement

[1] Cf. the impeachment of de la Pole in 1386.

[2] Cf. the protest of the Despensers against their sentence in 1321.

[3] *Rot. Parl.* ii. 169, no. 38; 170–1, no. 49; 171–2, no. 58.

[4] Ibid., p. 173.

on one of the petitions ordered an inquiry to be held by certain wise men of the Council.[1] Thus a common petition, drafted in general terms, was used to lay information against particular persons and to bring about a particular inquiry, conducted *ex parte regis*.

The case of Sir John Lee, recorded on the Parliament Roll of 1368,[2] shows that by that time the Commons had gained the confidence necessary for a direct accusation. Lee was steward of the household. Complaint was made that he had caused persons to be unlawfully arrested and brought before the Council; that he had extended the jurisdiction of the household courts beyond the verge; and that he was the patron of an informer and professional champion who brought false appeals of felony. It was also alleged that he had wrongfully acquired certain wardships and manors for his own use. Before the statute of 1352 these charges would probably have ranked as treasons, under the general term of 'accroaching the royal power'.[3] The accusations were cast in the form of five petitions, one from William Latimer of Dorset and the others from an anonymous source, styled *petitions des plusours*. The charges were examined before the King, Lords, and certain of the Commons; at the request of the Lords, they were explained (*monstrez*) by Thorpe, Chief Justice of the Common Bench. On one charge, at least, Lee spoke in his own defence. His answers were deemed insufficient and he was sentenced, presumably by the Lords, to be imprisoned until he made fine and ransom at the king's pleasure. Though the details of the procedure are obscure, it seems clear that Lee was tried on information laid in parliamentary petitions and in the presence of certain of the Commons.

[1] *Rot. Parl.* ii. 171. Another of the common petitions was endorsed: *Soient les marchantz appellez en Parlement, et eient lour respons.*

[2] Ibid., pp. 297–8.

[3] e.g. Sir John Gerberge, 1348; for the assault of a private person on the king's highway he was indicted for usurping the royal power (Hale, *Hist. Plac. Coronae*, pp. 80–1).

The part played by Thorpe suggests that the trial was *ex parte regis* and that the Commons had no share in what we would now call the prosecution. On the other hand, the later and separate judgement given by the Council on Latimer's petition[1] may indicate that the attendance of some of the Commons was deemed necessary at the hearing of the other charges. It is not too much to conclude that the petition is beginning to take on the appearance of an indictment.

Thus by the end of Edward III's reign principle and precedent had developed in contrary directions. On the one hand a long series of statutes maintained Magna Carta and the principle that every subject was entitled to trial according to the forms of common law; on the other, owing mainly to the clumsy and archaic procedure of the ordinary courts, the practice of trying men without appeal or indictment by neighbours was developed by the Council and even by Parliament itself. The new practice was growing up less for the benefit of the Crown than for subjects, and it owed its strength to a steady resolution to punish the king's ministers for abuse of power. This resolution was formulated in a demand made by the Commons in 1371. They presented a petition complaining that the chief officers of state had too long been clerks, and, therefore, not *justiciables* at law, and they requested that laymen should be appointed in future.[2] The principle that the king's ministers must answer for their misdeeds in the king's courts is clearly implied, though the place and form of trial remained undetermined.

It remains to discover how procedure by petition, adopted in Lee's case (1368), was translated into the

[1] 'Et puis du comandement le roi fust le dit Johan fait venir . . . devant le grant conseil et autre foitz examinez sur les pointz de la petition le dit William Latymer. . . . Par quoi de l'avys du conseil, eu consideration as pointz de la petition, le dit William fust accorde et assentu par le dit conseil . . .' (*Rot. Parl.* ii. 298). For the petition of Wm. Latymer, see ibid., p. 297.

[2] *Rot. Parl.* ii. 304.

formal procedure by indictment, through the Speaker in the name of the Commons, which was followed in the Good Parliament (1376). The change could hardly come naturally, as the way was barred by the long series of statutes insisting upon trials at common law. These enactments were too recent and too popular to be openly repealed, and to turn public attention from them it was necessary to seek for a new formula of prosecution. Where this formula was found cannot be definitely established, but the facts seem to point to Ireland, at least plainly enough to suggest an hypothesis. Evidence recently published shows that a burning question in the seventies was the misgovernment of Ireland by William of Windsor, king's lieutenant, and the chief ministers under him.[1] From 1371 angry complaints from the Anglo-Irish had been coming to England and a series of investigations had been set on foot.[2] Windsor himself was hand-in-glove with the persons generally blamed for abuses in England, as his wife was Alice Perrers, the king's mistress. Through her influence he was able to stave off judgement for a time, but just before Parliament met he and his officials were summoned to England to answer for their conduct.[3] A number of Anglo-Irish were also summoned, and they brought with them a great roll of eighty-four charges against Windsor and the Irish Chancellor, the Treasurer, and two barons of the exchequer.[4] The roll of indictments was supported by

[1] See my paper on 'William of Windsor in Ireland, 1369–76', with an appendix of documents printed from P.R.O., Parliament and Council Proceedings, Chancery, 47–50 Ed. III, Rolls 2 and 3 (*Proceedings of the Royal Irish Academy*, 1932). (*Supra*, pp. 146 seqq.)

[2] Ibid., pp. 56–62, 113–23. (*Supra*, pp. 148-56, 220-32.)

[3] *Cal. Pat. Rolls*, pp. 244–5. The first summons was for Feb. 1376; it was repeated for 27 April 1376 (*Cal. Cl. Rolls*, p. 295).

[4] *Windsor Documents*, loc. cit., pp. 83–102. (*Supra*, pp. 184–206.) The roll is headed: 'Ceux sont les articles mise a conseil nostre seigneur le roy en Engleterre par Richard Deere et William Stapelyn touchantz les mischiefs, tortz et disceitez faitz en Ireland par les ministres nostre dit seigneur le roy, illeoqes examinez par le court et par ceux qe sont venuz pur monstrer et

a long series of detailed charges presented to judges by special juries in Dublin and Drogheda (1373).[1] All this Irish business must have come up for consideration in Parliament or in the Council at an early stage of the session and, even before Parliament met, at least two important persons had full knowledge of the Irish accusations. The English Treasurer, Ashton, was one of the judges to whom the juries had made their presentments in 1373; he had been recalled from Ireland through Windsor's influence and was probably his enemy. More significant, probably, was the connexion with March, as he was not only one of the leaders of the opposition among the Lords, but also was closely connected with the Commons through de la Mare, their Speaker, who was his steward. The Anglo-Irish were most anxious to have him as king's lieutenant,[2] and it was probably through his influence that Windsor and the other officials had been summoned to Westminster. The suggestion, therefore, is that the Irish roll of accusations provided the model for the indictments put forward by the Commons in the Good Parliament.

If the hypothesis of an Irish model be accepted, it explains, not only the change in form, but also why no attention was paid to the statutes which guaranteed trial by due process of law. The English impeachments, or some of them, were probably presented in a great roll, like that brought from Ireland and perhaps directly copied from it.[3] The Irish accusations, as the title of

declarer les tortz, mischiefs et desceitez faitez, esteantz en la dite terre et iurrez sur lour serement de dire la verite selonc lour conissance.' Deere and Stapelyn were paid £10 for their trouble on 30 May 1376 (Devon, *Issues*, p. 199).

[1] Calendared in *Windsor Documents*, pp. 113–23. (*Supra*, pp. 220–32.)

[2] *Windsor Documents*, p. 99. (*Supra*, p. 203.)

[3] This is inferred from the last request of the Commons in 1376: 'Et sur ce mesmes les communes y baillerent avant en Parlement une grande rolle, ou une grande cedule, et une autre bille annexez a mesme le rolle, contenant entour XLI articles . . .' (*Rot. Parl.* ii. 360). The numeration of the roll (ibid., p. 329) suggests that ten sections of the original draft are missing.

the roll states, were based upon evidence drawn from presentments by juries and, therefore, it might be said, the forms of law had been preserved. It is true that two Irish officials, Holywood and Carlill, argued before the English Council that the charges brought against them were contrary to the statute of 1368,[1] and divers others, but the answer to this plea, which is not extant, may well have been a reference to the juries of Dublin and Drogheda.

The Irish officials were tried before the Council in July or August 1376,[2] and they may have borrowed part of their defence from the English who had been impeached in Parliament. It is, however, more probable that in the Good Parliament little opportunity was given for reasonable legal argument; as Gaunt said a few months later, the proceedings were carried through *en la chaluere de iour et saunz bone foye*.[3] Latimer alone seems to have challenged the whole procedure. He not only asserted his right to trial by peers,[4] but also put forward a claim to answer only those charges which were brought against him by particular persons.[5] The second protest shows that he fully understood the importance of the

[1] 42 Ed. III, c. 3. The protest ran: 'par estatut fait lan nostre seignur le roy qore est XLII, et autres diverses estatutz, ordinee est qe nul homme par accusement serra mys a respondre devant le conseil nostre dit seigneur le roy naillours sanz presentement devant justicz, ou chose de recorde, ou due processe et brief original, et, si riens soit fait a lencontre, qil soit voide en leye et tenuz pur errour . . .' (*Windsor Documents*, pp. 102, 108–9). (*Supra*, pp. 207, 215.)

[2] Ibid., p. 63. (*Supra*, p. 157.)

[3] *Anonimalle Chronicle*, p. 99. Gaunt was speaking of Latimer's trial.

[4] 'Qe salve a luy quan que doit estre salvez a luy come a un des pierres del roialme, tant en juggement doner come autrement en temps a venir . . .' (*Rot. Parl.* ii. 325; cf. ibid., p. 372).

[5] '. . . volents ent durra sa responce a celley qi en especial luy vorra surmettre aucune des choses avant dites. Et puis apres, partant qe nulle especiale persone vorroit apertement accuser le dit seigneur de mesmes les choses en Parlement, einz qe les communes vorroient maintenir les ditz accusementz en commune, le dit seigneur de Latymere, en excusation de sa persone et declaration de sa fame, dist . . .' (ibid. ii. 325). My thanks are due to Mr. J. G. Edwards for drawing my attention to the significance of this passage.

change from petition to indictment by the Commons. In offering to answer charges brought by individuals, he sought to reduce the indictment of the Commons to the level of private accusations brought before the Council.[1] Had he succeeded, his enemies would have run the risk of punishment under the statutes against false accusers[2] and the venue of the trial would probably have passed altogether from Parliament. When his plea was overridden, the common-law rights of subjects, jealously secured by statute, were openly set aside by Parliament in favour of a totally new procedure.

The other accused persons seem to have reserved their legal arguments until the following Parliament (January 1377). Then the Speaker demanded redress for those who had been impeached without due process of law, sentenced to certain penalties, and foreclosed from the common liberty which every loyal subject ought to have and to enjoy.[3] In spite of this and other protests,[4] there was no official condemnation of the procedure followed in the Good Parliament. It is true that the Speaker, de

[1] Cf. the case of *Rodeland* v. *Spinke*, already cited, *supra*, p. 255.

[2] Cf. the demand made (July–Aug. 1376) by the Irish barons of the exchequer that their accusers should be forced to find surety, in accordance with the statutes. When the surety was found they began to answer the charges brought against them (*Windsor Documents*, pp. 102, 109). (*Supra*, pp. 207, 215.)

[3] 'Qe pur ce que plusours gentz, si bien hommes comme femmes, estoient impeschez a derrain Parlement, et sanz meins due proces y feussent juggiez a certaines paines, et forcloses de commune libertee dont chescun loial lige le roy doit user et enjoier . . .' (*Rot. Parl.* ii. 374). Particular claims were made at the same time for Alice Perrers, foreclosed from common liberty 'par meinz vrai suggestion et sanz due proces' and for others 'torcenousement et par grante malice empeche'.

[4] The only detailed challenge of the legality of the proceedings in Parliament was that made by Windsor on behalf of Alice Perrers at the Parliament of Gloucester (1378)—'Errors dans le jugement d'Alice Perrers.' The first argument was that, contrary to statute, she had been 'mis a respondre sanz brief original, presentement, ou chose de record' (*Rot. Parl.* iii. 41). Her case has special complications as the details of the process against her in 1376 are obscure, and she was also condemned in 1377 (ibid. ii. 329; iii. 12 seqq.). In 1384 the proceedings of 1377 were reversed (ibid. iii. 186).

la Mare, was imprisoned for contempt,[1] a term which may have covered the general charge of overriding statutes and the ordinary process of law,[2] but he was never brought to trial, and his election as Speaker in October 1377[3] perhaps indicates a tacit acceptance of his line of action. Edward III's illness and death, the perils of the French war, and the need for a coalition of parties had combined to set political expediency above the law of the land.

Though the details of these first impeachments are uncertain,[4] and though the immediate Irish origin remains no more than an hypothesis, the main work of the Good Parliament is clear enough. In the face of Latimer's protests, Parliament had maintained the right of the Commons, as a body, to present an indictment. Perhaps they had been roused to action by a sermon preached by Brunton of Rochester, which bears all the signs of a contemporary political address.[5] His text was *Factor operis hic beatus*[6] and the theme was an appeal to his audience to be *non . . . tantum locutores sed factores*.[7] Into a significant rhetorical question it is hardly fantastic to read a condemnation of the older procedure by petition—'How will it profit to discuss parliamentary procedure and to expose the deeds of transgressors unless afterwards due penalties are awarded. . . .?'[8] Whether

[1] The release of de la Mare was ordered on 20 June 1377, as the king, by the advice of the Council, had remitted his contempt (*Cal. Cl. Rolls*, p. 7).

[2] Before the statute of 1352 he might have been charged with treason.

[3] *Rot. Parl.* iii. 5.

[4] See *supra*, pp. 243–4.

[5] Quoted by G. R. Owst, *Literature and Pulpit in Medieval England*, pp. 579 seqq. from MS. Harley 3760.

[6] '. . . this man shall be blessed in his deed', St. James i. 25.

[7] 'Amore Christi, et ob defensionem regni, in tanto discrimine constituti non simus tantum locutores sed factores . . . et ad istam finem sit omnis sermo, ut discant auditores quomodo bene debeant operari, et juxta bona opera premiari. . . .'

[8] 'Sed quid proderit puncta parliamenti tractare et facta transgressorum publice declarare, nisi post declarationem sequitur penalis executio debita in hac parte, cum frustra sint jura nisi sint qui jura debite exequantur.'

the sermon was preached in provocation or in defence,[1] it served to mark and to justify the change from a policy of complaint to a policy of action. The Good Parliament broke through the encirclement of statutes and achieved the transition from procedure by petition, with all its implications of grace and favour, to procedure by indictment, which is an assertion of right. Impeachment was already more than 'a criminal proceeding initiated by the House of Commons against any person';[2] it was a prosecution in which the Commons, as a whole, took over the functions of the jury of presentment.

The distinction is clearly indicated in the parliamentary trials of the years 1377 to 1386. Spencer, bishop of Norwich, was 'impeached' in Parliament on four charges presented (*monstrez*) by the Chancellor,[3] at the prayer of the Commons.[4] Here the proceedings were begun by petition and they must be contrasted with the impeachment of de la Pole in 1386 when 'all the commons, together and of one accord came before the king, prelates, and lords in the hall of Parliament to complain grievously against Michael de la Pole, . . . late Chancellor of England and there present to accuse him *par demonstrance de bouche*'.[5] In his able defence de la Pole did not challenge the legality of the procedure, but the distinction between it and proceedings on petition was underlined in one of the questions put to the judges in 1387. They were asked 'whether the lords and commons are able, *absque voluntate*

[1] The date of the sermon cannot be fixed precisely. Mr. Owst (op. cit., p. 579) suggests April 1376; Gasquet (*Old English Bible and Other Essays*, p. 64) hesitates in some confusion between a date during the session of the Good Parliament and one after the dissolution, at the time when William of Wykeham was in disgrace. The use of the future tense, as in the question quoted above, seems to indicate a call to action rather than justification after the event.

[2] Holdsworth, *History of English Law*, i. 379.

[3] 'Henry evesque de Norwiz estoit empeschez en ce Parlement de plusours choses, mais especialment de quatre articles a lui monstrez par le Chanceller d'Engleterre, en presence du roi mesmes et de monsieur de Lancastre en plein Parlement' (*Rot. Parl.* iii. 153).

[4] Ibid., pp. 152–3.

[5] Ibid., p. 216.

regis, to impeach (*impetere*) royal judges and officers for their offences in Parliament', and they replied that the Lords and Commons had no such right and that he who acted upon it should be punished as a traitor.[1] The question leaves no doubt that the significance of the change from petition to indictment was fully understood by Richard II and his advisers.

The later history of impeachment is not continuous. Henry IV was too feeble and Henry V too powerful to offer occasions for its employment. Though revived under Henry VI, the failure of Suffolk's trial[2] brought it into discredit and the savage alternative of attainder was accepted in its place. Under Yorkists and Tudors alike violent opposition to the Crown took the form of privy conspiracy and rebellion; a king strong enough to reign was strong enough either to protect his servants from Parliament or to punish them by its means. Impeachment was essentially a political weapon and it was not until the revival of political struggles in the seventeenth century that the practice of the earlier period was remembered.

There was not, as it is often implied,[3] a direct revival of impeachment in 1621. No one had been impeached since the break-down of Suffolk's trial in 1450;[4] the procedure was dead and forgotten, and the leaders of the attack on the king's servants were forced to rediscover for themselves essential parts of the medieval process. Their chief technical adviser was Coke, but at first his great legal knowledge served mainly to obscure the issue. His whole conception of the constitution was distorted by bitter prejudice and by the belief that the

[1] *Rot. Parl.* iii. 233. [2] Ibid. v. 176 seqq.

[3] For example, J. R. Tanner, *Constitutional Documents of the Reign of James I*, pp. 321–2.

[4] Stanley's case in 1459 can hardly be described as an impeachment. The Commons presented the king with a Bill in which they 'accused and impeached' Stanley of various charges. It was rejected by Henry VI (*le roi s'avisera*). His brother William Stanley was named in a general act of attainder. See *Rot. Parl.* v. 349 seq., 369–70.

forms and powers of Parliament were static and unalterable. In March 1621 he explained to the Commons that the judicature of Parliament was fourfold: '1. Coram domino rege et magnatibus; or rege et concilio: 2. coram magnatibus only: 3. coram magnatibus et communitate: 4. coram communitate.'[1] The cases he cited show that he did not understand the special character of procedure by impeachment.[2] Coke's extreme claim to rights of parliamentary jurisdiction helped to hurry the Commons into their rash judgement on Floyd, but even in the Lower House it did not pass unchallenged.[3] The normal view was probably that expressed by the Master of the Wards: 'Sorry, we [are] so uncertain in the power of this House. More puzzled this Parliament than ever before. Told, in the beginning of this Parliament, we [are] an absolute court: that, in some cases, we [are] to judge alone; in others, with the lords; in others, the lords alone.'[4]

It was in this state of confusion that proceedings were begun against Mompesson, Michell, and Bacon, and the confusion is reflected in the formal statements of the Commons. The delinquents were impeached at the *prayer* of the Commons or on their *complaint*;[5] the charges against them were forwarded by the Commons and supported by particular accusers who were liable to punishment for false suggestion.[6] In fact, as in Lee's

[1] *Journals of the House of Commons*, i. 545.

[2] Coke also cited the case of Sir John Lee (1368), 'punished by the lords, at the prayer of the commons' (ibid., p. 546).

[3] The king sent a message desiring them to examine precedents, with particular reference to that of 1 Henry IV, which was certainly the protest of the Commons in 1399 that they were not judges of Parliament, but petitioners (*Rot. Parl.* iii. 427). Coke argued that 'this record of 1 H. IV [is] but an ordinance, no statute', but Hackwill doubted whether a precedent could be found to support the claims of the Commons (ibid. i. 603–4).

[4] Ibid. i. 602.

[5] *State Trials*, ii. 1113, 1130–1, 1135. Cf. *Journals of the House of Commons*, i. 576.

[6] '. . . if not guilty, the commons desire that the accusers be punished' (*Journals of the Lords*, iii. 54).

case (1368), the Commons had done little more than to demand inquiry; though summoned to hear judgement, the whole conduct of the trial was outside their control.

By 1624 the Commons had gained more confidence, though the terminology of the records still indicates a certain timidity. The charge against Middlesex was *presented* by Coke and Sandys to the Lords;[1] though not the man but the articles of accusation were *presented*, the idea of indictment was becoming clear. This is suggested by the speech made by Coke to the Lords in which he described the Commons as 'inquisitors general of the grievances of the kingdom'.[2] Two years later (1626) the full procedure of impeachment was finally recovered in the heat of the attack on Buckingham. The debate in the Commons as to whether the House, like a grand jury, might accuse a man by common fame shows that the idea of a criminal indictment was at last plainly understood. A member argued that accusation, not calumniation, was allowed; 'the accusation in this House [is] proper. No subject, how great soever, but [is] questionable here, if he be grievous to the commonwealth.'[3] A message was sent to the Lords desiring a conference 'concerning the impeachment and accusation of a great peer of that House',[4] and afterwards it was formally declared that the Commons 'do accuse and impeach . . . Buckingham . . . of the said misdemeanours, misprisions, and crimes'.[5]

The proceedings against Buckingham were broken off by the king's dissolution of Parliament, but enough had been done to fix the process and to establish precedents.

[1] *Journals of the House of Commons*, i. 702.

[2] *Journals of the House of Lords*, iii. 307. Coke summed up with the words: 'this was the substance of this their crying complaint. . . . Their complaint is of a high lord, the lord treasurer . . .' (ibid., p. 309).

[3] *Journals of the House of Commons*, i. 847–8. Cf. Selden's citation of Suffolk's impeachment, with the remark: '. . . these cases are to be ruled by the law of Parliament, and not either by the common or civil law' (ibid., p. 848).

[4] Ibid., p. 857.

[5] *Journals of the House of Lords*, iii. 619.

In the *Judicature of Parliament*, published in 1640, Selden drew a distinction between procedure on impeachment and procedure on a general petition or complaint of the Commons.[1] At Strafford's trial the procedure of 1626 was followed and carried even farther than it had ever gone in the Middle Ages. As the Commons feared to entrust their secret evidence to the King's Council,[2] they claimed the right to conduct the prosecution; 'as we gave the charge,' it was said, 'so are we to mainteyn the charge'.[3] Strafford was accused before the Lords 'in the name of all the commons of England'; the trial was attended by a committee of the whole Lower House; the prosecution was conducted by the Speaker, Pym, supported by nine other accusers.[4] Though the Lord High Steward exercised an exclusive right of cross-examination,[5] the main conduct of the trial had finally ceased to be *ex parte regis* and had passed altogether under the control of the Commons.

Impeachment, as Selden said in 1626,[6] was ruled by the 'law of Parliament', a 'law' which might be defined as that part of parliamentary practice which was in general harmony with its own traditions and those of the common law. Though the 'law' had grown up under pressure of necessity, and though at one time or another it had run counter to the law of the courts, to the express injunctions of statutes or to the prerogative of the Crown, yet a sharp divergence from custom seldom had permanent results. What at first seems to be a mysterious selective purpose governing the growth of Parliament was, in fact, mainly common sense acting

[1] *Works*, ed. 1726, iii. 1591.

[2] 'For the prosecution, they had no mind to trust the King's Council; who neither knew their secret evidence, or, being informed, were like to apply and press it so vigorously as the business would require . . .' (Clarendon, *History of the Rebellion*, ed. Macray, i. 286).

[3] D'Ewes's *Journal*, ed. W. Notestein, p. 544. Cf. Baillie's *Journal*, i. 309: '. . . they shall manage the processe and witnesses as they find meet. . . .'

[4] *State Trials*, iii. 1414 seq.

[5] Baillie's *Journal*, p. 321.

[6] *Journals of the House of Commons*, i. 848.

upon strong traditions; this may be illustrated by a comparison of the first impeachments with the contemporary procedure of the appeal. In 1388 the Appellants boldly justified their attack on the king's servants by the claim that the high crimes contained in the appeal must be judged by the law and course of Parliament and that the other courts were no more than the executors of the ancient laws and customs of the realm and of the decrees of Parliament.[1] Their argument prevailed, the appeals were carried successfully to a conclusion, and within a dozen years the same procedure was twice used again.[2] None the less the appeal in Parliament was abolished by statute at the prayer of the Commons in 1399[3] and the only attempt to revive it was the disastrous 'impeachment' of the five members by Charles I. Impeachment, as we have seen, was another improvisation, devised in 1376 to satisfy the clamour of angry partisans, yet, unlike the appeal, it quickly hardened into a custom of the constitution. It survived, not only because its form was nicely adjusted to the distribution of function and power within Parliament itself, but because it could be shaped to fit the established legal habits of English society. By impeachment the principle of the ultimate responsibility of rulers to subjects was asserted: like all principles of action, it would have proved either purely destructive or sterile if it had not found expression through an institution fashioned by traditions of order and common life. Expression through Parliament was not enough. The appeal, though used with dramatic success in the Parliaments of 1388 and 1397, struck no roots; no more than a bastard slip of the court of chivalry, its form was alien both to Parliament and to the custom of common law. Impeachment had been provoked into being by the same violent demand for punishment, but it did not

[1] *Rot. Parl.* iii. 236. Cf. my paper on 'Forfeitures and Treason in 1388', loc. cit., pp. 83 seqq. (*supra*, pp. 134 seqq.), for a discussion of the appeal in Parliament.

[2] In 1397 and 1399.

[3] *Rot. Parl.* iii. 442.

depart from the main stock of constitutional practice. The links with procedure by petition and the close analogy to indictments at common law gave it a sort of protective colour which, within a few years, hid all appearance of revolutionary novelty. To devise a routine procedure for the trial of the king's ministers was perhaps the crowning achievement of Parliament in the fourteenth century. Impeachment was, in fact, a direct challenge to the royal prerogative, but, by discreet simulation of the 'ancient law of the land', a bridge was thrown up between normal usage and revolution. The ease with which it merged into the general body of parliamentary tradition helps to explain its remarkable vitality; that it lay in abeyance for nearly two centuries was due to circumstances rather than to inherent defects. In spite of a short and ill-recorded history, only a few half-understood precedents were necessary to guide the revival in the seventeenth century. It had grown naturally into the 'Law of Parliament' and its rebirth was a sign that, though the function of impeachment might seem to die, it could spring to life again at need as long as the forms of law and Parliament remained.

VIII

THE WILTON DIPTYCH[1]

IN 1929 the purchase of the Wilton Diptych for the National Gallery renewed and increased interest in this beautiful picture of the presentation of Richard II to the Virgin and Child, hitherto known to many only through the print issued by the Arundel Society. Various theories as to its date and meaning were put forward and discussed, but little evidence came to light which had not already been set out in the monograph of Scharf, published in 1882. Scharf used his collection of material more for illustration than for argument and he did not bring even all his own evidence under review when he reached the conclusion that the year 1381 was the date of the picture.[2] His method of inquiry was little suited to a problem where the evidence, though abundant, is indirect and circumstantial. No reference to the diptych in chronicles or records has yet been traced and all attempts to explain it must depend upon the interpretation of internal evidence in the light of contemporary events and relevant documents.

The natural starting-point for inquiry is the heraldry of the picture, and here it must be remembered that Richard's subjects could read a coat more easily than they could read a letter. In his reign coat armour and liveries were entering on a new phase of importance. Scropes and Grosvenors contended for a decade over the right to bear the golden bend on a field azure, and the political groupings of the court gave a partisan value to badges and signs. An artist would not have dared to

[1] This essay is reprinted, with the kind permission of the Editor, from the *Burlington Magazine*, June 1931.

[2] G. Scharf, *Description of the Wilton House Diptych, containing a contemporary portrait of Richard II*. Printed for the Arundel Society, 1882. The conclusion about the date and meaning appears on ibid., pp. 63–9.

employ heraldic devices merely as fanciful ornament; he probably learned his art as a painter of shields and pennons and knew that each detail must be used to convey a definite meaning. For this reason the heraldry of the diptych may be taken as valid evidence; the difficulty lies only in its interpretation. If an interpretation is accepted which assigns an approximate date to the picture, it then becomes possible to discuss the intention of the artist. This problem of intention, like everything else in Richard's reign, cannot be separated from chronology, as few kings in English history were swept in such shifting tides of policy, conspiracy, and war.

Before entering on an examination of heraldic detail certain preliminary arguments may be put forward on general grounds. It can hardly be doubted that the painting was executed either for Richard or in his honour and we may then adopt as limiting dates the years 1377 to 1399. As Richard is represented without a consort, it is also reasonable to assume that the work was done either before his first marriage or while he was a widower. It is possible that some special intention, a Crusade for example, might have made the representation of a queen inappropriate, but we would then expect her arms or other devices to appear in the blazonry of the picture or among the heraldic ornaments on the back of the panels. Richard's first wife was Anne of Bohemia, the daughter and sister of the Emperors Charles IV and Wenzel, and it is highly improbable that a painter would have omitted the imperial arms or her two collars—rosemary and ostrich—while she was queen.[1] A rich chasuble, presented by Richard to Westminster Abbey in 1389, provides an example of the association of the arms of the king and queen. It was embroidered with images of the Trinity, the Virgin, St. John the Baptist, the two royal saints, Edmund and Edward, and a certain abbess; also with

[1] Palgrave, *Ancient Kalendars and Inventories*, iii. 341, 357.

the arms of Edward the Confessor, Richard and Anne.[1] The chroniclers are agreed upon the king's devotion to his wife, and the omission of her arms and devices therefore suggests that the picture was painted either before their marriage in 1382 or after her death in 1394. It is, however, impossible to exclude at the outset the period of Richard's second marriage, 1396 to 1399, as the question of the arms and devices of Isabelle of France cannot be separated from the interpretation of the heraldry of the picture.

The heraldic evidence falls into three parts: the shield bearing the arms of Edward the Confessor, the badge of the white hart and the collar of broom cods.[2] The shield appears on the dexter panel of the diptych and it bears the quartered arms of England and France impaled with those of St. Edward. The arms of the Confessor were embroidered on the chasuble given to Westminster in 1389 and his cult was so closely bound up with the prestige of the monarchy that at first it would seem that they might have been borne at any period of the reign. It is, however, necessary to consider certain definite statements by contemporaries. Attention has often been drawn to the passage in Froissart stating that on the Irish expedition of 1394–5 Richard, to please the Irish, gave up the leopards and lilies of the English arms and assumed those of the royal saint.[3] This cannot be taken as a description of the shield on the diptych, as Froissart

[1] *An Inventory of the Vestry of Westminster Abbey*, edited by J. Wickham Legg (Society of Antiquaries, 1890), p. 86.

[2] The shield is surmounted by the crest of a crowned lion, *passant gardant*, standing on chapeau, helm, and mantle; this crest and its appurtenances appear on the seals of the Black Prince and are therefore of no value for the date. W. de Grey Birch, *Catalogue of Seals in the British Museum*, ii. 221–3.

[3] '. . . le roy Richard . . . quant auten il fut en Irlande, en toutes ses armoiries il laissa à porter les armes d'Angleterre, c'est-à-entendre les liépars et les fleurs de lis dont il est esquartellé, et prist celles du roy Edouard qui est saint, qui est une croix potencée d'or et de geules a quatre blans coulons ou champ de l'escu ou de la banière. . . .' Froissart, *Chroniques*, ed. Kervyn de Lettenhove, xv. 180.

obviously meant, not the impaling of two coats, but the substitution of one for another. What has hitherto been overlooked is that the St. Albans author of the *Annales Ricardi Secundi* has a concise description of the impaled arms. After an account of the Parliament of Shrewsbury, he states that the king became so proud that he changed his arms and added to his shield the arms of Edward the Confessor, bearing the arms of the saint on one half (*anterior pars*) and on the other (*pars reliqua*) the arms of his ancestors.[1] The Parliament of Shrewsbury met early in 1398, but the statement in the *Annales* immediately follows an account of the distribution of titles by Richard in the second or revenge Parliament of 1397. We know from an entry on the Parliament Roll that the new creations were made on 25 September,[2] and, as the order of events in the chronicle is confused at this point, it is more probable that the assumption of arms has been described out of its place and should be put back to the previous year.[3] The probability that the two events were closely connected is increased by the fact that the five new dukes—Hereford, Norfolk, Surrey, Aumarle, and Exeter—also assumed the arms of Edward the Confessor.[4]

[1] *Annales Ricardi Secundi* (Rolls Series), p. 223. 'Rex . . . sic superbivit . . . ut mutaret arma sua, quae pater et avus et patrui sui gestaverant et adderet scuto suo arma Sancti Edwardi: sic ut anterior pars arma Sancti plena forent, et pars reliqua esset recognitio armorum parentum ejus.'

[2] *Rot. Parl.* iii. 355.

[3] Holinshed (*Chronicles*, ed. 1577, p. 1097) also associates the two events, indicating a date just after the Christmas feast at Lichfield in 1397. Williams, in his edition of the *Traison et Mort*, remarks: 'On Saturday, September 29, when Richard had made the dukes, he added the arms of Saint Edward to his own and no one durst say him no. (Fabyan), p. 140, n. 1.' The statement does not occur in Fabyan and it has not been traced to any other source.

[4] Sandford, *Genealogical History of the Kings of England, 1677*, pp. 124, 191. Norfolk assumed the coat undifferenced, Surrey with a border *argent* and Exeter with a label of three points *argent*. Hereford may have assumed the arms at the same time: they were on his seal in 1399 (*British Museum Seals, ut supra*, iii. 384). No one of the four was using them on 1 May 1396 (Douet d'Arcq, *Inventaires et Documents: Collection de Sceaux*, iii. 284, 288–9, 292).

We are thus led to conclude that the arms were publicly assumed in England in the winter of 1397–8. There are, however, two earlier examples of their use which set the date farther back in the reign. The king's cousin, Edward, earl of Rutland and Cork (afterwards Aumarle), bore the arms, differenced with a label of three points, on his seal as Admiral as early as 9 March 1396.[1] The difference suggests that they had already been used by Richard, perhaps first as a substitute for his own in Ireland, where Rutland acted as his chief lieutenant.[2] We find them impaled with the royal arms on one of his signets, which bears a shield identical with that on the diptych.[3] Unfortunately, no exact date can be assigned to it; Tout puts it third on his list of Richard's signets and states that it was in use by 1395.[4] The evidence thus goes to show that the public assumption of the arms in 1397–8 was preceded by a use of them for special purposes which may go back as early as 1394.

The badge of the white hart with crown and chain appears repeatedly in the picture. Richard and the eleven angels wear it on the left breast; it is embroidered within circles of broom cods on Richard's robes; on the reverse of the panel of the kings the hart is lodged on a bank of grass and flowers. It is well known as Richard's badge or livery: his retainers were denounced in *Richard the Redeless* as the 'large laverers . . . that had hertis on hie on her brestis . . . they bare hem the bolder ffor her

[1] Douet d'Arcq, *ut supra*, iii. 299; G. Demay, *Le Costume au Moyen Âge d'après les sceaux*, p. 261, fig. 234. I owe this reference to the kindness of Dr. Previté-Orton.

[2] E. Curtis, *Richard II in Ireland*, *passim*.

[3] H. Maxwell Lyte, *Great Seal of England*, pp. 116–17. A royal warrant of 27 Oct. 1395 was issued 'souz nostre propre signet de Seint Edward'. Cf. T. F. Tout, *Chapters in the Administrative History of England*, v. 204, 448, Plate IV, fig. 6.

[4] Ibid., p. 204. Cf. p. 201, where Tout writes: 'The sequence of Richard's signets, if sequence there were, cannot be determined in the light of our present knowledge.'

gay broches'.[1] The Monk of Evesham states that the sign or *stigma* of the white hart with a crown and a gold chain was first given (*primo datum*) by the king at the Smithfield tournament in October 1390,[2] but this is not the earliest reference to the device itself. A tradition, not traced back beyond the sixteenth century, ascribes the badge to Richard's mother, Joan of Kent, and it was apparently on the seal of her eldest son, Thomas Holland, earl of Kent.[3] That it was used by the royal family early in the reign is suggested by the appearance of three brooches of the white hart set with rubies in a list of the king's jewels pawned to the City of London in September 1380.[4] In the inventories of chattels forfeited in 1387–8 by Richard's favourites were two pieces of plate engraved with a hart.[5] There is no record of livery collars among these forfeitures, though it would be natural to find them among the goods of men as closely associated with the king as de Vere and Burley. On the other hand among the forfeitures of the earl of Huntingdon, seized in January 1400, we find liveries of the King of France, Richard, and Henry IV and 'un livere de cerf ovesque iii baleys et ii safers, pris X livres'.[6] The

[1] *Political Poems*, ed. Th. Wright, i. 381. The date must be soon after the deposition, probably 1400.

[2] *Vita Ricardi Secundi*, p. 122. MS. Sloane 1776, f. 20, has a variant reading: 'Rex contulit pro suo signo liberatum cervi . . . in serico albo cum corona et cathena aurea ad demonstrandum suam regiam excellentiam extraneis predictis. . . .' Cf. Lambeth MS. 340, f. 77: '. . . datum est primum illud signum egregium de cervo albo cum corona aurea et cathena', another Evesham variant.

[3] Sandford, *ut supra*, pp. 124, 216. Kent's seal, 'a hind lodged under a tree with a ducal (?) coronet' was appended to a charter dated 8 February 1387. He used the same seal on 1 May 1396 (Douet d'Arcq, *ut supra*, iii. 289).

[4] Rymer, vii. 359, *Calendar of Letter Book H*, p. 159.

[5] 'Liber forisfacturarum Ducis Hibernie et diversarum personarum in parliamento tento apud Westmonasterium anno regni Ricardi secundi duo decimo adiudicatarum.' P.R.O. Miscellaneous Books, No. 66, f. 27. Among Bealknap's goods—'Un coupe dargent enorrey par tout oue j cerfe blance en la sumet, oue j eawer dargent ennorrey par tout par oue j cerfe blance en la sumet. . . .'

[6] P.R.O. E. 101. Exchequer K.R. Acc. 335/7. Cf. Vernon Harcourt,

evidence of the inventories points to the conclusion that great men did not wear even the king's livery until the last decade of the century. It is also significant that a tract on arms written for Anne of Bohemia has no reference either to liveries or to collars[1] and that the chroniclers write of the white hart and its adoption by the Cheshire guard as an innovation of the last phase of the reign. The author of *Richard the Redeless* looked back to a time when it was unknown and reminded the king that his lieges 'loved you fulle lelly or leverez begynne'.[2] We are thus led to accept the statement of Evesham that the livery of the white hart was not worn before the Smithfield tournament of 1390.

The collar of broom cods is treated with almost as much emphasis by the painter as the badge of the white hart, and it raises a question of greater importance. It is worn by Richard and the eleven angels and it is used to encircle the harts on the royal robe; it does not appear with the royal arms and other devices on the back of the panels. As long ago as 1842 John Gough Nichols asserted that the collar was French, the gift of Charles VI to Richard.[3] He also maintained that no member of the English royal family styled himself Plantagenet before Richard of York in the pedigree which he laid before

His Grace the Steward, pp. 445–6. Cf. the inventory of Gloucester's goods, seized at Pleshy in 1397, which contains neither collars nor liveries (*Archaeological Journal*, liv (1897), pp. 275 f.).

[1] *Tractatus magistri Johannis de Bado Aureo cum Francisco de Foveis in distinctionibus Armorum.* Edited by Ed. Bysshe with Upton's *De studio militari* and Spelman's *Aspilogia*, London, 1654. The author states that he wrote 'ad instanciam quarundum personarum et specialiter domine Anne quondam Regine Anglie . . .'. The MS. is in the British Museum, Add. 29901. This tract, written for Anne of Bohemia, is extant in at least five fifteenth-century MSS.: Add. 29901 in the British Museum and in the Bodleian Rawlinson B.107, B.10 and D. 225 (one MS. divided), and Laud Miscell. 723. The Laud MS. is an English translation, handsomely illustrated.

[2] *Political Songs*, loc. cit., p. 383.

[3] *Archaeologia*, xxix, 1842, 'Observations on the Heraldic Devices discovered on the effigies of Richard II and his Queen', pp. 41–7.

Parliament in 1460.[1] There was, therefore, no reason to use the *planta genesta* or broom as a rebus or badge. Scharf followed Nichols in accepting the collar as French, without either testing the evidence or realizing its full implications. If it be French, it must belong to the period of the Anglo-French *entente* and cannot be much earlier than Richard's second marriage in 1396.[2]

Nichols drew his information from two French historians, Favyn and Helyot, who, in patriotic anxiety to prove the antiquity of French orders of chivalry, were careless or unscrupulous in their use of evidence. André Favyn in *Le Theâtre de l'Honneur et de la Chevalerie*, maintained that *l'ordre de la Cosse de Geneste* was founded by St. Louis at his coronation, but the first document he puts forward is the gift in 1378 of the collar *de la cosse de Geneste*, by Charles V to his chamberlain.[3] He also states, on the authority of the Chronicle of Jean, duke of Berry—a work that has not been traced—that in 1389 Charles VI created Louis, king of Sicily, and Charles, prince of Tarentum, *chevaliers de l'Estoile et de la Cosse de la Geneste*.[4] A hundred years later Helyot in *L'Histoire des Ordres Monastiques, religieux et militaires*, repeated Favyn's story and cited as new evidence an account, which he

[1] *Rot. Parl.* v. 375. Anne Mortimer and Richard, earl of Cambridge, 'had issue and lefully bare Richard Plantaginet, commonly called Duc of York'. Cf. ibid., pp. 377–8. The first Great Seal of Richard I (1189–97) bears a curved spray like a broom plant on each side of the throne, but it does not appear on the second seal nor as the device of any of his successors (A. B. and A. Wyon, *Great Seals of England*, 1887, pp. 18–19 and Plate V). Nichol's conclusions are accepted by Round in his article on 'Plantagenet' in the *Encyclopaedia Britannica*.

[2] H. Moranville, 'Conférence entre la France et l'Angleterre' (*Bibl. de l'École des Chartes*, l (1889), pp. 355 f.). Negotiations for peace began languidly in 1389 and became more active in 1392. It was not until after the death of Anne and the proposal of a French marriage that both sides showed a determination to have peace. The *entente* may be dated from the 26 years' truce signed in March 1396, though at least a year of friendly negotiation had preceded it.

[3] Paris, 1620, pp. 581 f.

[4] The Order of the Star was founded in 1351 by King John. *Chroniques des règnes de Jean II et de Charles V*, ed. R. Delachenal, vol. iv, 1920, 'Miniatures de MSS. de Charles V', Plates II and III.

dated September 1393, for four collars of broom cods, one for the King of England and three for the dukes of Lancaster, York, and Gloucester.[1]

It is obvious that evidence thus drawn from uncritical and biased historians can have weight only if corroborated from other sources. We need not concern ourselves with the origin of the *Cosse de la Geneste*, though it may be noted that the great inventory of Charles V has not a single reference to a livery collar and that he does not wear one in any of the miniatures in his manuscripts.[2] On the other hand there is ample documentary evidence that the broom was the emblem of Charles VI and that the collar of cods was his livery. In a long inventory of jewels in the treasury of England in 1400 three collars of *genestes* are specifically called *del livere du Roi de France.*[3] This ascription is supported by Nicholas Upton, an English writer on heraldry; in *De Studio militari*, written before 1446, he says that the livery collar of the King of England is the SS collar and that of the King of France the collar of broom.[4] On the French side the evidence is equally definite. In Charles VI's inventories certain precious objects were marked with the *geneste*, including a *dragouer* (comfit-dish), enamelled with the arms of France encircled with branches of *geneste.*[5] When the arrangements for the marriage cortège of Isabelle were made in the Council at Senlis royal liveries were ordered to be embroidered round the neck and on the sleeves with a *chapelet de l'ordre du Roi a genestes.*[6] In the *Annales Ricardi Secundi* we have a detailed account of the wedding,

[1] Paris, 1719, vol. viii, chap. xxxvii, pp. 276 f. Helyot pretends to quote the document in full, but, as it will be seen, he altered the date and omitted part of the text.

[2] Delachenal, *ut supra. Inventaire de Charles V*, ed. J. Labarte, Paris, 1878.

[3] Palgrave, *Ancient Kalendars*, iii. 354, 357, e.g. no. 332. 'Un colare del livre du Roi du France contenant IX overages de genestres garnisez de IIII baleys, III saphire, XXVII perles, poisant VI unc et demi.'

[4] Edited by Ed. Bysshe, London, 1654. Book I, chap. xvii, p. 33.

[5] *Pièces inédites du règne de Charles VI*, ed. Douet d'Arcq, Paris, 1864, ii. 383, 397, 398.

[6] Ibid. i. 130. The Council sat on 29 July 1396.

and we are told that Charles wore round his neck a collar of his own livery and on his breast the hart, as livery of the King of England.[1] We cannot doubt that he was wearing the broom cods collar and the white hart just as Richard wears them in the diptych.

Finally, the story of Charles VI's gifts of his livery collars to Richard and his uncles is confirmed by the account for the wedding expenses of 1396, presented by Charles Poupart, *argentier du Roy*.[2] As it appears to assign limiting dates to the presentation of the collar and therefore to give the earliest date when Richard could have worn it, it is worth quoting in full:

'Compte particulier de Charles Poupart, argentier du Roy, de la recepte et mises faites par luy tant de plusieurs robes, joyaulx, etc., pour le Roy, pour Madame Ysabel de France . . . pours les nopces de lad. dame, qui furent faictes du roy d'Angleterre . . . et pour le fait de six colliers d'or garnis de pierrerie et perles, c'est assavoir: un pour le Roy, quatre autres que led. seigneur a envoyés en Angleterre pour donner de par luy aud. roy d'Angleterre, le 2e au duc de Lencastre, le 3e au duc de Glocestre et le 4e au duc d'Yort, et le 6e collier d'or en façon de cinq tuyaux garniz de pierrerie et perles pour led. seigneur. . .

'A Jehan Conpère, orfèvre a Paris, pour un collier d'or pour le Roy fait en façon de deux gros tuyaulx rons, et entre iceux tuyaux cosses de genestes doubles, entretenant par les queux, et autour d'ycelui collier sur lesd. cosses, fait 9 potences, garnies chacune de deux grosses perles l'un par l'autre, et entreux deux

[1] *Annales*, p. 190. L. Mirot (*v.* n. 2, *infra*) prints *Declaration du Trousseau d'Isabelle de France*, which included a bed and a velvet dress embroidered with *branches de geneste*, pp. 143, 146. At the wedding Charles VI gave to the duchesses of Lancaster and Gloucester, to the countess of Huntingdon, and to Joan, daughter of John of Gaunt, *colers de son liverée de broincoddes* ('L'Entrevue d'Ardres', by P. Meyer, *Annuaire-Bulletin de la Soc. de l'Histoire de France*, xviii (1881), p. 219; an English account of the wedding is preserved in MS. 46, Oriel College, Oxford).

[2] Published by L. Mirot in 'Un trousseau royal à la fin du XIVe siècle' (*Mémoires de la Société de l'Histoire de Paris et de l'Île de France*), 1902, xxix. 151, 154. The accounts of Charles Poupart are extant only in an eighteenth-century transcript, Bibl. Nat. MS. fr. 20684, fol. 467–78. The account for the wedding was not presented until 1398.

d'icelles potences autour dudit collier à 50 lettres d'or pendant a l'un d'iceulx tuyaux, qui font par dix fois, le mot du roy JAMES, et ou devant d'icelluy collier a un gros balay quarré environné de huit grosses perles de compte, et au derrière d'icelluy collier, a deux cosses de genestes d'or ouvertes, esmaillées l'une de blanc et l'autre de vert, ou a dedans en chascune d'elles cosses 3 semblables grosses perles, et lesd. tuyaux d'iceluy collier pooinssonnez de branches, fleurs et cosses de genestes, valant en tout 258 frans, 7s. 8d.

'Aud. Jean Compère, pour quatre autres colliers d'or, dont l'un est pareil au collier du Roy, pour le roy d'Angleterre, et les 3 autres pour le duc de Lancastre, l'autre pour le duc de Glocester et l'autre pour le duc d'Yhort, semblables à quelques perles un peu moins fortes, pour ce pour tout 830 frans, 3s. 4d.'

This extract makes it clear that it was his own livery that Charles was sending to England as a wedding gift to Richard and the uncles. The occasion cannot be earlier than the opening of marriage negotiations after Richard's return from Ireland in May 1395.[1]

There is nothing on the English side to set against this evidence. The inventories published by Palgrave do not contain a single reference to a livery collar before 1400 and there are none in the Book of Forfeitures of 1387–8.[2] It might fairly be argued that schedules of forfeitures were seldom complete and it is therefore fortunate that we have an inventory of the goods of Sir Simon Burley, drawn up for himself on 8 November 1387.[3] The list

[1] In a letter written in Ireland by Richard to Charles VI the question of a marriage alliance is raised; three French princesses are named as possible brides, but not one of them is the king's daughter, Isabelle. All Souls MS. 182, ff. 234, 235. The first embassy to treat of the marriage with Isabelle was appointed on 8 July 1395, Rymer, vii. 802.

[2] De Vere had *un hanap dargent senorre ove pesecoddes*, 'Liber forisfacturarum . . .', *ut supra*, f. 25, but no significance can be attached to the emblem in this form.

[3] P.R.O. E. 154. Bundle 1, No. 19. The roll begins: 'Conue soit a toutez gentz qe monsieur Simond de Burley ordaina affaire son inventore le VIII iour de Novembre lan XI de toutz les biens qe le dit monsieur Simond aveit si bien a la Meawes come a Baynardes Castell en Loundres, les queux biens sont contenuz en ycest rolle.'

was obviously intended to be exhaustive and it includes household stuff, clothes, furs, books, plate, arms for jousts, and arms for war. He had beds and robes embroidered with his device of stakes and with his arms, but nothing marked with the hart or broom cods and no livery collars or badges. No man of rank, except de Vere, was closer to the king or more prominent at court, and we must take the evidence of his inventory as decisive for the early period of the reign. An inventory of the jewels and plate which had belonged to Richard and other royal persons was drawn up on 20 November 1399.[1] It has a description of a number of livery collars, but not one of them is called the livery of Richard.[2] A significant incident occurred in the Parliament of 1394. Arundel complained that Richard was wearing the Lancastrian collar and the king replied that soon after Gaunt had returned from Spain (1389) he had taken the collar from his uncle's neck and put it on his own, saying that he would wear it as a token of love.[3] We may infer that he had then no collar of his own and that to please Gaunt he wore the Lancastrian SS collar for a time. There is, in short, no evidence that Richard wore a collar of his own and no evidence beyond the diptych that he ever wore any other collar than that of Lancaster.[4]

[1] Palgrave, *ut supra*, iii. 313–58.

[2] It is possible that 'II colers pour leverers embroidey ove plesance et ove turrety d'argent endorrey' (ibid., p. 353) may have been Richard's collar. There is no reference to a collar of Richard in the chronicles.

[3] *Rot. Parl.* iii. 313.

[4] Sir Thomas Markenfield on his tomb at Ripon wears a ludicrous collar of a hart lodged in park palings (J. R. Planché, *Journal British Archaeological Assoc.* xx. 285). An illumination in the Neville Book of Hours shows the same collar worn by the first earl of Westmorland and eight of his sons (MS. latin 1156, Bibliothèque Nationale, reproduced by C. Couderc, *Enlumineurs des MSS. du Moyen Âge*, Paris, 1927, Pl. LVII). Planché states that the design occurs on the seal of the bailiff of Derby and it may, therefore, be a livery collar of Henry IV as earl of Derby. These are the only examples of a collar of the hart which have been traced; both belong to the period 1425–30. Beltz, *Retrospective Review*, 1828, p. 501, says that at the Smithfield tournament of 1390 the king distributed 'his cognizance of the white hart,

Taking the English and French authorities together, we cannot avoid the conclusion that the broom cods collar was the livery of Charles VI and that its use by Richard cannot be put earlier than the marriage negotiations of 1395–6.

Thus the evidence from the heraldry of the diptych points to an artist at work in the closing years of the reign. One chronicler states that the badge of the white hart was first given in 1390, and the statement has indirect confirmation in the silence of earlier inventories. Richard's signet and the Admiral's seal show that the arms of Edward the Confessor were impaled with the royal arms, at least for special purposes, as early as 1395, though this may not have been generally known until the winter of 1397–8. A considerable body of evidence goes to prove that the broom cods collar was the livery of Charles VI, given to Richard at or before his wedding in 1396 and unknown in England before that date. We are, therefore, led to the conclusion that the work could not have been begun before the marriage negotiations of 1395, and may have been as late as the period from September 1397 to 1399.

The obvious objection to so late a date is the youthful appearance of Richard and the absence of the characteristic double beard, well known from the Westminster portrait, the effigy on the tomb, and the illumination of the Harleian manuscript of Creton.[1] The difficulty is made greater by the general resemblance of all the representations, each of which appears to be a portrait. It is specially hard to believe that the cunning-faced

pendent from a collar composed of cosses de genet . . .', but he is evidently misquoting the monk of Evesham, as he cites MS. Cotton Tib. C. IX, p. 25 (Hearne's text), which has no reference to the collar. Beltz may have confused some version of a passage in the Brut (E.E.T.S. ii. 343), where the harts are described as having crowns and chains 'about her nekkis'.

[1] Reproduced *Archaeologia*, xx. Cf. the miniature in MS. Cotton, Nero D. vi, f. 85, showing Richard giving a charter to the Earl Marshall; he is represented as a man of middle age, with red hair and a double beard.

copper effigy on the tomb, executed 1395–9,[1] belongs to the same time as the boyish and slightly built king of the diptych. Yet the evidence, drawn from a variety of sources, runs so flatly counter to an early date that we must conclude that the artist deliberately idealized his portrait of Richard, substituting a look of sensitiveness and hope for the sly cynicism of the effigy.

The first explanation that offers itself is that the diptych was painted as a wedding gift for the eight-year-old Princess Isabelle. The emphatic treatment of the French collar and its close association with the English livery of the white hart might be taken as a symbol of the marriage alliance and the Anglo-French *entente* thus secured. There are, however, too many objections to this theory. Isabelle's wedding presents were all carefully scheduled by the French when they claimed their restoration from Henry IV, and no object in any way resembling the diptych is mentioned.[2] Also if the work had been executed by a French artist for Richard, to celebrate the marriage, we would expect that a place would have been found for the bride herself and less attention given to the English arms and livery and to English saints.

In addition to these minor difficulties, the main objection to any suggestion of a secular occasion lies in the clearly religious significance of the picture. The English royal saints and St. John the Baptist present or dedicate the king to the Virgin and Child; he holds up his hands, not closed in prayer, but open in expectation; the Child points upwards to the banner which an angel holds with one finger pointed to Richard. The meaning of the picture seems to turn on the presentation of the banner;

[1] Devon, *Issues*, p. 270; Rymer, vii. 797–8. A contract for the effigies was drawn up on 24 April 1395. The work was to be finished by 29 September 1397, but the last payment (for gilding) was not made until 14 April 1399. Richard's robe bears the emblems of white hart, broom, and rising sun; these are not specified on the contract and were, no doubt, an afterthought.

[2] The schedule was published by Williams as an Appendix to *Traison et Mort*, pp. 108–13.

the red cross on a white ground may be either the banner of the redemption, or the crusading flag associated with St. George.[1] If it be admitted that the picture has a crusading significance we have at once an explanation of the idealization of Richard, of the offering of the banner, and of the general feeling of movement and expectation in the heavenly host round the Virgin and Child.

Scharf has already pointed out the resemblance of the banner to an illumination in a manuscript in the British Museum, entitled 'Un Epistre au Roy Richard' by 'un vieil solitaire des Celestins de Paris'.[2] Richard is seated on a throne hung with the arms of England; he is young and beardless and he is stretching out his hand to take a book from a kneeling monk. The monk offers the book with one hand and in the other he holds a banner, a red cross on a white ground, with the lamb and flag in black at the centre (Plate I *a*). On the opposite folio are painted the crown of thorns between the crowns of England and France (Plate I *b*).[3]

If Scharf had carried his examination of the manuscript beyond the illuminations at the beginning he would have found that it was primarily a plea for a crusade. On folio 35 there is another miniature of the banner (Plate I *c*) following the words: 'Comment le vieil solitaire presente au Roy dangleterre une nouvelle chevalerie du crucefix qui doit estre mandee oultremer devant les ii Roys qui par la grace de dieu ferront le saint passage.'

[1] In England St. George was beginning to be regarded less as a crusader than as a national saint, but on the Continent he was the patron of four crusading orders, e.g. the Order of St. George of Alfama, founded in 1201, received papal approbation in 1363 and united with the Order of St. George and Our Lady of Mompesa in 1399. W. G. Perrin, *British Flags*, chap. ii; Ashmole, *Order of the Garter*, pp. 76 f.

[2] Royal MS. 20. B. VI, f. 2. Scharf, *ut supra*, p. 65. It is reproduced in *British Museum Reproductions from Illuminated MSS.*, 1907, Series I, Plate XXV. One of the courtiers wears the Order of the Garter on his knee, showing that the painter was acquainted with English usage.

[3] Reproduced in *Catalogue of Western MSS. in the Old Royal and King's Collections in the British Museum*, iv, Plate 115.

RICHARD II OF ENGLAND, ENTHRONED, RECEIVING A BOOK
British Museum MS. Royal 20 B vi, f. 2

CROWN OF THORNS BETWEEN THE
CROWNS OF ENGLAND AND FRANCE
British Museum MS. Royal 20 B vi, f. 1v

BANNER OF RICHARD II
British Museum MS. Royal 20 B vi, f. 35

BANNER AND SHIELD OF THE ORDER OF THE PASSION
Bodleian MS. Ashmole 813, f. 1ᵛ

The author of the 'Epistre' was Phillipe de Mézières, a French *illuminé*, formerly chancellor of Cyprus, the friend and adviser of Charles VI.[1] The guiding idea of his life was the foundation of a new crusading order, the Order of the Passion; it was to draw its recruits from all the Christians of the west, to take the place of the older military organizations and to restore and govern the kingdom of Jerusalem. The plan was first worked out in detail at Avignon in 1367–8,[2] and from that time onward de Mézières let slip no chance to make his project known. After the murder of Peter I of Cyprus (1369), he came to Paris and entered the service of Charles V, as adviser on near eastern affairs. In this way he became the friend of Leo de Lusignan, the exiled king of Armenia, who was looking for Christian aid to recover his lands under the Taurus mountains from the emir of Aleppo. It may have been the generosity of Richard to Leo when he visited England in 1385[3] that first encouraged de Mézières to hope that the young kings of France and England would become the chief patrons of his Order of the Passion.

This hope is the main theme of the *Songe du vieil pelerin* and the *Oratio tragedia*, written for Charles VI in 1389.[4] When the English envoys came to Amiens to treat of peace in 1393, one of de Mézières's disciples, Robert the Hermit, had an interview with Lancaster.[5] Robert was the recognized go-between for Richard and Charles, visiting England freely between 1392 and 1396.[6] He

[1] N. Iorga, *Philippe de Mézières, 1327–1405, et la Croisade au XIVe siècle*, Paris, 1896.

[2] Ibid., p. 347.

[3] Anonymous of Westminster (Higden, ix. 76–7, 79–80); Devon, *Issues*, pp. 245–6.

[4] Iorga, pp. 468 f., 471 f.

[5] Froissart, xv. 192–3.

[6] De Mézières calls him: 'Robert L'Ermite du clos de Constentin en Normandie, singulier messaige de Dieu et de monseigneur saint Jaque aux roys de France en d'Engleterre sur le fait de la paix des ii roys et sur le fait de l'union de l'Église et du saint passage d'Oultremer.' 'Chevalerie de la Passion', f. 112b, extracts printed by Molinier, *Archives de l'Orient Latin*, 1881, i. 362. Robert was carrying letters to Charles VI from Richard as early as 1392 (Moranville, *ut supra*, pp. 375–6): he was again in England in 1395

was a member of the Order of the Passion and had been charged to make it known in England. 'L'Epistre au Roi Richard', written in 1395, was intended to press further the arguments for a crusade already put before the king at Eltham;[1] peace with France and the marriage with Isabelle were urged as preliminaries to the *saint passage*. We have evidence that Robert had some success in drawing recruits for the order in England. A list of members or patrons, compiled in 1395, contains twenty-five English names. Lancaster, Gloucester, and Huntingdon are claimed as patrons, and the members include York, Rutland, the Earl Marshal, Northumberland, and John Gilbert, bishop of St. Davids.[2] In the 'Epistre' de Mézières refers the king for information to Robert the Hermit and to 'le livre de la sustance abregie de la dite chevalerie que le vieil solitaire humblement et a grant devocion bailla nagaires a vostre tresame frere le conte de Hontintone (Huntingdon). . . . Et pour ce auxi que par vostre tresame oncle le duc de Wyork et par messir Iehan de Harlestone et autres tres vaillans chevalers,

and 1396 (Froissart, xv. 188–202, where there is a long account of the mission of 1395).

[1] The letter from Charles VI to Richard, delivered by Robert in 1395, was probably written by de Mézières, and, as Iorga has pointed out, is a summary of the 'Epistre', written very soon afterwards. It was published by Kervyn de Lettenhove in his edition of Froissart, xxv. 388 f.

[2] The full list of English names is as follows: 'Tous les dessus diz ont promis d'estre de la chevalerie. En Angleterre. Le duc d'Youlc, oncle du roy d'Engleterre, le conte de Rutherland, filz du dit duc, le conte Mareschal, le conte de Nortombelande, Mons. l'evesque de Saint David, Mons. le Despensier, Mons. Hue le Despensier, Mons. Loys Cliffort, Mons. Thomas West, Mons. Guillaume Helemann, Mons. Jehan Harlestone, Mons. Guillaume Feniston, Mons. Raoul de Persy, Mons. Hervy fil Hue, Mons. Symon Felbrig, Mons. Richart Albery, Mons. Hervy Guine, Mons. Thomas Herpignen, Mons. de Rochefort, Mons. Robert Morley, Piteux, escuier, Richart Chelmesinch, escuier du Roy.

Ceulx qui se sont offers de aidier a la dicte chevalerie et n'ont pas encore offert d'estre de la chevalrie . . . En Angleterre. Le duc de Glocestre, oncle du roy, Le duc de Lencastre, Le conte de Nornthone, frere du roy d'Engleterre.' (Arsenal MS. 2251, f. 113b–114a. Printed by Molinier, *ut supra*, pp. 363–4.)

vox loyaux subgies vostre debonnaurete en pourra estre enformee.'[1]

The book which de Mézières gave the Earl of Huntingdon makes it possible to carry our knowledge of his recruiting methods a stage farther. It can probably be identified as the manuscript known as Ashmole 813, now preserved in the Bodleian and entitled, 'La sustance de la passion de Jehus Crist en francois'.[2] It is a small folio containing four leaves of paper with a surface specially prepared, thirty-one leaves of paper bearing a French watermark of 1395, and twenty-three blank leaves of a later date. The handwriting belongs to the late fourteenth or early fifteenth century. There are six full-page pictures on the first paper and the thirty-one leaves of the paper of 1395 contain a French version of the rule of the Order, with prayers and arguments in justification. The manuscript is an illustrated copy of the third redaction of the rule, revised in order to use the Anglo-French alliance as an argument for a crusading order.[3] Another copy of the same redaction is preserved in the Arsenal Collection of Paris.[4] Molinier, the first modern scholar to examine de Mézières's work, has shown that the Ash-

[1] MS. Royal, 20 B, VI, f. 37.

[2] W. H. Black, *Catalogue of the Manuscripts bequeathed unto the University of Oxford by Elias Ashmole. . . .*, p. 45. A transcript of the MS., with pen and ink drawings was made by Ashmole in MS. 865 of the same collection, ff. 377–465; his 'Institution of the Order of the Garter' contains an abstract of the text and engravings of the pictures on a reduced scale, pp. 83–7. The autograph of Lord William Howard occurs on f. 1 and f. 2. Ashmole cites the MS. as 'ex vet. MS. in Bibliotheca Arundeliana', and no doubt it passed with other MSS., two of which are now in the British Museum (Arundel, 29 and 150), from Howard to his kinsman, Thomas Howard, second earl of Arundel.

My thanks are due to Dr. H. E. Craster and Mr. N. Denholm Young for their advice and help in examining the MS.

[3] Twenty reasons justifying the Order are given (ff. 4–15^{v}): the argument turns chiefly on the new hope of success given by the end of 'la vielle inimiste et haine mortele et aussi comme contraire en nature entre les Francois et Engles' (f. 11^{v}). The first and second redactions of the rule were issued in 1369 and 1384 and are extant in MS. 1056, 'Bibliothèque Mazarine'.

[4] MS. 2251.

mole manuscript is an abridgement of that in the Arsenal, containing not much more than one-third of the whole,[1] The portion which the two manuscripts have in common is entitled, 'La substance abregée de la chevalerie de la Passion de Jésus Christ en francois' in the Arsenal copy;[2] the other copy is, therefore, not only abridged from the longer manuscript, but its subject matter is an abridgement of the earlier Latin redactions of the rule. It thus answers exactly to 'la livre de la substance abregie', which de Mézières said he had given to Huntingdon.

For our purposes the interest of the manuscript lies in the six full-page pictures at the beginning of the volume (Plates D, and E). They are painted against a dark red background, with a green border, and represent the 'Prince de la chevaliere de la Passion'; a knight and a lady, each wearing a blue robe, a red hood, and a white mantle with a red cross; a knight in armour with the plate gorget over the *camail* which was then just coming into fashion; two squires and the banner and shield of the Order. The size and unusual position of the pictures —(all together on the first four folios)—imply a definite intention to make a display of the dress and badges to be worn by members; in fact the impression they leave is of poster work done not so much for adornment as for propaganda.[3] They are rougher in execution than the fine miniatures in the royal manuscript, but the two manuscripts show that de Mézières was making use of pictures to draw recruits for his order in England. Both appear to belong to the year 1395, the earliest date which the evidence permits us to assign to the diptych.

[1] *Archives de l'Orient Latin, 1881*, i. 335–64. The Ashmole MS. omits an introductory allegory (ff. 1–43), a plan of campaign (ff. 92–112), and the list of supporters (ff. 112–14).

[2] f. 44. 'La substance abregée' is written on ff. 44–91, Molinier, *ut supra*.

[3] The Arsenal MS., which formerly belonged to de Mézières's, house of the Celestines, was doubtless not intended for propaganda purposes. It has no ornaments except some rubrics and one or two letters in colour (Molinier, *ut supra*, p. 346).

DRESSES FOR MEMBERS OF THE ORDER OF THE PASSION

Bodleian MS. Ashmole 813, ff. 1v and 2v

PLATE 4

DRESSES FOR MEMBERS OF THE ORDER OF THE PASSION

Bodleian MS. Ashmole 813, ff. 2^{v} and 3^{v}

Finally, there is a certain, though limited coincidence of detail between the manuscripts and the diptych. The banner of the Order was a cross with the symbol of the lamb on a white ground. It is thus illustrated in both manuscripts but with some interesting variations. On the second folio of the royal manuscript the monk holds a white flag with a red border, three-pointed in the fly; on the thirty-fifth folio the flag is square, with a border of red and gold. The Ashmole banner is rectangular; the ground is white, with a white floral pattern like damask and a fringe of green and yellow. These variations suggest that the emblems, probably existing only on paper, had not yet become fixed, a suggestion supported by the use of the future tense in the description in the Ashmole manuscript.[1] In the diptych the flag is long like a standard, floating and forked in the fly. The lamb is not painted on the banner, but it is carried in the arms of St. John. Further, the signs of the Passion are represented by the crown of thorns and nails on the nimbus of the Christ, corresponding in idea, though not in execution, to the crown of thorns on the first folio of the royal manuscript.[2] Lastly, both in the royal manuscript and in the diptych, Richard is painted as young and beardless and this at a time when he certainly wore a double-pointed beard and was certainly not less than twenty-eight years of age. This coincidence of detail can hardly be accidental when considered in relation to

[1] Ashmole, 813, f. 23^{v}. 'Le champ de la baniere commune de la sainte chevalerie sera blanc et en milieu aura une crois vermelle. . . . Et en milieu de la crois aura un compas . . . tel compas des paintres de France est apele philatiere. Cestui compas sera tout rempli de coulour noire representant la doulour de la passion de nostre Seigneur . . . ou quel compas noir aura l agnus dei bien figure de coulour doree resplendissant representant la gloire de Jesus Crist resussitant. . . .'

[2] Mr. S. C. Cockerell and Mr. Kenneth Clark, to whom I am much indebted, tell me that the representation of these symbols on the nimbus is very unusual. Their appearance both in the Royal MS. and the diptych is, therefore, less probably merely coincidence. Mr. Clark points out that they are not punched into the gold but drawn on with a stylus.

the theme of the diptych. A crusading picture with the liveries of England and France united and executed between 1396 and 1399 cannot be traced to any other origin than de Mézières's propaganda for the Order of the Passion.[1]

[1] A discussion of the later history of the diptych by my friend Mrs. R. L. Poole will be found in the *Antiquaries Journal*, April 1931. I am indebted to her for much advice and encouragement, but she is in no way responsible for the conclusion here set forth.

IX

HENRY KNIGHTON AND THE LIBRARY CATALOGUE OF LEICESTER ABBEY[1]

IN the library catalogue of Leicester Abbey there are a series of references to the chronicler Knighton;[2] six of these describe books acquired by the abbey through him and two refer to the chronicle or *Compilatio de eventibus Angliae* of which he wrote or compiled all except the concluding section.[3]

The references to Knighton's books are as follows:

f. 26ᵛ. (Subject heading: *Summe.*)

Summa Bartholomei de proprietatibus rerum in asseribus per h. Knyton. 2° fo. vici potencia.

f. 27ᵛ. (Subject heading: *Penitencialia.*)

Penitenciale aliud—Quere in oratione exposita per h.k.

f. 31ᵛ. (Subject heading: *Specula.*)

Speculum ecclesie Iohannis Beleth[4] in asseribus nudis 2° fo.—significans: ympraríum glossum in eodem. Speculum eiusdem de officio ecclesie per h. de knyton.

f. 32. (Subject heading: *Elucidaria.*)

Elucidarium—Quere in lapidare[5] per henricum knyton.

[1] Reprinted from the *E.H.R.* xlv. 103–7, by permission of the editor.

[2] 'Registrum librorum monasterii beate Marie de pratis Leycestrensis Renovatum tempore Fratris Willelmi Charite tunc precentoris' (Bodley MS. Laud 623). My thanks are due to Mr. V. H. Galbraith for help in transcribing portions of the manuscript.

[3] *Chronicon Henrici Knighton*, edited J. R. Lumby, 1889 and 1895 (Rolls Series).

[4] John Beleth (*fl.* 1182?) was the author of *Racionale divinorum* [*officiorum*], also in the Leicester library (fo. 31ᵛ). In addition to the *Speculum ecclesie*, the library possessed *Summa de ecclesiasticis officiis Iohannis Beleth* (f. 25ᵛ) and *Penitenciale Iohannis Beleth* (fo. 27ᵛ).

[5] Probably contained in the volume described as follows on fo. 34 under *Gramatica*:

Liber qui incipit dactile quid latitas in quaternis. 2° fo.—presens sicut icit

Marbotus de lapidibus.//De Miraculis beate Marie.// lucidarius.

f. 33. (Subject heading: *Materie diverse.*)
Liber meditacionum Iohannis howden[1] per h. Knytton.
Liber meditacionum Iohannis Howden per salow. . . .[2]
. . . .
Oracio dominica exposita per h. Knytton.

The references to the Chronicle are of greater interest:

f. 24^v. (Subject heading: *Chronicalia.*)
cronica Leycestrensis in asseribus cum albo coopertorio 2° fo. et dicentes pax.

f. 46^v. (Description of position: *in septimo stallo.*)
Cronica henrici Knygtton 2° fo. et dicentes.

The words *et dicentes pax* occur on line 6, page 5, volume i of Lumby's edition; they are also the first three words on the second folio of the Cotton manuscript, Tiberius C. vii, the text used by Twysden and badly damaged in the fire of 1731. Lumby believed that both this manuscript and Claudius E. iii, the only other extant medieval text of the Chronicle, were derived from a lost original. He based this opinion on 'some corrections made by a later hand in the margin' of the Tiberius manuscript.[3] The identification of the manuscript with the copy described in the *Registrum* makes it almost certain that the damaged Cotton manuscript is the original version, retained by the house in which it was written until the eve of the dissolution; the marginal notes, which appear to be mainly verbal corrections, were perhaps added by some member of the convent, possibly from rough copies of the author's.

Attention should be drawn to the misleading way in which the contents of the manuscript catalogue are described by Nichols in his *History and Antiquities of the*

[1] Usually known as Hoveden. A Latin poet who died *c.* 1275: he was chaplain to Eleanor, mother of Henry III.

[2] Galfridus Salow was probably a member of the house. He gave it fifteen books, covering a wide range of subjects.

[3] Introduction, vol. ii, p. xxv.

County of Leicester.[1] He printed the *Tabula* (folios 1–3) or list of authors, omitting eighteen names; he added a few additional details from the *Registrum* itself but without any indication that he was not copying the text of the *Tabula* as it was before him, or indeed that the *Registrum* existed at all. He also summarized the list of service books, rentals, and books procured or copied by William Charite, described in some detail on folios 47–51. In his brief comment he remarks:

'Many books are referred to some other arrangements: Many have only 2 folia. The first words of some are given; and, after all our inquiries, many of the writers here enumerated must remain as unknown as they are uninteresting: and perhaps posterity has very little reason to regret the loss of the library of Leicester Abbey. . . . From this Catalogue it seems to be rather doubtful whether in the library of this religious house there might be any one complete collection of all the Holy Scriptures. Supposing *Bible*, in the first article, to have included both the Old and the New Testament, it was a tome *defective* and *worn* (*defect' et usitat'*).'

The opening sentences of this quotation show how completely Nichols misunderstood or misrepresented the catalogue; it hardly ever gives the first words of manuscripts, but usually quotes the opening words of the second folio as an identification mark. It seems almost incredible that Nichols believed that most of the books so carefully described had only two leaves: it may be that this remarkable blunder and his gratuitous statement about the Bible were not only due to ignorance but to *odium theologicum*. Apart from a long list of separate books of the Old and New Testament, the *Registrum* contains on its first leaf, a place too obvious to be missed,

[1] London, 1815, ii, App. 101–8. Becker (*Catalogi Bibliothecarum Antiqui*, Bonn, 1885) merely refers to Nichols: Gottlieb (*Über Mittelalterliche Bibliotheken*, Leipzig, 1890) prints the summary of the contents on fo. 1, but probably had not examined the manuscript as he accepts the date, 1482, contradicted by internal evidence, given by Warton (*History of English Poetry*, edited Hazlitt, 1871, i. 184).

a list of no less than twenty-two Bibles, only two of which are styled *defecte et usitate*.

The manuscript is a volume of 51 folia, measuring 15½ by 10½ in. and written in a clear hand of the late fifteenth or early sixteenth century. The original pagination (folia 90–140) shows that it was once part of a much larger volume, described three times in the *Registrum* as follows:

f. 49v. (Heading: *Libri et Rotule evidenciarum nostrarum, valde necessarii.*)

Est alius liber vocatur liber de terris dominicalibus in quo continentur terraria de terris nostris dominicalibus et terraria de aliis terris nostris in diversis locis et villis.//Item Registrum omnium librorum nostrorum.

f. 50. (Heading: *Libri quos Frater Willelmus Charite scribi fecit.*)

Item liber vocatur liber de terris dominicalibus cum multis aliis in eodem compilavit et scribi fecit. 2° fo. in quira et Rod'.

f. 50v. (Heading: *Libri quos propria manu scripsit et compilavit.*)

Item unus liber vocatur liber de terris dominicalibus primo scriptus in paupiro quem librum predictus W. cum multis aliis libris postea compilavit et scribi fecit in pergameno 2° fo. in quira Et Rod'.

Charite's statement that he copied the *liber* from paper on to parchment suggests that he was using an older catalogue, a suggestion borne out by the word *renovatum* in the title at the beginning of the subject catalogue. An entry under *Sermones* may refer to the original *Registrum*:

f. 29v. (Subject heading: *Sermones.*)

Liber sermonum in quo Registrum librorum in asseribus cum albo coopertorio 2° fo. quare sicut rote

Dilataciones communes fere in omni materia viciorum et virtutum et de hiis que spectant ad ultimum

Brevis meditacio Anselmi. Sextum capitulum de disciplina claustralium

Tractatus de Compoto.//Sermones iij vel. iiijor notabiles. Registrum librorum in fine.

The contents of the manuscript are faithfully set out in the paragraph preceding the *Tabula* or list of authors:[1]

f. 1. Contenta huius Registri sequentis prout sequuntur in ordine. Primo tabula facta per fratrem Willelmum Charyte de nominibus omnium doctorum, auctorum sive compilatorum quorum libri, volumina, tractatus etc. notantur in isto registro. Deinde omnes biblie pertinentes huic monasterio; postea libri biblie glossate cum diversis doctoribus in eisdem. Deinde iiij^{or} doctores ecclesie scilicet Augustinus etc.; tunc alii diversi doctores, auctores et compilatores sicut stant in ordine; postea Historialia, Cronicalia, Vite Sanctorum, Epistole et Omelie doctorum; tunc Summe, Penitencialia, Sermones, Volumina, Concordancie, Constitutiones, Specula, Testamenta prophetarum, Elucidaria, Proverbia, Ysagoge Philosophorum, Responsa Philippi secundi cum multis aliis. Tunc libri de gramatica, de poetria, de sophistria, de logica, de philosophia, de arithmetica, de musica, de geometria, de astronomie, de instrumentis, de phisica naturali. Tunc libri de iure civili et de iure canonico. Tunc registrum de omnibus libris qui sunt in libraria et scriptoria [*sic*] prout dividuntur in ix stallis.[2] Tunc Registrum omnium librorum in choro, in capella, in firmaria et apud Ingwardby, prout dividuntur inter conventum. Ultimo Registrum diversorum librorum et rotulorum concernentium evidencias nostras ut patet in fine huius Registri.

It is fortunately possible to fix the date within four years. It must be as late as 1492/3, as one of the books catalogued is described as 'breve opusculum per quod aliquis potest plane cognoscere quomodo redditus nostri decreverunt a tempore Edwardi Regis III usque ad annum octavum anni H. VII' (fos. 50, 50^{v}); it cannot be later than 27 October 1496 when John Penny, described as *capellanus* on folio 48, is called abbot in a letter patent: it was probably before 15 June in the same year, when

[1] Printed by Nichols, ii. 101. I have slightly modified the punctuation of the original.

[2] These nine *stalli* suggest comparison with the nine *distinctiones* described in the catalogue of Dover Priory: 'tota hec biblioteca in nouem separatis distinccionibus secundum nouem primas alphabeti literas . . . diuiditur (*Ancient Libraries of Canterbury and Dover*, ed. M. R. James, 1903, p. 407).

a *congé d'élire* was issued to the prior and convent.[1] The date must therefore lie between 1492 and 1496.[2]

It is difficult to come to any conclusion about the size of the library or the arrangement of the books. There are no shelf-marks and the position classification *in stallis* is obviously incomplete. Even a preliminary examination shows that the *Tabula*, the *Registrum*, and the position classification differ from each other in many details, discrepancies most easily illustrated by the differences in numbers. About 344 names of authors are on the *Tabula*; about 1,016 volumes are described in the *Registrum*; 249 volumes, repeated for the most part from the *Registrum*, are recatalogued according to their position. At the end 172 service books, 28 rolls, 19 rentals, and 4 confused and over-lapping lists of over a score of books, made or procured by Charite himself, are catalogued separately.

Though it is tempting to accept the high figure of 1,016 as an indication of the size of the library, it is perhaps an over-estimate, even if the service books and rentals are included in the reckoning. The attempt to compile a subject catalogue and Charite's eagerness to insert his own books as often as possible caused the same volumes to be entered on the *Registrum* more than once. An elaborate system of cross-references and the listing of the contents of a number of books has swollen the *Registrum* so that it covers forty folia of the whole catalogue. Books may have been lost or sent to Oxford[3] before Charite began his work, or his classification by

[1] *Cal. of Pat. Rolls, Henry VII, 1494–1509*, pp. 56, 77.

[2] A note on fo. 1 in a later hand runs as follows: 'Registrum hoc compositum fuit per Willelmum Charyte qui vixit Anno 1482. Scriptus autem hic liber ad annum octavum Regis Henrici septimi, ut patet folio 139' (new pagination fo. 50). The annotator evidently confounded the *opusculum* with the catalogue.

[3] Some books may have been sent to St. Mary's College, Oxford, founded in 1435 as a place of study for Austin canons. It had a special connexion with Leicester from the time of its foundation. No books are mentioned in the inventory of the goods of the college (1541), printed in Wood's *City of Oxford*, ed. A. Clark, vol. ii, appendix A.

position may be incomplete, as his failure to describe the contents of one of the nine *stalli* suggests. If to the number of books *in stallis* and *in scriptoria* is added that of service books and other miscellaneous books, we find that there must have been at least 450 volumes in the possession of the house in Charite's time. It is possible that a detailed analysis of the *Registrum* will show that at one time Leicester Abbey owned more than 1,000 volumes and was, in fact, one of the larger libraries of fifteenth-century England.

X

BIBLIOGRAPHY OF THE PUBLISHED WORKS OF M. V. CLARKE

The Medieval City State, an Essay on Tyranny and Federation in the later Middle Ages. London: Methuen, 1926.

Medieval Representation and Consent, a study of Early Parliaments in England and Ireland with special reference to the Modus Tenendi Parliamentum. London: Longmans, 1936.

[*The Chartulary of Tristernagh Abbey*. Edited for the Irish Manuscript Commission. Unfinished, but in process of completion by Miss K. M. E. Murray, B.A., B.Litt., and Miss J. S. A. Macaulay, B.A., B.Litt.]

REVIEWS

'Henry VII's Relations with Scotland and Ireland, 1485–98', by Agnes Conway. C.U.P. 1932. *English Historical Review*, xlviii. 473–5.

'L'Avènement du régime démocratique à Bruxelles pendant le moyen âge, 1306–1423', par F. Favrisse. Brussels, 1932. Ibid. xlix. 120–1.

'Ormond Deeds', ed. Edmund Curtis. 'The Red Book of Ormond', ed. Newport B. White. 'Calendar of Ormond Deeds, 1172–1350', vol. i, ed. E. Curtis. Ibid. xlix. 329–32 and *Bulletin of the Institute of Historical Research*, xiii. 95–7.

'Calendar of the Ormond Deeds, 1350–1413', vol. ii. *English Historical Review*, li. 518–20.

'The Mission of Rinuccini, 1645–9', by M. J. Hynes Dublin, 1932. Ibid. xlix. 364–5.

'Life of John, First Baron Darcy of Knayth, 1280–1347', by R. F. D'Arcy. London, 1933. Ibid. l. 166–7.

'Gerald Fitzgerald, the Great Earl of Kildare, 1456–1513', by Donough Bryan. Dublin, 1933. Ibid. l. 169.

'View of the Present State of Ireland' (vol. iv of the Complete Works of Edmund Spenser), ed. W. L. Renwick. London, 1934. Ibid. li. 548.

INDEX

LIST OF SUBSCRIBERS

Mrs. ABELL, 2 Race View, Lahore, India.

Mrs. E. D. ADRIAN, 48 Grange Road, Cambridge.

Miss C. M. ADY, 40 St. Margaret's Road, Oxford.

Mrs. J. O. BARRETT, 120 Wingrove Road, Newcastle-on-Tyne, 4.

Miss A. BEARDWOOD, 802 North 24th Street, Philadelphia, Pennsylvania, U.S.A.

Miss A. F. BEAUCHAMP, Somerville College, Oxford.

Professeur CHARLES BÉMONT, de l'Institut, Paris, France.

P. V. M. BENECKE, Esq., Magdalen College, Oxford.

Sir JAMES BERRY, Kirby Gate, Westmead, Roehampton, London, S.W. 15.

Professor R. R. BETTS, University College, Southampton.

B. H. BLACKWELL, Ltd., 50 & 51 Broad Street, Oxford.

The Misses J. E. & F. M. BLOMFIELD, Somerville College, Oxford.

T. S. R. BOASE, Esq., Hertford College, Oxford.

BOWES & BOWES, Ltd., 1 & 2 Trinity Street, Cambridge.

Mrs. GUSTAV BRAUNHOLTZ, 22 Old Road, Headington, Oxford.

Mrs. R. F. BRETHERTON, 'Merifield', Cumnor Hill, Oxford.

Miss J. D. BROWNE, 32 Saddlewood Avenue, Didsbury, Manchester.

Hon. A. M. BRUCE, White Gables, Sandfield Road, Headington, Oxford

Miss E. C. BRUCE, Loughton, Essex.

Miss A. F. BULL, 4 Walberton Avenue, Cosham, Hants.

Miss H. M. CAM, Girton College, Cambridge.

Lady IRIS CAPELL, 21 Empire House, Thurloe Place, London, S.W. 7.

Miss G. M. CARTER, 70 Main Street West, Hamilton, Ontario, Canada.

C. R. CHENEY, Esq., The University, Manchester.

Dr. I. J. CHURCHILL, Fircroft, 22 Mays Hill Road, Shortlands, Kent.

B. E. CLARKE, Esq., Homeside, Wimbledon Common, London, S.W. 19.

Miss L. T. M. CLARKE, 36 Cheniston Gardens, London, W. 8.

Miss E. R. COCHRANE, Fresden, nr. Highworth, Wiltshire.

Mrs. H. CONSTANT, Cowcroft, Ogbourne St. George, Marlborough, Wilts.

Miss M. J. CROOK, 98 Woodstock Road, Oxford.

Miss D. M. CROWFOOT, Somerville College, Oxford.

Miss H. DARBISHIRE, Somerville College, Oxford.

Miss R. J. DEBES, Headbourne Worthy Rectory, Winchester.
N. DENHOLM-YOUNG, Esq., Magdalen College, Oxford.
Miss D. L. DOUIE, 16 Old Elvet, Durham.
Miss E. EVANS, Somerville College, Oxford.
H. O. EVENNETT, Esq., Trinity College, Cambridge.
Miss V. FARNELL, Somerville College, Oxford.
Professor H. G. FIEDLER, The Lane House, Norham Road, Oxford.
Miss J. M. V. FOSTER, Rothesay, New Brunswick, Canada.
A. B. GILLETT, Esq., 102 Banbury Road, Oxford.
Dr. ROSE GRAHAM, 12 Ladbroke Gardens, London, W. 11.
Miss M. C. GRIFFITH, Milleen, College Road, Galway, Ireland.
Miss E. GURNELL, 35 Valkyrie Road, Wallasey, Cheshire.
H. B. HANNA, Esq., Royal Belfast Academical Institution, Belfast.
Herr HANS HARTINGER, Dorotheenstrasse 19, Berlin, N.W. 7, Germany.
Miss M. HARTLEY, Somerville College, Oxford.
W. HEFFER & SON, Ltd., 3 & 4 Petty Cury, Cambridge.
L. W. HENRY, Esq., The Grove, Harrow-on-the-Hill.
J. W. F. HILL, Esq., 2 Lindum Terrace, Lincoln.
Miss R. M. T. HILL, University College, Leicester.
HODGES, FIGGIS & Co., Nassau Street, Dublin.
Mrs. J. E. HODGSON, Haslemere, Blyth Road, Bromley, Kent.
Miss N. D. HURNARD, 49 Woodstock Road, Oxford.
The INTERNATIONAL UNIVERSITY BOOKSELLERS, Gower Street, London, W.C.
Miss E. M. JACK, 2 Ashburnham Gardens, Eastbourne.
Miss E. M. JAMISON, Lady Margaret Hall, Oxford.
Miss N. M. E. JOACHIM, 11 Rawlinson Road, Oxford.
Miss M. F. W. JOSEPH, 53 Linden Gardens, London, W. 2.
Miss E. M. JOWETT, 34A Clanricarde Gardens, London, W. 2.
Mrs. N. KALDOR, 15 Mecklenburgh Square, London, W.C. 1.
Miss K. M. KENYON, Kirkstead, Godstone, Surrey.
Dr. T. P. C. KIRKPATRICK, 11 Fitzwilliam Place, Dublin.
O. KYLLMANN, Esq., 10 Orange Street, London, W.C. 2.
G. LAPSLEY, Esq., Trinity College, Cambridge.
Miss M. M. LASCELLES, Somerville College, Oxford.
Miss B. A. LEES, 8 Norham Road, Oxford.
Miss M. D. LEGGE, 115 Banbury Road, Oxford.
F. A. LEPPER, Esq., 'Ridgrove', Hester's Way, nr. Cheltenham.
R. S. LEPPER, Esq., Elsinore, Carnalea, Co. Down, Northern Ireland.
Mrs. R. G. C. LEVENS, The Red House, Hinksey Hill, Oxford.
Dr. N. B. LEWIS, 40 Westbourne Road, Sheffield, 10.

Miss H. G. LIDDELL, 51 Thurleigh Road, London, S.W.12.
Dr. A. G. LITTLE, Risborough, Sevenoaks, Kent.
Miss H. L. LORIMER, Somerville College, Oxford.
Miss J. S. A. MACAULAY, 6 The Garden, Orchard Road, Sutton, Surrey.
Miss M. E. MACAULAY, 74 Westbourne Road, Sheffield, 10.
K. B. McFARLANE, Esq., Magdalen College, Oxford.
C. J. McKISACK, Esq., 9 Mount Pleasant, Belfast.
Miss M. McKISACK, Somerville College, Oxford.
Miss E. MACLENNAN, 31 Oriole Parkway, Toronto, Canada.
Mrs. I. McMASTER, 6 High Street, Eton, Windsor.
B. MANNING, Esq., Jesus College, Cambridge.
Miss E. M. MERRIFIELD, 6 South Road, The Park, Nottingham.
E. MILNER, Esq., Bluff, Ossett, Yorks.
Miss M. F. MOOR, 10 Church Street, Old Headington, Oxford.
W. MULLAN & SON, Belfast.
Miss K. M. E. MURRAY, Upper Cranmore, Heyshott, Midhurst, Sussex.
J. N. L. MYRES, Esq., Christ Church, Oxford.
Professor N. NEILSON, Mount Holyoke College, South Hadley, Mass., U.S.A.
Mr. & Mrs. F. W. OGILVIE, Lennoxvale House, Belfast.
PARKER & SON, Ltd., Oxford.
Rev. T. M. PARKER, Pusey House, Oxford.
Mrs. J. PARSONS, 19B Pembridge Square, London, W. 2.
Dame EMILY PENROSE, 14C Belsize Park Gardens, Hampstead, London, N.W. 3.
Miss D. PLEYDELL-BOUVERIE, 7 Warwick Square, London, S.W. 1.
Miss P. D. POOL, 13 Wadham Gardens, London, N.W. 3.
A. L. POOLE, Esq., St. John's College, Oxford.
Professor M. K. POPE, 32 Wilbraham Road, Manchester, 14.
Professor G. R. POTTER, 21 Slayleigh Lane, Sheffield, 10.
Dr. C. W. PREVITÉ-ORTON, St. John's College, Cambridge.
Miss J. PRESTON, 5 Ferrand Lane, Bingley, Yorks.
Miss E. S. PROCTER, St. Hugh's College, Oxford.
Professor B. H. PUTNAM, Mount Holyoke College, South Hadley, Mass., U.S.A.
Miss H. J. PYBUS, Newnham College, Cambridge.
Miss M. RHYS, Gwynva, Barton Lane, Headington, Oxford.
Miss E. ROBINSON, 610 Park Avenue, New York City, U.S.A.
Miss E. M. C. ROWLEY, c/o *The Daily Mirror*, Geraldine House, Rolls Buildings, Fetter Lane, London, E.C. 4.
Miss I. M. RUSSELL, Stubbers, North Ockendon, Essex.

Miss F. M. SACHSE, St. Cyprian's School, Capetown, South Africa.
Miss M. SEAVER, Lisroyan Malone, Belfast.
Miss M. C. SHARP, 3 Tedworth Square, Chelsea, London, S.W. 3.
Mrs. RAWDON SMITH, 17 Greenbank Drive, Liverpool, 17.
Mrs. C. M. SNOW, Southerway, Old Headington, Oxford.
Mrs. R. D.-N. SOMERSET, 120 Banbury Road, Oxford.
Miss E. STARKIE, Somerville College, Oxford.
A. STEEL, Esq., Christ's College, Cambridge.
Miss M. B. STONEDALE, Somerville College, Oxford.
Miss L. S. SUTHERLAND, Somerville College, Oxford.
Miss M. N. THOMAS, 42 Matthew Green Road, Wokingham, Berks.
Miss G. SCOTT THOMSON, 23 Carlisle Mansions, Carlisle Place, Westminster, London, S.W. 1.
J. THORNTON & SON, 11 Broad Street, Oxford.
Miss I. D. THORNLEY, 6 Cholmeley Crescent, Highgate, London, N. 6.
Professor J. EADIE TODD, University College, Belfast.
Miss HELEN WADDELL, 32 Primrose Hill Road, London, N.W. 3.
Dr. E. W. AINLEY WALKER, 1 Church Walk, Oxford.
Mrs. C. C. J. WEBB, Walnut Tree House, Marston, Oxford.
Mrs. O. WESTERN, 23 Langland Gardens, Hampstead, London, N.W. 3.
Miss J. K. BAKER WILBRAHAM, 76 Elm Park Gardens, London, S.W. 10.
Miss P. L. WINGFIELD, 6 Learmonth Gardens, Edinburgh.
Miss B. W. WOODALL, Yotes Court, Mereworth, Maidstone, Kent.
E. L. WOODWARD, Esq., All Souls College, Oxford.
The WORKERS' EDUCATIONAL ASSOCIATION OF S. ADELAIDE, S. Australia.

UNIVERSITY AND OTHER LIBRARIES

England

BIRMINGHAM PUBLIC LIBRARY: Reference Department.
BIRMINGHAM UNIVERSITY.
BRISTOL MUNICIPAL LIBRARIES.
BRISTOL UNIVERSITY.
CAMBRIDGE: Newnham College.
CAMBRIDGE: St. John's College.
HULL UNIVERSITY COLLEGE.
LEEDS PUBLIC LIBRARY.
LIVERPOOL UNIVERSITY.
LONDON: Bedford College.
LONDON: Birkbeck College.

LONDON: His Majesty's Stationery Office.
LONDON UNIVERSITY.
LONDON: Westfield College.
MANCHESTER UNIVERSITY.
OXFORD: Balliol College.
OXFORD: Brasenose College.
OXFORD: Christ Church.
OXFORD: Corpus Christi College.
OXFORD: Jesus College.
OXFORD: Lady Margaret Hall.
OXFORD: Faculty of Modern History Library.
OXFORD: The Nettleship Library.
OXFORD: New College.
OXFORD: St. Hugh's College.
SHEFFIELD UNIVERSITY.

SCOTLAND

EDINBURGH UNIVERSITY.
GLASGOW: Mitchell Library.
GLASGOW UNIVERSITY.

IRELAND

BELFAST: Linenhall Library.
BELFAST PUBLIC LIBRARY.
BELFAST: Queen's University.
DUBLIN: National Library of Ireland.
CITY OF DUBLIN PUBLIC LIBRARIES.

WALES

ABERYSTWYTH: University College of Wales.
CARDIFF CENTRAL LIBRARY.

STRAITS SETTLEMENTS

SINGAPORE: Raffles College.